TEXAS
POLITICS

The fifth edition of this popular text is now expanded and updated to better fit the needs of a stand-alone Texas politics course. Jillson continues to approach the politics of the Lone Star State from historical, developmental, and analytical perspectives, while giving students the most even-handed, readable, and engaging description of Texas politics available today. Throughout the book students are encouraged to connect the origins and development of government and politics in Texas—from the Texas Constitution, to party competition, to the role and powers of the Governor—to its current day practice and the alternatives possible through change and reform. This text helps instructors prepare their students to master the origin and development of the Texas Constitution, the structure and powers of state and local government in Texas, how Texas fits into the U.S. federal system, as well as political participation, the electoral process, and public policy in Texas.

Texas Politics offers instructors and students an unmatched range of pedagogical aids and tools. Each chapter opens with an engaging vignette and a series of focus questions to orient readers to the learning objectives at hand and concludes with a chapter summary, a list of key terms, review questions, suggested readings, and web resources. Key terms are bolded in the text, listed at the end of the chapter, and included in a glossary at the end of the book. Each chapter includes "Let's Compare" boxes to help students see how Texas sits alongside other states, and "Pro & Con" boxes to bring conflicting political views into sharper focus. Tables, figures, and photos throughout highlight the major ideas, issues, individuals, and institutions discussed.

Cal Jillson is professor in the department of political science at Southern Methodist University. His recent books include *American Government: Political Development and Institutional Change*, 8th edition; *Lone Star Tarnished: A Critical Look at Texas Politics and Public Policy*, 2nd edition; *Pursuing the American Dream: Opportunity and Exclusion Over Four Centuries*; and *Pathways to Democracy: The Political Economy of Democratic Transition*. He is frequently cited in local and national media on a range of political issues.

 A range of further resources for this book are available on the companion website: www.routledge.com/cw/jillson

"I've taught from all four editions of Cal Jillson's Texas Politics and am now looking forward to the fifth edition. I've organized my Texas government course to the Jillson text and it works like a charm, be it for a full semester or a shorter summer session."

—Gary Brown, *Lone Star College-Montgomery*

"Ounce per ounce this new Jillson 300-page edition, is among the better reads on Texas politics. The mandated essentials for Student Learning Objectives are presented in clear, to-the-point, prose; good tool for government teachers and students of rough-and-tumble Texan politics."

—Jose Angel Gutierrez, *University of Texas-Arlington*

"Jillson's text offers an excellent description and analysis of politics and political institutions in Texas. Students will appreciate the accessible and lively writing style. Brief but thorough, this textbook is well suited to the task of introducing students to Texas government."

—Daniel Sledge, *University of Texas-Arlington*

Praise for Previous Editions

"Cal Jillson has provided students with a concise yet thorough introduction to the often Byzantine intricacies of the Texas government. Especially helpful are the special features in each chapter that bring abstract concepts into contemporary and concrete focus. Students who use this book will find it engaging, timely, and relevant, and will be spurred to further independent exploration of their state's institutions, warts and all—a critical step toward becoming actively participating democratic citizens."

—Kevin T. Holton, *South Texas College*

"Cal Jillson has masterfully developed a Texas Politics book that combines readability with scholarship and enables the student to understand much of the institutional structure and unique character of Texas within the Federal context. Jillson provides needed insights to understanding Texas institutions and the interactions of interest groups within those institutions. He does so in an enjoyable readable format while addressing the important Texas state-mandated student learning outcomes and the significance of Texas politics for everyone. Texas Politics is reflective of the myriad of interesting stories which made Texas what it is today."

—Ray Sandoval, *Richland College*

"Texas Politics is a well-written and documented text that will be an asset to any professor or student interested in Texas politics. As mentioned in the Preface, one will find a broad 'range of pedagogical aids and tools' that will be helpful in the classroom."

—Morris D. Drumm, *Texas Christian University*

TEXAS
POLITICS

Governing the Lone Star State

CAL JILLSON
Southern Methodist University

Fifth Edition

Routledge
Taylor & Francis Group

NEW YORK AND LONDON

Please visit the companion website
at www.routledge.com/cw/jillson

This edition published 2016
by Routledge
711 Third Avenue, New York, NY 10017

Simultaneously published in the UK
by Routledge
2 Park Square, Milton Park, Abingdon, Oxon OX14 4RN

Routledge is an imprint of the Taylor & Francis Group, an informa business

First edition published 2007 by The McGraw-Hill Companies, Inc.
Fourth edition published 2014 by Routledge.

Library of Congress Cataloging in Publication Data
A catalog record for this book has been requested

ISBN: 978-1-138-84200-7 (pbk)
ISBN: 978-1-315-73189-6 (ebk)

Typeset in ITC Giovanni
by Florence Production Ltd, Stoodleigh, Devon, UK

"Texas is a state of mind. Texas is an obsession. Above all, Texas is a nation in every sense of the word . . . . Like most passionate nations Texas has its own private history based on, but not limited by, facts."

John Steinbeck, *Travels with Charley*,
1962, pp. 201–202

BRIEF CONTENTS

CONTENTS

Special Features

OPENING VIGNETTE

LET'S COMPARE

PRO & CON

TEXAS LEGENDS

TIMELINES

TABLES

FIGURES

PREFACE

Texas Politics: Governing the Lone Star State was a joy to write. That joy turned to quiet satisfaction as teachers and students of Texas politics found the first four editions of this book accessible, informative, and, yes, fun. In this thoroughly revised and expanded fifth edition, we treat Texas politics as serious business, but we also recognize that it is a great show. Decisions that Texas political leaders make about taxes, education, health care, and child services directly affect the quality of people's lives and their prospects of future success and security. But for the serious political junkie, it does not get any better than watching Ted Cruz redefine the Republican Party, watching the Democrats try to get up off the mat one more time, and watching demographic change reshuffle the partisan deck of Texas politics. I have tried to capture the structure and dynamics, the poetry and the prose, the good, the bad, and the ugly of Texas politics.

This book has been designed as a stand alone text to fulfill the revised requirements of the Texas Government course. All of the topics and student learning outcomes (SLOs) mandated for the Texas Government course are treated in a thorough yet engaging way to enhance the teaching environment for faculty and the learning environment for students. My goal is to help teachers and students understand and enjoy Texas politics.

Texas Politics approaches the politics of the Lone Star State from historical, developmental, and analytical perspectives. Each chapter opens with a discussion of the origins and development of the subject of the chapter, whether that subject is the Texas Constitution, the status of party competition in the state, or the role and powers of the Governor. Once we know how some aspect of Texas politics has developed over time, we can ask how and how effectively it works today. And then, inevitably, the discussion must shift to alternatives, to political change and reform. This text will allow teachers to share with their students the evolution of Texas politics, where we stand today, and where we seem to be headed.

In this new fifth edition, I have revised and expanded the text while still keeping in mind that my goal is to help teachers open and sustain an interesting conversation with their students. Faculty know too much that is fascinating and students have too many interesting questions for any book to try to anticipate and address them all. What I have done in the space that I have allowed myself is to describe how Texas politics works, how it came to work that way, and what general range of possibilities, both for continuity and for change, the future seems to hold. Where the conversation goes from there is up to students and their teachers, as it should be.

To students, I have tried to say more than that politics is important because it affects your lives in important ways and continuously. I have tried to provide a sense of how politics works and how people can become involved in it so that when an issue arises that you feel strongly about you will feel empowered. Politics is not just a spectator sport. It is a game that we are all entitled to play. Those who play Texas politics do not always win, but those who do not play almost always lose. To faculty teaching Texas politics, I have tried to help you communicate to your students what we know as political scientists and how much fun we had discovering it and sharing it.

Instructors and students will find an unmatched range of pedagogical aids and tools built into *Texas Politics*. Each chapter opens with a thought provoking vignette and a number of focus questions and concludes with a chapter summary, a list of key terms, suggested readings, and web resources. Each chapter's opening vignette is a compelling story that goes to the heart of a key issue to be covered in the chapter. It is intended to be an eye-opener, to capture student interest, before the content of the chapter puts the story conveyed in the vignette in its full context. The focus questions are listed at the beginning of the chapter and then again in the margins of the chapter where the information answering the question is to be found. Key terms are bolded in the text, listed at the end of the chapter, and included in a Glossary at the end of the book. Each chapter presents several carefully designed tables or figures to highlight the major ideas, issues, and institutions discussed. Each chapter also contains three pedagogical features guaranteed to capture student attention and spark classroom conversation and debate. A "Let's Compare" feature compares Texas to other states on some important dimension or issue, such as urbanization, voter turnout, gubernatorial powers, and tax rates. A "Pro & Con" feature presents both sides of a controversial topic like voter I.D. laws, campaign contribution limits, or legislator compensation in a way intended to open a classroom debate. Another feature, "Texas Legends," introduces students to the great names of Texas politics, not just Sam Houston and LBJ, but Sarah T. Hughes, names that students should know but may not yet know.

In addition, Routledge hosts a companion website that includes a number of useful resources for both students and instructors. Students looking for extra study aids will find practice quizzes, flash cards, chapter summaries, and internet links to online resources. To help instructors with classroom preparation, the companion website includes an instructor's manual with a wealth of tips and aids, as well as a testbank with a range of question types, and all attuned to the course's SLOs. The companion website can be found at www.routledge.com/cw/jillson

Texas Politics is organized in ten chapters. Chapters 1 and 2 trace the state's political history and place Texas within the broader context of American federalism. Chapter 1 describes the history and settlement of Texas and the cultural, economic, and political developments to the modern period. Chapter 2 describes the constitutional history of Texas, lays out the major provisions of the Texas Constitution, and describes how Texas fits into the American federal system.

Chapters 3 through 5 deal with political behavior. Chapter 3 deals with voters, campaigns, and elections. Key topics include voter registration, turnout, campaign finance, and the conduct of Texas elections. Chapter 4 describes the resources and activities of interest groups in Texas and the generally ineffectual attempts to regulate them. Chapter 5 describes structure, history, and prospects of Texas political parties.

Chapters 6 through 9 detail the major political institutions of Texas: the legislature, the Governor and the executive branch, the judicial system, and local governments. Chapter 10 describes the budgetary process, major sources of tax revenues, and the major programs and expenditures of Texas state government. Special attention has been given to recent controversies over school finance, immigration, and redistricting. The personalities and issues of the 2012 and 2014 Texas elections are explored throughout.

The 2014 elections have been covered in detail because they ushered in great change. After 14 years as governor, Rick Perry declined to run for re-election, setting off a general scramble for high office in the state. The race for governor, in which Attorney General Greg Abbott (R-Houston) bested state Senator Wendy Davis (D-Fort Worth), drew national attention. Long-time Lieutenant Governor David Dewhurst faced three challengers in the Republican primary; state Senator Dan Patrick, Land Commissioner Jerry Patterson, and Agriculture Commissioner Todd Staples. Dan Patrick ultimately emerged victorious. Finally, George P. Bush, upon whom many future Republican hopes are pinned, was elected Land Commissioner. As a result, all six state-wide executive offices have new incumbents. We explore what happened and what it all means.

Finally, I would like to give special thanks to the Routledge team that brought this edition of the book to print. Michael Kerns, as Acquisitions Editor, continues to have faith in the book. Lillin Rand and Olivia Marsh gently but very efficiently coordinated the development of this project, Rachel Hutchings kept the reader front of mind as she copy-edited the manuscript, and the rest of the Routledge team who brought the book to press.

Equally important were the reviewers who kept this project focused on the major issues of Texas politics. Present at the creation were: Nancy Bednar, Del Mar College; Bob Bezdek, Texas A&M University, Corpus Christi; Paul Blakelock, Kingwood College; Gary Brown, Montgomery College; Cecillia Castillo, Texas State University, San Marcos; Brian Farmer, Amarillo College; Robert Holder, McLennan Community College; Timothy Hoye, Texas Women's University; Jerry Polinard, University of Texas, Pan American; and Robert E. Sterken, Jr, The University of Texas at Tyler. Each is a Texas politics expert in his or her own right and I was proud to have their advice and guidance. Special thanks go to Gary Brown who was always there when we needed a really well-trained eye really fast.

Southern Methodist University has, as always, been supportive of my work and the Political Science Department has created a great working environment. Harold Stanley, Dennis Simon, and Matt Wilson teach me something about Texas politics every day. Beyond all of these, my wife Jane has provided the peace, security, and support that make life a joy.

Chapter 1

TEXAS AND THE TEXANS: THEN AND NOW[1]

Prior to the decisive Battle of San Jacinto, and after a heated argument with General Sam Houston, Pamelia Mann led her oxen "out of harm's way."

Courtesy of **EPICArt**® by Native Sun Productions

PAMELIA MANN AND HER OXEN

Texas women have a reputation for strength and determination that goes far back into Texas history. In modern times, we think of Barbara Jordan, Ann Richards, and Kay Bailey Hutchison as Texas women strong enough to part a sea of Texas men, but few Texas women have shown the fierce determination of Pamelia Dickinson Mann.

Pamelia Mann was born around 1800, probably somewhere in the Upper South. By the time she arrived in Texas in early 1834, she was on her third husband, one Marshall Mann, and had two sons, Flournoy Hunt and Samuel Allen, from the earlier marriages. Pamelia dominated her husbands and was universally described as a force of nature that few tried to challenge.

She is most famous for two interactions, one with Sam Houston and one with Mirabeau B. Lamar. The interaction with Sam Houston occurred just before the Battle of San Jacinto. Pamelia and her family fled their home and joined the civilians under the protection of Houston's army during the "runaway scrape." Houston's army, with Pamelia's permission, had commandeered a yoke of her oxen to help pull wagons and guns east. Pamelia's understanding was that the army was withdrawing toward Nacogdoches and the safety of Louisiana beyond. When Houston ordered the army south toward San Jacinto and a pitched battle with Santa Anna's forces, Pamelia feared for her livestock.

Pamelia rode up to General Houston, shouting "General, you told me a damn lie. You said that you was going on the Nacogdoches Road. Sir, I want my oxen." Houston demurred, arguing that the oxen were needed to extract cannon stuck in the mud, at which Pamelia cursed and upbraided the general in the presence of his troops, leaving most observers slack-jawed. When she had had her say, she dismounted, cut the oxen loose, and led them away. She was followed by a teamster intent on retrieving the beasts, but he returned with a torn shirt and no oxen.

After independence, the Manns relocated to the new settlement of Houston, where they built the Mansion House Hotel and ran a livery stable across the street. Pamelia was the driving force in the family, managing the hotel, while Marshall ran the stable until his death in late 1838. As one of only 40 women among 1,000 men in Houston, Pamelia was soon married again, this time requiring her new husband, one Tandy Brown, just six years older than her eldest son, to sign what today we would call a "prenup" leaving her in complete control of her property. Both Pamelia and Brown died of yellow fever in late 1840.

Still, her last years were full of adventure. Between 1837 and 1840, she was involved in no fewer than 18 legal disputes. In two-thirds of these she was the defendant. In the most significant case, she was accused of forgery, tried, and sentenced to death by hanging. President Lamar, having succeeded Houston, responded to a petition for clemency—remember Pamelia is one of very few women in the city—by pardoning and releasing her from jail. Texas women are tough and shrewd, but it is safe to say that they don't make them like Pamelia Mann anymore.

Source: Andrew Forest Muir, "In Defense of Pamelia Mann," Texas Folklore Society; Mody C. Boatright, ed., *Mexican Border Ballads and Other Lore*, 1946.

Focus Questions

Q1 Where does the larger-than-life Texas mystique come from?

Q2 How has the geography of Texas affected the state's development?

Q3 How has the Texas economy evolved over the state's history?

Q4 How has the ethnic mix of the Texas population evolved over time?

Q5 What factors will determine the future prosperity and stability of Texas?

Texas is a big, complex, multifaceted, and utterly fascinating state. In both myth and reality, Texas is larger-than-life. It is the second largest state in the union (behind only Alaska) and the second most populous (behind only California). No other state can summon an equally romantic history, beginning with the Alamo, a decade as the independent Republic of Texas, the cattle drives, the oil fields, and J.R. Ewing's "Dallas." Only California, Florida, and New York can boast anything similar—a brand name—an image that has implanted itself in the popular mind.

Q1 Where does the larger-than-life Texas mystique come from?

Throughout its history, Texas has attracted a volatile mix of adventurers, talented rascals on the rebound, and hardworking men and women searching for a fresh start. As early as the 1820s, the message *G.T.T.* (Gone to Texas) was scribbled on log cabins and boarded-up storefronts of Americans looking for a new beginning.[2] Stephen F. Austin, the founder of **Anglo** Texas, was born in Connecticut and schooled in Kentucky before settling in Texas. Sam Houston was born in Virginia and raised in Tennessee where he became governor before scandal drove him into Indian country and then on to Texas. Bowie came from Kentucky, Crockett from Tennessee, Fannin and Lamar from Georgia, and Travis from South Carolina. A few found Texas by traveling south: Anson Jones from Massachusetts, David Burnet from New Jersey, and Deaf Smith from New York.

Anglo A Spanish term referring to non-Hispanic whites.

History did not treat Texans gently. Texans had to fight for independence against a dangerous and arbitrary Mexican government. After ten rocky years of independence and fifteen as an American state on the distant frontier, Texas threw in its lot with the Confederacy. The **Civil War** left Texas defeated, occupied, and deeply traumatized. **Reconstruction** produced a sullen standoff between white Texans and their state government. Once white Texans regained control of their state in the 1870s, they wrote a constitution designed, above all else, to make government too weak and diffused to threaten them further. Modern Texans depend on that same government to confront and solve the vastly more complex problems of the 21st century. We will ask whether this 19th-century constitution serves Texas well today.

Civil War The U.S. Civil War, pitting the northern states against the southern states, occurred between 1861 and 1865.

Reconstruction The period of post–Civil War (1867 to 1872) military occupation of the South during which the North attempted to reconstruct southern social, political, and economic life.

In Chapter 1 we describe the people, culture, geography, and economy of Texas. How did Texas, a late arrival as the 28th state, become "the great state of Texas," or what Texas humorist Molly Ivins simply called "the great state" (assuming, apparently, that the Texas part was obvious)? Who settled Texas? When did they come? Where did they come from and where did they settle? How did they wrestle a living from the land? And what kind of society and polity did they intend to build?

ORIGINS AND SETTLEMENTS

The land that became Texas had been home to native peoples for at least 12,000 years.[3] Only in the 16th and 17th centuries did European exploration, conquest, and colonization impinge upon these first Texans. As late as 1800, between 20,000 and 30,000 Native Americans, including mighty tribes like

Rio Grande Spanish for Grand River, the Rio Grande forms Texas's southern border with Mexico from El Paso to Brownsville.

the Comanche and Apache, lived in and ranged across Texas. About 3,500 Spanish Mexicans lived north of the **Rio Grande**, about half in San Antonio and most of the rest in La Bahia (Goliad) and Nacogdoches. Anglos and blacks numbered only in the dozens.[4]

By 1900, 2.35 million whites and 620,000 blacks lived in Texas. About 71,000 Hispanics (4 percent of the total population) lived in South Texas, most between the Neuces and the Rio Grande, and the Indians largely were gone (0.5 percent). The Anglo settlement of Texas (or conquest of northern Mexico, depending upon your taste and perspective) was one of the most stunning population movements in history.

Native Peoples

The first Texans were big game—*really* big game—hunters. They tracked mammoth and giant bison across the plains of what today is north central Texas. As the last ice age receded about 7,000 years ago, these prehistoric animals disappeared and the native peoples became hunters and gatherers focusing on smaller animals, including deer and gazelle, as well as fish, nuts, berries, and useful plants. Settled agriculture began among some native tribes, especially in east and northeast Texas, around 400 AD. Hunting, fishing, and gathering from nature were still important, but crops of corn, beans, and squash provided flexibility and variety to native diets.

Intruders arrived early in the 16th century. The Spanish came first, but others, more numerous and more powerful, followed. Native people successfully resisted the Spanish attempts to draw them to the missions of early Texas, but they could not resist the rising Anglo immigration of the 19th century. The Caddo, Tonkawa, and Karankawa of Central and East Texas were subdued by the 1850s.[5] By the late 1870s, the Apache and the Comanche were forced from the Hill Country and High Plains north into Oklahoma and west into New Mexico.[6]

Spanish Explorers and Mexican Settlers

The Spanish explorer Alvar Nunez Cabeza de Vaca is one of history's most intriguing figures. Initially shipwrecked in Florida, his party built barges and put to sea only to wreck again on Galveston Island. Cabeza de Vaca spent nearly eight years (1528–36) living among and trading with native tribes throughout Texas and the Southwest as far as the Gulf of California. His tales of prosperous lands and cities of gold piqued the interest of Spanish officials in Mexico City. Francisco Vasquez de Coronado was dispatched to make a more systematic survey. Coronado and a force of 2,000 Spaniards and Mexican-Indians spent nearly three years (1540–42) exploring Texas and the Southwest, penetrating as far as central Kansas. Coronado's failure to find the fabled Seven Cities of Cibola cooled Spanish interest in their northern provinces for more than a century.[7]

A brief incursion into Texas in the 1680s by the French trader and explorer, Rene-Robert-Cavelier, Sieur de La Salle, finally spurred the Spanish to expand their mission activities beyond the **Rio Grande Valley** as far north as San Antonio and as far east as Nacogdoches.[8] Still, as the 19th century dawned, Texas remained the lightly populated northernmost province of Spanish Mexico. Then, in 1810, Mexico rebelled against Spain and after a decade of warfare won independence in 1821. Even as Mexicans celebrated independence, an Anglo tide was rising in Texas.

Rio Grande Valley Texas's four southernmost counties, often referred to simply as "the valley," are heavily Hispanic. The phrase is sometimes used more expansively to refer to all of South Texas.

American Settlers

Americans began drifting into Texas in small numbers beginning about 1800. The first major Anglo settlement, organized by Moses Austin and carried forward by his son, Stephen F. Austin, was established in 1823. Austin was authorized by Mexican authorities to offer up to one square league (4,428 acres) to settlers willing to occupy and work the land. Settlers were expected to be (or be willing to say they were) Catholics, to become Mexican citizens, and to forswear slavery. As Anglo numbers grew, Mexican authorities worried about how to control these independent, even rebellious, immigrants. Attempts to limit immigration and to enforce laws requiring Catholicism and prohibiting slavery irritated the Anglos and tensions grew.[9]

Mexican authorities worried that too many Americans would come and that their loyalties would remain with their homeland. The worry that the U.S. had designs on Texas was never far from Mexican minds. They had reason to worry. In 1832 Sam Houston, often seen as an unofficial U.S. agent, wrote to his old friend President Andrew Jackson, to report: "I have travelled near five hundred miles across Texas, and am now enabled to judge pretty near correctly of the soil, and the resources of the country, and I have no hesitancy in pronouncing it the finest country of its extent upon the globe." Texas boosterism and braggadoccio developed early.

The election of Antonio Lopez de Santa Anna as president of Mexico in 1834 was initially seen as promising. Texans believed that Santa Anna supported their autonomy within a loose federal state. But Santa Anna soon sought to consolidate power by centralizing control over all of Mexico, including Texas. Hostilities broke out between Texans and elements of the Mexican Army near San Antonio in October 1835. The first fight was the famous "Come And Take It" skirmish in which residents of Gonzales, about 70 miles east of San Antonio, defended a small cannon against Mexican cavalry sent to seize it. A wild Texan charge (it would not be the last) dispersed the Mexicans and retained the cannon, at least for a time.

By early 1836, Santa Anna had crossed the Rio Grande at the head of a large army. The real fight for Texas was about to begin. The Texans were bloodied early, first at the Alamo (March 6, 1836) and then in the slaughter at Goliad (March 27, 1836). These early defeats sent thousands of panic-stricken Anglo Texans fleeing eastward in what came to be known as the "Runaway Scrape." General Sam Houston's ragtag Texas army also retreated eastward, stopping

Hulton Archive/Getty Images

General Sam Houston later served as President of the Republic of Texas, U.S. Senator, and Governor of Texas.

where possible to train the unruly volunteers in marching, close order drill, and firing by platoons.

Confident of victory, Santa Anna divided his force, sending three columns in pursuit of the bedraggled Texans. One column was sent to capture the provisional government of Texas and another was to find and destroy the Texas army. The last was to drive the fleeing civilians across the Sabine and out of Texas. Santa Anna accompanied the lead elements in pursuit of Houston's army. Yet, within weeks, the Texans had outmaneuvered Santa Anna's force, caught them napping (literally), and routed them at San Jacinto (April 21, 1836). Santa Anna himself was captured on April 22 and forced to sign treaties recognizing Texas's independence and withdrawing the remaining Mexican armies south of the Rio Grande. A tentative independence had been won, but danger and uncertainty lurked all about.

The **Republic of Texas** experienced a decade-long rollercoaster ride of independent nationhood. Continued immigration and expansion vied with two Mexican invasions, frequent flirtations with bankruptcy, hyperinflation, and political instability to shape the new nation's future. Once Texas

Republic of Texas Texas was an independent nation from 1836 until it became a U.S. state on December 29, 1845.

began to stabilize under the strong hand of President Sam Houston in the early 1840s, the U.S. grew wary of Texas as a competitor for influence over the West. To forestall this competition, U.S. President James K. Polk welcomed Texas into the Union on December 29, 1845. Polk's action sparked the Mexican-American War (1846–48) and secured for the U.S. not only Texas but all of the American Southwest and California.[10]

The Slaves

Spain and Mexico outlawed slavery by the 1820s, so Anglos were reluctant to bring slaves into Texas before the 1830s. Once Texas secured its independence many southern slaveholders moved to Texas. Texas entered the union as a slave state and the expansion of slavery in Texas continued through the 1850s. Most Texas slaves worked on cotton plantations east of a line running from Dallas through Austin to Corpus Christi.

No figure bulks larger in Texas history than Sam Houston. He is our flawed George Washington, though a comparison to Houston's mentor, Andrew Jackson, might be more apt. All three were men whose military accomplishments paved their way to political careers. Washington was born into the plantation aristocracy of Virginia, while Jackson and Houston were the rough products of the early 19th-century frontier.

Sam Houston was born on March 2, 1793, the fifth of nine children, to Samuel and Elizabeth (Paxton) Houston in Virginia's Shenandoah Valley. The senior Sam Houston planned to move his family to Tennessee, partially to escape growing debts, but died before the move could be accomplished. His family moved on without him, settling in Maryville, Tennessee, in 1807. Young Sam Houston did not take to school, farm work, or clerking in his brother's store, so he left home at 16 to live among the Cherokee. They named him "The Raven."

Houston returned to Maryville in 1812 and before long enlisted in the army to fight the British in the War of 1812. Houston rose quickly through the ranks, capturing the attention of General Andrew Jackson, especially by his heroic actions in the 1814 Battle of Horseshoe Bend, where he was wounded three times. Jackson acted as sponsor and mentor to Houston until Jackson's death in June 1845.

Once he recovered from his wounds, Houston studied law and opened a law practice in 1818 in Lebanon, Tennessee. Soon he was appointed local prosecutor and militia captain in Nashville and his political career took off like a rocket. He was elected twice to the U.S. House and, in 1827 at the age of 34, he was elected Governor of Tennessee. Then it all came crashing down. On January 22, 1829, the 36-year-old Houston married 19-year-old Eliza Allen of a prominent local family. Within weeks the marriage collapsed, Eliza returned to her family, and by April Houston had resigned the governorship and fled again to the Cherokee, now in the Arkansas Territory. Soon Houston had a new Indian name, which translated as "the Big Drunk."

By late 1832, Houston was in Texas and immediately swept up in the coming revolution. In 1833 and 1835, Houston attended conventions considering Texas's political and military options. He was commissioned a Major General in the Texas Army in November 1835 and at the March 1836 convention that declared Texas independence he was appointed Commander-in-Chief of Texas military forces—such as they were. Within days, the Alamo, under the command of Travis and Bowie, fell and Fannin's troops, captured near Goliad, were slaughtered. Houston, initially with fewer than 400 men under his command, retreated east before Santa Anna's superior forces. By the time Houston's army reached Jan Jacinto its numbers had grown to 900, though the Mexican force was nearly twice that. Yet, in the mid-afternoon, "siesta time," of April 21, 1836, Houston ordered an attack and in less than twenty minutes won a decisive victory. By the end of the day, the Mexicans counted 630 dead, 203 wounded, and 730 captured. Santa Anna was captured the next day and soon forced to sign the Treaty of Velasco recognizing Texas independence.

In the fall of 1836, Houston was elected the first President of the Republic of Texas. Since there was a one term limit on the presidency, he served in the Texas Congress in 1839–40, before being elected to the presidency again in 1841. Despite the tumult, 47-year-old Sam Houston married 21-year-old Margaret Moffette Lea of Marion, Alabama. They had eight children. When Texas was admitted to the Union in late 1845, Houston was elected to the United States Senate, where he served from February 21, 1846 through March 4, 1859. Houston unsuccessfully sought the governorship of Texas in 1857, but won it in 1859. He ran both times as a Unionist, arguing for negotiation of regional differences, rather than secession and war. Houston warned that the South would lose a war with the populous and industrialized North, but secession and war came anyway. When Texas voted to secede in February 1861 and joined the Confederacy in March, all officeholders, including Governor Houston, were required to take an oath of allegiance to the Confederacy. Houston refused and resigned, choosing to retire to his Huntsville home, rather than to fight either his state or his nation. Sam Houston died at Huntsville on July 26, 1863.

In February 1861, Texas seceded from the United States to become the west-ernmost member of the Confederate States of America. Though Governor Sam Houston opposed secession, a majority of Texans embraced the Confederate cause. The Civil War and Reconstruction had a tremendous impact on Texas. Following Reconstruction, white Texans struggled to restore and then main-tain the social, political, and economic primacy that they had enjoyed before the Civil War.

THE POLITICAL CULTURE OF TEXAS

These formative decades stamped Texas political life with a distinctive feel and character. By the time Texas won its independence from Mexico in 1836, Anglo Texans outnumbered Texans of Spanish or Mexican origin by ten to one. Anglo immigrants brought to Texas assumptions about and attitudes toward politics that they had learned in the United States. Most of the immi-grants came out of the American South.

Scholars use the term **political culture** to denote widely shared attitudes toward politics.[11] These shared attitudes broadly define what citizens should expect from government and what roles they should expect to play in poli-tics and governance. Political scientist Daniel Elazar has traced the roots of the American political culture back into the colonial period. By the 1830s, this American political culture (in the U.S. and Texas) had matured into a broad commitment to democratic capitalism for white men. Democratic capitalism joins elements of equality and community with elements of competition and hierarchy. Intriguingly, Elazar identified three regional **political subcultures** that draw from the broader American political culture, each in a distinctive way.

New England and the northern states draw most heavily from the egalitarian and communitarian strains (think town meetings) to form what Elazar called a moralistic political culture. Today, we would probably call this a communitarian political culture, as moralistic tends to have strong religious overtones for us. Citizens in a moralistic political culture take politics seriously, participate at high levels, and approve higher taxes so that more public needs can be met. The Middle Atlantic and Middle Western states draw most heavily from the competitive strain (think Lincoln, rail-splitter to president) to produce an individualistic political culture. Citizens in an individualistic political culture assume that politics, like business, is a competitive arena in which advancement can be sought, services can be delivered, contracts can be awarded, and benefits can be received. The South draws most heavily from the hierarchical strain (think *Gone with the Wind*) to produce a traditionalistic political culture. In a traditionalistic political culture, participation is low, government is small and taxes low, elites govern, and the maintenance of social order is paramount.

The first Anglo Texans came mostly out of the American South and settled in East Texas and the Gulf Coast region. The dominant southerners

Political culture Widely held ideas concerning the relationship of citizens to their government and to each other in matters affecting politics and public affairs.

Political subcultures Distinct regional variations produced when some elements of the national political culture are emphasized and others deemphasized.

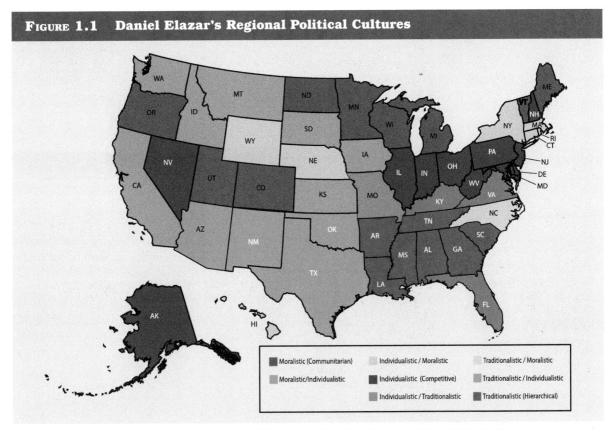

| FIGURE 1.1 | Daniel Elazar's Regional Political Cultures |

Legend:
- Moralistic (Communitarian)
- Moralistic/Individualistic
- Individualistic / Moralistic
- Individualistic (Competitive)
- Individualistic / Traditionalistic
- Traditionalistic / Moralistic
- Traditionalistic / Individualistic
- Traditionalistic (Hierarchical)

Source: Adapted from Daniel J. Elazar, *American Federalism: A View from the States* (New York: Harper Collins, 1984), 124–125.

favored states' rights and the leadership of established elites. Midwesterners came somewhat later, in smaller numbers, and settled in North Texas, the Panhandle, and West Texas. They favored small government, low taxes, and individual opportunity. History, migration and immigration, urbanization, and economic change have mixed and modified these regional political sub-cultures. Nonetheless, scholars and political observers agree that the Texas political culture has always been, and remains, Southern traditionalism with an admixture of western and midwestern individualism.[12]

As we shall see throughout this book, despite historic change, the Texas political culture has been remarkably stable.[13] The Texan political culture highlights small government, low taxes, and personal responsibility. Texas was once a rural agricultural state in which planter interests dominated the ruling Democratic party. Today, Texas is an urban industrial state in which business interests dominate the ruling Republican party. But throughout, political participation has been limited, citizens have been disengaged, the lobby has dominated Austin, and taxes have rested lightly on the state's social and economic elite.[14] The state motto, "Don't Mess With Texas," might well be "Let the Big Dogs Hunt."

THE PHYSICAL GEOGRAPHY AND EARLY ECONOMY OF TEXAS

Q2 How has the geography of Texas affected the state's development?

Texas is a vast and varied state. It spans more than 267,000 square miles. At its widest points, it is 773 miles from east to west and 801 miles from north to south. On this broad canvass, wave after wave of immigrants found their future.[15]

The geography of Texas presents three main regions. South Texas, often called the Lower Rio Grande Valley, or simply "the Valley," is semiarid brush country south of an arc that runs from Corpus Christi to San Antonio to Del Rio. The rest of Texas is separated into two distinct regions, with several sub-regions in each, by the Balcones Escarpment. The **Balcones Escarpment** is a geological faultline that runs east from Del Rio to San Antonio and then north to the Red River, passing west of Austin, Killeen, and Fort Worth. It separates the humid, well-watered, lowlands of East Texas from the drier, upland, prairies and plains of West Texas.

Balcones Escarpment
A geological faultline that separates the lowlands of East Texas from the prairies and plains of West Texas.

South Texas

South Texas was home to many Native-American tribes and to the first European settlers in Texas. The limited natural resources of this harsh land supported their modest needs. By 1720, cattle ranches operated on both sides of the Rio Grande.[16] Indian raids, cattle rustling, and the political instability surrounding the war for Mexican independence resulted in cattle ranging free throughout South Texas. Before the American Civil War, these famed longhorns fed Texans and modest herds were driven east to New Orleans and, somewhat later, much larger herds were driven north to midwestern markets and railheads. The famed Chisholm Trail started south of San Antonio and ran through Austin, Waco, and Fort Worth, then through the Oklahoma Indian Territory to Abilene, Kansas.

King Ranch Founded in 1853 by Captain Richard King, the 825,000 acre King Ranch south of Corpus Christi epitomizes the huge dry land cattle ranches of Texas.

The ranching culture looms large in the Texas mind, if not so large as it once did in the Texas economy. The legendary **King Ranch**, south of Corpus Christi, still covers an expanse of 825,000 acres, larger than the state of Rhode Island.[17] Adjacent to the King Ranch was the relatively modest Kenedy Ranch at just 400,000 acres. Increasingly, though, these historic ranches are being divided up, sold off, and set to other purposes. The majority of the sparse, mostly Hispanic, population has remained desperately poor. Nonetheless, parts of "the Valley" became a thriving truck farming economy of citrus fruits and vegetables once Anglo farmers introduced large-scale irrigation in the 1920s.

FIGURE 1.2   Texas Counties: Major Regions of the State

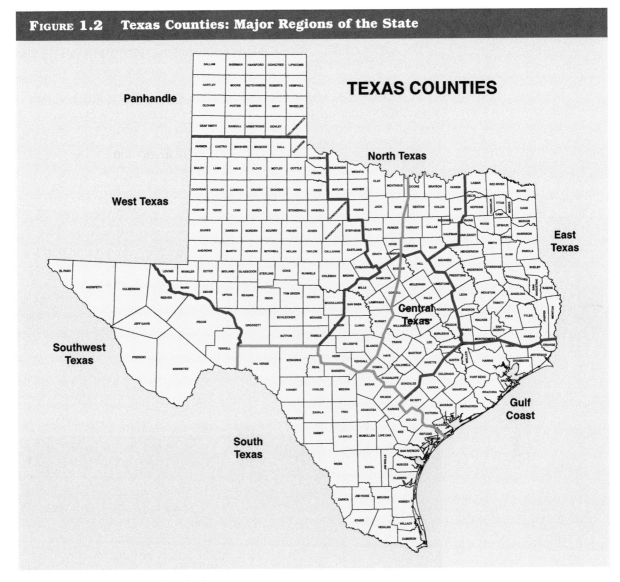

Source: Texas Natural Resources Information System.

San Antonio has always been the urban anchor of South Texas. The oldest city in Texas by several decades, the first mission, called San Antonio de Valero and later called the Alamo, was founded on the east side of the San Antonio River in the 1690s. The city itself, the villa of San Fernando de Bexar, was laid out on the west side of the river in 1730 and the next year thirty families from the Canary Islands became its founding population. For the next century and a half, San Antonio remained principally a garrison town of military installations for defense of the frontier and outfitters for westward exploration.

The arrival of the railroads sparked more rapid growth and opened the possibility of a more diverse economy. In early 1877, the Galveston, Harrisburg, and San Antonio Railroad linked San Antonio to Houston and the Gulf and in 1881 the International and Great Northern arrived, linking San Antonio through the Midwest to the rest of the nation and to the Mexican trade through a spur to Laredo. A sleepy outpost of 12,256 in 1870, San Antonio grew to 20,550 in 1880 and 37,653 in 1890. As other railroads arrived and economic development followed, San Antonio became the most populous city in Texas in 1900 and remained so through the first third of the 20th century.[18] Only in the past couple of decades has the economy of San Antonio really expanded beyond the military and tourism to manufacturing, health care, and the biosciences.

East Texas

Q3 How has the Texas economy evolved over the state's history?

East Texas was the population and wealth center of the state for much of the 19th century. White immigrants from the American South and their slaves brought a rich cotton culture to East Texas in the 1820s and 1830s. Prior to the Civil War and for decades thereafter, agriculture, especially "King Cotton," rivaled and even surpassed ranching as a mainstay of the Texas economy. The cotton culture was a slave-based economy and society of plantations and small towns. Even after slavery ended and cotton gave way to poultry, timber, and oil and gas,

© Eduardo Garcia/Getty Images

The Texas Gulf Coast is a commercially bustling place.

the social structure of East Texas remained rural and segregated. Economic leadership passed to other regions of the state, especially to Houston and the Upper Gulf Coast.

The Gulf Coast

The Gulf Coast, from the Louisiana border to Corpus Christi, is low grasslands and swamps with plentiful rainfall. During the 19th century, the Gulf Coast was an extension of East Texas. Cotton, rice, and grains were the principal crops. Although the wealth of early Texas was in the Colorado and Brazos River valley plantations, they had to export through the gulf ports of Houston and Galveston. Houston and Galveston grew up together and in competition from their founding in the 1830s until 1900 when nature decided the contest. The brothers John and Augustus Allen bought land and laid out a town on Buffalo Bayou in 1836 and named it for Sam Houston, the hero of that year's famous battle at nearby San Jacinto. Two years later, Michael Menard bought land and laid out a city on the east end of Galveston Island. Both sought to capture the seaborne trade into and out of Texas. The Allens bet that the lucrative cotton, sugar, and hide trades would converge at Houston for shipment down Buffalo Bayou to the Gulf. But Buffalo Bayou was shallow, serpentine, and frequently obstructed. Menard bet on Galveston's natural harbor in the Gulf. Galveston won early, Houston won eventually.

For decades Houston served as a transshipment point for Galveston. Oxcarts, flat boats, and shallow-hulled steamers brought the products of the interior's plantations, ranches, and farms to Houston. Once gathered in Houston, these products made their way down Buffalo Bayou on small steamers to the deep water port at Galveston where they were transferred to bigger Gulf and ocean-going vessels, sailing ships initially, but steamers by mid-century. In 1850, the first federal census to include Texas counted Galveston with 4,177 residents to Houston's 2,396.

Houston and Galveston were the centers of early railroad construction in Texas. During the 1850s, nine small roads connected the Colorado and Brazos Rivers to Houston and Galveston. The Civil War generally stopped railroad construction in Texas, but the 1870s saw a boom that soon connected all of the state's major cities. The Houston and Central Texas Railroad reached Austin and Corsicana in 1871 and Dallas in 1872. The goods of the interior flowed to Houston, but from there they had to go to Galveston for export, unless the Gulf could be brought to Houston and some thought that it could.

In 1869, the Buffalo Bayou Ship Channel Company began work to straighten and deepen the channel. Near the end of the century, first Galveston and then Houston won congressional appropriations to improve their channels and ports. Galveston built jetties that allowed its port to be deepened to 25 feet but a devastating hurricane and flood in 1900 leveled the city and raised concerns about its ongoing vulnerability.

At around ten in the morning on January 10, 1901, the Spindletop oil well, located just a few miles south of Beaumont on the Gulf Coast, came in. In a matter of days, Spindletop was producing more oil than all other U.S. oil wells and in a matter of weeks the Beaumont field was producing more than the rest of the world's oil fields combined. Though production at Spindletop trailed off within just a few years, it sparked a Texas oil boom that continues today.

Spindletop A.F. Lucas's Spindletop well near Beaumont came in on January 10, 1901, kicking off the 20th-century Texas oil boom.

The 20th century brought tremendous change to the Gulf Coast. On January 10, 1901, A.F. Lucas brought in the **Spindletop** oil field near Beaumont. Oil wells had been operating in Texas for decades, but Spindletop was much bigger and more productive. With Galveston in rubble and the oil fields booming, how to improve Houston's access to the Gulf became a critical question.

Houston began work to deepen a cut through Galveston Bay and Buffalo Bayou to 18.5 feet by 1908 and 25 feet by 1914. In the 1920s and 1930s, the role of the Houston Ship Channel expanded as oil moved to economic center stage. The great East Texas oil field came on-line in the 1920s. Pipelines brought the oil to refineries along the Ship Channel, eight of them by 1930, and to ships waiting in the channel. Nineteen-thirty was the first U.S. census that showed Houston to be the state's most populous city at nearly 300,000.[19] With Houston at its core, the Gulf Coast became an energy, petrochemical, manufacturing, and shipping center for Texas and the nation.

North Texas

Like Houston and Galveston, Dallas and Fort Worth also grew up as sibling competitors, though Dallas was always the older brother. Dallas was founded by John Neely Bryan in 1842 at a natural ford of the Trinity River. Bryan's trading post grew into a county seat by 1846. Fort Worth began as an army post in 1849 named to honor the service of General William J. Worth in the recent Mexican War. By 1870, Dallas had about 3,000 residents, ranked fifth and slightly behind Waco, but the railroads were about to arrive. In addition, North Texas had the benefit of some of the state's best farm land, the Black and Grand Prairies, so as soon as transportation was in place the locus of cotton production shifted to these fertile lands.

Railroads did not arrive in Dallas on their own; they were brought by the civic leaders of Dallas, led by William Gaston. The Houston and Central Texas Railroad initially planned to pass eight miles east of Dallas, but Gaston raised funds and contributed land to lure the railroad through the city. Similarly, financial incentives and legislative pressures were used to bring an east/west line, the Texas and Pacific Railroad, through Dallas as well. By 1900, Dallas had become a cotton trading and agricultural equipment manufacturing center, and, just as importantly, a banking and insurance center for the region.

Prior to the Civil War, Fort Worth was a military post and the last stop before the unsettled West. After the war, the massive cattle drives out of South Texas passed through either Dallas or Fort Worth, headed for the Kansas railheads. The arrival of the railroads in Fort Worth in 1876 diversified the city's economy and made it the services center for West Texas, just then beginning to be settled. By 1890, Dallas was, briefly, the state's most populous city at 38,000, while Fort Worth had climbed to fifth, at more than 23,000, less than

4,000 behind Houston. Fort Worth continued to thrive as the Armour and Swift meat-packing companies built plants in the city.

But Dallas took the higher-end development. Dallas's position as a banking center convinced the new United States Federal Reserve system to locate one of its twelve regional branches in Dallas in 1913 and in the same year Ford built a major auto assembly plant in Dallas. The Ford plant was expanded and then replaced with a larger plant in 1925. World War II ushered in a period of tremendous growth in and around the Dallas–Fort Worth "Metroplex." North American Aviation came to Dallas and Convair to Fort Worth to build the B-24 and many related aerospace industries, including Temco, Chance, Vought, and Bell Helicopter, followed in their wake. Population more than doubled between 1940 and 1960 and manufacturing employment grew even faster. The postwar years brought rapid expansion of defense, construction, as well as aerospace, and the Texas oil industry expanded into oil services, pipelines, shipping, and petrochemicals.[20]

The Hill Country

Originally settled by German immigrants beginning about 1840, this beautiful but difficult area of central Texas remains distinctive today. Never easy for agriculture, the Hill Country became home to ranchers that ran sheep, goats, and cattle as the terrain and foliage allowed. In recent decades, the region's beauty has drawn vacationers and retirees. Fredericksburg remains the ethnic German heart of the Hill Country.

West Texas

After the Apache and Comanche were subdued in the late-1870s, this rugged country was settled by farmers and ranchers, many of them from the American Midwest. By the mid-1880s, large ranches overspread West Texas, the railroads had arrived, and cattle moved to the urban markets of the Midwest and East by the tens of thousands. After World War II, ranching gave way to large-scale irrigated agriculture on the high plains of West Texas. Today, the Panhandle and high plains are the heartland of Texas agriculture and of its modern cotton culture. From the wheat fields of the Panhandle, through the heavily irrigated cotton to the south, the oil and gas fields of the **Permian Basin**, and the ranch lands of lightly populated Southwest Texas, the cowboy, vaquero, rancher, farmer, roughneck traditions of Texas still live.

Permian Basin A geological formation in West Texas, around Midland, where oil discoveries were made in the 1920s that remain productive today.

BECOMING MODERN TEXAS

Texas is no longer an overwhelmingly Anglo, sparsely populated, rural state defined by cattle, cotton, and oil. This old Texas has receded before a new Texas that is vibrantly urban and vastly more diverse. The new Texas is urban, majority-minority, and vibrantly entrepreneurial. It has great potential, but that potential will not be realized automatically. Texas's political authorities and citizens will have to see the future coming and respond thoughtfully to insure that "the great state" continues to merit that appellation in the 21st century.

Texas is changing rapidly, though its politics do not seem to be keeping up. Since independence was achieved in 1836, Texas has conceived of itself as an Anglo Republic. For most of the state's history, Anglos comprised two-thirds or more of the state's population and more of its social and economic leadership. Those days are, at least as far as the ethnic and racial make-up of the population is concerned, though not yet the social and economic leadership of the state, passing into history.

Cultural Diversity

Q4 How has the ethnic mix of the Texas population evolved over time?

Dramatic social change has been a constant in Texas history. Figure 1.3 puts contemporary social change in historical perspective. We see that as late as

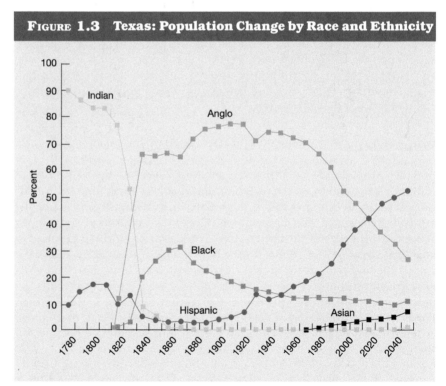

FIGURE **1.3**   **Texas: Population Change by Race and Ethnicity**

Source: Population estimates prior to 1850 are compiled from best available sources. U.S. Census Bureau, Texas: Race and Hispanic Origin: 1850 to 1990, Table 58. Randolph B. Campbell, *Gone To Texas: A History of the Lone Star State* (New York: Oxford University Press, 2003), pp. 470, 472. Projections for 2020 to 2050 come from the Population Estimates and Projection Program, Texas State Data Center, UT, San Antonio. See http://txsdc.utsa.edu/tpepp/2012allcntymigtot.csv

1800, Indians comprised 80 percent of those living in what would become Texas, with Hispanics comprising the remaining 20 percent. But huge change was coming.

Though data are sketchy for the first half of the 19th century, it is clear that the Indian presence in Texas plummeted, the Hispanic presence lagged, while Anglo and black numbers soared. By 1850, Anglos accounted for 65 percent of Texans and blacks for another 26 percent. Indian and Hispanic numbers had fallen to 5 percent and would drift even lower as the end of the century approached. Anglo numbers continued to rise throughout the 19th century. In 1900, Texas was about 75 percent Anglo, 20 percent black, and 4 percent Hispanic. Native-American numbers were vanishingly small. In 1940, when the U.S. Census began reporting Hispanics separately from whites, Anglos were still 74 percent, blacks 14.4 percent, and Hispanics 11.5 percent.

After 1950, slowly at first, but then more rapidly, the racial and ethnic make-up of Texas began to change. The Anglo share of the population began to fall, the black share continued its slow decline, and the Hispanic share began to rise more quickly. Population data from the U.S. Census Bureau and the Texas State Data Center show that Anglos were 66 percent of the population as late as 1980, 61 percent in 1990, 52 percent in 2000 (they fell below 50 percent in 2005), 44 percent in 2015, and are projected to be 41 percent by 2020 and just 27.5 percent by 2050. Blacks have held steady at about 12 percent since 1980, but will slowly decline in coming decades. Projections suggest that blacks will make up 11 percent of the Texas population in 2030 and 10 percent by 2050.

The Hispanic share of the Texas population has doubled since 1970 and will continue to grow rapidly. In 1970, Hispanics composed 18 percent of the population; by 2015 it was 39 percent. Almost 30 percent of Texans speak Spanish at home. A majority of Texans will be of Hispanic heritage by 2040.

Asian Americans, a relatively new presence in Texas, constitute 3.5 percent of the population, but that will more than double, to 8 percent by 2050. Native Americans remain a small proportion of the Texas population. The federal government recognizes three tribes, comprising about one-half of 1 percent of the state's total population. The Alabama-Coushatta live in East Texas, the Tigua in West Texas, and the Kickapoo on the New Mexico border near Eagle Pass.

Urbanization

The first U.S. Census to include Texas was conducted in 1850 and reported that Texas was just 4 percent urban (towns of 2,500 or larger). Most Texans lived in small rural towns and on plantations, farms, and ranches. The Let's Compare box on p. 18 shows that in 1900 Texas was still overwhelmingly rural. Only 17 percent of Texans lived in urban settings, compared to 73 percent of New Yorkers, 55 percent of Pennsylvanians, and 40 percent of Americans. Texas urbanized slowly through the early 20th century, until preparations for World War II spurred an exodus from rural Texas to the military bases and industrial plants in the urban triangle joining Houston, Dallas–Fort Worth, and San Antonio. Today, Houston, San Antonio, and Dallas are three of the ten largest cities

| | | LET'S COMPARE | THE MOVE TO THE CITIES IN TEXAS AND OTHER LARGE STATES |

Texas urbanized slowly and late, but then with a vengeance in the 1940s and 1950s. By 1960, Texas was more urbanized than the nation as a whole and it remains so today. Only 17 percent urban in 1900, Texas is 85 percent urban today, while the U.S. as a whole is 81 percent urban.

In 1900, the South was still mainly agricultural as a glance at Florida, Georgia, and North Carolina, in addition to Texas, will show. New York State was already 73 percent urban, while Illinois, Pennsylvania, and California had already broken 50 percent and Ohio was not far behind. In 1920, the U.S. as a whole broke 50 percent urban and six of the ten largest states in the nation were over 60 percent urban. The South still lagged, with Florida the only southern state more than one-third urban and Texas at just

32 percent urban. The 1930s, a decade consumed by the Great Depression, saw urbanization stagnate in the big, northern, industrial states, but creep forward in the still predominantly agricultural South as displaced farm labor drifted into the cities.

The war years of the 1940s, which brought high demand for oil and petrochemicals and new military bases and war industries to Texas, spurred a human flood out of the countryside and into Texas cities. Texas's urban population jumped 18 percent, from 45 to 63 percent, just 1 percent below the national average, during the 1940s and then continued rapid growth, reaching 75 percent by 1960 and 80 percent by 1970. Eighty-five percent urban today, Texas is one of the most highly urbanized large states in the nation.

	1900	1910	1920	1930	1940	1950	1960	1970	1980	1990	2000	2010
Nation	40	46	51	56	57	64	70	74	74	75	79	81
CA	52	62	68	73	71	81	86	91	91	92	94	95
TX	17	24	32	41	45	63	75	80	80	80	83	85
NY	73	79	83	84	83	86	85	86	85	84	88	88
FL	20	29	37	52	55	66	74	82	84	85	89	91
PA	55	60	65	68	67	71	72	72	69	69	77	79
IL	54	62	68	74	74	78	81	83	83	85	89	88
OH	48	56	64	68	67	70	73	75	73	74	77	78
MI	39	47	61	68	66	71	73	74	71	71	75	75
NC	10	14	19	26	27	34	40	46	48	50	60	66
GA	16	21	25	31	34	45	55	60	62	63	72	75

Source: U.S. Census Bureau, Urban and Rural Population: 1900–90, www.census.gov/population/census data/urpop0090.txt. 2000 data came from U.S. Census Bureau, *Statistical Abstract of the United States, 2014*, p. 35, Table 30.

in the country and fully 70 percent of Texans live in a triangle that connects these three cities. All three of the cities have minority-majority populations

Economic Diversification

As late as 1900, fully two-thirds of Texans were employed in agriculture.[21] The Texas economy expanded through most of the 20th century, but it also showed its vulnerability to unexpected shifts in commodity prices. In addition to Texas agriculture, oil and gas buoyed Texas up through the 1970s. However, when the oil price boom of the 1970s and early 1980s collapsed, dragging down the commercial property market, the banks, and then the whole Texas economy, state leaders vowed to diversify. They thought, rightly, that strength in business services, aerospace, computer and communications technology, health care, and biotechnology would cushion the boom and bust cycle of commodity prices.

Even this new, more diverse, Texas economy has experienced its ups and downs in recent years. The stock market collapse of early 2001 and the attacks of 9/11 later that year devastated the airline and hospitality industries and slowed the national and state economies. Corporate corruption, of which Houston's Enron provided the most glaring example, did further damage. The high-tech industries around Dallas, Austin, and Houston took a beating in 2001 and 2002, but they have rebounded and will be a major factor in the state's future growth. The bust in the housing market and the deep recession of 2008 and 2009 hit Texas hard, though not as hard as most other states.

Table 1.1 highlights both the painful job losses caused by the deep recession of 2008–09 and the resiliency Texas showed in the recovery. Texas lost nearly 400,000 jobs, with goods producing jobs in construction and manufacturing being particularly hard hit. Financial and business services were also badly affected. As the recovery continues, jobs for medical assistants, respiratory therapists, and physical therapy aides are expected to grow by 35 percent in the coming decade. Some teaching fields, such as special education in both elementary and middle schools, will grow by 40 percent. Jobs in energy extraction are also expected to grow by 50 percent.[22]

FUTURE CHALLENGES

Texas has a mythical self-image as a place where an individual willing to work hard can make a life and maybe a fortune. But while Texas is home to great wealth, it is also home to great poverty. Texas ranked only 24th among the 50 states in median household income in 2012, with 17.6 percent of Texans and 25.8 percent of Texas children living below the federally designated poverty line. Only eleven states, mostly in the deep South and Southwest, have a greater proportion of poor citizens than Texas.[23] Texas also has among the highest teen birth rates in the U.S. and a higher proportion of children without health insurance than all but one other state. The future prosperity of Texas depends upon ensuring that more Texans are healthy, well-educated, and profitably employed.

Q5 What factors will determine the future prosperity and stability of Texas?

Pro-Business Climate

Texas is generally rated near the top in the quality of its "business climate." It is home to 52 Fortune 500 companies, more than all the states but California

Table 1.1 Texas Employment by Industry Sector, 2010–2014			
Industry Sector	2010	2012	2014
Goods Producing			
Agriculture*	59,825	58,637	57,162
Natural Resources	205,900	261,800	302,500
Construction	543,700	572,900	625,500
Manufacturing	819,500	856,500	880,700
Service Providing			
Trade, Transportation, and Utilities	2,032,900	2,146,700	2,293,200
Information	198,900	197,000	205,300
Financial Activities	621,300	650,600	691,400
Professional and Business Services	1,226,000	1,368,200	1,494,400
Education and Health Services	1,371,800	1,461,200	1,511,000
Leisure and Hospitality	1,014,500	1,080,500	1,173,900
Government	1,850,400	1,781,200	1,833,900
Other Services	359,100	379,000	404,800
TOTAL EMPLOYMENT	10,303,825	10,814,237	11,473,762

* Agricultural employment is available only in the Texas Quarterly Census.

Source: Texas Labor Market Review, April 2010, May 2012, and April 2014, p. 2 and Texas Quarterly Census of Employment and Wages, 4th quarter 2009, 2nd quarter 2012, and 3rd quarter 2013. Both are at the Texas Workforce Commission website, www.tracer2.com.

and New York. Texans expect government to facilitate freedom and opportunity, mostly by staying out of people's way, and by keeping government small, taxes low, and regulations light. These are core preferences of the Texas political culture and are unlikely to change.

Texas often rates much lower, sometimes near the bottom, on "quality of life." Generally, a high quality of life involves good schools, attractive cities and towns, low pollution, and abundant outdoor recreation. Texas ranks in the mid-40s on education spending, but even lower on the arts, health, welfare, and environmental spending. The state's political leaders, often imagining that they must pick between a good business climate and an attractive quality of life, usually pick a good business climate. Future Texans will demand a better balance.

Educated Workforce

Texans understand that a strong economy requires an educated workforce. Yet, spending the money that it would take to insure excellent schools comes hard to Texans. Texas ranks 29th among the states on the proportion of adults with Bachelor's degrees at 26.4 percent (below the national average of 28.5 percent).

Pro & Con   The Tradeoff Between Taxes and Services

Virtually all of us would like to keep more of what we earn. But most of us realize that we must pay some taxes to fund national defense and air traffic control at the national level and schools and roads at the state and local levels. Arguments arise over what kinds of taxes—income, sales, property—we should have, how high or low they should be set, and who should pay them. But pay them we must.

Texas has always been a low tax state and remains so today. The highly respected Tax Foundation reported that in 2013 state tax collections per person in the U.S. was $2,556, while Texas collected just $1,955. Texas ranked 2nd among the 50 states. Low taxes are a good thing in the abstract, but, as a practical matter, the question always is whether you are collecting the revenues needed to fund key state services.

Conservatives generally argue that low taxes leave money in the pockets of those who earned it, spur entrepreneurship and business creation, and create jobs that allow hard-working people to take care of themselves and their families. As evidence that a low tax, business friendly, environment is working in Texas, conservatives point to decades of rapid population growth and job creation at rates above the national average and above that of any other large state. People are moving to Texas, voting with their feet as the saying goes, because they think opportunities are brighter here.

Progressives (who generally do not want to be called liberals) argue that Texas has serious problems that it is failing to address for lack of understanding and revenue. As exhibits A and B they point to Texas's low ranking among the states on educational attainment and access to health care. According to the Texas Legislature's own 2012 Texas Fact Book, Texas ranks 50th in the proportion of residents over 25 with a high school degree and in the proportion of the population not covered by health insurance. We are number three in teenage births per 100,000 of population.

Would Texas do better if it revised its tax structure to bring in more revenue so that it could increase spending on education, health services, and more? Progressives believe that increasing spending on education, particularly for the disadvantaged and minorities, and increasing broad access to health care services would make for a smarter, healthier, more productive workforce. Conservatives generally believe that public schools are inefficient, public health care programs like Medicaid are wasteful, and raising taxes would kill jobs. What do you think? Can Texas thrive on its current course—a firm commitment to small government, low taxes, and personal responsibility? Or must Texas change course, increase taxes and revenue, improve education and health care, especially for the coming Hispanic majority, so that they can help carry Texas forward? ¿Que opine usted?

But shockingly, Texas ranks last, tied with Mississippi and California, among the states on the proportion of adults over 25 who have graduated from high school (or passed a GED). The national average is 85.9 percent, while Texas graduates 81.1 percent. Texas must do better.

Education reform and funding were the top issues during the 2005 regular legislative session and three special sessions in 2005 and 2006. In May 2006, the Texas legislature finally passed and the governor signed an education reform and funding bill that lowered local property taxes and replaced the money with an expanded business tax, a dollar a pack increase in the tax on cigarettes, and a number of smaller tax increases. Despite endless talk and

TIMELINE: THE ROAD TO TEXAS INDEPENDENCE

February 18, 1823	1825	1829	April 6, 1830	1834	1835
Stephen F. Austin's empresario contract is approved	Green DeWitt, Haden Edwards, and Martin DeLeon establish colonies west, east, and south of Austin's	Mexican government outlaws slavery, spawning discontent in Texas	Mexican government forbids further Anglo immigration to Texas	General Santa Anna becomes dictator of Mexico	Texans win the battles of Gonzales, Goliad, Conception, and San Antonio

years of political wrangling, Texas public schools ended up with little new money. The recession of 2009 and 2010 depressed state revenues, leading the 2011 regular session of the Texas Legislature to cut $4 billion from public education and another $1.5 billion from school maintenance and construction. In the 2013 legislative session, about two-thirds of the money cut in 2011 was restored. Nonetheless, in the most recent data, Texas ranked 38th among the states in funding per student. More money for schools will be necessary to insure that the workforce of the future is well trained.

Inclusion and Empowerment

As Texas continues to evolve ethnically and economically, it must insure that all of its citizens are included and empowered. By 2050, Anglos will constitute just 27.5 percent of the Texas population. Those that Anglo Texans have traditionally called minorities—blacks, Hispanics, Asians—will make up three-quarters of the population, and Hispanics alone will be the new majority. Texas will not thrive unless most, ideally all, of its citizens thrive.[24]

The demographic future of Texas puts a heavy responsibility on all Texans. Anglo Texans, who will control most of the state's wealth long after their numbers wane, will be challenged to finance a state education system that prepares all Texans to contribute their full measure to our future prosperity. Texas's traditional minorities, and especially Hispanic Texans, will be challenged to increase their overall educational achievement and to enter more fully into the political community through naturalization (for those not already citizens), voter registration, voting, and office-holding.

Chapter Summary

When history first took notice of Texas it was home to dozens of Native American bands and tribes. They lived by hunting, fishing, and gathering as they were without horses, cattle, or domesticated animals beyond dogs. The Spanish arrived early in the 16th century and quickly established a broad but thin control of Texas. Almost three centuries later, as the 19th century opened, there were no more than 3,500 Spanish Mexicans north of the Rio Grande.

March 2, 1836	March 6, 1836	March 27, 1836	April 1836	April 15, 1836	April 21, 1836	May 14, 1836
Texas Declaration of Independence signed at Washington-on-the-Brazos	Alamo falls	Slaughter at Goliad ordered by Santa Anna	Texas citizens flee east in the "Runaway Scrape" as Mexicans advance	Texas government flees as Santa Anna burns Harrisburg	Texans defeat the Mexican army under Santa Anna at San Jacinto	Santa Anna signs Treaties of Velasco acknowledging Texas independence

Anglos began streaming into Texas, 90 percent of them out of the American South, after the Louisiana Purchase brought the U.S. to its eastern border. By 1820, even before Austin led his settlers across the Sabine, Anglos outnumbered Spanish Mexicans. After Texas independence in 1836, Anglo immigrants and their slaves reached a floodtide that did not abate for decades. The Civil War and Reconstruction left Texas devastated socially, economically, and psychologically. Cotton farming and cattle ranching were the basis of the Texas economy until oil took the leading role early in the 20th century.

By 1900, Texas was overwhelmingly Anglo; the black population was shrinking and the Hispanic population had not yet begun to expand. Anglo dominance of the Texas society, economy, and politics extended through the first two-thirds of the 20th century, but the ground was shifting. The Mexican Revolution of 1910–21 triggered a slow growth in Texas's Hispanic population and the Great Depression and World War II moved Texans of all sorts from the countryside to the cities. The Texas economy, always heavy on natural resources, diversified into manufacturing, aerospace, banking, insurance, and technology. Just as importantly though, after 1970 the pace of demographic change picked up speed. By 2015, Texas was 45 percent Anglo, 39 percent Hispanic, 11 percent black, and about 4 percent Asian. By 2050, Hispanics will outnumber Anglos by two-to-one in the Texas population and work-force.

Texas Anglos have always been predominantly conservative and they have put their stamp on the state. Scholars use the term political culture to denote broadly held ideas about the relationship of citizens to their government and to each other in matters of politics and public policy. Texas and the South are said to have a traditional political culture in which small government, low taxes, personal responsibility, and elite leadership are the organizing principles of state politics. Even as Texas evolved from predominantly Anglo, rural, and agricultural, to a diverse, urban, commercial and industrial state, it has retained its small government culture. But the challenge of the 21st century in Texas is to expand inclusion and enhance equity as Anglo Texans go from being a large and dominant majority to being less than 30 per cent of the population by 2050. For Texas to be healthy and prosperous in the 21st century, all Texans must be educated, empowered, and involved.

Key Terms

Anglo 3	Political subcultures 8
Balcones Escarpment 10	Reconstruction 3
Civil War 3	Republic of Texas 6
King Ranch 10	Rio Grande 4
Permian Basin 15	Rio Grande Valley 5
Political culture 8	Spindletop 14

Review Questions

1. Explain the origins of the special pride that many Texans, both the native born and transplants, have in their state.
2. Assess how the geography of Texas has affected the economic development of the state.
3. Differentiate the general political culture of the United States from the regional political subculture of the South and especially Texas.
4. Summarize the political and public policy issues raised by the rapid population growth and demographic change in modern Texas.
5. Describe the potential conflicts involved in trying to balance economic development with an attractive quality of life in Texas.

Suggested Readings

Rodolfo Acuna, *Occupied America: A History of Chicanos*, 5th ed. (New York: Pearson Longman, 2004).

Bryan Burrough, *The Big Rich: The Rise and Fall of the Greatest Texas Oil Fortunes* (New York: Penguin Press, 2009).

Randolph B. Campbell, *Gone To Texas: A History of the Lone Star State* (New York: Oxford University Press, 2003).

Gregg Cantrell, *Stephen F. Austin: Empresario of Texas* (New Haven, CT: Yale University Press, 1999).

T.R. Fehrenbach, *Lone Star: A History of Texas and the Texans* (New York: Macmillan, 1968).

Paul Ganster and David E. Lorey, *The U.S.–Mexican Border Into the 21st Century* (New York: Rowan and Littlefield, 2008).

David M. Hart, "The Politics of 'Entrepreneurial' Economic Development Policy of States in the U.S.," *Review of Policy Research* (2008), 25: 149–168.

Joel Lieske, "The Changing Regional Subcultures of the American States and the Utility of a New Cultural Measure," *Political Research Quarterly* (2010), 63: 538–552.

Gary Moncrief and Peverill Squire, *Why States Matter* (New York: Rowman and Littlefield, 2013).

Joel H. Silbey, *Storm Over Texas: The Annexation Controversy and the Road to the Civil War* (New York: Oxford University Press, 2005).

Web Resources

1. **http://www.lsjunction.com/**
   The Lone Star Junction website contains great resources on Texas history and politics. It rewards exploration.

2. **http://texashistory.unt.edu/**
   Like the Lone Star Junction, the University of North Texas's Portal to Texas History is well worth exploring.

3. **http://www.census.gov/**
   The U.S. Census Bureau website contains an extraordinary range of information on population, income, race, and ethnicity, most of it by state.

4. **http://www.texas.gov/**
   The general website for the state of Texas.

5. **http://www.texasalmanac.com/**
   Published every year since 1957, a comprehensive source for all things Texas.

6. **http://www.pewhispanic.org/**
   A key site for research and data on the rise of the Hispanic population in the U.S.

7. **http://www.cfed.org/**
   Corporation for Economic Development (CFED) created the Development Report Card for States.

8. **http://www.itif.org/**
   Like CFED, the Information Technology and Innovation Foundation compares states on its New Economy Index.

Chapter 2

THE TEXAS CONSTITUTION AND AMERICAN FEDERALISM

BOB BULLOCK AND THE INCOME TAX

Democratic theory understands constitutions to be superior to regular laws. Both have their roots in the authority of the people, but in somewhat different ways. Constitutions are written documents that layout the structure, powers, and processes of government and must be ratified by a vote of the people before they can go into effect. Constitutions can be amended or changed, but the amendment process also requires popular approval. Laws, on the other hand, can be passed by elected representatives of the people, usually legislatures and governors, without direct popular involvement. Constitutions, then, are superior to and more fundamental than regular laws.

The distinction between constitutions and laws became critical to the political prospects of one of Texas's leading public officials, Bob Bullock, when he got crosswise of the income tax issue in the 1980s and 1990s. Texas, then as now, was one of only seven states that do not levy an income tax and most Texans like it that way. But for more than one hundred years, often when recessions hit and state revenues decline, Texas politicians have flirted with the idea of an income tax. As early as 1907, Texas Governor Thomas M. Campbell proposed both an income tax and an inheritance tax, losing the income tax but winning a modest inheritance tax. As Texas and the nation struggled under the Great Depression of the 1930s, Governor Ross Sterling in 1931 and Miriam "Ma" Ferguson in 1933 proposed income tax legislation—both failed.

More recently and more famously, Bob Bullock, one of the most interesting Texas politicians of the last quarter of the 20th century, pushed an income tax for several years. Bullock was boisterous, aggressive, determined, and opponents rarely crossed him. Like Sam Houston in some ways, Bob Bullock was a flawed giant. Like Houston, Bullock was a heavy drinker and he could claim five wives to Houston's three. But also like Houston, he spent his adult life serving Texas. Bullock served in the Texas House (1957–59), and as Secretary of State (1971–73), but his greatest contributions were made as Comptroller of Public Accounts (1975–91) and Lieutenant Governor (1991–99).

As Comptroller, Bullock was responsible for tracking revenues and insuring that the state budget remained in balance. Revenues were plentiful in the 1970s, but energy prices and severance tax revenues began to decline in the early 1980s and then crashed devastatingly in the mid-1980s. Bullock warned that tax reform would be necessary and in late 1985 he said, "We need new revenue. Yes, I'm talking about an income tax. It's political death to anyone who mentions it, but you have to think about it." Shortly after being elected Lieutenant Governor in 1990, Bullock again advocated an income tax and tried to push a bill through the 1991 regular session of the Texas Legislature. Not only did he fail, he faced enough blowback that he thought it wise to seek cover. What to do!

If pushing an income tax bill had cost him support, maybe advocating a constitutional amendment prohibiting an income tax could help rebuild that support. Bullock proposed an amendment requiring that both houses of the legislature and a majority of Texas voters had to agree before an income tax could go into effect. Even then the amendment required that two-thirds of the revenue raised from an income tax go to reduction of property taxes and the remaining one-third go to public education. The amendment was adopted in November 1993—Bullock had saved Texas from an income tax, voters relaxed, and Bullock was safe. It's good to be flexible, light on your political feet, and to know the difference between laws and constitutions.

Focus Questions

Q1 What restraints does federalism impose on Texas politics?

Q2 How do the U.S. and Texas Constitutions share political authority in Texas?

Q3 What similarities and differences have characterized Texas's seven constitutions?

Q4 What are the basic principles and key provisions of the current Texas Constitution?

Q5 Should constitutional reform be on the political agenda in Texas?

Federalism A form of government in which some powers are assigned to the national government, some to the states, and some, such as the power to tax, are shared.

Constitution Basic or fundamental law that lays out the structure of government, the powers of each office, the process by which officials are elected or appointed, and the rights and liberties of citizens.

ederalism is an American invention. For most of human history, people thought that governments had to be highly centralized, as in monarchy or tyranny, or highly decentralized, as in loose confederations of sovereign states. The U.S. Founders thought that carefully written constitutions allowed two levels of government, national and state, to act over the same territory and people simultaneously. Yet, the Founders were practical men; they knew that shared powers invited conflict. The struggle between national and state actors for the power and resources to define and address the dominant issues of American political life is a permanent feature of American federalism.

The United States Constitution and the fifty state constitutions, including the Texas Constitution, derive their authority from popular sovereignty: the freely granted approval of the people. **Constitutions** are basic or fundamental law, superior to, and controlling of, the everyday acts of government. Constitutions describe the structure of government, the powers of each office, the process by which officials are elected or appointed to office, and the rights and liberties of citizens. Constitutions both award and limit political authority.

The U.S. Constitution and the fifty state constitutions all mandate similar institutions. All employ separation of powers, checks and balances, bicameralism, and the explicit protection of individual liberties through a bill of rights. All have a chief executive, a bicameral or two-house legislature (except Nebraska, which gets by with a unicameral legislature), and a judicial system of trial and appellate courts. All explicitly protect the rights and liberties of citizens.

Despite these structural similarities, states vary widely in how they understand the balance of power in American federalism. These debates are as old as the nation; older than Texas. Before the ink on the U.S. Constitution was dry, Alexander Hamilton, speaking for much northern opinion, argued that the national government was supreme over the states. Thomas Jefferson, speaking for much southern opinion, argued that national powers were narrowly limited. Regional opinions hardened over the first half of the 19th century.

The Anglo settlement of Texas came overwhelmingly out of the American South. As an independent nation from 1836 to 1845, Texas was even more prickly about "states' rights" than the rest of the South. When the Civil War came, Texas unhesitatingly joined the Confederacy. Texas historian T.R. Fehrenbach, author of the iconic *Lone Star: A History of Texas and the Texans* (1968), placed Texas deep in the states' rights tradition, writing that as the Civil War approached, "All evidence shows that then (and afterward) much southern educated opinion felt that the Union was designed originally as a confederacy, in which sovereign states possessed an inherent right to come and go."[1] While Fehrenbach is undoubtedly correct, after all, the secession vote was 46,153 Yes to 14,747 No, not all Texans took the strong states' rights view. As the debate over secession raged, Governor Sam Houston reminded his fellow citizens that Texas "entered not into the North, nor into the South, but into the Union."[2]

Houston also warned his fellow Texans that northern numbers and industrial capability would overwhelm the South, but the war came anyway and the South did lose. The Confederacy was structured around state sovereignty and limited national powers. Nonetheless, Texas Governor Pendleton Murrah complained regularly about "federal encroachment" by the Confederate government in Richmond.

Joseph F. Zimmerman, a leading student of American federalism, has argued that though state sovereignty survived the Civil War, the idea of secession did not.

> The question of whether a state may secede from the Union was answered by the defeat of the Confederate States of America in the Civil War. In Texas v. White, Chief Justice Salmon P. Chase of the U.S. Supreme Court declared in 1869 that, "the Constitution . . . looks to an indestructible Union, composed of indestructible States."[3]

Chief Justice Chase's view is widely held today, though still somewhat grudgingly in parts of the South.

Not surprisingly, states also vary in the powers given to their governments, the concentration or diffusion of those powers, and the precise limits and checks employed. As we shall see below, the Texas Constitution limits political power more than most state constitutions, distributes power broadly through a diffuse political system, and encourages political officials to check each other at every turn. By design, the Texas Constitution makes indecision easy and decision difficult.

In this chapter, we describe the balance of constitutional authority between the national and the state governments in the American federal system. We trace Texas constitutionalism from its origins in Spanish Mexico, through the tumult of independence, statehood, and the American Civil War. We then explore the current (we cannot really say modern) Texas Constitution of 1876. We close with a discussion of the prospects for constitutional reform in Texas.

TEXAS: A STATE IN THE AMERICAN FEDERAL SYSTEM

The U.S. Constitution defines the balance of power in American federalism.[4] Article VI contains the famous "**supremacy clause**," which declares "this Constitution, and the laws of the United States which shall be made in pursuance thereof; . . . shall be the supreme law of the land; and the judges in every state shall be bound thereby, anything in the Constitution or laws of any State to the contrary notwithstanding." This seems pretty definitive: national power trumps state power.

In practice, federalism is murkier than the supremacy clause suggests. The national government is a government of **enumerated powers**, powers specifically allocated to it in the Constitution. Within these areas of enumerated

Q1 What restraints does federalism impose on Texas politics?

Supremacy clause Article VI of the U.S. Constitution declares the U.S. Constitution, federal laws, and treaties to be the supreme law of the land.

Enumerated powers The specifically listed, or enumerated, powers of the Congress and president found in Article I, section 8, and Article II, section 2, of the U.S. Constitution.

power—foreign policy, national defense, interstate and foreign commerce, immigration and naturalization, and a few others—national authority is supreme. But where authority is not granted to the national government by the U.S. Constitution, state governments enjoy complete or plenary powers, unless specific powers are denied them by their state constitution. Traditionally, states have made most policy regarding education, public safety, health care, transportation, family law, business regulation, and much more.[5]

National Powers

Q2 How do the U.S. and Texas Constitutions share political authority in Texas?

Necessary and proper clause The last paragraph of Article I, section 8, of the U.S. Constitution states that Congress may make all laws deemed necessary and proper for carrying into execution the powers specifically enumerated in Article I, section 8.

The U.S. Constitution grants a number of specific or enumerated powers to the national government. Article I, section 8, and Article II, section 2, give the national government the exclusive power to conduct foreign policy; raise, support, and command an army and navy; establish a national currency; set uniform rules for naturalization and bankruptcy; and regulate interstate and foreign commerce. Moreover, Article I, section 8, concludes with the **"necessary and proper" clause**, or elastic clause as it is sometimes known. The elastic clause gives the national government broad discretion to act in regard to its enumerated powers. It declares that Congress has the power "to make all laws which shall be necessary and proper for carrying into execution the foregoing [enumerated] powers, and all other powers vested by this Constitution in the government of the United States, or in any department or officer thereof." The U.S. Supreme Court interpreted the "necessary and proper"

AP Photo/J. Scott Applewhite

The U.S. Supreme Court is the final arbiter of the meaning of the U.S. Constitution and of its relationship to state constitutions and laws.

clause expansively in *McCulloch v. Maryland* (1819). Chief Justice John Marshall wrote: "Let the end be legitimate, let it be within the scope of the Constitution, and all means which are appropriate, which are plainly adopted to that end, which are not prohibited but consistent with the letter and spirit of the Constitution are constitutional."

Amendments to the U.S. Constitution also expanded national power over the states. The 13th (1865), 14th (1868), and 15th (1870) Amendments gave Congress the power to end slavery, define American citizenship, and ensure the right of black men to vote. The 19th Amendment (1920) gave Congress the power to enforce female suffrage, the 24th (1964) to suppress the poll tax, and the 26th (1971) to enforce the right of 18- to 20-year-olds to vote. Finally, the "due process" and "equal protection" clauses of the 14th Amendment have been used to make the rights and liberties outlined in the U.S. Bill of Rights apply against the state as well as the national governments.

Powers Reserved to the States

Many among the founding generation worried that the new national government might oppress the states and their citizens. The very first Congress proposed, and the states adopted, ten amendments to the new Constitution—the Bill of Rights. The 10th Amendment declared that "the powers not delegated to the United States by the Constitution, nor prohibited by it to the states, are reserved to the states respectively, or to the people."

The political scientist Joseph Zimmerman has explained the scope and variety of the **reserved powers** of the states by dividing them into three categories: "the police power, provision of services to citizens, and creation and control of local governments."[6] States are operating within their general "police power" when they act to promote public health, welfare, safety, morals, and convenience. States also provide a wide range of public services, including police and fire protection, road construction, and education. And states have the constitutional authority to create and regulate local governments. The reserved powers of the states give them the authority, if they choose to use it, to govern much of daily life.

> **Reserved powers** The 10th Amendment to the U.S. Constitution declares that powers not granted to the national government by the Constitution are reserved to the states or their citizens.

Moreover, the 11th Amendment (1798) to the U.S. Constitution explicitly recognizes the **sovereign immunity** of the states. The 11th Amendment says "the judicial power of the United States shall not be construed to extend to any suit in law or equity, commenced or prosecuted against one of the United States by citizens of another state, or by citizens or subjects of any foreign state." This means that states, as sovereign entities, cannot be forced to appear in the courts of another sovereign, whether the Federal courts, the courts of another American state, or those of a foreign nation. Similarly, states cannot be sued in their own courts unless state law expressly provides for such suits. Despite these explicit constitutional protections, states have had to fight to maintain their powers and prerogatives in the federal system.

> **Sovereign immunity** The 11th Amendment to the U.S. Constitution declares that states cannot be sued in their own courts, the courts of other states, other nations, or in federal courts except as their own state laws or federal law explicitly allows.

Pro & Con   What Does the 10th Amendment Really Mean?

Throughout American history, advocates of a robust national government have pointed to Congress's power to tax and spend for the general welfare, to regulate commerce, and to do those things "necessary and proper" to carrying out their responsibilities. States' rights advocates have countered that the national government is a government of limited and specifically "enumerated" powers. They also have pointed to the 10th Amendment, "The powers not delegated to the United States by the Constitution, nor prohibited by it to the states, are reserved to the states respectively, or to the people," to demonstrate that all power not explicitly given to the national government remains with the states and their citizens.

The question of the relative priority of federal versus state authority plagued the Founders during the Constitutional Convention, was one of the central points over which ratification was fought, and has surfaced time and again throughout American history. In the 1860s we fought a bloody Civil War over just this issue—national versus state authority within the federal system.

For most of American history, the claims of state officials that federal officials construed their powers too broadly and thereby infringed on state powers protected by the 10th Amendment were taken seriously in the nation's courts. All of that changed during the "Great Depression," in 1937 to be exact. President Franklin Roosevelt moved aggressively to deal with the depression, using new legislation and regulation, backed by unprecedented spending, to stimulate the economy, but the Supreme Court resisted, striking down major parts of his agenda. FDR responded by trying to "pack" the Court with new and more compliant members. Some of FDR's fiercest opponents were Texans, including Vice

President John Nance "Cactus Jack" Garner. Garner stood for limited government and states' rights, so when the Supreme Court acceded to Roosevelt's demand for more national power to fight the depression, Garner was outraged. After 1937, the Court wholly abandoned its traditional role of limiting federal power. Only in the mid-1980s did the Court begin to challenge federal powers, but only occasionally on the basis of the 10th Amendment.

How then can states push back against unwelcome actions by the federal government? One option is nullification. The South long argued that states can render federal laws null and void within their boundaries if they believe the laws are unconstitutional—meaning touching matters beyond the scope of the Congress's enumerated powers. Nullification would involve a state government declaring an act of Congress void and the federal courts upholding that claim. The Supreme Court has declared a federal law an unconstitutional violation of the "reserved powers" of the states under the 10th Amendment only twice in the last half century. Not very promising.

Informal nullification occurs in a variety of ways, most involving state and public reluctance to comply with a particular federal statute. State resistance to federal marijuana laws and the Obama health care law, for example, is well within the American traditions of political bargaining, popular democracy, and federalism. If state authorities challenge federal authorities carefully, or if state authorities find some support in the federal courts, federal authorities might react by bargaining with them or at least limiting enforcement.

Can you think of any issues besides marijuana use and Obamacare where state and federal powers come into conflict?

Shared Powers

While some powers belong exclusively to the national government, such as the power to make war, and others belong exclusively to the states, such as the power to create local governments, other powers are shared. Both the national and state governments have the power to tax, borrow, and spend; to build and maintain roads and highways; to regulate commerce within their respective jurisdictions; and to administer social services. The Founders expected some conflict between the national government and the states, but they sought to limit conflict between the states.

Relations among the States

Article IV, sections 1 and 2, of the U.S. Constitution require the states to respect each other's civil acts, deal fairly with each other's citizens, and return suspected criminals who flee from one state into another. Broadly, these constitutional provisions were intended to push down on the boundaries between states to promote the growth of a national community of rights and opportunities.

Full Faith and Credit. Article IV, section 1, of the U.S. Constitution requires that "Full Faith and Credit shall be given in each State to the public Acts, Records, and Judicial Proceedings of every other State." Through this simple provision, the Founders sought to create a national legal system by requiring the states to recognize and respect each others' legal acts and findings. Think how important it is, for example, that marriages, divorces, and adoptions executed in one state are recognized and respected when persons or families move. Nonetheless, over the course of American history, social issues such as religious toleration, slavery, and gay marriage have strained the reciprocity and cooperation between the states.

Privileges and Immunities. Article IV, section 2, of the U.S. Constitution declares that "the Citizens of each State shall be entitled to all Privileges and Immunities of Citizens in the several States." The U.S. Supreme Court has declared that the "privileges and immunities" clause guarantees that citizens visiting, working, and conducting business in other states enjoy "the same freedom possessed by the citizens of those States in the acquisition and enjoyment of property and in the pursuit of happiness; and . . . the equal protection of the laws." Again, the point is to promote movement and opportunity by ensuring that newcomers have the same rights and responsibilities as established residents.

Extradition. Article IV, section 2, provides for a legal process called extradition. "A person charged in any state with treason, felony, or other crime, who shall flee from justice, and be found in another state, shall on demand of the executive authority of the state from which he fled, be delivered up, to be removed to the state having jurisdiction of the crime." In Texas history, the smart criminals headed for Mexico, the stupid ones for Louisiana. Extradition requests remain a staple of television police dramas.

Historically, the U.S. Constitution gave the national government responsibility for military and foreign policy and left Texas and her sister states in charge of their own "internal police." But as the nation has grown in size, population, wealth, and complexity, the boundary line between the national government's "supremacy" within its areas of constitutional responsibility and the states' "reserved powers" has shifted and blurred.

During the 19th century, domestic policy was state and local policy. But the economic and social problems accompanying the Great Depression of the 1930s convinced most Americans that the national government had to play a larger role in social and economic policymaking. National influence over state governments and policy grew through the 1970s. Beginning with the Reagan administration in the 1980s, conservatives in the executive branch, Congress, and the courts sought to restore some domestic policy responsibilities to the states. This process has been called **devolution**.

Nonetheless, the federal government continues to guide and direct the states in myriad ways. Fully 35.5 percent of the funds that Texas state government spends each year comes from the federal government and these funds always have strings attached. In addition, the federal government frequently requires action by the states, in regard to education reform, pollution control, and prisoner treatment, among many other issues, without providing the funds to comply. These requirements are called **unfunded mandates** and are a particular irritant to the states.

Devolution The return of political authority from the national government to the states.

Unfunded mandates States frequently complain that the federal government mandates actions, such as improving education, without providing sufficient funds to fulfill the mandate.

THE CONSTITUTIONAL HISTORY OF TEXAS

Q3 What similarities and differences have characterized Texas's seven constitutions?

Table 2.1 shows that Texans have lived under seven constitutions, five since statehood.[7] Hispanic and Anglo Texans lived under the Spanish imperial government of New Spain before Mexico achieved its independence in 1821. In 1824, Mexico adopted a federal constitution; in 1827, authorities in Mexico City approved a provincial constitution that rolled Texas into the northern Mexican province of Coahuila. Texas's independence brought adoption of the hastily prepared 1836 Constitution of the Republic of Texas. Texas's annexation to the United States in 1845 required another new constitution.

Secession, military defeat, reconstruction, and readmission brought a series of short-lived Texas constitutions between 1861 and 1869. As soon as Reconstruction ended, Texans overturned the hated Constitution of 1869 and replaced it with a new constitution that made Texas state government weaker,

TABLE 2.1 The Seven Constitutions of Texas	
Constitution	**Years in Effect**
Coahuila y Tejas	1827–35
Republic of Texas	1836–45
U.S. Statehood	1845–61
C.S.A. Statehood	1861–65
Presidential Reconstruction	1866–69
Congressional Reconstruction	1869–76
Modern Texas	1876–present

more diffuse, and in the minds of its authors, less dangerous. The Texas Constitution of 1876 remains in effect today.

1827 Coahuila y Tejas *Constitution*

Spain ruled Mexico for nearly 300 years, until a decade-long revolution (1810–21) established Mexican independence. Neither Spain nor Mexico established stable government on its lightly populated northern frontier.[8] Mexico attempted to do so by wrapping Texas into the northern Mexican state of Coahuila. Texans enjoyed a modest representation in the *Coahuila y Tejas* legislature, one of ten members initially and two of twelve once the provincial Constitution was completed in 1827. Texans felt outnumbered and ignored. They twice petitioned to be a separate Mexican state, but were turned down both times.

1836 *Republic of Texas Constitution*

Texans declared their independence from Mexico on March 2, 1836. In the chaotic days that followed the fall of the Alamo, as Houston struggled to build an army, Texas political officials worked to produce a new constitution. The Republic of Texas Constitution, adopted on March 17, 1836, reflected basic U.S. principles, including separation of powers, checks and balances, and bicameralism.

Reading of the Texas Declaration of Independence by Charles and Fanny Normann. Collection of the Joe Fultz estate, Navasota, Texas. Courtesy of the Star of the Republic Museum

The Texas Constitutional Convention of 1836 met at Washington-on-the-Brazos. The convention was called to order on March 1 and approved the new constitution on March 17.

The president was limited to a single three-year term, but while in office he enjoyed many of the powers of the U.S. president. He was commander-in-chief of Texas military forces, though he was prohibited from commanding in person without the formal permission of the Congress. He was empowered to negotiate treaties and make senior appointments with the advice and consent of the Congress, and he had power to grant reprieves and pardons. The Congress of the Republic of Texas was made up of a House and Senate. Members of the House served one-year terms and senators served three-year terms, with one-third of the Senate elected annually. Supreme Court justices and state judges were elected by a joint-ballot of the Congress for a four-year term, and were eligible for re-election.

For individual Texans, slavery and freedom stood side-by-side in the Republic of Texas Constitution. Slavery was legalized and free blacks were forbidden to live in Texas without the express permission of Congress. All white men were assured a broad array of rights and liberties, including a homestead if they did not already possess one. All white men enjoyed the right to vote and to stand for office if they so chose.

The Constitution concluded with a Declaration of Rights (again addressed mostly to white men) that followed closely the U.S. Bill of Rights. It guaranteed freedom of speech, press, and religion. It guaranteed the right against self-incrimination, the right to a speedy trial, and the right against cruel and unusual punishment. It also guaranteed citizens against imprisonment for debt and declared that "monopolies are contrary to the genius of free government."

1845 U.S. Statehood Constitution

Texas joined the United States of America as the 28th state in 1845. The statehood Constitution was modeled on the U.S. Constitution and the constitutions of southern states already in the Union, particularly Kentucky and Louisiana.[9] Universal, white, male suffrage and slavery were again embraced. On the one hand, all white men, including Hispanics, which counted as progressive in 1845, were permitted to vote and to hold state and local office. On the other hand, slavery and the rights of slaveholders were reinforced. The legislature was forbidden to emancipate slaves without compensation or to prohibit immigrants to Texas from bringing their slaves with them.

The governor's term was cut to two years, but re-election was permitted, so long as a governor served no more than four years in any six-year period. The legislature was to meet biennially (every other year) rather than annually. Members of the Texas House served two-year terms and members of the Senate served four-year terms. The Texas judiciary was comprised of district courts of original jurisdiction and a three-member Supreme Court to hear appeals.

The governor appointed, by and with the advice and consent of the Senate, the secretary of state, the attorney general, and members of the judiciary. The legislature, by joint-ballot, elected a state treasurer and a comptroller of public accounts. The Bill of Rights, moved to the front of the document as Article I, included all of the protections afforded by the Constitution of 1836 and more.

In addition to protection of individual rights and liberties, the Constitution of 1845 sought to protect citizens against predatory corporations and business practices. Monopolies were again prohibited, as were state chartered banks, and corporations were required to secure a legislative charter.

Finally, the Constitution of 1845 included a restrictive amendment procedure. Amendments had to be approved by a two-thirds vote in each house of the legislature in two consecutive sessions of the legislature — got that. Only one amendment, but an important one, ever passed. In 1850, Texas adopted a "plural executive," making most senior executive branch officials, including the state treasurer, comptroller, and land commissioner, elected as opposed to appointed officials like the governor and the lieutenant governor. The idea was to enhance popular control by diffusing executive power across a number of independently elected officials.

1861 C.S.A. Statehood Constitution

When Texas seceded from the Union and joined the Confederate States of America (C.S.A.), it needed a new constitution. The 1845 Constitution was simply amended to remove references to the U.S.A. and insert references to the C.S.A. Slavery was, of course, retained and slave-owners were forbidden to free their slaves without state government approval.

1866 Presidential Reconstruction Constitution

Within days of General Lee's surrender at Appomattox, President Lincoln was assassinated and Andrew Johnson became president. Lincoln was, of course, a Republican, but he had reached across party lines to select Johnson, a Tennessee Unionist senator, former Democrat, and slaveholder, as his running mate in the wartime election of 1864. Lincoln intended Johnson's selection as a signal to the nation that unity could and would be restored. But with Lincoln dead, President Johnson was left alone to shape post-war policy. Johnson required only that southern states renounce slavery and secession before rejoining the Union. Texas again sought lightly to revise its 1845 Constitution.

The Constitution of 1866 abolished slavery, renounced the ordinance of secession and the right of secession for the future, and repudiated wartime debts. However, blacks were denied the right to vote, hold office, serve on juries, or attend the public schools.[10] Republicans in Congress were outraged and grew increasingly assertive. In 1867, they seized control of the reconstruction process from President Johnson and demanded that new constitutions be written to assure equal rights to the former slaves. Most southern states, including Texas, resisted and the U.S. Congress eventually responded with force.

1869 Congressional Reconstruction Constitution

In March of 1867, Congress disbanded the southern state governments and divided the South into five districts for military occupation, with one composed of Texas and Louisiana. Each state was required to ratify the 14th

TEXAS LEGENDS   JOHN H. REAGAN: TEXAS'S RETURN TO THE UNION

John H. Reagan (1818–1905) had a keener understanding of constitutions and federalism than perhaps any other Texan of the 19th century. Like Sam Houston, Reagan's understanding of these issues was emotional, political, and legal. Houston was a generation older than Reagan, so secession and the Civil War ended Houston's role in Texas politics and nearly ended Reagan's.

Reagan was born in Sevierville, Tennessee, near modern day Gatlinburg, on October 8, 1818. He moved to Texas at 19 and worked as a surveyor and tutor while he read the law. He earned his law license in 1846 and was first elected to the Texas House in 1847. Though defeated for re-election in 1849, he was immediately elected district judge in Palestine where he served to 1857. He was elected to the U.S. House in 1857, where he served as a moderate unionist until he returned to Texas when it became clear that the state would secede. He was elected to the Confederate Congress in 1861 but served only a matter of weeks before President Jefferson Davis appointed him Post Master General of the Confederacy. Reagan was a respected member of President Davis's cabinet throughout the war and was, in fact, captured with Davis by union troops on May 10, 1865, near Irwinville, Georgia.

Reagan was imprisoned at Fort Warren in Boston. During his imprisonment, he wrote an open letter to Texas advising that it work cooperatively with the national government to foreswear slavery, renounce secession and the legal acts of the Confederacy, and accept some political role for the newly freed slaves. Otherwise, he warned, union power, perhaps including extended military occupation, would be imposed. Better, he argued, to give the North what it demanded, return to full representation in Congress, and resist from there. Texas leaders ignored Reagan, resisted federal demands, and ultimately suffered the fate that Reagan had predicted. For a time, Reagan's counsel got him denounced as a Yankee sympathizer.

As the weight of Reconstruction pressed hard on Texas, Reagan's reputation revived and before long he became known as the "Old Roman." He played a leading role in the Constitutional Convention of 1875 before being re-elected to his old seat in the U.S. House where he would serve until 1887. In Congress, Reagan chaired the prestigious Committee on Commerce from 1877 through 1887. Reagan served four years in the U.S. Senate before returning to Texas when Governor James S. Hogg appointed him to the new Texas Railroad Commission. He chaired the Railroad Commission from 1897 to 1903 when he retired. John Henninger Reagan died on March 6, 1905.

Few 19th-century Texans served in high political office as long or as well as Reagan. Like Houston, he was a unionist, but unlike Houston, he chose to serve the Confederacy once Texas decided to join. But having served in the Confederate cabinet throughout the war, he saw clearly that continued resistance to key northern aims, like granting political rights to the freedmen, was both futile and dangerous, so he advised compliance. Though many of his fellow citizens initially denounced him, the "Old Roman" persevered and Texas came again to admire him and to raise him to high office. Though not as famous today as Sam Houston, John H. Reagan deserves to be ranked with the Texas Legends.[11]

Amendment and to draft a constitution that insured the political equality of black men. With white men who had actively supported the Confederacy barred from voting, black and white Republicans controlled the Constitutional Convention of 1868. Divisions soon emerged among Republicans over whether to move incrementally or immediately to black equality. Democrats opposed black equality. Moderate Republicans wanted to go slow while radical Republicans, led by convention chair Edmund J. Davis, favored full equality. Radicals won. Black men were assured equal rights with white men, including the right to vote, stand for office, serve on juries, and send their children to public schools.

The new Constitution centralized power in the hands of the governor and gave him a four-year term. The governor appointed most executive, judicial, and local officials; commanded the state militia; and controlled the state police. Salaries were generous, the state legislature met annually, and a new public school system required high taxes.[12] Most Republicans approved the new Constitution while those Democrats still eligible to vote were ready to adopt anything that would end military occupation and secure readmission to the Union. The Constitution was approved by the lopsided vote of 72,446 to 4,928.

In a much closer contest, radical Republican E.J. Davis narrowly defeated moderate Republican A.J. Hamilton (39,901 to 39,092) for the governorship. Davis used the full powers of the governor's office to restore order to postwar Texas, constitute loyal local governments, and provide free public education to all children. Davis' use of the state militia and police to protect the freedmen against violence offended many whites, and the high taxes required by the new public school system confirmed the worst fears of his opponents. As soon as Texas statehood was restored and former confederates returned to the electorate in 1872, Democrats returned to power in the legislature. In 1873, Democrat Richard Coke ousted Davis from the governorship.

1876 Texas Constitution

Initially, Governor Coke and the Democratic leaders in the legislature sought only modest reforms to the Constitution of 1869. They acknowledged that the powers of government were great, but promised to use them in the interest of the state's resurgent white majority. Despite extensive debate, the politicians were unable to forge a proposal that could pass popular muster. White Texans had had their fill of a government strong enough to order them about. The legislature finally admitted defeat and called for a constitutional convention.

The Constitutional Convention of 1875 was determined to return to Texas's traditional preferences for limited government, low taxes, and local control, and to fasten them down in explicit constitutional provisions.[13] Delegates believed that the purpose of a constitution was to restrict political power. They proceeded very systematically to do precisely that. The governor's term was reduced from four years to two, his salary was cut from $5,000 to $4,000, and his power to appoint most statewide and local officials was removed.

The legislature was to meet biennially, the length of the sessions was strictly limited, and the legislator's pay was cut to just five dollars a day for the first sixty days of the session and two dollars a day thereafter—a decision meant to encourage them to get their work done and go home. The Texas Supreme Court was divided into two high courts. The new Supreme Court was limited to hearing appeals in civil cases and a Court of Appeals (renamed the Court of Criminal Appeals in 1891) was created to hear appeals of criminal cases. Finally, the administration of local schools, along with some state funds, was returned to local officials. Texas voters overwhelmingly approved the new Constitution, 136,606 to 56,652, in February 1876.

The Constitution of 1876, though frequently amended, still governs Texas. Texas elites have always favored small government, low taxes, and an open field for entrepreneurship and competition. And with the singular exception of the Republican Reconstruction Constitution of 1869, when the traditional Texas elites were temporarily sidelined, they have prevailed. Now we ask how well the Texas Constitution works today.

THE TEXAS CONSTITUTION TODAY

All fifty state constitutions, including the Texas Constitution, have the misfortune of being compared to the U.S. Constitution. The U.S. Constitution, in just 4,300 words in the original document, 8,500 including its twenty-seven amendments, defines the structure and powers of the national government and the federal system. State constitutions are almost invariably longer, more detailed, and more frequently amended. As a result, they enjoy less respect than the U.S. Constitution.

The average state constitution is over 39,000 words and has been amended 147 times. Alabama holds the dubious distinction of having the longest and most frequently amended constitution, at 376,000 words and 880 amendments. California's constitution, at nearly 67,000 words, has been amended more than 527 times. The Texas Constitution is about 89,000 words and has been amended 483 times (as of November 2013).[14]

Bill of Rights

Q4 What are the basic principles and key provisions of the current Texas Constitution?

Article I of every Texas constitution since statehood has been dedicated to guaranteeing an extensive list of personal freedoms. As we have seen, there has always been lots of overlap between the U.S. Bill of Rights and the Texas Bill of Rights. Both guarantee freedom of speech, press, religion, assembly, and petition. Both guarantee rights to a speedy trial before a jury of one's peers and protections against unreasonable searches, seizures, and double jeopardy.

But the Texas Bill of Rights offers some protections that the U.S. Bill of Rights does not. For example, in Texas, "no person shall be outlawed," "no person shall be committed . . . except on competent medical or psychiatric testimony," and "no person shall be imprisoned for debt." While these provisions protect a relative few, below we discuss a number of special bill of rights provisions that impact all Texans. Moreover, Texans have, in recent decades, turned to the protection of gender and victim's rights. Texas added an equal rights amendment to the Constitution in 1972. Eighteen other states have ERA provisions in their constitutions and four more have narrower equal rights provisions.[15] Victims' rights provisions were added in 1989 and 1997. Victims of crime have the right to be present at all stages of the legal process, to confer with prosecutors, and to receive restitution and compensation where appropriate.

Who Knew?

As late as 1960, all 50 states had laws against homosexual conduct, also called anti-sodomy laws, and in 2003 Texas was one of 14 states that still had such a law in force. In 2003, in a case called *Lawrence v. Texas*, the Supreme Court declared the Texas law unconstitutional. The Texas legislature declined to remove the law from the books but did insert a note in the Texas Penal Code saying that the law had been declared unconstitutional. Very helpful.

LET'S COMPARE	THE TEXAS CONSTITUTION TO NINE OTHER STATE CONSTITUTIONS

State constitutions are not only less awe-inspiring than the U.S. Constitution, they are almost always longer, more detailed, and, hence, more frequently amended. The U.S. Constitution, in force since 1789, is 8,500 words long, including amendments, and has been amended only 27 times in its history. The shortest constitution (see table below), Illinois's at 16,400 words, is twice as long as the U.S. Constitution, the average state constitution at 39,000 words is four times as long, and Texas's constitution at 89,000 words is ten times as long.

Both the federal and state constitutions are foundational documents that limit, define, and structure politics within their respective jurisdictions. But the logic of the federal constitution is one of enumerated powers, meaning that powers not specifically granted are withheld. The powers that are granted in the federal constitution are usually granted in broad terms, such as the power to tax, raise an army, and regulate commerce. State constitutions, on the other hand, assume plenary or general grants of power unless power is specifically denied. Hence, state constitutions tend to be longer and more detailed, specifying what powers are withheld. This is especially so in southern state constitutions, where great care is taken to limit power. Alabama has the longest and most frequently amended constitution, at 376,000 words and 880 amendments. The more detailed a constitution is, the more frequently it will have to be amended to keep all of its provisions up to date.

The Texas Constitution of 1876 is the second longest among the 50 states, at 89,000 words, and the third most frequently amended, at 483 and counting.

State	Effective Date	Word Length	Amendments	Amendments Per Year
Alabama	1901	376,000	880	7.69
California	1879	67,048	527	3.95
Florida	1969	56,705	121	2.74
Illinois	1971	16,401	12	0.29
Massachusetts	1780	45,283	120	0.52
New York	1895	44,397	220	1.88
Oklahoma	1907	81,666	193	1.78
Pennsylvania	1968	26,078	30	0.68
Texas	1876	89,000	483	3.49
Wyoming	1890	26,349	100	0.80

Source: *Book of the States* 2013 (Lexington, KY: Council of State Governments, 2013), Vol. 45, Table 1.1, p. 12.

Legislative Branch

Article III of the Texas Constitution authorizes a Senate and a House of Representatives. It limits the Texas legislature to biennial sessions of no more than 140 days. It requires a balanced budget and limits member salaries to $7,200 annually plus a modest per diem for days that members are actually in

Attorney General, now Governor, Greg Abbott successfully defended before the U.S. Supreme Court Texas's right to display the Ten Commandments on the Texas State Capital grounds.

regular session, special session, or engaged in committee work. The explicit idea behind limiting the time the legislature is in session, the amount of money they can spend, and the salaries that legislators can draw for their work is to keep government small, cheap, and unobtrusive.

Executive Branch

Article IV of the Texas Constitution describes an executive branch in which power is both limited and fragmented. Although the governor is described as the state's "chief executive officer," he or she shares executive authority with five other statewide elected officials, two key policymaking boards, and dozens of independent boards and commissions. The lieutenant governor, comptroller of public accounts, attorney general, agriculture commissioner, commissioner of the General Land Office, and the Texas Railroad Commission are all elected statewide, while the fifteen members of the State Board of Education are elected in single-member districts. Moreover, the legislature has made most administrative agencies independent of the governor's direct control.

Judicial Branch

Article VI describes the Texas judiciary. The judicial system in Texas includes seven different kinds of courts, including two courts of final appeal; the Texas Supreme Court deals with civil cases and the Texas Court of Criminal Appeals deals with criminal cases. Texas judges are elected to four- or six-year terms and judicial vacancies are filled by gubernatorial appointment.

Local Government

Articles IX (Counties) and XI (Municipal Corporations) describe the role and powers of local governments in Texas. Local governments come in three basic types: county governments, municipal or city governments, and special districts. Under a legal principle known as "**Dillon's Rule**," local governments are subject to state authority as outlined in the Constitution.

Dillon's Rule A legal concept holding that local governments are the creatures or creations of state governments.

Amendments

Constitutional amendments must be approved both by the legislature, in regular or special session, and the voters. A proposed amendment must receive an absolute two-thirds vote in both houses of the Texas legislature (100 votes in the House, 21 in the Senate). Then it must be approved by a majority of voters in the next statewide election. Texans have adopted 483 amendments and rejected 177, for an overall pass rate of 73.2 percent. Some states, California most famously, allow citizen initiatives to place potential amendments on the ballot. Texas does not.

SPECIAL RIGHTS PROVISIONS OF THE TEXAS CONSTITUTION

States like Texas often are criticized for their long, frequently amended, and, arguably, outdated constitutions. But in the sprawling Texas Constitution there are certain nuggets, many buried deep in Texas history, that provide critical protections to individual citizens. For example, many of the early settlers who scribbled GTT on the walls of their Kentucky or Alabama cabins and headed for Texas were escaping debts. To assure these settlers of a new start in Texas, early Texas Constitutions promised, as we saw above, that no one could be imprisoned for debt and, further, that homesteads could not be seized for debt. These provisions, or their direct descendants, remain in the Texas Constitution today. We find them not only in Article I, but throughout the document, especially in Article XVI, which is a grab-bag of General Provisions. Let's look closer at a number of provisions that help define the Texan's place in their community and state.

First, modern constitutional protections against creditors found in Article XVI, sections 49–51 allow most Texans to protect most of their real and personal property. Even in bankruptcy, your homestead, meaning the main home in which you live, up to ten acres in the city and 200 acres in rural areas, with buildings and improvements irrespective of value, are exempt from claims by general creditors. So is personal property, meaning furniture, clothing, jewelry, cars, and the like, up to $60,000 for couples and $30,000 for an individual. Critically, retirement accounts, including IRAs, 401k, 403b, and educational IRAs, are generally protected. For most Texans, most of their net worth is in their home and retirement accounts, so this is a broad set of asset protections.

Second, Texans enjoy a general protection, found in Article XVI, section 28, against garnishment, meaning seizure, of wages to pay debts except under particular circumstances, including spousal and child support, repayment of student loans, and repayment of federal obligations to the Internal Revenue Service. However, creditors can gain access to cash and cash equivalents, including checking and savings accounts, as well as investments not in retirement accounts, so once paychecks are deposited in the bank they are fair game.

Third, some creditor claims are privileged in the Texas Constitution and the Texas Property Code. Article XVI, section 37, of the Texas Constitution permit original contractors, though not subcontractors, described as "mechanics, artisans, and materialmen," to assert a claim ("a lien") or interest in a building or property upon which materials or labor were expended without prompt payment. Texas lien laws are complicated, often said to be more beneficial to property lawyers than to contractors. Nonetheless, a property lien can be sufficiently troublesome to a property or business owners, especially if they should decide to sell their property, that the mere threat of one might prompt settlement discussions.

Fourth, few constitutional provisions have more practical importance for more Texans than the Article XVI, section 15, "Community Property" provisions. The community system of marital property holding and rights, which has its historical roots in Spanish and Mexican law, assumes that property acquired before marriage or acquired after marriage by gift or inheritance remains separate, but that all property acquired during the marriage is held in common. Community property rules tend to benefit women, since women often make less than men during marriage, if a marriage ends in divorce. On the other hand, Texas alimony or spousal support rules are less generous to stay-at-home or lower earning spouses than are those of many other states.

While the constitutional provisions discussed above seem relatively generous, other provisions seem less generous. Article I, section 4, secures religious liberty—up to a point. It reads, "No religious test shall ever be required as a qualification to any office, nor shall anyone be excluded from holding office on account of his religious sentiments, provided he acknowledge the existence of a Supreme Being." In the 1980s Texas Attorney General Jim Mattox stipulated in court that the provisions requiring officeholders to acknowledge "the existence of a Supreme Being" was unconstitutional and unenforceable, but the provision remains in the Texas Constitution today.

Finally, in 2005, the Texas Legislature and voters approved a constitutional amendment prohibiting gay marriage in the state. Texas already had a law in force prohibiting gay marriage, but, as we have already seen, politicians and voters see constitutional prohibitions as sturdier than regular laws. In a conservative state, politicians can benefit by upping the ante from mere law to constitutional amendment on an emotional and controversial topic like gay marriage.

THE PROSPECTS FOR CONSTITUTIONAL REFORM IN TEXAS

Is Texas well served by a 19th-century constitution written by and for a rural, agricultural, racist society still reeling from military defeat, social dislocation, and economic turmoil? Some argue that after 140 years and 483 amendments, the Texas Constitution of 1876 is a shambles. Advocates of constitutional reform promise a shorter, clearer, more effective constitution. The reforms most frequently mentioned are consolidating executive authority, moving to annual legislative sessions, rationalizing the judiciary, and modernizing county government.

But Texans have always been wary of strong (fearing that strong really means expensive) government. Nonetheless, political scandal occasionally has opened the door to constitutional reform, but never very far. When Governor James Ferguson was impeached for corruption and removed from office in 1917, his successor, Governor William P. Hobby, proposed civil service and judicial reform but neither passed. In 1921, Hobby's successor, Pat M. Neff, called for a constitutional convention to modernize the constitution but the legislature ignored him.[16] Governor John Connally proposed major constitutional reforms, including an extension of the governor's term from two years to four and a move to annual legislative sessions, but the legislature again failed to respond. Soon, however, new scandals brought talk of reform back to the top of the political agenda.

Q5 Should constitutional reform be on the political agenda in Texas?

Sharpstown scandal 1972 scandal in which Houston financier Frank Sharp and a number of prominent Texas politicians were accused of trading political for financial favors.

Constitutional Convention of 1974 and Its Aftermath

In the early 1970s, Texans seemed primed for constitutional reform. The Watergate affair in Washington and **Sharpstown scandal** in Austin produced a wave of reform sentiment. In 1972, Texas voters approved a constitutional amendment creating a constitutional revision commission to produce recommendations for submission to a constitutional convention. The convention was to be composed of the members of the Texas House and Senate meeting as one body. House Speaker Price Daniel, Jr. (right), son of former Governor and Senator Price Daniel, presided over the Constitutional Convention, though most insiders knew that Lieutenant Governor Bill Hobby had done most to bring it about.

The convention labored from January to July 1974 to produce a new constitution. The result was a sleek new document of just 17,500 words. It called for major institutional reforms, including an annual meeting of

Courtesy of Texas State Library and Archives Commission

Price Daniel, Jr. presided over the ultimately unsuccessful Texas Constitutional Convention of 1974.

TIMELINE: THE BATTLE OVER FEDERALISM

	1789	1791	1798	1819	1831	1861
National Federalism	U.S. Constitution adopted	Bill of Rights adopted		*McCulloch v. Maryland* adopts broad view of necessary and proper clause		Lincoln prepared to defend the Union
The States' Rights View		10th Amendment adopted	Kentucky and Virginia Resolutions challenge national power		Senator John C. Calhoun's (SC) Fort Hill address advocated nullification	Eleven states secede from the Union

Right-to-work Legal principle prohibiting mandatory union membership.

the legislature and appointment of state judges. But other issues, especially a **right-to-work** provision opposed by organized labor, a gambling provision opposed by conservatives, and a school funding provision opposed by rural interests, doomed the convention's work. The revised constitution fell three votes short of final passage in the convention and, hence, never reached the voters.

The 1975 regular session of the Texas legislature repackaged major elements of the constitutional convention's work into eight separate amendments and submitted them to the voters for approval. Among these proposals were streamlining executive and judicial institutions, annual legislative sessions, modernizing county government, and tax reform. Conservative Democratic Governor Dolph Briscoe opposed the reforms, claiming that they could lead to an income tax, and all eight proposals went down to a two-to-one defeat.

The Future of Constitutional Reform in Texas

Reformers tried again in the early 1990s, but they did not get far. Senator John Montfort started the conversation in the early 1990s and Representative Rob Junell and Senator Bill Ratliff continued it later in the decade. They developed a plan to reduce the number of statewide elected officials to four (the governor, lieutenant governor, comptroller, and attorney general) and empower the governor to appoint the key executive branch department heads. Legislative terms were extended to four years for the House and six for the Senate. Proposals were also made to streamline the courts and to move from elected to appointed judges who would then stand for confirmatory election to

1865	1868	1885–1930	1932–1939	1954–1970	1964–1968	1980s	1990s	2009
Union forces defeat secession	*Texas v. White* declares the Union Perpetual		FDR's New Deal expands national power over commerce and social services		LBJ's Great Society expands national power over civil rights and voting			Obama's stimulus and health care bills expand national power
		Supreme Court limits national power over the states		South seeks to nullify desegregation orders		Reagan's New Federalism seeks to return power to the states	Devolution Revolution continues	

subsequent terms. These proposals, while widely discussed, never even made it out of committee. One hears nothing of constitutional reform in Texas today.

Still, constitutional reform is a foundational democratic process and so it is meant to be difficult. In democratic theory, a constitutional convention is understood to be the whole people meeting to consider and reconsider the foundations of their government—not a process to be undertaken lightly. Because the convention represents the whole people, many believe that no prior limitations can be placed on it—everything is on the table—including the structure and process of government, the sources of government funding (including the income tax), the scope and jurisdiction of the courts and of local governments, and even the Bill of Rights and the liberties of individual citizens.

Now the fact that Texas is bound by the U.S. Constitution does place some limits on state constitutional reform. The U.S. Constitution guarantees Texas a republican form of government and the provisions of the U.S. Bill of Rights would still apply in Texas. And citizens of Texas would, of course, get to vote on whether to adopt a new constitution once it was proposed. Constitutional reform is serious and fundamental business and, as such, deserves the thoughtful attention of citizens and public officials.

Chapter Summary

Federalism is a system of government that divides power between a national government and a series of subnational governments—in the U.S., these are the fifty states. The U.S. Constitution declares the national government "supreme" within the areas of its enumerated powers and reserves to the states all remaining political authority not denied to them by their own state constitutions. Not surprisingly, the national and state governments have struggled throughout American history to define the boundaries of American federalism.

All constitutions define and limit the powers of government. The U.S. Constitution and all fifty state constitutions do this by granting some powers, denying others, and deploying institutional features such as separation of powers, checks and balances, and bicameralism to limit and restrain government. Some states have sought to accomplish their public purposes through a broadly empowered, well-funded, and active set of state and local political institutions. Some have gone another way.

Texans have always favored limited government, low taxes, and local control. These commitments were evident in the Republic of Texas Constitution of 1836 and the U.S. Statehood Constitution of 1845. Texas's Civil War experience of military defeat, occupation by Union forces, and centralized government under the hated Constitution of 1869 deepened the people's commitment to limited government. Hence, limiting, even minimizing, government power was the dominant goal of the Constitution of 1876.

The Constitution of 1876, amended no less than 483 times, highlights a plural executive, a diffuse bureaucracy, a part-time legislature, and an elected judiciary that culminates in dual high courts. While several attempts, especially in the 1970s, have been made to modernize and streamline the Texas Constitution, each has foundered on the fear that modern really means intrusive and expensive.

To this day, Texans are wary of powerful government, high taxes, and intrusions upon their individual rights and liberties. Yet, some Texans wonder whether their state government can provide excellent schools, a healthy economic environment, and an attractive quality of life without significant constitutional reform. We will explore these issues in the remainder of the book.

Key Terms

Constitution 28	Reserved powers 31
Devolution 34	Right-to-work 46
Dillon's Rule 43	Sharpstown scandal 45
Enumerated powers 29	Sovereign immunity 31
Federalism 28	Supremacy clause 29
Necessary and proper clause 30	Unfunded mandates 34

Review Questions

1. Describe several ways in which the American federal system constrains or limits political or policy choices that Texas might otherwise make.

2. Enumerate the personal rights and liberties protected in the Texas Constitution that are not protected in the U.S. Constitution.
3. Explain the underlying logic of "enumerated" powers in the U.S. Constitution and how that differs from the underlying logic of state constitutions like that of Texas.
4. Summarize the basic principles and key provisions of the current Texas Constitution.
5. Assess the strengths and weaknesses of the constitutional reform proposals most frequently directed toward the current Texas Constitution.

Suggested Readings

Dale Baum, *The Shattering of Texas Unionism: Politics in the Lone Star State During the Civil War Era* (Baton Rouge, LA: Louisiana State University, 1998).

Ann O'M. Bowman and Richard C. Kearney, "Power Shift: Measuring Policy Centralization in U.S. Intergovernmental Relations, 1947–1998," *American Politics Research* (2003) 31: 301–325.

Timothy J. Conlan and Paul L. Posner, "Inflection Point? Federalism and the Obama Administration," *Publius: The Journal of Federalism* (2011) 41: 421–446.

William T. Gormley, "Money and Mandates: The Politics of Intergovernmental Conflict," *Publius: The Journal of Federalism* (2006) 36: 523–540.

Margaret Sweet Henson, *Lorenzo de Zavala: The Pragmatic Idealist* (Fort Worth, TX: Texas Christian University Press, 1996).

Janice C. May, *The Texas State Constitution: A Reference Guide* (Westport, CT: Greenwood Press, 1996).

Carl H. Moneyhon, *Texas After the Civil War: The Struggle of Reconstruction* (College Station, TX: Texas A&M University Press, 2004).

Saundra K. Schneider, William G. Jacoby, and Daniel C. Lewis, "Public Opinion Toward Intergovernmental Policy Responsibilities," *Publius: The Journal of Federalism* (2011), 41: 1–30.

Christopher Wlezien and Stuart N. Soroka, "Federalism and Public Responsiveness to Policy," *Publius: The Journal of Federalism* (2011), 41: 431–453.

Joseph E. Zimmerman, *Interstate Relations: The Neglected Dimension of Federalism* (New York: Praeger, 1996).

Web Resources

1. **http://www.tsha.utexas.edu/handbook/online.html**
   The Handbook of Texas Online is a joint project of the General Libraries of UT, Austin and the Texas State Historical Association. This site provides the text of, and articles about, Texas constitutions.

2. **http://www.capitol.state.tx.us/txcon.st/toc.html**
   From the Research Division of the Texas Legislative Council, here is an updated version of the Texas Constitution including all amendments.

3. **http://ww2.lafayette.edu/~publius/**
   Publius is the leading scholarly journal dealing with American federalism.

4. **http://www.csp.org**
   Website for the Council on State Governments contains a wealth of comparative data and topical discussion.

5. **http://www.ncsl.org/**
   Website for the National Conference of State Legislatures contains political and policy data on the states.

6. **http://www.census.gov/govs/www/index.html**
   U.S. Census data on state and local government finance, employment, and policy.

Chapter 3

POLITICAL PARTICIPATION IN TEXAS: VOTERS, CAMPAIGNS, AND ELECTIONS

DEMANDING HISPANIC EQUALITY:

HERNANDEZ V. TEXAS

Sometimes even deeply flawed men and women leave an outsized mark on their times and on the lives of the people around them. In mid-20th-century Texas, two men, one a murderer and the other a lawyer whose personal demons would soon overwhelm him, changed the legal place of millions of Hispanics in Texas and throughout the nation. In 1950, Texas was a segregated society, requiring separation of blacks and whites in most public places. But Hispanics occupied a tenuous middle ground, legally considered white, their actual rights—what schools their children would attend, whether they sat on juries, or were allowed to vote—were determined by Anglos, i.e. non-Hispanic whites.

In 1951, Mexican farmworker Pedro "Pete" Hernandez killed his employer, Joe Espinosa, after a brief altercation in a bar. Hernandez's mother convinced two San Antonio civil rights attorneys, Gustavo C. "Gus" Garcia and Carlos Cadena, to handle the case which came to be known as *Hernandez v. Texas*. There was little doubt that Hernandez was guilty of the killing and he was duly convicted. Because the trial was held in the small East Texas town of Edna in Jackson County, the jury was all white (meaning all Anglo; remember, Hispanics are white but not Anglo). Garcia and Cedena filed an appeal in federal court, arguing that the all white jury was a denial of Hernandez's 14th Amendment promise of "equal protection of the laws" and the 6th Amendment right to "a speedy and public trial by an impartial jury" of his peers.

Hernandez's lawyers argued, first before the appeals court and then before the Supreme Court, that Hispanics were a "class apart," discriminated against even though legally classed as white. Many Hispanics worried that their position might be worsened if the Supreme Court extended the "separate but equal" doctrine that defined the black place in American society to Hispanics as well. Instead, on May 3, 1954, the Supreme Court, citing the 14ᵗʰ Amendment, ruled that Pete Hernandez deserved a new trial before a jury of all of his peers. Remarkably, just two weeks later, the Supreme Court ruled in the far more famous case of *Brown v. Board* that segregating blacks and whites in public schools was unconstitutional for the same 14ᵗʰ Amendment reasons. Together, *Hernandez v. Texas* and *Brown v. Board* made clear that treating blacks, whites, and Hispanics differently before the law was unconstitutional.

While *Hernandez v. Texas* marked a huge win for Texas Hispanics, establishing their claim to equal treatment before the law, tragedy also marked the case. Pete Hernandez was reconvicted, but that is no tragedy because he was guilty. But within a decade Gus Garcia, the brilliant but troubled lawyer that argued *Hernandez v. Texas* before the Supreme Court, was dead. Garcia succumbed to alcoholism soon after winning the case and to mental illness in subsequent years. He died of liver failure on June 3, 1964. Gus Garcia, weak in some ways, was strong enough to change the state of Texas.

Focus Questions

Q1 What means have been used to limit suffrage in Texas history?

Q2 What laws and rules govern the right to vote today?

Q3 Which Texans exercise their right to vote and which do not?

Q4 How are political campaigns conducted in Texas?

Q5 What kinds of elections do we have in Texas?

Political participation
All of those activities, from attending campaign events, to voting, and even running for office, by which individuals and groups undertake to affect politics.

Healthy democratic politics assumes the full and informed participation of citizens in the discussion of public issues and the selection of government officials. Active citizens are the irreplaceable participants in democratic politics. **Political participation** refers to all of the opportunities we have as individuals or as members of groups, associations, or political parties to join in shaping our common life. Intelligent candidates conducting informative campaigns before watchful citizens who cast thoughtful votes on election day are the democratic ideal.

Opportunities for political participation in Texas are extensive. Talking, instant-messaging, and tweeting about politics with friends and neighbors, studying the issues, joining civic groups, attending school board meetings, protesting at the local court house or the state capitol, stuffing envelopes for a candidate, giving money to a political party, voting, and stepping forward as a candidate for office are all forms of political participation. There are many ways, available to you and every other citizen, to make your voice heard and your opinions and interests felt on matters of public interest.

Yet, in politics, as in the rest of life, the ideal and the real often diverge. In real politics, candidates often are intelligent, but they do not always, or even usually, conduct informative campaigns. Rather, campaigns are often mud baths, filled with charge and countercharge, as issues fade into the background. Citizens do not always watch closely, turn out to vote on election day, or make well-informed decisions. Some citizens are disengaged and ill-informed, others are turned off by the negative tone of campaigns, and many stay home on election day. Hence, the support, goodwill, and legitimacy that should greet newly elected public officials are often replaced by alienation, skepticism, and suspicion.

Unfortunately, skepticism and suspicion about state politics has often been well-founded. Article I, section 2 of the U.S. Constitution gave the states the principal responsibility for registering voters, structuring campaigns, and holding elections. Many states, including Texas with its traditionalistic political culture and dominant Anglo elite, used this authority to exclude most poor and minority citizens from politics. Over the course of the 20th century, the federal government forced Texas and other states, usually much against their will, to treat their citizens equally.

Eric Schlegel/Getty Images News

Spectators cheered as Democrats, led by Wendy Davis, maneuvered to kill an anti-abortion bill in the final hours of the 2013 legislative session.

Past discrimination is not just of historical significance. Modern scholarship contends that today's voter turnout reflects historical patterns of discrimination as well as socio-demographic characteristics of the population such as racial and ethnic diversity, income, and education. States with a history of discrimination and poverty tend to have lower turnout today even if they have ceased overt discrimination.[1] Ominously, few states, very few states, have lower voter turnout than Texas.

THE EVOLUTION OF SUFFRAGE IN TEXAS

Q1 What means have been used to limit suffrage in Texas history?

Suffrage Another term for the legal right to vote.

Today, virtually every adult citizen of Texas is allowed to register and to vote. It was not always so. The Texas Constitutions of 1836 and 1845 granted **suffrage**—the legal right to vote—to white men and Hispanic men and denied it to blacks, Indians, and women. Hispanics, while legally citizens and entitled to vote, were subject to frequent discrimination. The South's defeat in the Civil War brought an end to slavery and a demand, embodied in the 13th, 14th, and 15th Amendments to the U.S. Constitution, that black men be recognized as citizens with the right to vote and stand for political office. Once Reconstruction ended, private groups and public officials worked systematically and over a period of decades to limit black and Hispanic participation in Texas public life.[2]

Post–Civil War Exclusion

From our contemporary perspective, it is difficult to think our way back to an understanding of post–Civil War politics. Once Anglo Texans regained control of state politics in the 1870s, they moved systematically to control where they could not immediately eliminate black and Hispanic political participation. Means fair and foul were employed and there were few laws to distinguish one from the other. Post–Civil War Texas law permitted men of all races and ethnicities to vote if they met simple age, residency, and citizenship requirements. In fact, like many other western and midwestern states at the time, Texas law allowed aliens to vote if they merely declared an intent to become U.S. and Texas citizens. There were no formal voter registration requirements, no campaign finance or spending regulations, and candidates and parties prepared their own ballots, each a distinctive color, with just the names of their candidates on it. Finally, the elections themselves were overseen by local officials, usually led by the county judge and sheriff.

Blacks and Hispanics were managed votes by the 1890s. White elites worked through black "'fluence men" in East Texas and the local "jefes" of South Texas. In East Texas, black voters were feted in "owl meetings" on election eve. Democratic Party election managers "provided roast beef in unlimited quantities; but they were careful not to be too generous with the jug, for there was yet work to be done." When the polls opened next morning, "the revelers of the night before came down to the polling place to vote," with their easily identifiable party ballots in hand.[3] In South Texas, "goat barbecues" were used to treat the next day's voters. The South Texas patrons had an additional advantage in the state declarant alien voter laws. "Under this law the local Democratic chieftain could summon as many votes as he might need and aliens were imported in droves from Mexico. . . . Tales of the 'wet' and the 'muddy' vote of the Rio Grande Valley became legendary, and there is ample evidence that they rested on a foundation of truth."[4]

But controlling minority voters is messy and, sometimes, expensive business. Excluding them from the electorate was cleaner, at least from the perspective of late 19th- and early 20th-century Anglo elites, but that was the work of decades. "Not until the new 'black codes' and signs went up in the 1890s and early 1900s was the transformation complete."[5] However, once in place, the impact of the new system was profound. Alwyn Barr and others note that, "the decline in Negro voter participation from about 100,000 in the 1890s to approximately 5,000 in 1906 suggests the effectiveness" of the restored Anglo control.[6]

Restrictions on Voter Registration

Texas had no voter registration law until 1891 and the 1891 law applied only to cities of over 10,000. The state had no truly secret ballot until the middle of the 20th century. This lack of legal structure and protection made it easier for elites to manage who voted and how they cast their ballots.[7]

The voter registration system in place in 1900 was intended to be open to well-heeled whites and closed to all others. The voter registration rolls were open for just four months each year, October 1 through January 31. Campaigns occurred in the late summer and fall, with elections in November, so the voter lists were locked down nine months before the election was held. Generally, only the social and political elite, who followed politics year-round and knew the importance of electoral outcomes, were registered. By 1900, only about 5 percent of adult black men in Texas were registered to vote. And then the rules were tightened.

Poll Tax

Early 20th-century Texas was a largely rural society in which exchanges of labor and barter of goods meant many poor families saw little real money over the course of a year. In 1902, Texas adopted a **poll tax** of $1.50, later raised to $1.75, to register to vote. A small farm might clear $300 in a good year, so paying the tax to register to vote involved no small calculation. The impact was immediate. Registered voters in Houston dropped by more than half, from 76 percent of the potential electorate to 32 percent and similar declines were registered elsewhere.[8] Most poor Texans decided to save their money and forego their vote. Most, but not all.[9]

Poll tax In 1902 Texas adopted a poll tax of $1.50 to discourage the poor and minorities from voting.

In addition, the poll tax gave Anglo elites and their election managers new ways to monitor and control even the shrunken Texas electorate. After 1903, voters had to bring a numbered poll tax receipt to the polling place where it would be attached to their ballot. The numbered receipt identified each voter's ballot. Not until 1949 did good government groups, including the League of Women Voters, secure legislation "Providing for a secret ballot in all Texas elections through a numbered detachable stub system."[10] The numbered detachable stub effectively severed the link between individual poll tax receipts and ballots. After 1949, poll workers detached the numbered stub of the poll tax receipt before attaching it to the ballot, thus finally establishing the integrity of the secret ballot in Texas.

White Primary

In 1903, Governor Jim Hogg and the Texas legislature, led by Representative Alexander Terrell, sought further to limit minority influence in Texas politics. The Terrell election law altered the process by which parties nominated candidates by moving from party conventions to party primary elections. Texas was one-party Democratic, so winning the Democratic Party primary was tantamount to election. In 1906, the Texas Democratic Party held its first **white primary**. Only whites were permitted to vote in the Democratic Party primary, insuring that most blacks and Hispanics had no role in choosing the state's officeholders.[11]

Anglo leaders were very much aware that their white primary could be seen as an affront to the 15th Amendment to the U.S. Constitution, which had given black men the right to vote in 1871, so in 1910 the Texas House voted to encourage the amendments repeal. Repeal, of course, did not occur and in 1924 black leaders sued the state of Texas, arguing that the 15th Amendment to the U.S. Constitution prohibited racial discrimination in voting. In 1927, the U.S. Supreme Court declared, in *Nixon v. Herndon*, that the state of Texas could not exclude blacks from voting in state sanctioned primary elections. Democratic Party officials responded by arguing that the Democratic Party in Texas was a private organization, not an official organ of Texas government, and could define its membership as it saw fit. In the 1935 case of *Grovey v. Townsend*, the Supreme Court accepted the Texas Democratic Party's argument and the white primary was, for a time, restored.[12]

Anglo control of voter registration and turnout was complete from the early 20th century into the 1940s. While black citizens and interest groups, led by the National Association for the Advancement of Colored People (NAACP), struggled in the courts to overturn the white primary, the Hispanic vote remained in play. Two stories from Texas in and around the 1930s, one from history and one from fiction, both equally compelling, highlight the mechanisms for controlling the Hispanic vote.

The prominent historian Robert A. Caro, author of the four volume (eventually to be five volume) *The Years of Lyndon Johnson*, described a young LBJ working San Antonio Congressman Maury Maverick's 1934 campaign. Johnson and an aide, Luther E. Jones, were staying at the Plaza Hotel. In Caro's telling,

> Johnson was sitting at a table in the center of the room—and on the table were stacks of five-dollar bills. "That big table was just covered with money—more money than I had ever seen," Jones says. . . . Mexican-American men would come into the room, one at a time. Each would tell Johnson a number—some, unable to speak English, would indicate the number by holding up fingers—and Johnson would count out that number of five-dollar bills, and hand it to him. "It was five dollars a vote," Jones realized. "Lyndon was checking each name against lists someone had furnished him with."[13]

The beauty of this system was that it was completely verifiable. Texas matched the voter's poll tax number with the number on his ballot.[14]

White primary In 1906 Texas Democrats held their first white primary, meaning that only whites were permitted to vote in the Democratic primary.

Nixon v. Herndon (1927) U.S. Supreme Court held that Texas could not exclude blacks from voting in state sanctioned primary elections.

Grovey v. Townsend (1935) U.S. Supreme Court found that the Democratic Party in Texas was a private organization and could exclude blacks from its primary elections.

Minnie Fisher Cunningham (1882–1964) was the driving force behind the woman suffrage movement in Texas. A native Texan, born in New Waverly near Huntsville in Walker County, her once prominent family had fallen on hard times after the Civil War. Educated by her mother, Minnie taught school for a year before entering the pharmacy program at the University of Texas Medical Branch at Galveston. The second woman to earn a pharmacy degree from UT, she worked for a year as a pharmacist in Huntsville. Finding out that her untrained male colleagues made twice what she did, she later declared "made a suffragette out of me."

She married Bill Cunningham in 1902. The couple moved to Galveston in 1902 and adopted two children, but the marriage was unhappy so Minnie poured most of her energy into community work. In 1910 she was elected president of the Galveston Equal Suffrage Association. She dedicated the next decade to winning women's suffrage in Texas and the nation. In the process, she became a shrewd political strategist. In 1915 she was elected to the first of four annual terms as president of the Texas Woman Suffrage Association. Local chapters proliferated throughout Texas. Cunningham helped lead the impeachment of Governor James "Pa" Ferguson for corruption and then helped block a Ferguson comeback by promising his successor, Governor Bill Hobby, that women would "clean house" with a broad anti-corruption campaign if given the vote in state and local primary elections. The legislature approved women's primary election suffrage in 1918 and women supported Hobby over Ferguson. In addition, Annie Webb Blanton, the first female president of the Texas State Teachers Association, ran for State Superintendent of Education and won, becoming the first woman to win statewide office in Texas.

Still, the anti-suffrage forces were not done. Though Cunningham and her colleagues worked hard to pass full female suffrage in 1919, Texas male voters defeated it two-to-one in the general election. Despite the loss, national suffrage leaders recruited her to Washington, D.C., to lobby Congress on behalf of the 19th Amendment. She was one of a core group of national woman suffrage leaders to meet with President Woodrow Wilson in the Oval Office to demand his support. Wilson did swing in behind the 19th Amendment and it passed both houses of the Congress. Cunningham returned to Texas to lobby the Texas Legislature for ratification. Texas joined the border states of Oklahoma, Arkansas, and Tennessee as the only southern states to ratify the 19th Amendment. With female suffrage won, Cunningham joined other national leaders in founding the League of Women Voters.

Minnie Fisher Cunningham made two runs for statewide office in Texas. In 1928 she ran for the U.S. Senate as a liberal against the Ku Klux Klan endorsed Senator Earle B. Mayfield. Though she finished fifth of six in the Democratic primary, Mayfield was forced into a runoff by Thomas T. Connally. She endorsed and campaigned for Connally and he won. In 1944 she ran as a liberal alternative to the conservative incumbent Governor Coke Stevenson. Stevenson easily won re-election, but Cunningham did finish second in a field of nine candidates.

She remained a liberal democratic activist to the end. In 1952 and 1956, she supported the Democrat's presidential nominee, Illinois Governor Adlai Stevenson, even as Texas Governor Allen Shivers was leading conservative Democrats to the Republican nominee, Dwight D. Eisenhower. She was a founding member of the liberal journal, *The Texas Observer*, and she stood with Senator Ralph Yarbrough, John Kennedy, and LBJ on civil rights when many conservative Democrats would not. Minnie Fisher Cunningham is a true Texas Legend.

Rural Texans of the same time period were a little more direct in managing the Hispanic vote. Edna Ferber's *Giant*, a 1952 novel set in the big ranch country of South Texas in the 1920s through the 1940s, has Bick Benedict, the patriarch of the sprawling Reata Ranch, explaining South Texas elections to his Virginia-born wife, Leslie. Bick explains that, "There are about four million whites in Texas. And about a million Mexicans. . . . It's really exciting at election. Regular old times, guns and all. They lock the gates and guard the fences, nobody can get out." Leslie asks why. "So they'll vote right of course honey. So they won't go out and get mixed up with somebody'll tell them wrong. This way they vote like they're told to vote."[15] This rough but eminently workable system was about to be upset by what some Texans delight in calling an overbearing and intrusive federal government.

Federal Intervention

Federal intervention on behalf of poor and minority voters began in the mid-1940s but took decades to complete. The first big step was taken in a case argued by Thurgood Marshall, later to be the first black justice on the U.S. Supreme Court, on behalf of the NAACP. In 1944, the Supreme Court overturned its finding in *Grovey* to declare in *Smith v. Allwright* that political parties are "agencies of the state" and must abide by the 15th Amendment's prohibition on racial discrimination in voting. Despite this important ruling, several stout lines of defense against minority voter registration and political participation remained in place.[16]

Smith v. Allwright (1944) U.S. Supreme Court overturned *Grovey*, declaring that political parties are "agencies of the state" and must abide by the 15th Amendment's prohibition on racial discrimination in voting.

Restrictive voter registration procedures and the poll tax limited minority participation into the 1960s, but then change came on in a rush. Texas resisted at every turn.[17] In 1964, the 24th Amendment to the U.S. Constitution made the poll tax unconstitutional for national elections. Texas responded by developing a dual ballot, one for national elections where no poll tax was required, and another for state elections where the poll tax was still required. In 1966, the U.S. Supreme Court, in *U.S. v. Texas*, declared the poll tax unconstitutional in state elections too. While Texas was forced to abandon the poll tax in 1966, a sullen Texas legislature refused to ratify the 24th Amendment until 2009.

U.S. v. Texas (1966) U.S. Supreme Court struck down the poll tax in state elections.

Finally, in 1971, President Nixon, Congress, and three-quarters of the states approved the 26th Amendment to the U.S. Constitution, giving the vote to young people aged 18 to 21. To hold down youth voting, particularly in towns and counties with colleges and universities, conservative Texas legislators passed a law requiring college students to register and vote where their parents lived, rather than where they lived during the academic year. Federal courts struck down the student registration and voting law at their first opportunity.[18]

By the early 1970s, the federal courts had struck down state laws requiring annual voter registration, an early end to voter registration, lengthy residence requirements, and youth registration where their parents lived.

The Voting Rights Act and Its Amendments

The **Voting Rights Act** (VRA) of 1965, along with the Civil Rights Acts of 1964 and 1965, broke the back of racial segregation. The VRA required federal officials to facilitate minority voter registration, and required nine southern states with histories of racial discrimination in voting to submit any proposed changes to electoral laws to a **preclearance** process run by the U.S. Department of Justice. Preclearance was intended to block any changes that would, intentionally or not, dilute minority voter influence. Most provisions

Mark Wilson/Getty Images

Congressional leaders look on as President George W. Bush signs the 2006 extension of the Voting Rights Act.

of the VRA were intended to be permanent, though funding levels and some specific enforcement provisions require periodic renewal. The VRA was reviewed and renewed in 1970, 1975, and 1982. In 1975, provisions were added requiring Texas and other states with large numbers of voters for whom English is not their native language to provide bilingual ballots and other assistance.

In 2006, President Bush and the leadership of both parties in Congress promised to extend the VRA for another twenty-five years. Southern Republicans in the House, led by representatives from Georgia and Texas, staged a revolt that threatened the renewal. Some opponents of renewal argued that great progress had been made in minority voter registration, participation, and office holding over the past forty years and that it was unfair to subject southern states to special scrutiny any longer. Others opposed the language assistance provisions, arguing that knowledge of English is a requirement of citizenship and so should not be necessary for those truly eligible to vote. Eventually, the revolt was quelled and the VRA was renewed by a vote of 390 to 33 in the House and 98–0 in the Senate. President Bush signed the bill on July 27, 2006.

More recently, in the innocuous sounding case of *Northwest Austin Municipal Utility District No. 1 v. Holder*, a small Texas water utility district sued to have the preclearance requirement of the VRA overturned. Lawyers for the utility board argued that there had never been a charge of discrimination in their district and that a half century after the VRA's initial passage, southern political districts no longer deserved special scrutiny. In June 2009 the U.S. Supreme Court exempted the water district from preclearance, but allowed the VRA to stand.

In a momentous 2013 case called *Shelby County v. Holder*, the U.S. Supreme Court struck down section 5, the preclearance provision, of the VRA. Chief Justice John Roberts, writing for the majority of a court divided 5–4,

Voting Rights Act Law requiring federal officials to facilitate minority voter registration and participation in states with a history of discrimination.

Preclearance The Voting Rights Act requires states and communities with a history of racial discrimination in voting to seek prior approval from the Justice Department for changes to their election codes to insure against dilution of minority electoral impact. The U.S. Supreme Court struck down preclearance in 2013.

declared that the formula deciding which states were subject to preclearance was outdated. He reminded Americans that other provisions of the VRA still made discrimination illegal and that Congress could revise the preclearance formula to bring it up to date. Few knowledgeable observers believe that the deeply divided Congress will pass a new preclearance formula.[19]

Texas officials were joyous. Governor Perry and Attorney General Abbott immediately declared that two laws—the 2011 redistricting law and the 2011 Voter I.D. law—that had been denied preclearance by the federal courts would be implemented immediately. The preclearance requirement on states with a history of discrimination blocked more than 1,000 discriminatory provisions over the past 25 years, fully 20 percent of them, more than 200, from Texas. So, is preclearance no longer needed because a great deal of progress has been made in U.S. race relations since the VRA was originally passed, or, has a valuable tool in fighting discrimination been lost?

MODERN VOTER REGISTRATION AND TURNOUT

Q2 What laws and rules govern the right to vote today?

Initial passage of the VRA in 1965 convinced Texas officials that federal officials were serious about equal voting rights for all citizens. In 1967, the Texas legislature designated the Secretary of State as the state's chief elections official, responsible for interpreting legislation, monitoring compliance, and distributing funds to local election officials. Local election officials, usually the county tax assessor-collector or a designated county election administrator, actually set up and conduct elections. In 1971, the state legislature adopted a thoroughly modern system of permanent voter registration.

Voter Qualifications

To be a qualified voter in Texas, one need only be a U.S. citizen over 18 years of age (though you can register at 17 years and 10 months if you will be 18 by election day) and a resident of the state and county for at least 30 days. Qualified voters must have been registered at least 30 days before the election. Texans do not register as Democrats, Republicans, or independents, as voters in more than half the states do. Texans simply register to vote and then on election day they decide which party to support.[20] In 2014 Texas had 14 million registered voters, which is about 74 percent of the state's voting age population of 18.9 million.[21]

Voter Registration

The Texas Secretary of State's website (see the Web Resources section at the end of this chapter) provides easy-to-follow information on how to register to vote. Texas voters can register at any time during the year, either in person or through the mail. In fact, a new voter can be registered by his or her spouse,

Pro & Con   The Texas Voter ID Law

After years of tumultuous debate, the 2011 Texas Legislature passed and Governor Perry signed a voter ID bill. The voter ID bill requires voters to present an approved form of photo identification, such as a Texas driver's license, a U.S. passport, a military ID or, since this is Texas, a concealed carry permit, in addition to the standard voter registration card. Proponents of the voter ID law claim that it is necessary to combat illegal voting and guarantee the integrity of Texas elections. Opponents of the Texas voter ID law claim that it could disenfranchise 600,000 to 800,000 otherwise eligible voters, mostly elderly, poor, and minorities, who do not have and might have trouble getting an appropriate photo ID.

Texas is required to submit all changes in its election code to the U.S. Department of Justice so they can check to see that the changes are not discriminatory toward minorities. The Justice Department refused to "preclear" the Texas law, even though similar laws had been permitted in Georgia, Indiana, and other states. The Justice Department decision, written by Assistant Attorney General Thomas E. Perez and dated March 12, 2012, made two key points. First, he said, "According to the state's own data, a Hispanic registered voter is at least 46.5 percent . . . more likely than a non-Hispanic registered voter to lack this identification." And second, he said, "We note that the state's submission did not include evidence of significant in-person voter impersonation not already addressed by the state's existing law." Some scholars also contend that tight voter ID laws can limit turnout. Thad Hall and Kathleen Moore, in an article entitled, "Election Administration: Setting the Rules of the Game," write that "Very strict voter identification laws most effect the low-income voter, but all voters are subject to the vagaries of how a given set of poll workers will implement the new law when the voter arrives at the polls."[22]

Texas Attorney General Greg Abbott responded by appealing to a three-judge panel of the D.C. Circuit Court of Appeals, for approval of the voter ID law. The case went before the court in July 2012. In late August 2012, the court struck down the Texas voter ID law, agreeing with the plaintiffs and the Justice Department that the law would have imposed "strict, unforgiving burdens on the poor and racial minorities." Governor Perry responded that, "Today, federal judges subverted the will of the people of Texas and undermined our effort to ensure fair and accurate elections." Texas immediately vowed another challenge, this one before the U.S. Supreme Court and, as Texas frequently does, it upped the ante for the next round by asking the court to overturn section 5, the preclearance provision, of the Voting Rights Act (VRA).

Governor Perry and Attorney General Abbott charged that the Voting Rights Act "preclearance" provisions are outmoded and unnecessary. While Texas once discriminated against minorities, it does no longer and has not for a long time. Nonetheless, the Justice Department and a three-judge federal panel in Washington found intent to discriminate in violation of the Voting Rights Act. Who's right? Slavery and segregation are far in Texas's past, so should the Justice Department and the federal courts still engage in close oversight of the states' electoral practices? Can Texas blacks and Hispanics, who give most of their votes to the Democrats, trust Republican officials to protect their voting rights? Or do poor and minority Texans need federal officials to keep a close eye on Texas political elites? What do you think?

parent, or child if that person is a registered voter. Registration, once established, is permanent so long as the voter's address remains the same. Voters who move within the same county can revise their voter registration information online. If you move from one county to another, you must reregister, but, again, the process is quite simple. Twenty-four States allow online voter registration but Texas does not.

Motor Voter A 1995 law, also known as the National Voter Registration Act, that permits persons to register to vote at motor vehicle and other state government offices.

In 1995, the U.S. Congress passed the National Voter Registration Act (better known as the **Motor Voter** law). Motor Voter allows qualified voters to register while they are getting or renewing a driver's license or applying for some other public service. The hope was that making voter registration more convenient would increase registration and, more importantly, turnout. It did, modestly.[22] In 2002, Congress passed—and President Bush signed—the Help America Vote Act (HAVA). HAVA established a new federal agency, called the Election Assistance Commission (EAC), to assist states in improving their voter-registration, vote-casting, and vote-counting systems.

HAVA required each state, including Texas, to construct a statewide voter registration list. Each voting location is required to have at least one computer with access to the statewide list to check eligibility if a voter's name does not appear on the precinct's voter list. Voters whose eligibility is unclear must be allowed to cast a provisional ballot, which is counted when the voter's eligibility is confirmed, and the state is required to develop a system through which voters can check to see whether their provisional ballot has been counted. Finally, states must comply with education requirements to assure that new voters know how to use electronic, optical scan, and punch card voting systems. Congress spent more than $3.9 billion on new voting equipment between 2003 and 2008, with $190 million going to Texas, but questions remain about the accuracy and vulnerability to tampering of the new voting equipment.[23]

Moreover, federal law requires that voter rolls be kept up to date, which involves insuring that duplicate names are purged and the deceased are removed. Unfortunately, Texas pursues this responsibility in a low-budget and inefficient manner that in 2012 threatened to remove 1.5 million names, at least 20 percent of whom were legitimate eligible voters.[24]

Voter Turnout

Voter turnout That portion of the eligible electorate that actually turns up to cast a vote on election day.

Voter turnout is the proportion of the citizen voting-age population (CVAP) that actually cast a ballot in a given election. American elections, even hard-fought presidential elections, have rarely reached 60 percent in recent decades. Off-year elections for the U.S. Congress and many top state races average around 40 percent. And countless local and special district elections attract less than 10 percent of potential voters.

Even by these modest U.S. standards, Texans are poor voters. Texans average 6 to 10 percent under national averages. Texans have for decades averaged about 50 percent turnout in presidential elections and 30 percent in gubernatorial and congressional elections. Major metropolitan elections, such as those for mayor in Dallas, Houston, and San Antonio, usually draw between 10 and 20 percent of eligible voters. Special elections, such as those for constitutional amendments, municipal charter reform, and school bond elections, usually draw from 5 to 15 percent of eligible voters. In 2012, Texas turnout trailed the national average by 10.4 percent, 51st among the 50 states and D.C.

Two aspects, one historical and one current, of Table 3.1 demand our attention. The historical point is that before the federal government intervened in the mid-1960s to demand that Texas cease voter suppression, Texas voter turnout

TABLE 3.1	U.S. and Texas Turnout (among Citizen VAP) in National Elections			
Election Year	U.S. Turnout	Texas Turnout	Texas Shortfall	Texas Ranking
Presidential Elections				
1960	63.1	41.2	−21.9	44
1964	61.8	44.6	−17.2	44
1968	60.7	48.7	−12.6	48
1972	55.4	45.3	−10.1	43
1976	53.5	46.3	−7.2	44
1980	52.6	44.9	−7.7	44
1984	53.1	47.2	−5.9	44
1988	50.2	44.2	−6.0	45
1992	55.2	49.1	−6.1	46
1996	48.9	41.1	−7.8	47
2000	51.2	43.1	−8.1	48
2004	58.3	50.3	−8	48
2008	61.7	52.4	−9.3	48
2012	56.5	46.1	−10.4	51
Congressional Elections				
1962	46.3	26.1	−20.2	43
1966	45.4	20.8	−24.6	50
1970	43.8	27.5	−16.3	46
1974	36.2	18.5	−17.7	49
1978	34.9	23.3	−11.6	47
1982	38.1	26.4	−11.7	48
1986	33.4	25.5	−7.9	45
1990	33.1	26.8	−6.3	43
1994	36.0	31.3	−4.7	44
1998	32.8	24.3	−8.5	46
2002	34.2	27.3	−7.4	49
2006	43.6	33.5	−10.1	51
2010	41.8	31.4	−10.4	51
2014	36.3	28.5	−7.8	50

Source: U.S. Bureau of the Census, *Statistical Abstract of the United States* (Washington, D.C.: Government Printing Office), 1975, #729, p. 451; 1984, #439, p. 265; 1990, #444, p. 265; 1994, #451, p. 289; 1995, #462, p. 291; 2002, #396, p. 255; 2004–05, #410, p. 258; 2007, #406, p. 257; 2008, #405, p. 257, 2010, #400, p. 247, 2014 #419, p.267. 2014 comes from personal communication between the author and Curtis Gans, Director of the Center for the study of the American Electorate.

trailed the national average by about 20 percentage points. Within a single decade, though Texas continued to trail the national average, it did so only by 7 to 10 points. More recently, however, the Texas shortfall has been creeping up again. In 2014, 36.3 percent of the eligible voting-age population in the U.S. cast a ballot, while in Texas only 28.5 percent did—this was 50th among the 50 states and D.C.—the lowest in the nation. Only one State, Indiana at 28.0, lagged Texas.

LET'S COMPARE   TURNOUT AMONG 2012 ELIGIBLE VOTERS BY AGE

Young people take a while to find their place in society. Often they are mobile, perhaps away at school, looking for a first job, or just moving from one apartment to the next. Parents are less mobile but just as busy, building a family, working for the next promotion, maybe even going back to school to buff credentials. Grandparents, at least the younger ones, own their own home, are in their peak earning years, and have been around the track a few times. Political participation, perhaps especially voting, requires time, energy, and confidence, all of which sum to a sense of understanding and empowerment.

The table below highlights a number of interesting points. One is that, as noted above, turnout increases with age until old-age begins to make getting around difficult. Nationally, voters 65 to 74 turnout at almost twice the rate of voters 18 to 24, 73.5 percent to 41.2 percent. Turnout begins to slip among voters over

75 but still remains high compared to younger voters. Another obvious point is that Texans 18 to 64 are poor voters. Texans 18 to 24 do terribly, fully 15 points below the national average for this age group; 25 to 44 do badly, ten points below the national average; and 45 to 64 do poorly, five points below. Only older Texans, 65 and above, reach and modestly exceed the national average for their age group including the critical 25 to 44 and 45 to 65 categories, Texas has the lowest turnout among the ten largest states.

So what do we make of this? Should we worry that young people vote in lower proportions than older people? Maybe. Should we worry that Texans 18 to 64 are poor voters compared to their peers nationally? Probably. Finally, do we think these low turnout levels in Texas are just the way it is, or are they intended, built-in, an element of Texas law and regulation, a product of the Texas political culture?

	18–24	25–44	45–64	65–74	75+	Total
National	41.2	57.3	67.9	73.5	70.0	61.8
California	41.6	53.5	62.9	68.3	67.0	57.5
Texas	**25.4**	**47.3**	**62.6**	**74.6**	**72.6**	**53.8**
New York	39.6	56.3	64.7	66.6	61.8	58.7
Florida	41.9	56.0	64.5	69.9	69.7	60.8
Pennsylvania	42.1	59.4	65.7	68.8	68.9	61.6
Illinois	35.3	58.0	69.3	74.7	65.1	61.5
Ohio	46.3	58.8	67.9	70.4	73.7	63.1
Michigan	44.0	62.3	73.0	78.4	74.3	66.8
North Carolina	50.0	66.9	72.1	79.4	75.0	68.9
Georgia	40.2	60.0	68.4	72.5	61.8	61.9

Source: United States Census, Voting and Registration, by Age, for States, November 2012, http://www.census.gov/hhes/www/socdemo/voting/publications/p20/2012/tables.html. Table 4c.

Texas public officials have done at least a few things to improve turnout by making voting easier and more convenient. Absentee ballots, obtained and returned by mail, have long been available to citizens who knew in advance that they would be away from home on election day or otherwise unable to make it to the polls. In the late 1980s, the Texas legislature approved early voting. County election officials set early voting dates, beginning as much as three weeks before and concluding four days before the official election day. The record for early voting was set in the 2008 General Election at over 66 percent. In 2012, 63 percent of Texas voters cast their ballots before election day and in 2014 54 per cent voted early.

THE DECISION TO VOTE (OR NOT)

Voting is a function of knowledge, experience, and confidence. Citizens who are older, well-educated, economically secure, and embedded in their community tend to vote in large numbers. Citizens who are younger, less well-educated, economically insecure, and new to their community tend to vote

Q3 Which Texans exercise their right to vote and which do not?

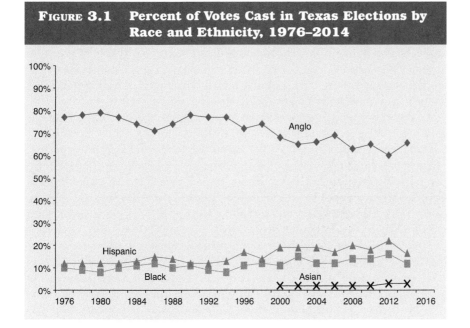

FIGURE 3.1 Percent of Votes Cast in Texas Elections by Race and Ethnicity, 1976–2014

Note: Data is unavailable for 1978 and 1984. Average of votes cast by race and ethnicity in the previous and subsequent election has been inserted.

Source: Derived by the author from U.S. Census data. Go to Census, click on "V" in the alphabetical list. Data for 1976 comes from "Registration and Voting in 1976—Jurisdiction Covered by the Voting Rights Act Amendments of 1975," Table 1. Data for later years comes from "Reported Voting and Registration, by Race and Spanish Origin (Hispanic Origin after 1986), for States," 1980, Table 5; 1982, Table 4; 1988, Table 4; 1990, Table 4; 1992, Table 4; 1994, Table 4a; 1998, Table 4a; 2000, Table 4a; 2002, Table 4a; 2004, Table 4a; 2006, Table 4b; 2008, Table 4b; 2010, Table 4b; 2012, Table 4b.

in much smaller numbers. Not surprisingly, politicians respond to those who vote, ignoring substantially, if not completely, those who do not vote.

Who Votes

In Texas, voter turnout varies by age, income, education, race, and ethnicity. Let's look first at age. Only about 40 percent of Texans aged 18 to 24, compared to 62 percent of all Texans and 70 percent of Texans 65 to 74, are even registered to vote. And as the Let's Compare box shows, young Texans turn out to vote at just a third the rate of older voters and turnout rates in Texas are low to begin with. Voting is a habit, so it is best to register and get in the habit of voting while you are young.

Income and ethnicity have big impacts as well. Wealthy Anglos vote at much higher rates than poor blacks and Hispanics. Even when one controls for income, Anglos vote at slightly higher rates than blacks and significantly higher rates than Hispanics. Though Anglos make up only 46 percent of the population while Hispanics make up about 38 percent and blacks 11.5 percent, Anglos still control statewide elections.

How can this be? First, one must be a citizen to vote. While 98 percent of Anglo and black Texans are citizens, only 70 percent of Hispanic Texans are citizens. Second, even among Hispanic citizens, voter turnout is significantly lower than it is for Anglo and black citizens. Figure 3.1 shows that while the numbers are changing slowly, Anglos still cast about two-thirds of the votes in statewide elections. Blacks cast about 14 percent of votes, a little above the black proportion of the Texas population. The Hispanic vote is increasing, but it is still just 20 percent of votes cast in recent elections.[25]

Analysts speculate in each election about whether the increasing Hispanic presence in the population will show up in electoral results. It will, eventually, but only as several processes play themselves out. First, some significant portion of the 30 percent of Texas Hispanics who currently are not citizens must become naturalized American citizens. Second, the 45 percent of Hispanic citizens not currently registered to vote must register. And third, turnout among Hispanic registered voters, currently just about two-thirds of Anglo turnout, must increase. When Texas Hispanics do vote, they vote about two-to-one Democrat.[26]

Low levels of voter registration and turnout are not without their costs. Politicians represent their constituents. Ideally, a politician would represent every person in his or her constituency with equal care and attention. But most politicians are more likely to listen to those they think support them, vote for them, or contribute to their campaign. How receptive would you expect a politician to be to each of three groups of constituents if one group consistently supports him, the second group splits its vote, and the third group mostly does not vote at all?

Illegal immigration is a different, though related, political issue. Yesterday's illegal immigrant might become tomorrow's legal(ized) citizen and voter. Democrats seek to represent the interests of Hispanic Americans in family unification (bringing additional family members to the U.S.) and civil liberties (not being targeted for special scrutiny) without appearing to be dismissive of border security. Republicans tend to focus on border control, as both law enforcement and national security issues, while trying not to alienate Hispanic voters or employers who depend on the labor of illegal immigrants.[27]

Hence, the immigration debate nationally—and in Texas—has focused on three key issues: border security, a guest worker program, and a path toward citizenship for illegal immigrants already in the country. U.S. House Republicans passed a bill in 2006 calling for tight border controls, with no guest worker program and no path to citizenship. The Senate, following President Bush's lead, passed a "comprehensive" immigration bill also requiring increased border security, but establishing a guest worker program, and a path to citizenship for most of the 11 million illegal immigrants now in the U.S. Though Congress partially funded a 700-mile border fence just before the 2006 congressional elections, it failed to pass comprehensive immigration reform in 2007. Immigration was once again a hot issue in the 2012 Republican presidential nomination contest, with the focus being principally on border control. When Romney lost the Hispanic vote by 71 percent to 29 percent, some Republicans began looking for a more attractive message, while others held firm behind border security first.

Why Texans Don't Vote

We often think of Texas as a wealthy state, and, in some sense, it is. But Texas is also a state in which great poverty lives just out of sight of great wealth. Wealthy people participate in politics in all kinds of ways, including lobbying, voting, and contributing to campaigns, while poor people usually do not. Just a few formal and informal barriers are sufficient to dampen voting, especially among the poor, in Texas.

Formal restrictions. Few formal or legal restrictions on voting exist in Texas. But, there are a few. Political scientist Michael McDonald has done a state-by-state study of the number of potential voters rendered ineligible by felony conviction. Texas allows former felons to re-register after they have completed all of their prison, parole, and probation time. McDonald reports that 487,484 felons and former felons were ineligible to vote in Texas during the 2012 elections.[28]

While Texas formally excludes only felons and a few others from the electorate, it fails to take actions that other states have taken to increase voter turnout. Some states cluster elections to enhance voter interest, allow voters to register up to and including election day, and schedule elections over several days to facilitate voter turnout. Texas has yet to adopt any of these reforms. Moreover, Texas's new Voter I.D. law, discussed in this chatper's Pro/Con box, will make voting more difficult for some—exactly how many is hotly debated.

Informal restrictions. Historical and cultural barriers act to limit political participation in Texas. A century and a half of violence, intimidation, and legal exclusion of minority voters, reluctantly lifted under federal pressure, has left a legacy of non-participation. Lessons once learned are not easily forgotten. In the voting rights case of *Seaman v. Upham* (1982), Federal Judge William Wayne Justice of the Eastern District of Texas noted that "A century of neglect, sometimes benign, frequently malign, has created a climate of alienation and apathy, mixed with deep-seated resentment in many of the minority communities of Texas."[29] Many minorities continue to believe that the state's politics are, if not closed to them, at least they are still unwelcoming and unresponsive to them. In 2012, Priscilla Swofford, a black woman from Alief, northwest of Houston, declared that, "Whether you vote or not, the people on top, if they don't like how you voted, they gonna give it to the other person. Our voice really doesn't mean anything at the bottom. Only the people with big bucks have a voice." A Hispanic woman, also from Alief, said, "They don't know me personally, and I don't know them. So at the end of the day I'm not going to pay attention to it. At the end of the day, they are going to do what they want. I don't think our vote actually counts."[30] The same alienation and apathy also affect poor white voters.

Language also acts as a barrier for some Hispanic voters. While the VRA of 1975 requires that the needs of language minorities be addressed, voters not comfortable with English and not familiar with the electoral process still might be intimidated and discouraged.

Finally, voter turnout is highest in visible, important, competitive elections. Many Texas elections are quiet, even lazy, affairs. Elections in which Texans are asked to decide on a dozen statewide elected officials and perhaps two dozen obscure local county commissioners, city council persons, and judges also depress turnout. So do non-competitive elections in which one party dominates.

POLITICAL CAMPAIGNS

Q4 How are political campaigns conducted in Texas?

Campaigning in Texas takes time, stamina, money, and, perhaps most importantly, a thick skin. Before looking at modern campaigns, we should glance back at past campaigns to see how much things have changed. Candidates have always been required to demonstrate the knowledge and experience to confront the major issues of the day and to shape a vision for the future. One of the first campaign reports we have from early Texas came from no less a figure than Rutherford B. Hayes, a future President of the United States. Hayes visited Texas in 1849, just a few years after the states' admission to the Union, in the middle of a campaign for the U.S. Senate. In the 19th century state legislatures, rather than voters, selected U.S. senators so the campaigning occurred in Austin. Hayes reported to his diary that one "Colonel Kinney, . . . being Senator from San Patricio and a candidate for United States Senator," appealed to his fellow legislators with a show of horsemanship that involved "riding through the streets of Austin in every variety of posture."[31] Despite his trick riding skills, Colonel Kinney lost to incumbent U.S. Senator Thomas Jefferson Rusk of Nacogdoches.

Another classic Texas campaigner of the old school was James Stephen Hogg. Hogg was, as he must have been, a big man. A populist who campaigned against corporate and railroad interests and for Texas farmers and small businessmen, Hogg dominated late 19th-century Texas politics. He served as Attorney General (1887–91) and then Governor (1891–95), leaving office in debt before becoming wealthy late in life through his law practice and investments. On the stump, Hogg was a force to behold in a state just emerging from its frontier days. Texas in the late 19th century was overwhelmingly rural and agricultural; speeches were given from court house steps or wagon beds, often as the sun beat down. Hogg presented as "a man of the people: here was a man who spoke a language all might understand, who removed his coat when he made a public address and threw his suspenders off from his shoulders, letting them dangle about his knees, who drank water out of the pitcher provided him . . ." and as the overflow from the pitcher soaked and cooled his shirt front, the farmers and the small town men in the crowd could not doubt that Jim Hogg was one of them.[32]

Well into the mid-20th century, most political campaigns in Texas required going door-to-door and meeting your neighbors. Even statewide campaigns mostly involved driving from county seat to county seat and giving impromptu speeches from the courthouse steps. Lyndon Johnson's use of a helicopter in his 1948 Senate campaign presaged the future, but that future had not yet arrived for most Texas politicos.

In fact, in 1948 a budding young Texas politician named Dolph Briscoe, a future governor about to make his first race for the Texas House, went to see his Uvalde neighbor John Nance "Cactus Jack" Garner to ask his political blessing and for any pointers he might have to offer. Garner was a former Speaker of the U.S. House of Representatives, two-term vice president under FDR, and mentor to a couple generations of Texas politicians including Sam Rayburn. Garner looked Briscoe up and down and said, "Young man, there are 40,000 voters in this district. If you go out, shake the hands and ask for the vote of over half of them, you might get elected."[33] Garner was right and Briscoe did get elected.

Ben Barnes, another famous Texas politician of mid-century, tells a similar story about his first campaign. Just 21 years old, Barnes declared in 1960 for an open Texas House seat around Brownwood in West Texas. "For three months, I woke up with the Baptists and went to bed with the drunks, spending 18-hour days trying to shake every hand in the district. . . . Campaigns at that time were won with sweat and shoe leather, not attack ads and focus groups."[34] Barnes won his race and within a few years was the youngest Speaker in the history of the Texas House. Texas politics have changed a great deal since Briscoe and Barnes, let alone Kinney and Hogg, entered the arena.

In local races it is still common for candidates to knock on doors and go to neighborhood meetings.[35] But in statewide races, candidates depend upon teams of professional campaign managers, hundreds (if not thousands) of activists and volunteers, and a multimedia strategy of yard signs, fliers, radio, television, Twitter, and YouTube to get their name and message before the

Dallas Morning News/Rex Curry

Campaign volunteers call voters, asking them to support Kay Bailey Hutchison in her ultimately unsuccessful bid to unseat Governor Rick Perry in the 2010 Republican primary.

voters. As professional managers have taken over campaigns, costs have rapidly escalated.

Campaign Staff: Professionals and Amateurs

Major statewide races, such as those for governor, lieutenant governor, and U.S. senator, are organized and managed by a professional team of campaign strategists, pollsters, media specialists, and fundraisers. Oftentimes, these campaign professionals are drawn not just from Texas, but from around the nation. Top campaign managers and their firms are the hired guns of modern politics.

Well-known candidates have established histories and records, but the campaign team can gauge public opinion on the major issues of the day, select the issues and issue positions that put the candidate in the best light, and design a media campaign that will present the candidate most effectively. The campaign team also engages in opposition research: studying the opponent's personal background, issue positions, and past political statements and votes, looking for weaknesses that might be exploited during the campaign.

Most voters do not see candidates for statewide office in person, but they can hardly avoid their campaign commercials and materials. Television, radio, and print advertisements have become increasingly targeted. Campaign operatives pour over survey data to determine which television programs and which radio stations their supporters watch or listen to regularly. They also try to determine which issues—jobs, taxes, immigration, the environment—concern them most. Campaigns work very hard to find clusters of like-minded voters and target them with messages that will resonate with them and hopefully move them to the polls.[36] Campaigns usually find it much easier to identify and turn out their base voters than to mobilize non-voters or convert opponents.

Every campaign, especially local campaigns but even well-funded state-wide races, depends on amateurs, part-timers, and volunteers. Most people do not have the time, money, or inclination to dedicate themselves to politics. They can, however, make a modest contribution of time to take part in a phone bank, stuff campaign fliers into envelopes, or put up yard signs. Young people, on the other hand, have more energy and fewer obligations than older people and are always welcome in political campaigns.

When volunteers do not appear in sufficient numbers, the inner-LBJ in most Texas politicians can be summoned. In Texas cities, get-out-the-vote money, also called street money or walking around money, can boost volunteerism. In South Texas, campaigns can hire politiqueras, temporary paid campaign workers to go door to door for $100 to $200 on election day to pass out fliers, urge a vote, and even arrange a ride to the polling place.[37]

Campaign Finance

A few candidates have personal wealth and are willing to put it to work in support of their political ambitions. Most have to raise campaign money from others and virtually all of them hate it. Political fundraising is awkward, time consuming, and fraught with moral ambiguity. Politicians commonly say that donors neither expect nor receive anything for their contributions, but most citizens cannot help but wonder.

The 2002 Texas campaigns for governor and lieutenant governor put a spotlight on the role of personal wealth in campaigns. Most spectacularly, Democrat Tony Sanchez, a first-time candidate, poured nearly $70 million of his own money into a losing campaign to unseat incumbent Republican Governor Rick Perry. Perry spent nearly $30 million to hold his seat. In the lieutenant governor's race, Republican David Dewhurst drew heavily on his personal fortune in winning a $12 million race against Democrat John Sharp. Other statewide races cost anywhere from $1–7 million. Personal fortunes do not insure victory, but they certainly streamline and simplify the campaign process.

The 2006 governor's race was less about personal wealth and more about traditional fundraising prowess.[38] Governor Perry faced an unusual electoral challenge in 2006. The Democratic Party nominated former Houston city council member and one-term congressman Chris Bell. In addition to Bell, Perry faced two prominent independent candidates.

AP Photo/David J. Phillip

Republican Ted Cruz, with his father Rafael and daughter Caroline, became the first Hispanic to win a U.S. Senate seat from Texas in 2012.

One was popular entertainer and political novice, Kinky Friedman. The other was popular Republican Comptroller Carole Strayhorn. She decided to run as an independent when it became clear that she could not beat Perry in the Republican primary.

As the incumbent Republican governor of a red state, Perry was considered the favorite throughout the race. He raised more than half of the $46 million raised by the four major candidates and entered the post-Labor Day stretch run of the campaign with a war chest of $10 million on hand.[39] While Perry's three challengers ultimately held him to less than 40 percent of the total vote, none ever posed a serious threat to him.

In 2010 Rick Perry drew the two most credible opponents that he had faced in more than a decade and dispatched them with relative ease. In the $40 million Republican primary, Perry faced popular Republican Senator Kay Bailey Hutchison and new-comer Debra Medina. Despite Medina's libertarian bent, Perry rode the "tea party" wave to defeat Senator Hutchison by more than 20 points, though he had to spend out to do it.

After the primary, Perry trained his sights on Bill White, the Democratic nominee and former three-term mayor of Houston. Perry also turned to a familiar group of big donors to refill his campaign coffers for the general election contest.[40] As Democrats dared to hope for the first time in two decades, Perry turned on the afterburners. Perry entered the final six weeks of the campaign with $10 million on hand to White's $2.7 million.[41] When the dust cleared, Perry had spent $40 million to White's $25 million and won 55 percent to 42 percent.

In fact, the campaign contribution "late train" ran for more than a month after the voting to allow donors to show their love. It's good to be the governor.

In 2010, Rick Perry raised $39 million, with the largest donors concentrated in the fields of energy and natural resources ($6 million), finance ($5.4 million), ideological and single issues groups ($3.6 million), and miscellaneous business groups ($3.4 million). The largest personal donations came from the traditional big Republican contributors, including Bob and Doylene Perry (no relation, $1.5 million), Harold C. Simmons ($600,000), and Brit and Amanda Ryan ($450,000).

Remarkably, 66 percent of Perry's contributions, totaling more than $26 million, came in contributions of $10,000 or more. Another 20 percent, totaling over $8 million, came in donations of $1,000 to $10,000. Ten percent came in amounts between $100 and $1,000 and just 2.3 percent came in amounts of $100 or less. Large donors completely dominate the process of funding statewide campaigns in Texas. Small donors are not excluded, their money will be taken, but they clearly are marginal to the process.

Perry's Democratic challenger, former three-term Houston mayor Bill White, raised $25 million. Forty-one percent of White's contributions came in amounts of $100,000 or more, but $3 million of that came from White himself and $2 million came from the Democratic Governors Association. Several unions also made contributions in amounts ranging from $135,000 (American Federation of Teachers, AFT) to $500,000 (American Federation of State, County, and Municipal Workers, AFSCME). Far fewer wealthy individuals wrote six-figure checks to White than did to Perry.[42] Republican Greg Abbott declared his candidacy for governor on July 14, 2013. Abbott began the campaign with a $20 million war-chest that he had saved from earlier campaigns. Democrat Wendy Davis did not officially declare until October 3, though she began fundraising as soon as the 2013 legislative session adjourned. By July 2014, Abbott had raised an additional $28 million and had a total of $36.6 million on hand for the stretch run. Davis raised $18.2 million and had $9 to 12 million on hand. Overall, Abbott raised about $45 million to Davis's $30 million. Critically, Abbott's financial advantage allowed him to buy 251 hours of television campaign ads to Davis's 105 hours from July to November 2014. Abbott won by 20 points.[43]

Texas U.S. Senate races also tend to be very expensive; none more so than the 2012 Republican primary and runoff between Lt. Governor David Dewhurst, the early favorite, and Tea Party darling Ted Cruz, a former Solicitor General of Texas. Dewhurst went into the fight with four successful statewide races and ten years as presiding officer of the Texas Senate under his belt, while few Texas voters had ever heard of Ted Cruz. Moreover, while both had personal wealth to draw on, Dewhurst's fortune of more than $200 million was far greater than Cruz's modest millions. But Cruz proved to be a dogged grass roots campaigner who captured the attention of the Tea Party wing of the Republican primary electorate. As his support grew, so did his fundraising.[44]

Over the course of the Republican primary race and runoff, Dewhurst outraised Cruz three to one. Dewhurst raised $33 million, $25 million of it from his own bank account. Cruz raised $10.2 million, with $1.4 million of it his own money. But SuperPAC spending, much of it late in the contest, favored Cruz, $8 million to $6.5 million for Dewhurst. Dewhurst's SuperPAC support came mostly from inside Texas, from familiar Republican establishment donors like Bob Perry of Houston and Harold Simmons of Dallas, while Cruz benefited from high profile national money from FreedomWorks and South Carolina Senator Jim DeMint.[45]

Fully two-thirds of campaign money goes to buy television time. Texas has twenty-seven major media markets in which serious statewide campaigns must compete. A single thirty-second ad on a major urban television station in an attractive time slot, say leading into the local news, costs about $10,000. Running such an ad statewide, just once, costs about $150,000. Campaign professionals know that a commercial must run six or eight times before its message penetrates the consciousness of a busy and distracted voter. Obviously, costs pile up quickly. A well-funded gubernatorial campaign plans to spend at least $1 million a week on television from Labor Day to mid-October and then dump what is left into the final two weeks.[46]

Luckily (or not), Texas has some of the most permissive campaign finance laws in the country. The Texas Campaign Reporting and Disclosure Act of 1973, as amended over the years, allows Texans, and we really mean wealthy Texans, to give unlimited amounts of money to Texas state politicians, so long as those contributions are publicly recorded. In practice, reporting often occurs after the election and there are no enforcement provisions to insure that campaign finance reports are timely, accurate, and complete.

In 2006, Judge Mike Lynch presided over a trial in which Congressman (now former Congressman) Tom DeLay, his political action committee, and the Texas Association of Business (TAB) were charged with illegally using corporate money in the 2002 Texas legislative elections. Judge Lynch dismissed some of the charges against TAB, describing Texas election law as an "archaic, cumbersome, confusing, poorly written document in need of a serious legislative overhaul."[47] (Note to students: If it was a little later in the semester and you had read a little further in this book, you would be smiling now. But since it is early in the semester, just ask yourself, why would elected politicians write campaign finance laws that judges find too "archaic, cumbersome, confusing, (and) poorly written" to enforce?) In 2008, the TAB pleaded guilty to a misdemeanor charge of unlawful campaign expenditure and a slap on the wrist $10,000 fine to conclude their part of the case. DeLay was convicted on two counts related to money laundering in 2010. In 2011, DeLay was sentenced to three years in federal prison on a conspiracy charge and ten years probation on a money laundering charge. In 2013, a Texas appeals court overturned DeLay's conviction.[48]

DeLay's conviction now seems almost quaint. In the wake of the U.S. Supreme Court's Citizens United case (2010), Texas mega-donors, long active nationally, kicked it into hyperdrive. Texans donated almost $300 million to candidates, PACs, SuperPACs, and political parties during the 2012 election cycle. Not surprisingly, more than three-quarters of it went to Republican candidates and conservative causes. And, because conservative control of Texas is secure, 40 percent of the total went out of state.

The largest Republican and conservative donors were businessmen and investors. Harold and Annette Simmons of Dallas gave $18 million, while Houston's Bob Perry tossed in $16 million. Though Bob Perry died in 2013 and Harold Simmons died in 2014, legions of wealthy conservatives were eager to step into their places. The largest Democratic and liberal contributors were lawyers, plaintiffs lawyers the right would point out, and professionals. There were fewer of them and they tended to give less. Married trial lawyers Steve Mostyn and Amber Anderson of Houston gave $3.3 million, while Tom and Lynn Meredith of Austin gave more than $2 million. Nonetheless, the Democrats' great disadvantage was summarized by Houston lawyer Steve Susman. Explaining why virtually all of his contributions go out of state, Susman said, "In Texas, supporting a Democrat is throwing your money away, basically."[49]

Style and Tone

Even in a well-funded campaign, money is not in endless supply. Campaign officials must decide what kind of spending, particularly what kind of advertising, is likely to bring the greatest bang for the buck. Increasingly, American political campaigns, including those in Texas, depend on mudslinging and attack ads. We tend to think of this as a modern phenomenon, but it has ever been thus. Noah Smithwick, a prominent pioneer and diarist in early Texas, lamented the rough treatment meted out to the hero, Sam Houston, writing, "General Houston . . . was assailed through the newspapers; every incident of his life . . . being mercilessly dragged to the light and perverted to heap ignominy upon him." James Morgan, another of Houston's contemporaries, admitted that much of the criticism lodged against Houston was true, but concluded that "Old Sam H. with all of his faults appears to be the only man for Texas—he is still unsteady, intemperate, but drunk in a ditch is worth a thousand of Lamar and Burnet."[50]

While you can find a fair amount of mudslinging in most Texas elections, the 2002 gubernatorial election was particularly memorable. The Democratic challenger, Tony Sanchez, set off a real donnybrook by running a campaign commercial charging incumbent Republican Governor Rick Perry with abuse of power in trying to avoid a traffic ticket. Perry responded with thoroughly scurrilous charges that Sanchez had allowed banks under his control to launder Mexican drug money. As if that were not enough, another Perry commercial presented two former Drug Enforcement Agency (DEA) agents speculating broadly, and with no apparent evidence, that Sanchez had somehow been involved in the 1985 murder of DEA agent 'Kiki' Camarena. Perry won re-election, but both candidates were demeaned in the process.

By Texas standards, the 2010 campaign had a moderate tone, until Perry closed in for the kill in late October. Perry coasted through the campaign, leading by six to ten points most of the way, refusing to debate and even to meet with newspaper editorial boards. White pounded away with charges of cronyism, patronage, and the evils of a political machine built up over Perry's ten years in office. Perry was ominously quiet until after Labor Day when he began running ads touting the relative strength of the state economy and declaring Texas "open for business." Then in late October the Perry campaign released a slashing ad in which Joslyn Johnson, the wife of a Houston police officer slain by an illegal immigrant in 2006, accused Bill White of running Houston as a sanctuary city, thereby contributing to her husband's death. Though the White campaign howled and newspaper fact-checkers picked the ad apart, the damage was done. Rick Perry's campaigns are nothing if not ruthlessly efficient.

The 2014 will be remembered more for the picture that the Republican primary gave us of the state's near-term political future than for the general election results. In the November general election, the entire Republican slate, top to bottom, Abbott for governor to George P. Bush for land commissioner, won by twenty points.[51] 2014 was a shockingly broad and deep defeat for the Texas Democratic Party from which they will not recover quickly.

The real fight had occurred months earlier in the Republican primary. Greg Abbott was barely opposed in the Republican primary and cruised to an early victory. The races for lieutenant governor and attorney general were hotly contested and when the dust cleared two tea party candidates, Dan Patrick, a Houston senator, and Ken Paxton, a McKinney senator, had defeated establish candidates, David Dewhurst and Dan Branch, respectively, by two-to-one margins. It was a strikingly clear signal that the tea party or populist wing of the dominant Republican party had thrust the establishment wing aside.[52] Though George P. Bush campaigned tentatively, he won the race for land commissioner in a walk. Many believe that he will be prominent in the state's politics for years to come.

TYPES OF ELECTIONS IN TEXAS

Q5 What kinds of elections do we have in Texas?

Texans participate in three types of elections—primary elections, general elections, and special elections. Primary elections select party candidates for office, general elections select officeholders from among the party nominees, and special elections decide special issues or fill vacant offices. Primary and general elections are partisan elections. Special elections are generally nonpartisan, though partisanship often intrudes.

Primary Elections

Primary elections A preliminary election in which voters select candidates to stand under their party label in a later general election.

Closed primary A primary election that is open only to registered members of the sponsoring political party.

Open primary A primary election that is open to the participation of any registered voter, irrespective of party affiliation.

Texas two-step Name popularly given to the Texas primary election process where voters cast ballots during the day and return during the evening to conduct other party business.

About a dozen states nominate candidates for office in caucuses and conventions, but the rest use primary elections. **Primary elections** can be organized in different ways. Most states employ a **closed primary** in which only voters registered with the party may participate. Some states use an **open primary** in which voters get to decide on election day in which party's primary they will participate. And three states, Louisiana, Washington, and California, employ a "Top 2" system allowing voters to pick any candidate running in each race. The top two vote-getters, irrespective of party, advance to the general election. In Louisiana, the second round of voting is necessary only if no candidate receives a majority in the first round.

Texas, few will be surprised to hear, uses an unusual mixed primary and caucus system. The Texas primary process, often called the **Texas two-step**, occurs in two stages: the first stage is open, the second closed. Texas permits registered voters to choose the party primary in which they wish to participate on election day (so it is open at this point). As soon as the polls close on primary election day, each precinct holds a caucus which anyone who voted at that precinct earlier in the day is entitled to attend to do other party business.

While the evening caucuses are more important for the Democrats than for the Republicans, both parties hold them.

The second stage of the primary process in state elections (though not in presidential contests) is the runoff stage. Texas primary election rules require a majority to win. In a race with three or more candidates, no candidate might win a majority of the vote, in which case a runoff election between the top two vote-getters is required. Runoff primaries are held two months after the first primary and are supposed to be closed to persons who voted in the other party's primary (so runoff primaries are at least partially closed). Voter turnout in party primary and runoff elections often runs in the single digits.

Since 1986, Texas has held its primary elections in early March in even-numbered years. Legal scuffling over partisan redistricting led to the 2012 primary being pushed back to late May, but the Texas primary is usually held in March. In presidential election years (2008, 2012, 2016, etc.), the presidential primary gets most of the attention though state and federal legislative races are also held. In off-year elections (even-numbered years off the presidential cycle, 2006, 2010, 2014, etc.), the gubernatorial and other statewide office primaries, along with all of the Texas and federal legislative races, are held. Minor parties, defined as those receiving less than 20 percent of the vote in the last general election, are permitted to avoid the expense of a primary election by picking their candidates in a state party convention.

General Elections

General elections are held on the first Tuesday after the first Monday in November of even-numbered years. In the general election, voters choose among the winners of the major party primaries and the minor party nominees selected in convention. In the general election, a plurality of the votes cast for that office, even if less than a majority, is sufficient to win. There are no runoffs in the general election.

Finally, the general election ballot allows voters the option of casting a "straight ticket" or party ballot. The voter can mark a box at the top of the ballot to vote for all of one party's candidates. Texas is one of 14 states that allow **straight-ticket voting.** Voters are also permitted to mark the straight-ticket box, but then go selectively down the ballot and vote for some candidates of other parties. Sixty to sixty five percent of Texans vote a straight ticket.

General election A final or definitive election in which candidates representing their respective parties contend for election to office.

Special Elections

Special elections are employed for a variety of purposes, such as to fill vacancies caused by resignation or death, or to decide on constitutional amendments, local bond issues, or other non-recurring issues. Special elections are conducted on a non-partisan basis to avoid the need for major party primaries and minor party conventions. Most special elections are low-visibility, low-turnout, affairs.

While most special elections are sleepy affairs, one type of special election—those for an open U.S. Senate seat—have jolted Texans wide awake. The field is often large and the outcomes unpredictable. When Senator Morris Shepherd died unexpectedly in 1941, Governor W. Lee "Pappy" O'Daniel narrowly beat

Straight-ticket voting Voting for all of the candidates of one party, often by marking a box at the top of the ballot designating the favored party.

Special election Special elections are held to decide constitutional amendments, local bond proposals, and other non-recurring issues.

TIMELINE: WOMEN IN TEXAS POLITICS

1821	1831	1875	1903	1920	1924
Jane Long accompanies her husband James on a filibuster in Mexican Texas	Mary Austin Holley writes *Texas*, the first book in English about Texas	Woman suffrage is raised but ignored in the Texas Constitutional Convention	Texas Woman Suffrage Association is organized in Houston	19th Amendment to the U.S. Constitution approves female suffrage	Miriam Ferguson is elected the first female Governor of Texas

LBJ in a crowded field of twenty-nine. Johnson swore that Pappy had out stole him and that it would never happen again. Sure enough, LBJ won a hotly contested Senate race against former Governor Coke Stevenson in 1948 as charges of vote stealing in South Texas filled the air. In 1957, when Senator Price Daniel resigned to return and run for governor, Ralph Yarborough, a liberal, won the open Senate seat when two conservatives split the vote. Even more remarkably, when LBJ resigned his Senate seat to become Vice President under John Kennedy, John Tower emerged from a field of seventy candidates, almost all Democrats, to become the first Republican to win a statewide race since Reconstruction. Finally, Senator Kay Bailey Hutchison won her seat in a 1993 special election. Given this history, you can see why her claim that she was going to resign from the Senate to run for governor in 2010 (she ultimately ran and lost in the Republican primary to Rick Perry without resigning her Senate seat) created a certain amount of excitement.

ELECTORAL REFORM POSSIBILITIES

How concerned should we be that most Texans do not participate in elections and that those who do tend to be led by about 200 big contributors? And if we are concerned, what might we consider doing to broaden participation and insure that votes count for at least as much as dollars?

First, while turnout is low among all Texans, it is especially low among Hispanics. That will change over time, but it will not change very fast unless policymakers enact programs to encourage non-citizens to become citizens, then to register to vote, and finally to turn out on election day. Second, turnout for all Texans, including new citizens, has improved slightly since early voting was initiated in the late 1980s, but clustering elections so voters thought of them as more important and allowing citizens to register to vote right up to and on election day might help as well. Third, the Wild West approach to campaign finance in Texas may convince many citizens that their little contribution and, perhaps, even their vote are of no consequence. Texas law allows unlimited campaign contributions. According to watchdog group Texans for Public Justice, Rick Perry raised $102.8 million from 2001 through December 31, 2010. Perry raised almost $51 million from 204 mega-donors who gave him $100,000 or

1934	1961	1966	1981	1990	1993
Texas Legislature defeats a bill to allow jury service by women	President Kennedy names Sarah T. Hughes of Dallas as federal judge	Barbara Jordan of Houston is the first black woman elected to Congress from the South	Kathy Whitmire is elected first female mayor of Houston	Ann Richards is elected Governor of Texas	Kay Bailey Hutchison is elected to the U.S. Senate from Texas

more.[53] Proponents of the current system say that money is political expression and should not be limited while critics argue that big money can sometimes buy elections and can often rent politicians.

Chapter Summary

Political participation encompasses all of the actions that citizens undertake to influence politics. The most common forms of political participation include talking and reading about politics and voting. Many citizens also belong to civic, labor, professional, and business groups that monitor politics and some of those groups have PACs and hire lobbyists. Fewer citizens make the deeper commitment to work in a campaign, contribute money, serve on an advisory committee, or stand for office. In general, U.S. political participation rates are lower than European rates, and Texans participate at rates well below the U.S. average.

Historically, Texas actively restricted political participation by minorities and poor whites. For decades, these restrictions, including the poll tax and white primary, as well as more direct discouragements, were legal, if not just, and very effective. From the mid-1940s through the mid-1960s, from *Smith v. Allwright* through the initial passage of the Voting Rights Act, federal authorities steadily forced Texas authorities to open political participation and voting to all legally eligible citizens. Though Texas political authorities claim that the recently implemented Voter I.D. law was not designed to reduce turnout, especially minority turnout, many wonder.

In recent decades, most formal restrictions have been removed, but voter turnout in Texas remains 6 to 10 percent below U.S. averages. In modern Texas, citizens with good educations and incomes and strong ties to their community vote in significantly higher rates than those without these advantages and attributes. Anglos and blacks turn out at approximately equal rates, while Hispanics turn out at substantially lower rates.

Texas selects its political leaders through partisan primaries and party conventions. Party nominees face off in general elections. Local races still involve door-to-door campaigning, talks at the local civic clubs, and weekend barbecues. Statewide elections, especially for high-profile offices like governor, are expensive, often raucous, affairs. Campaign professionals manage these contests, there are no limits on campaign contributions or spending, and the mud flies thick and fast.

Finally, Texas law allows unlimited contributions to state, though not federal, races. The result is that big donors dominate Texas politics. In top statewide races, half to two-thirds of contributions come from a couple hundred big donors. Citizens and voters, knowing that major races are being funded by big donors, wonder whether the races and the politicians in them are not being bought—or at least rented—in the process.

Key Terms

Closed primary 76	*Smith v. Allwright* 58
General election 77	Special election 77
Grovey v. Townsend 56	Straight-ticket voting 77
Motor Voter 60	Suffrage 54
Nixon v. Herndon 56	Texas two-step 76
Open primary 76	*U.S. v. Texas* 58
Political participation 52	Voting Rights Act 59
Poll tax 55	Voter turnout 62
Preclearance 59	White primary 56
Primary elections 76	

Review Questions

1. Summarize the means, legal and illegal, that Anglo Texans and their elected representatives have employed to limit political participation among minorities and the poor.
2. Analyze the differences in voter turnout levels among Texans by race, ethnicity, age, and income.
3. Describe the kinds of elections we have in Texas and the kinds of issues considered and decisions reached in each.
4. Assess the historical and contemporary relevance of the Voting Rights Act (VRA) to Texas politics and elections.
5. Describe several key reforms that have been proposed for the Texas electoral and campaign finance systems and assess their relative merits.

Suggested Readings

Ben Barnes, *Barn Burning, Barn Building: Tales of a Political Life from LBJ to George W. Bush* (Albany, TX: Bright Sky Press, 2006).

Adam Berinsky, "The Perverse Consequences of Electoral Reform in the United States," *American Politics Review* (2005), 33: 471–491.

William D. Berry, Richard C. Fording, Evan J. Ringquist, Russell L. Hanson, and Carl Klarner, "Measuring Citizen and Government Ideology in the American States: A Re-Appraisal," *State Politics and Policy Quarterly* (2010), 10: 117–135.

Mary Fitzgerald, "Greater Convenience but No Greater Turnout," *American Politics Research* (2005), 33: 842–867.

George N. Green, *The Establishment in Texas Politics: The Primitive Years, 1938–1957* (Norman: University of Oklahoma Press, 1984).

Darlene Clark Hine, *Black Victory: The Rise and Fall of the White Primary in Texas* (Columbia: University of Missouri Press, 2003).

Michael Lind, *Made in Texas: George W. Bush and the Southern Takeover of American Politics* (New York: Basic Books, 2003).

Jason D. Mycoff, Michael W. Wagner, and David C. Wilson, "The Empirical Effects of Voter ID Laws: Present or Absent," *PS: Political Science and Politics* (2009), 42: 121–126.

Cynthia Rugeley and Robert A. Jackson, "Getting on the Rolls: Analyzing the Effects of Lowered Barriers on Voter Registration," *State Politics and Policy Quarterly* (2009), 9: 56–78.

Sue Tolleson Rinehart, *Claytie and the Lady: Ann Richards, Gender, and Politics in Texas* (Austin, TX: University of Texas Press, 1994).

Web Resources

1. **http://www.texas.gov**
   Texas Online is the state's general web portal. It provides access to many online services and helpful links.

2. **http://www.tsha.utexas.edu/handbook/online**
   The Handbook of Texas Online is sponsored by the Texas State Historical Association and UT Austin. It is an encyclopedia of Texas history, geography, and culture.

3. **http://www.sos.state.tx.us**
   The Texas Secretary of State's website contains extensive information on voter registration, turnout, and election results.

4. **http://www.followthemoney.org**
   National Institute on Money in State Politics is a non-partisan organization that tracks fundraising and spending in state elections.

5. **http://www.lwv.org**
   The League of Women Voters focuses on voter information and education.

6. **http://www.fec.gov**
   Independent federal government agency charged to oversee campaign finance rules.

7. **http://elections.gmu.ed**
   George Mason University Professor Michael McDonald's fine voter registration and turnout website.

Chapter 4

INTEREST GROUPS IN TEXAS

REPRESENTATIVE KRUSEE'S CAMPAIGN FUNDS

Texas State Representative Mike Krusee (R-Round Rock), served in the Texas House from 1993 through 2009. Representative Krusee was a competent and respected member of the legislature. He supported Governor George W. Bush's agenda during the 1990s, while he learned the legislative ropes and made himself an expert on transportation issues. When Republicans took control of the House in 2003, Speaker Tom Craddick named Krusee chairman of the Transportation Committee, where he worked hard to support Governor Perry's toll road program.

Support for toll roads offended some of his constituents and after narrowly winning re-election in 2006, he announced he would not stand for another term in 2008. Nothing too unusual here, but when Krusee concluded his House service in January 2009, he launched a new career as a paid lobbyist, again, nothing unusual here as dozens of former members serve as lobbyists. What is somewhat unusual is that former Representative Krusee had about $300,000 in his campaign bank account when his legislative service concluded and he continued to draw on it in his post-legislative career.

Texas Ethics Commission rules specify the uses that former legislators can make of left-over campaign and officeholder account funds—including donations to charities, to other candidates and campaigns, and to the Texas state treasury. State law forbids converting these funds to personal use, but according to reports in the *Austin American-Statesman*, Krusee spent nearly $200,000 on memberships, travel, hotels, meals, and equipment.[1] Krusee did not try to hide these expenditures, reporting them regularly to the Texas Ethics Commission, and he explained that the expenses were incurred for memberships and participation in groups he originally joined as a legislator. Soon after reports of these expenditures appeared in the press, the government watchdog group, Texans for Public Justice, filed a complaint with the Texas Ethics Commission charging that at least $94,000 of the expenses were personal, not officeholder, or even former officeholder, expenses.

How do you suppose the Texas Ethics Commission decided this complaint, for the watchdogs or the former legislator? In fact, they did not decide it at all; in mid-2014 the case remained unresolved. Should former legislators be able to continue spending from their campaign accounts even after they have left office, or should these funds be required to go, in relatively short order, to charity, other candidates and campaigns, or the Texas treasury?

Focus Questions

Q1 Why do the U.S. and Texas Constitutions protect interest groups?

Q2 Which Texas interest groups tend to be best organized?

Q3 How do interest groups try to influence the political process?

Q4 What roles do interest groups play in political campaigns?

Q5 Have we done enough to regulate interest groups in Texas?

Americans have always been concerned that narrow private interests, whether based in religion, ideology, partisanship, or profit, might overcome the broad public interest. The founding generation, led by James Madison, worried that highly motivated groups of citizens, like the commercial elites in the cities, or the holders of government debt, might work to skew government policy to their benefit and to the detriment of the broader public. Madison famously defined "factions," what we would call interest groups today, as "a number of citizens, whether amounting to a majority or minority of the whole, who are united by . . . some common impulse of passion, or of interest, adverse to . . . the permanent and aggregate interests of the community."[2]

Q1 Why do the U.S. and Texas Constitutions protect interest groups?

James Madison was not alone in his concern about the impact of clashing interests on the common good. Sam Houston warned his fellow Texans and the nation of the dangers posed by clashing sectional interests. Speaking in Tremont Hall, Boston, on Washington's birthday, 1855, he urged his listeners to send to Congress and the presidency "men who will care for the whole people, who will . . . reconcile conflicting interests. This can be done, and let us not despair and break up the Union."[3] Despite Houston's best efforts, conflicting interests became more strident, party conflict deepened, and civil war came. But despite the potential hazards of factions and interests in democratic politics, Madison, Houston, and most Americans with them have recognized that free people must have the right to join together, express their views, and press those views on government.

Interest groups Organizations that attempt to influence society and government to act in ways consonant with their interests.

Both the United States and Texas Constitutions protect the right of citizens to make their views known and to press their interests on government. The 1st Amendment to the U.S. Constitution declares that, "congress shall make no law . . . abridging . . . the right of the people peaceably to assemble, and to petition the Government for a redress of grievances." Similarly, Article 1, section 27, of the Texas Constitution declares that, "citizens shall have the right, in a peaceable manner, to assemble together for their common good and to apply to those invested with the powers of government for redress of grievances or other purposes, by petition, address, or remonstrance."

The most prominent contemporary definition of **interest groups** comes from David B. Truman's classic study of the governmental process. In terms similar to Madison's, Truman defined an interest group as "any group that, on the basis of one or more shared attitudes, makes certain claims upon other groups in society."[4] Others highlight the interplay of interest groups and government. Graham Wilson noted that "interest groups are generally defined as organizations, separate from government though often in close partnership with government, which attempt to influence public policy."[5]

Pluralism The belief that the interest group system produces a reasonable policy balance.

Elitism The belief that the interest group system is skewed toward the interests of the wealthy.

Despite the prominence of modern interest groups, politicians and scholars continue to ask whether they strengthen or weaken democracy. Two general answers have been offered. **Pluralism** suggests that groups arise to represent most interests in society and that the struggle between groups produces a reasonable policy balance. In this view, interest groups play a positive, even necessary, role in democratic politics. **Elitism** contends that effective, well-funded interest groups are much more likely to form, win access, and exercise influence on behalf of the wealthy and prominent than the poor and humble. In this view, the playing field is tilted in favor of the wealthy and powerful and, hence, democracy is at risk.

In this chapter we evaluate the organization, activities, and effectiveness of interest groups in Texas. We describe the kinds of interest groups active in Texas and how they seek to influence the political process. We ask what legal restraints are in place to regulate and control their activities and what additional reforms might be advisable. As we shall see, interest groups and their lobbyists play an influential, even dominant, role in Texas government and politics.

INTEREST GROUPS IN TEXAS

Both nationally and in Texas, the interest group world is tilted toward occupational or economic groups that represent corporate, business, and professional interests. In the traditional political culture of Texas, these interests tend to be especially well-organized, well-funded, and influential. They play offense.

Labor, public interest groups, and social equity groups tend to be less well-organized, less well-funded, and much less influential. They play defense.[6] As we explore the world of Texas interest groups, we will find that elitism is a better guide than pluralism.

Business Interests

Groups that represent business come in many shapes and sizes, but together they are the dominant force in Texas politics. They work to promote a strong business environment—which usually means protecting the competitive position of the state's largest businesses, encouraging support for new and expanding businesses, and discouraging business taxation and regulation. A few very prominent groups represent business in general, while most represent narrower sectors or types of businesses.

Peak associations, such as the Chamber of Commerce, which in Texas is known as the Texas Association of Business (TAB), represent the interests of business throughout the state. The TAB was established in 1922 and is a force in Texas politics. Its website unabashedly says, "our business is business, and TAB has been on the forefront of each legislative initiative that has made Texas the best business climate in America."

Trade associations, such as the Texas Oil and Gas Association, Texas Hotel and Lodging Association, and the Texas Good Roads and Transportation Association, represent particular business sectors. Finally, most major corporations, including ExxonMobil, Texas Instruments (TI), and Electronic Data Systems (EDS), lobby the Texas state government. These companies and their employees pay taxes into the state's coffers, support or oppose candidates and officeholders, and have information that state officials need to do their jobs. The associations and their representatives have never had much trouble getting the attention of Texas officials.

Since business lobbyists are sure public officials are listening, they can afford to speak softly. One famous story from mid-century, told by Robert Caro, a well-known biographer of LBJ, concerned a Johnson protégé named Alvin Wirtz. Wirtz was a former state senator, a named partner in a top Austin law firm, and the top business lobbyist of the 1940s and 1950s. Caro says that, "As a lobbyist . . . the most he might say to a legislator was, 'I just want you to know that I have been employed by a group to help pass this bill. There is a great deal of interest in seeing that it is passed. I hope you'll vote the courage of your convictions.'"[7] Legislators generally assured Senator Wirtz that they would surely vote their convictions and then proceeded to do precisely what he expected of them.

As if to prove that these are still the good old days in Texas, a similar exchange occurred in the 2011 Texas legislature. Governor Perry and majorities in both houses declared themselves in favor of a "sanctuary cities" bill. Such a bill would authorize police in Texas to question anyone they stopped about their immigration status. Though both the House and Senate passed versions of the bill, it died in the final chaotic days of the regular session and had to be brought up again in the subsequent special session. However, two of Texas's most prominent businessmen, both big Rick Perry supporters, Bob Perry of Houston-based Perry Homes and Charles Butt, head of the HEB/Central Market grocery chains, hired super-lobbyist Neal "Buddy" Jones to help kill the bill because they considered it bad for their

Q2 Which Texas interest groups tend to be best organized?

Peak associations Peak associations, such as the U.S. Chamber of Commerce, represent the general interests of business.

Trade associations Associations formed by businesses and related interests involved in the same commercial, trade, or industrial sector.

Texas Association of Business

Bill Hammond was named President and Chief Executive Officer of Texas Association of Business & Chambers of Commerce (TABCC) on April 1, 1998.

particular businesses. Jones, apparently channeling Alvin Wirtz, emailed Rep. Pete Gallego (D-Alpine), saying, "Just want to tell you that Charles Butt and Bob Perry have asked me to call every member of State Affairs [the committee controlling the bill] and ask them not to pass the sanctuary cities bill."[8] State Affairs obligingly bottled up the bill until the special session was over.

Professional Interests

Like business, Texas professions are well-organized and influential. While there are no peak associations representing all of the professions, the most prominent **professional associations**, including the Texas Medical Association, the Texas Bar Association, the Texas Association of Realtors, and the Texas Federation of Teachers, are well represented in Austin. Only occasionally, as in the case of medical malpractice reform, do the professional associations—in this case, the associations representing doctors and lawyers—go toe-to-toe. Usually, each quietly and effectively works its own side of the street.

In addition to the prominent and well-funded associations representing the doctors, lawyers, realtors, and teachers, there are dozens of other professional associations. They represent the accountants, architects, engineers, dentists, nurses and pharmacists, barbers, hair dressers and cosmetologists, surveyors, plumbers, and many more. The goal of interest groups representing professions is to keep incomes up by limiting entry into the profession, usually through some sort of licensing procedure, in exchange for modest state regulation and oversight. These groups generally dominate state policy that affects them because they care more than anyone else, they know the issues better than anyone else, and they are eager to serve on the state boards that regulate their professional activities.[9]

Professional associations
Organizations formed to represent the interests of professionals in occupations like medicine, law, accounting, and cosmetology.

Agricultural Interests

Farming and ranching are still important parts of the Texas economy, but not nearly as important as they once were. While they have to fight harder for attention, when issues that matter to rural Texans come before state government, the Texas Farm Bureau speaks for the bigger producers and the Texas Farmers Union speaks for the smaller family farms and ranches. Commodity producers, including cattle, cotton, grain, poultry, sheep, and timber, have their own associations ready to act when their interests come into play.

Who Knew?

There are 181 members of the Texas Legislature, 150 in the House and 31 in the Senate. In the 2013 regular session of the legislature, just over 1,900 lobbyists were paid between $328 million and $155 million to advance the interests of their clients. That is 10 lobbyists and $1 to 2 million in influence peddling per legislator. Texas legislators are outmanned and overmatched.

Organized Labor

In states like Michigan, Pennsylvania, and New York, organized labor shapes state policy on workplace safety, employment security, and workers' rights. Not so in Texas. In Texas, business shapes labor policy. Texas is one of twenty-five mostly southern, midwestern, and western right-to-work states. These states prohibit the closed or union shop, in which a majority vote of a business' workers to join a union requires every worker in the business to join the union, pay dues, and abide by union rules. Right-to-work laws weaken unions in relation to management and owners. They allow individual workers to decide whether to join the union. Some do, and some—wanting to save the union dues—do not, and the union is weakened as a bargaining unit. In 2014, only 4.8 percent of Texas's 11.4 million workers (compared to 11.1 percent nationally) were members of a labor union.

There are pockets of union strength in Texas. The Texas chapter of the American Federation of Labor and Congress of Industrial Organizations (AFL-CIO) and the Oil, Chemical, and Atomic Workers of Texas are strong in the Houston-Beaumont-Port Arthur area. The Service Employees International Union (SEIU) had some success in organizing janitors and health care workers in Houston in 2006 and 2007. Texas unions can affect local and regional issues and elections, but they usually struggle when they attempt to operate in Austin. They lose most direct confrontations with business interests.[10]

Table 4.1 presents one obvious way to think about the relative clout of Texas business and labor. Who hires the most lobbyists to represent their needs to government. Not surprisingly, the energy and natural resources sector spend the most money, between $31 and $62 million in 2013, though Ideological and

TABLE **4.1**	Texas 2013 Lobby Contracts by Interest Represented			
Interest Group	Max. Value of Contracts	Min. Value of Contracts	No. of Contracts	Percentage of Max. Value
Energy/Natural Resources/Waste	$62,516,987	$31,407,000	1,311	19%
Ideological/Single Issue	$47,049,984	$19,235,000	1,583	14%
Health	$46,474,988	$21,725,000	1,165	14%
Miscellaneous Business	$40,759,990	$19,440,000	998	12%
Communications	$21,014,996	$10,430,000	393	6%
Finance	$17,999,996	$8,360,000	448	5%
Lawyers/Lobbyists	$16,284,997	$9,275,000	328	5%
Construction	$12,166,997	$5,617,000	324	4%
Transportation	$12,134,997	$5,370,000	331	4%
Insurance	$11,964,998	$6,055,000	246	4%
Computers/Electronics	$10,999,997	$5,070,000	269	3%
Real Estate	$9,869,997	$4,380,000	310	3%
Agriculture	$7,204,998	$3,340,000	181	2%
Other	$5,859,998	$2,730,000	160	2%
Labor	$5,574,999	$2,690,000	121	2%
Unknown	$400,000	$160,000	13	<1%
TOTALS	$328,278,919	$155,284,000	8,172	100%

Source: Texans for Public Justice. http://www.tpj.org/reports/Top%20Lobbyists%202013.pdf

Texas NAACP president Howard Jefferson opposed a state voter ID law at a news conference on July 6, 2012. The NAACP national convention, held in Houston from July 7 through 12, also focused on voter participation.

Single Issue groups let more contracts. Following the energy industry and (mostly) conservative interest groups, comes the huge health care, communications, and finance industries. Agriculture appears near the bottom of the table and at the very bottom, between "Other" and "Unknown," comes "Labor." That pretty much tells you all you need to know about interest group influence in Texas.

Ethnic Groups

Texas is a majority-minority state, but the state's interest group structure is still very much dominated by Anglo interests. While prominent minority interest groups have operated in Texas for nearly a century, they have generally not prevailed in the Texas legislature and courts. Their successes usually came when Congress and the federal courts weighed in. The National Association for the Advancement of Colored People (NAACP) and the League of United Latin American Citizens (LULAC) have operated in Texas since 1915 and 1929, respectively.[11] The NAACP initially focused on voting and political access while LULAC focused on equal educational opportunity.

The period of greatest success for the NAACP, LULAC, and related groups came from the mid-1940s through the mid-1960s. The national NAACP and its Texas chapter won a series of voting rights victories, including *Smith v. Allwright* (1944), which opened up the Democratic party primary to blacks. LULAC and the newly formed G.I. Forum (composed of Mexican American G.I.s who had recently returned from World War II and were insisting upon equality) prevailed in a case, *Delgado v. Bastrop ISD* (1948), which declared that Mexicans could not be segregated in public schools. LULAC prevailed again in *Edgewood ISD v. Kirby* (1989), which mandated equalization of school funding between rich and poor districts.

Neither the NAACP nor LULAC have been particularly effective in recent years. In fact, LULAC has been challenged by two newer and more aggressive organizations, La Rasa and the Mexican American Legal Defense and Education Fund (MALDEF). Like the unions, interest groups representing minorities have been most effective in areas where their numbers are concentrated. The NAACP has been most effective in the state's urban centers, especially Houston and Dallas, while LULAC, La Rasa, and MALDEF have been most effective in South Texas, especially San Antonio and the Rio Grande Valley. At the capitol, they strain to be heard over the louder voices of business and the professions.

Religious Groups

For most of the 20th century, religion was important to many Americans, but it was not an organized political force. A series of Supreme Court rulings prohibiting state-sanctioned prayer and religious symbolism in the public schools seemed to many religious people to threaten the complete exclusion of religion from public life. By the late 1970s, Christian conservatives had begun to organize and push back.

Religious groups have been strongest in the Midwest and South and very strong in Texas. Since 1994, Christian conservatives have controlled the state's Republican Party and are central to Governor Greg Abbott's support coalition. Christian conservatives, often represented in court by the Liberty Legal Institute, campaign for prayer in the public schools, faith-based social policy initiatives, abstinence-based sex education, strict limits on access to abortion services, home schooling, charter schools, private school vouchers, and defense of traditional marriage.

Religious conservatives are not unchallenged in Texas. The moderate Baptist General Convention of Texas elected an Hispanic president in 2004, a black president in 2005, and a female president in 2007. The Catholic Church and the Interfaith Alliance have worked extensively in local communities to improve education, alleviate poverty, act as a liaison between those in need and social service agencies, and help with employment, language training, and health care. The Texas Freedom Network stands for separation of church and state and worries about prayer in the schools and faith-based social programs. But in Texas, religious conservatives are close to power, whispering in the governor's ear, while religious moderates and secularists whisper earnestly to the Democrats about the dangers of mixing religion and politics.[12]

AFP/Karen Bleier

Single Issue Groups

Some groups are tightly focused on one or a few related issues. The best example of a prominent single issue group is the National Rifle Association (NRA). While a national group, the NRA is powerful in Texas. The NRA favors a broad understanding of the gun owner's rights and opposes government restrictions on those rights. The Texas Constitution protects the right to bear arms but allows the legislature to regulate the right to prevent crime. In Texas, this means arming honest citizens so they can better resist the criminals.

David A. Keene, President of the National Rifle Association, addressed the 142nd annual NRA convention, May 4, 2013, in Houston. Seventy thousand members attended the three-day event.

Texas's strong support for the right to bear arms came under close scrutiny in the 2000 presidential campaign. In 1995, Governor George W. Bush signed a bill that gave Texans the right to carry concealed weapons. In 1997, he signed an amendment to the concealed-carry law that stripped out provisions forbidding concealed weapons in churches. The amendment required churches to post signs if they wanted to exclude guns. On September 16, 1999, seven people were shot and killed in a Fort Worth church. Vice President Al Gore, then about to become the Democratic nominee for president, criticized George W. Bush, about to become the Republican nominee for president, for supporting the 1995 law and the 1997 amendments.[13]

The most recent debate over guns in public places came in the wake of 24-year-old Fausto Cardenas's January 21, 2010 visit to the Texas state capitol. Cardenas entered the capitol to seek a meeting with Senator Dan Patrick (R-Houston). When his request to meet Senator Patrick was denied, Cardenas walked out of the capitol, took out a gun, and fired several shots into the air before he was subdued by state troopers. Under the 1995 law described above, anyone with a valid concealed-carry permit can bring a gun into the capitol. The *Wall Street Journal* reported the story by observing that, "Lawmakers in firearm-friendly Texas are embroiled in a debate over how to make the state Capitol safer: get rid of guns or encourage even more."[14] Governor Perry contributed to this discussion in a 2011 South Carolina speech in preparation for his first presidential campaign, saying "I'm actually for gun control—use both hands."[15]

Abortion is another highly contentious issue that has spawned single issue groups on both sides. The Texas chapter of the National Abortion Rights Action League favors "a woman's right to choose," or simply "choice." Supporters of the pro-choice position envision a situation in which abortion is legal and women and their doctors decide when it is appropriate. The Texas Right to Life Committee lobbies the Texas legislature to regulate the timing and circumstances under which abortions are available. Pro-life interest groups play an influential role in Texas politics while pro-choice groups have a very rough time. In 2005, Texas passed a law requiring written parental approval for unmarried women under 18 to secure an abortion. In 2011, Texas passed a law requiring women to view a sonogram of the foetus and to hear a description of its development before choosing an abortion. The 2013 legislature banned Planned Parenthood from the state's Women's Health Program and forced the closure of a number of clinics that provided abortion services.

Public Interest Groups

Many groups claim to pursue the public interest, rather than partisan, ideological, or economic interests. Like the single issue groups, the most prominent public interest groups are national groups with Texas chapters. The best example of a non-partisan public interest group is the Texas League of Women Voters. The League of Women Voters works to enhance voter awareness and participation. Despite their claims to the contrary, most public interest groups lean to the right or the left. Examples on the left, in the sense that they support

Helen L. Montoya/San Antonio Express-News

Texas women protesting exclusion of planned parenthood from state health programs.

an activist government, are the Center for Public Policy Priorities, Texans for Public Justice, Common Cause, and Public Citizen. These and similar groups work for the rights of children and the poor, consumer safety, environmental protection, and open government. The "good government" groups are often patronized and, more often, ignored by the powers that be in Texas politics.

On the right are the Texas Public Policy Foundation, the Conservative Coalition Research Institute, Empower Texans, and the Texas Eagle Forum. These groups produce advocacy and research that support core conservative principles of small government, low taxes, and modest regulation. The Texas Eagle Forum works for traditional values, law and order, small government, and low taxes. Conservative leaders are more likely to growl than to plead if they feel public officials are drifting from the approved path. In the summer of 2006, Lt. Governor David Dewhurst and Senator Kay Bailey Hutchison, both now out of office, both suggested the need for a guest worker program as part of their re-election campaigns. Cathie Adams of the Texas Eagle Forum told Gardiner Selby of the *Austin American-Statesman* that "Dewhurst and Hutchison seem to speak for corporations. 'What we are up against [Adams said] is the taxpaying citizen versus the elites who are only looking out for the cost of doing their own business . . . . This is hurting. I'm sorry that maybe our voices haven't been loud or clear enough.'"[16] In the 2011 legislative session, Michael Quinn Sullivan of Empower Texans expressed much the same sentiment, saying, "If they do the right thing only because they're scared, that's fine. Let's make them scared."[17]

Behind Empower Texans and a number of other conservative policy and political groups is Midland oil and gas entrepreneur Tim Dunn. A longtime donor and vice chairman of the conservative Texas Public Policy Foundation, Dunn founded Empower Texans and an affiliated nonprofit called Texans for Fiscal Responsibility in 2006. Dunn supports a libertarian agenda of limited government, low taxes, light regulation, and personal responsibility that reflect, he claims, his West Texas roots.[18]

INTEREST GROUP ACTIVITIES AND RESOURCES

Q3 How do interest groups try to influence the political process?

Texas state governments, with the singular exception of the strong state government created by the post–Civil War Reconstruction Constitution of 1869, were designed to be weak and diffuse so that they could not dictate to private individuals and interests. This is particularly true of the Texas Constitution of 1876, the current constitution, with its weak governor, part-time legislature, elected judges, and diffuse and under-funded bureaucracy. Interest groups wield great influence in Texas because, oftentimes, they are better organized, better informed, and better funded than Texas state government.

Interest groups use a variety of tools in their attempts to influence the elected and appointed officials of state government. Most groups have knowledge and expertise that the public officials need. Some groups have deep pockets, some have many members, and some have a small number of influential and well-connected members. Other groups have influential leaders or well-established ties to important economic and ideological networks. Interest groups and their lobbyists engage in **lobbying**, meaning that they deploy their resources to influence the making and implementation of public policy in Texas.

Lobbying To attempt, often on behalf of an organized group, to influence the making or implementation of public policy in ways favorable to the group's interests.

The American League of Lobbyists'
Code of Ethics (Key Elements)

- Conduct lobbying activities with honesty and integrity.
- Comply fully with all laws, regulations, and rules applicable to the lobbyist.
- Conduct lobbying activities in a fair and professional manner.
- Avoid all representations that may create conflicts of interest.
- Vigorously and diligently advance the client's or employer's interests.
- Have a written agreement with the client regarding terms and conditions of service.
- Maintain appropriate confidentiality of client or employer information.
- Ensure better public understanding and appreciation of the nature, legitimacy, and necessity of lobbying in our democratic governmental process.
- Fulfill duties and responsibilities to the client or employer.
- Exhibit proper respect for the governmental institutions before which the lobbyists represent and advocate clients' interest.

Source: *State Legislatures*, "Tools of the Trade," May 2013, p. 33.

Benny Frank Barnes, later known simply as Ben Barnes, was born in Gorman, Texas, on April 17, 1938. His family had a peanut farm in nearby Comanche County, in West Central Texas about 100 miles southwest of Fort Worth. Barnes graduated from high school in DeLeon, Texas, before briefly attending Texas Christian University in Fort Worth and Tarleton College in Stephenville. After marrying his high school sweetheart, Martha Morgan, he moved to Austin and enrolled in the University of Texas to study business administration.

Barnes's meteoric political career began in 1959 when he was barely 21 years old. Ben Sudderth, the state representative from his home district, unexpectedly announced his retirement. Barnes rushed home to announce his candidacy for the position, and campaigned tirelessly from January 1960 through the May 7 primary, which he won by a near two-to-one margin. At 22 he was on his way to the state legislature where he became chair of the powerful Rules Committee at 24 and Speaker at 26. Ben Barnes was the youngest man ever elected Speaker, fully three years younger than Sam Rayburn had been when elected at age 29.

Barnes came of age in Texas politics when the Democratic Party was unchallenged in Texas and led by Texans nationally. Sam Rayburn was Speaker of the U.S. House and Lyndon Johnson, the Senate Majority Leader, had been elected Vice President on the Kennedy ticket in 1960. Johnson protégé John Connally was elected Governor of Texas in 1962. Barnes cast his lot with the dominant Johnson/Connally wing of the Democratic Party. As Speaker, Barnes worked closely with Connally on an agenda of improved education, especially colleges and universities, to support high tech business and job growth in Texas. After two years as Speaker, Barnes was elected Lt. Governor in 1969 at age 30.

No politician in Texas history ever rose to the edge of greatness faster than Ben Barnes. With Lyndon Johnson and John Connally having left the presidency and governorship in early 1969, Barnes was the presumptive leader of the Democratic Party in Texas. He was widely expected to run for governor in 1972 and was expected to win easily. So evident was his political charisma and potential that former President Johnson declared in 1970 that Barnes would be the next Texan to win the presidency. Many agreed, but then the wheels came off.

Ben Barnes lived his life on the edge of political scandal, but was taken down by a scandal in which he was not directly involved. The Sharpstown Scandal of 1971 revolved around a banker named Frank Sharp. Sharp's bank made loans to Governor Preston Smith, Speaker Gus Mutcher, and others so they could buy bank stock and then sell it back at a quick profit. No one made much money on this little scheme, but federal authorities discovered it, indictments, trials, and convictions followed and the whole Democratic leadership of the state was tainted. While Barnes was never indicted in the Sharpstown case and apparently had nothing to do with it, he was known to play the game hard, and so he took part of the blame.

Ben Barnes, unable to get clear of the scandal, ran third in the Democratic primary for governor in 1972. He left elective politics upon completion of his term in early 1973. Barnes went into the property development business where he prospered until the energy, banking, and property market bust of the mid-1980s. Like John Connally, his sometime real estate investment partner, Barnes declared bankruptcy in the late-1980s. But not to worry—today Ben Barnes is one of Washington D.C.'s most powerful Democratic lobbyists, business consultants, and fund raisers. Cats and Texas politicians always land on their feet.

TABLE 4.2 The "Rainmakers" of the Texas Lobby				
Lobbyist	Contracts Max. Value	Contracts Min. Value	No.of Contracts	Lobbyist's Background
Andrea McWilliams	$3,845,000	$1,960,000	46	Ex-House aide
Stan Schlueter	$3,075,000	$2,035,000	23	Ex-House member
Dean R. McWilliams	$2,745,000	$1,410,000	31	Ex-Senate aide
Randall H. Erben	$2,475,000	$1,335,000	25	Ex-Asst. Sec. of State
Michael Toomey	$2,400,000	$1,325,000	26	Ex-House member
Mignon McGarry	$2,320,000	$1,325,000	24	Ex-Senate aide
Ron E. Lewis	$2,250,000	$1,175,000	27	Ex-House member
Robert D. Miller	$2,125,000	$1,115,000	31	Ex-House aide
Robert E. Johnson, Jr.	$1,970,000	$1,300,000	15	Son of Ex-House member
Christopher S. Shields	$1,950,000	$965,000	29	Ex-Governor aide
Walter Fisher	$1,900,000	$1,025,000	21	Ex-Parliamentarian
Frank R. Santos	$1,850,000	$975,000	21	Ex-House aide
John R. Pitts	$1,830,000	$870,000	41	Ex-Lt. Governor aide
Bill Messer	$1,700,000	$835,000	26	Ex-House member
Demetrius McDaniel	$1,635,000	$$835,000	19	Ex-House aide
Royce Pabst Poinsett	$1,570,000	$900,000	17	Ex-Governor aide

Source: Texans for Public Justice, "*Texas' Top Lobbyists.*"

Lobbying Government Officials

Lobbyists Hired agents who seek to influence government decision making in ways that benefit or limit harm to their clients.

Texas Ethics Commission Created in 1991, the TEC administers the state's ethics, campaign finance, and lobbying laws.

Most major interest groups hire one or more **lobbyists** to defend their interests in Austin. Just over 1,900 lobbyists registered with the **Texas Ethics Commission** (TEC) prior to the 2013 legislative session.[19] TEC records (which record ranges rather than precise dollar amounts) indicate that lobbyists earned between $328 and $155 million representing clients before the Texas legislature.[20]

Most of the top professional lobbyists have a detailed knowledge of Texas government and policy. They are often former members of the legislature, like Stan Schlueter, former chair of the House Calendars Committee, or former senior staff to the legislature, like ex-Speaker's aide Rusty Kelley. Others cut their teeth in the governor's office or in a key element of the bureaucracy. Former officials know the legislative and bureaucratic process and they have networks of former colleagues and friends who will assure them a respectful hearing.

One major interest group, the Texas Cable and Telecommunications Association (TCTA), learned a costly lesson in Texas "pay-to-play" politics in 2005. Texas phone companies, led by SBC Communications and Verizon Communications, pushed for legislation, called SB5, allowing them to offer statewide internet-based television services without negotiating separate agreements with Texas cities as the cable companies are required to do. The cable companies opposed the bill, arguing that it would give the phone companies an unfair competitive advantage.

The phone companies fertilized the legislative process by contributing $156,000 to Governor Perry and spending as much as $10.2 million on lobbying. The cable companies gave Governor Perry only $25,000 and spent $1.7 million on lobbying. The phone company's bill passed in the second special session of 2005 and the responses of interested observers and participants were instructive. Andrew Wheat, research director for Texans for Public Justice (a left-leaning public interest group), said:

> Nobody is shocked to learn that moneyed interests call the shots in Austin. Yet it is truly boggling that a single special interest has the "stroke" to push its legislation through the special session . . . The only way to adequately recognize this feat is to rename the Capitol "SBC Arena."

Wheat was right to point to SBC's impressive "stroke" with the governor and the legislature, but he was wrong to say that nobody was "shocked to learn that moneyed interests call the shots in Austin"—the cable companies certainly were shocked. Tom Kinney, chairman of the TCTA, said "The cable industry chose to stand by the merits of our position—namely, create regulations that treat each player in the telecom market equitably—rather than spend huge amounts of money on lobbyists and political contributions." It did not take the cable lobby long to rethink its strategy. A little more than two months later, Representative Todd Baxter (R-Austin) resigned his seat in the Texas House and on the House Regulated Industries Committee to become the top lobbyist for the Texas cable industry. Kinney observed that Baxter's "experience at the Capital will serve TCTA well."[21] Lesson learned.

Though Baxter's lobbying effort failed to overturn SB5, in mid-2012, a full seven years after the law was enacted, the federal courts overturned it as a denial of the cable companies' First Amendment rights. But these were seven costly years, during which competitive opportunities were limited, expensive new hires had to be made, campaign contributions had to be increased, and court costs mounted. What is the lesson here—stand by your principles or pay up and avoid the hassles?

In 2007, a similar fight broke out between Texas liquor wholesalers and package store distributors. Since Texas legalized liquor by the drink in 1971, liquor wholesalers have sold to package stores and package stores have enjoyed a monopoly on selling liquor to bars and restaurants. In the ten weeks prior to the 2007 regular session, the wholesalers lubricated the Texas political establishment with $1.7 million, $100,000 apiece to Governor Perry and Speaker Craddick, $75,000 to Lieutenant Governor Dewhurst, and amounts ranging from $40,000 to $1,500 to a majority of the House and Senate, to get the law changed. The wholesalers also spent $1.1 million on lobbyists, while the package store owners responded with $635,000 on lobbying contracts.

Despite outspending the package store distributors, the wholesalers lost when Rep. Kino Flores (D-Mission) refused to bring the bill up in his

LET'S COMPARE — LEGISLATOR/LOBBYIST RELATIONSHIP REPORTING REQUIREMENTS

The story about Representative Kino Flores's indictment and conviction, while more brazen than most, is not as uncommon as we might wish. Other Texas elected officials, from both the executive and legislative branches, have been investigated for and sometimes convicted of seeking personal benefit from their public service. In a state like Texas, where unlimited political contributions are legal and money can be moved from campaign accounts to officeholder expense accounts, checking the influence of money is no easy task.

One way that states seek to check the influence of money is to require legislators to report their relationships and financial contacts with lobbyists. Texas is one of seven states requiring legislators to report financial contacts with lobbyists. Fourteen more states require disclosure of benefits accepted from lobbyists by spouses or spouses and family members.

Twenty-eight states have no legislator reporting requirements, though most of these do require lobbyists to report some financial contacts with legislators. Surely the public needs to know when financial relationships exist between lobbyists and legislators, whoever is required to report it.

But financial relationships are harder to monitor than one might think, especially for a part-time legislature like Texas's where legislators have professions, businesses, and jobs which bring them into contact with people who have interests before the state. How do you limit business and financial contacts between legislators and lobbyists without unfairly denying either or both a legitimate economic opportunity? On the other hand, if a legislator is offered a piece of a business opportunity by a lobbyist or other person with interests before the legislature or the state, is it enough that the business relationship simply be reported?

No Legislator Disclosure Required		Legislator Only	Legislator + Family
Arizona	Montana	Alaska	Colorado
Arkansas	Nebraska	Illinois	Connecticut
California	Nevada	Indiana	Kentucky
Delaware	New Hampshire	Maryland	Louisiana
Florida	New Jersey	Oklahoma	Massachusetts
Georgia	New York	**Texas**	Missouri
Hawaii	North Dakota	Virginia	New Mexico
Idaho	Pennsylvania		North Carolina
Iowa	Rhode Island		Ohio
Kansas	South Dakota		Oregon
Maine	Vermont		South Carolina
Michigan	West Virginia		Tennessee
Minnesota	Wyoming		Washington
Mississippi			Wisconsin

Source: National Council of State Legislatures, "Personal Financial Disclosure for Legislators: Lobbyist Connection Requirements."
See http://www.ncsl.org

Licensing and Administrative Procedures Committee. Does this mean that Texas politicians cannot be bought, or just that sometimes the deep-pocketed special interests have to pay more than once before getting their way? Suzy Woodford of Common Cause Texas observed that the fight

> shows that in Texas, we have a pay-to-play system. We have no limits on the amount of money that . . . individuals, their PACs, and their officers can contribute. So it clearly demonstrates to the average Joe that if you don't have the big bucks . . . the item you care about is not even going to be considered.[22]

Kino Flores soon came to a bad end. In 2009 he was indicted on 16 counts of tampering with or falsifying government records and three counts of perjury. The Travis County District Attorney, charged with prosecuting wrongdoing in state government, argued that Flores had failed to report $847,000 in income over six years from at least seven properties and from gifts to himself and his son. Some of the gifts came from persons with interests before the legislative committee that Flores chaired before he was removed in 2009. In 2010, he was convicted on 11 counts of tampering with state records and perjury. The charges carried prison terms and fines ranging up to two years on each felony count and $10,000 in fines. He was sentenced to five years of probation, a $1,000 fine, and 400 hours of community service. He is no longer in the legislature, but he did keep the $847,000. Texas is a forgiving state.[23]

Unlike the highly visible and well-funded fight between the phone and cable companies, or the liquor wholesalers and package stores, most lobbying is low profile, even behind-the-scenes. The most potent resource that most lobbyists have, especially during the crush of the legislative session, is information. A lobbyist representing an interest group will have all of the information that is available to that group. They may offer the legislator only, or at least mostly, that information that supports the group's policy position, but the interested legislator can get the rest of the information from a competing lobbyist. Lobbyists also testify before legislative committees and often participate directly in the discussions and negotiations that lead to the final legislative product.

Lobbyists work to establish a personal, as well as a professional, relationship with legislators. They hold an endless series of receptions, lunches, and dinners for legislators throughout the session. At the end of the session, they host parties and contribute to the purchase of gifts for the legislative leaders and committees with whom they worked most closely. There are state laws governing lobbyist expenditures, but they are weak and their weakness is no accident.[24]

Lobbyists and other interest group representatives are integral to the consultative, deal-making, legislative process, but their work does not end when the legislature adjourns. Laws have to be implemented and bureaucratic decisions about rules, regulations, and procedures that govern implementation can be critical. A group that opposed a particular piece of legislation might gain back some of what it lost in the legislature if its representatives can shape the way the bureaucracy administers the law.[25] Alternatively, a group that supported the legislation, seeing it administered in unintended ways, might appeal to the courts for a judgment on the law's real meaning.

Lobbying the Public

While most interest groups and all lobbyists prefer to make their case directly to politicians and decision makers, groups also lobby the public. They do this through newspaper and television advertising, direct mail, and public meetings intended to educate, inform, and rally citizens to the group's issue positions and legislative proposals.

Once citizens are informed and engaged, they can be organized in mail, phone, and e-mail campaigns. They might also be taken to Austin to meet with their legislators, address committees where appropriate, and even rally and demonstrate on the capitol steps. If television cameras can be attracted, all the better. Lobbying the public is intended to encourage citizens to supplement the efforts of professional lobbyists, or, where professional help is too expensive, to bring the pressure of public opinion directly to bear against elected officials and bureaucrats.

Campaign Support

Q4 What roles do interest groups play in political campaigns?

Wealthy individuals, interest groups, and their lobbyists know that if they contribute to a candidate's campaign or political committee, that candidate will meet with them and listen to them once elected.[26] On the other hand, statewide elected officials, legislative leaders, committee chairs, and many others take contributions from interests on all sides of major public issues. Contributors know that while making a contribution gets them a hearing, it does not necessarily buy them a vote.

Political action committee Legal entity, often associated with interest groups, through which campaign contributions and other forms of support can be given to parties and candidates.

Most interest groups make their contributions through a **political action committee** or PAC. Regulation of PACs in Texas is far looser than are federal regulations or regulations in most other states. Texas PACs (there were 1,364 in 2012) are required to register with the TEC, name a treasurer, and file regular reports. Those reports must identify persons who give more than $50 to a Texas campaign, but unlike federal campaigns, where contributions are limited to $2,500, there are no limits on the amount that an individual or PAC can contribute in Texas.[27]

Electioneering To take an active part in working for the election of a particular candidate or party.

Some interest groups and PACs have the resources to engage in active **electioneering** and try to shape elections more generally, by participating in candidate recruitment, voter registration and mobilization, polling, and advertising. One prominent Texas PAC, Tom DeLay's Texans for a Republican Majority (TRMPAC), raised more than $532,000 to target twenty-three Texas House districts in 2002. Most of their preferred candidates won, giving the Texas House a Republican majority for the first time since the early 1870s. Subsequent charges that TRMPAC had accepted illegal corporate contributions led to the indictment and conviction of some TRMPAC officials, the demise of TRMPAC itself, and Tom DeLay's resignation from Congress—but the election results stood. DeLay's convictions were overturned in 2013, but both sides have vowed to continue the fight.

Not surprisingly, the largest political donors in the U.S. often are Texans. Houston home builder Bob Perry had been making major political contributions since the first Bill Clements gubernatorial campaign in 1978. He helped fuel the rise of Governor Clements, but also of Tom DeLay, George W. Bush, and most of today's prominent Republican elected officials.

In 2006, Bob Perry gave $16 million, 92 percent to Republican candidates and causes; $6.7 million in Texas contests and $9.3 million in other state and national contests. Most of Bob Perry's national contributions were not to candidates, where federal law limited contributions to $2,400, but to groups called 527s which are independent expenditure groups that can support causes and candidates without expenditure limits. Little wonder that Texas politicians show so little interest in limiting contributions to state contests.[28]

Finally, a 2010 decision by the U.S. Supreme Court, a campaign finance case called *Citizens United v. Federal Election Commission*, had significant implications for Texas's already wide open campaign spending system. *Citizens United* overturned a century-old prohibition on direct spending by corporations and unions to advocate or oppose the election of particular candidates. While corporations and unions still cannot give more than $5,000 to individual federal candidates, they can spend unlimited amounts advocating for or against individual candidates so long as they do not coordinate with any candidate's campaign. Such direct spending on elections by corporations and unions has long been illegal in Texas, but in the wake of the *Citizens United* decision the TEC broke records in declaring that, "It is our position that corporations are allowed to make all types of direct campaign expenditures."[29] Anyone surprised?

Between 2009 and mid-2012, Bob Perry contributed $13.1 million to Texas candidates and PACs. He was the number one contributor to all six Texas statewide elected officials and to the Speaker of the Texas House. He gave $1.7 million to Governor Rick Perry, $550,000 to Attorney General Greg Abbott, $300,000 each to Lt. Governor David Dewhurst, Comptroller Susan Combs, and Agriculture Commissioner Todd Staples, and lesser amounts to the others. And, because his coffers were still quite full, he gave $20.5 million to conservative SuperPACs in the 2012 presidential cycle.[30] Bob Perry, 80, died in 2013.

Litigation

Interest groups are nothing if not tenacious. If they lose on an important issue before the legislature and executive branch, they often look to the courts. Bureaucrats make policy by deciding precisely how to implement legislation, and courts make policy by judging whether legislative intent was constitutional and, if so, whether it has been followed.

Powerful interest groups attempt to shape the judiciary by recruiting favorable candidates for judicial office, contributing to their campaigns, and supporting them for re-election. Weaker interest groups have to take the judiciary as it is, but they can sometimes prevail by suing to insure that the letter of the law is applied. The NAACP, LULAC, and MALDEF have all won major victories in the Texas courts over the years. While victories expanding civil liberties, political access, and equal opportunity have not been frequent, they

Erich Schlegel

Anti-tax and small government lobbyist Michael Quinn Sullivan bears down on Representative Allen Fletcher (R-Tomball).

have been important, and sometimes the courts are the only means that the politically weak have to move a system that usually pays them little heed.

INTEREST GROUPS AND LOBBY REFORM

Q5 Have we done enough to regulate interest groups in Texas?

Texas has had laws on the books to regulate the activities of interest groups and lobbyists for more than a century. As early as 1903, four years before the national Congress passed a similar bill, Texas outlawed corporate campaign contributions. In 1907, Texas instructed lobbyists to use no inducements other than sweet reason to influence legislation. New laws requiring interest groups and their lobbyists to register with the legislature and report on various aspects of their activities were passed in 1929, 1957, 1973, and again in 1983. Each was riddled with loopholes, lacked enforcement provisions, and was generally ineffective. New laws were passed in 1991 and updated in 1997 and 2003, but Texas remains the Wild West as far as effective regulation of interest groups, lobbyists, and campaign contributions are concerned.[31]

Generally, ethics laws try to control, or at least record, the benefits, gifts, and contributions that lobbyists shower on legislators and, to a lesser extent, on bureaucrats and judges. Lobbyists buy meals and drinks for legislators, push benefits and gifts their way, and make campaign contributions to them. Texas law does not forbid gifts, gratuities, and contributions, it merely requires that a public record of them be kept. In fact, as we shall see below, it barely requires that.

Pro & Con   Legislator Compensation: Low Pay v. Officeholder Accounts

Legislators around the country receive varying levels of pay for their service. California legislators receive $90,526 annually, Pennsylvania pays $83,801, and New York pays $79,500, while Mississippi pays $10,000, South Carolina pays $10,400, and Arkansas pays $15,869. Most also pay a daily expense amount, ranging from under $100 to around $175, for each day actually spent on legislative business. Texas pays its legislators $7,200, among the very lowest in the nation, and a per diem of $150 a day. Why does Texas pay its legislators so little?

First, legislator pay is set in the Texas Constitution and can only be raised by constitutional amendment. The Texas Constitution of 1876 set legislator pay at $5 a day for the first sixty days of the session and $2 a day thereafter. The message, clear to every legislator, was get your work done and go home. Amendments adjusted legislator pay to $10 a day in 1930 and $25 a day in 1954. In 1960, an amendment was approved setting legislator pay at $4,800 annually plus a per diem of $12 a day when on actual legislative business. Finally in 1975, the annual salary was raised to $7,200, where it remains today, and the Texas Ethics Commission was empowered to set the daily per diem—now $150 a day.

No one argues that a legislator, let alone a legislator and his or her family, can live on $7,200 a year plus per diem. And no one thinks legislators should be expected to spend their own money defraying political expenses. So where are legislators to look for more money. The answer has been that the public, really the lobby, should provide funds to cover political expenses beyond $7,200 a year and per diem. Texas candidates and officeholders can take contributions from citizens, corporations, union, PACs, and other groups into two accounts—campaign accounts and officeholder accounts.

The Campaign Finance Guide produced by the Texas Ethics Commission for the guidance of candidates and officeholders defines a campaign contribution as intended for use in campaigns and officeholder contributions as intended to support officeholders in their official and political activities. However, the boundaries between a legislator's campaign account and officeholder account is paper thin. In Ethics Commission reports, legislator's are not required to distinguish between campaign and officeholder contributions or expenses. Both kinds of contributions are listed as "political contributions" and both kinds of expenses are listed as "political expenses."

As a practical matter, Texas legislators can use campaign contributions to defray officeholder expenses. Most campaign contributions come from interested parties—wealthy individuals, PACs, now SuperPACs, and political and ideological groups—and if legislators are depending on these groups for living expenses, how independent would you expect them to be when their donors come to them for favors. The Texas Observer ran an article, provocatively entitled "Lifestyles of the Corrupt and Elected," in which the authors, Dave Mann and Abby Rapoport, explored the use of campaign funds to pay for rent and cars in Austin, attendance at policy conferences in attractive locations, hotels, meals, and any other expenses that plausibly can be related to legislative business.[32]

Do you think paying legislators a pittance and then allowing them to make up the rest of what they need to meet their expenses in contributions from wealthy individuals, lobbyists, and interest groups is a good idea? Can we depend on our legislators to remain unbiased while they are taking rent money from interest groups, or would we be better off paying them a reasonable wage and demanding that they put the public interest before the interests of private parties—no matter how generous?

TIMELINE: ETHICS REFORM IN TEXAS

1900	1903	1907	1957
The Waters-Pierce scandal, involving loans to Senator Joseph Weldon Bailey, sparks discussion of ethics reform	Texas passes corporate campaign contribution limits	Lobbyists instructed to use no inducements other than reason	Lobbyists required to register for the first time

Perhaps most glaringly, while thirty-five states have sitting-out periods designed to at least slow the revolving door between the legislature and the lobby, Texas does not. A Texas legislator can turn around and lobby his former colleagues the day after he or she leaves office. Moreover, conflicts of interest are masked because lobbyists do not even have to indicate the bills on which they are lobbying.[33]

The Lobby Registration Act of 1973 and the Ethics Law of 1991 form the basis of Texas's modern regulatory structure. The 1973 **Lobby Registration Act** required groups and individuals attempting to influence state government to register and file reports on their activities. The 1991 Ethics Law required any person who spends more than $500 or receives more than $1,000 in a calendar quarter for activities designed to influence legislative or executive branch activities to register with the TEC. The law further required lobbyists who spend more than $50 on a legislator to name the legislator and detail the expenditures. Unfortunately, the TEC is a small agency with thirty-seven staff members and a budget of just over $2 million. The TEC is led by an eight-member commission. Each commissioner serves a four-year term. David Reisman was named executive director of the TEC in 2004.

One of the classic stories about legislative ethics in Texas involved Lonnie "Bo" Pilgrim of Pilgrim's Pride chicken fame. Chicken processing plants are dangerous places. So as the 1989 Texas legislature mulled a bill relating to workplace safety, Bo Pilgrim was allowed on the Senate floor where he proceeded to pass out $10,000 checks, perhaps to encourage senators to think about the bill in detail. Public embarrassment led the House Speaker, Gib Lewis (D-Fort Worth), long an opponent of stronger ethics legislation, to support new legislation.[34]

The 1991 Ethics Law charged the TEC to receive complaints about violations of the ethics rules, conduct investigations, and issue findings. Nonetheless, the 1991 Act left some gaping loopholes. First, members of the TEC are appointed by the governor, lieutenant governor, and Speaker of the House from a list of candidates declared acceptable by the legislature. Hence, TEC members are, almost by definition, friendly with the politicians they are appointed to scrutinize. Second, the TEC requires a super-majority of three-quarters to initiate important actions. Complaints that are not upheld are kept secret; neither the charge nor the Commission's findings is ever made public.

Third, because Texas legislators receive only $7,200 a year, plus a modest *per diem* when the legislature is actually in session or they are engaged in official

Lobby Registration Act
A 1973 Texas law requiring groups and individuals attempting to influence state government to register and report on certain of their activities.

1973	1991	1995	2003
In the wake of the Sharpstown Scandal, the Lobby Registration Act and the Campaign Reporting and Disclosure Act pass	In the wake of $10,000 checks being handed out on the Senate floor, the Texas Ethics Commission is established. Lobbyists required to file regular reports	Judicial Campaign Fairness Act passed	TRMPAC campaign finance scandal leads to modest TEC reform

legislative business, they search for money to meet their living expenses while in Austin. Current law permits legislators to accept unlimited amounts of money from lobbyists and others, deposit it into their campaign accounts, and then to draw on those accounts to cover living expenses in Austin. Clearly, accepting money for these expenses from lobbyists guarantees that legislators will be beholden to them.

It gets worse. In 2004 and 2005, Bill Ceverha, a former official of TRMPAC and at the time a current member of the State Employees Retirement System board, accepted two checks from Houston real estate developer Bob Perry (no blood relation to Gov. Rick Perry, but the top Republican donor in Texas). Ceverha incurred more than $1 million in legal fees and civil penalties for his role in TRMPAC's illegal fund raising for the 2002 state legislative races. Ceverha was forced to declare personal bankruptcy and to appeal to friends and associates for assistance. Perry felt sorry for Ceverha and made charitable gifts to him to help defer legal expenses.

Ceverha, as required by Texas law, filed reports with the TEC on which he listed the first of these gifts as a "check." When public advocacy groups demanded more information—for example, how much the "check" was for— the TEC ruled that state disclosure laws do not require that the amount of cash gifts be disclosed. Clean-government types howled and eventually Perry and Ceverha announced that two checks, totaling $100,000, had passed from Perry to Ceverha.[35] Sage old veterans of Texas politics just smiled and shook their heads. "Let the big dogs hunt."

Chapter Summary

Interest groups and their lobbyists are an integral part of American and Texan political life. The U.S. and Texas constitutions explicitly assure citizens that they have the right to assemble, share their views in speech and writing, and petition their government for redress of grievances. Nonetheless, Americans and Texans worry that powerful interest groups and effective lobbyists may skew public policy toward narrow private interests rather than toward the broader public interest.

In Texas, this concern is particularly acute. Organized interests, along with their PACs and lobbyists, are particularly numerous, well-funded, aggressive, and effective. Business and professional groups, like the Texas Association of

Business, the Texas Oil and Gas Association, and the Texas Medical Association, wield decisive influence. Labor, civil rights, and environmental groups do the best they can, but they are at distinct disadvantages when it comes to numbers, money, talent, and relevant expertise.

Some Texas business and professional interests, led by the oil and gas industry and including conservative activist groups like Empower Texans, are particularly influential. They wield money, prestige, and expertise to protect and enlarge their interests. Their goals are reflected in and aided by the commitment of the state's political culture to limited government, low taxes, and personal responsibility. This same political culture often works against those, like unions and minority groups, who approach state government for more spending on education, health care, and even transportation and water infrastructure.

The dominant interest groups tend to lobby government officials directly and to come to the support of elected officials in their campaigns. Less effective groups are left to demonstrate, lobby the public, and appeal to the courts. Texas's very permissive campaign finance system, which allows unlimited contributions and demands only modest reporting requirements, gives the established interests and their agents a formidable role in Texas politics.

Hence, calls for reform of the Texas interest group system have been steady, if mostly unheeded. A series of reforms have been made over the past half century, mostly under the pressure of scandal, but enforcement provisions have been written not to press too hard on wayward politicians. Critics still call for several types of reforms. First, reforms that would expand the budget and staff of the Texas Ethics Commission and give teeth to its enforcement powers are necessary. Second, unlimited campaign contributions allow a couple hundred wealthy donors to exercise dangerous influence over Texas electoral and political processes. Third, allowing Texas legislators to convert campaign contributions, most of which come from wealthy donors and lobbyists representing interest groups, to cover day-to-day political expenses is asking for trouble. While other reforms might be needed, these seem critical and would constitute a good start.

Key Terms

Electioneering 98	Peak associations 85
Elitism 84	Pluralism 84
Interest groups 84	Political action committee 98
Lobby Registration Act 102	Professional associations 86
Lobbying 92	Texas Ethics Commission 94
Lobbyists 94	Trade associations 85

Review Questions

1. Analyze the plusses and minuses, the benefits and the costs, that interest groups bring to U.S. and Texas politics.

2. Discuss how low legislator pay and no limits on campaign contributions relate to the traditional political subculture of Texas.
3. Explain which interest groups are most influential in Texas and what assets they possess that make them so.
4. Describe the differences between how interest groups lobby public officials and how they lobby the public more generally.
5. Evaluate the key reforms that have been proposed to govern interest groups and the role that they play in Texas elections and politics.

Suggested Readings

Virginia Gray, David Lowrey, Matthew Fellowes, and Andrea McAtee, "Public Opinion, Public Policy, and Organized Interests in the American States," *Political Research Quarterly* (2004), 57: 411–420.

Benjamin Marquez, *LULAC: The Evolution of a Mexican American Political Organization* (Austin, TX: University of Texas Press, 1993).

H.C. Pittman, *Inside the Third House: A Veteran Lobbyist Takes a 50-Year Frolic Through Texas Politics* (Austin, TX: Eakin Press, 1992).

Guadalupe San Miguel, Jr., *Let Them All Take Heed: Mexican Americans and the Campaign for Educational Equality in Texas, 1910–1981* (Austin, TX: University of Texas Press, 1987).

Dennis Shirley, *Valley Interfaith and School Reform: Organizing for Power in South Texas* (Austin, TX: University of Texas Press, 2002).

Susan Webb Yackee, "Private Conflict and Policy Passage: Interest-Group Conflict and State Medical Malpractice Reform," *Policy Studies Journal* (2009), 37: 213–231.

Christopher Witko and Adam J. Newmark, "Business Mobilization and Public Policy in the U.S. States," *Social Science Quarterly* (2005), 86: 356–367.

Web Resources

1. http://www.ethics.state.tx.us/
   Website of the Texas Ethics Commission.

2. http://www.tpj.org/
   Website of Texans for Public Justice.

3. http://www.texasaflcio.org/
   The Texas AFL-CIO, top labor organization in the state.

4. http://www.texmed.org/
   The Texas Medical Association.

5. http://www.lulac.org/
   The League of United Latin American Citizens.

6. http://www.txoga.org/
   The Texas Oil and Gas Association.

7. http://www.alldc.org/
   American League of Lobbyists.

Chapter 5

POLITICAL PARTIES IN TEXAS

RESIDENTS, CITIZENS, AND VOTERS: WHO COUNTS MOST?

Once a decade, the United States government conducts a census of the population. Following the census, all of the electoral districts, from school board districts to congressional districts, must be redrawn to create equal member districts. Equal member districts insure that every vote counts equally—one man, one vote—in electing public officials. But, of course, it's more complicated than that.

First, as we shall see later in the chapter, politicians get extremely nervous over redrawing electoral boundaries—redistricting—because they won in the old district and they want to be sure that any changes do not leave them with voters less likely to support them. Second, though all residents are counted in a census, not everyone is entitled to vote. Obviously, children cannot vote and neither can residents, whether here legally or not, who are not citizens. These distinctions are particularly important in Texas because both the age and citizenship profiles of Hispanics in Texas dramatically affect their electoral clout. Hispanics comprise about 38 percent of the Texas population, but 48 percent of the population under 18; hence, many more Hispanics than Anglos and blacks are too young to vote. In addition, 30 percent of Hispanics in Texas are not U.S. citizens and, as a result, are not eligible to vote.

This showed up clearly when Dallas sought to draw new electoral boundaries for its fourteen city council districts. In 2010, 42.4 percent of Dallas' total population was Hispanic, compared to 28.8 percent Anglo, and 25 percent black. But the voting age population in the city was 36.8 percent Hispanic, 34 percent Anglo, and 25 percent black. Moreover, while 90 to 95 percent of Anglos and blacks in Dallas were U.S. citizens, the census reported that just 140,000 of the roughly 330,000 Hispanic adults in Dallas were citizens. And Hispanics who are entitled to vote turnout at lower rates than Anglos and blacks.

As a result, over the last decade, the Dallas city council, rather than reflecting the city's population, has reflected its voting population—producing just 4 Hispanic council members, 4 black council members, and 7 Anglo council members. Political clout reflects not just numbers, but citizenship, voter registration, and turnout as well. Not surprisingly then, politicians pay closest attention to voters, some attention to citizens because they might become voters if they are not already, and little attention to mere residents.

Focus Questions

Q1   How are the Texas Democratic and Republic Parties organized?

Q2   How does Texas law treat minor-party and independent candidates?

Q3   Why was Texas a one-party Democratic state for so long?

Q4   What led to the rise of the Republican Party in the late 20th century?

Q5   Is the power shift from Democrats to Republicans in Texas permanent?

Political parties, like interest groups, are sets of like-minded people who work to make their government more responsive to their values, goals, and policy preferences. But political parties and interest groups differ in how they organize and act to affect politics. As we saw in the previous chapter, interest groups usually focus on a narrow range of issues that are of particular interest to their members and try to influence office-holders to act favorably on those issues. **Political parties** adopt attractive policy positions, recruit and train talented candidates, and support those candidates in elections. Their ultimate goal is to win majority control of government so that they can appoint senior officials and influence all of the issues that come before the government.[1]

Many scholars and an increasing number of politicians argue that political parties should articulate clear policy positions, campaign on them during elections, and then seek to implement those positions once elected. In this **responsible party model**, parties are expected to campaign on ideologically coherent platforms so voters know what they will get if they vote for the party and it wins control of the government. Other scholars and many politicians still believe that a **big tent model** is more realistic and more effective. The big tent model encourages parties to blur contentious issues and present

Political parties Organizations designed to elect government officeholders under a given label.

Responsible party model Sees political parties as organizations that campaign on coherent ideological platforms and then seek to implement their policies if elected.

Big tent model Sees political parties as organizations that appeal to the broadest range of potential voters rather than seeking to implement a coherent ideological program.

themselves as a comfortable home for most, if not all, voters. If the goal of political parties is to win elections (and it is), does it usually make sense to frame the party's appeal narrowly, appealing to the base of the base, or broadly, appealing to the base but also trying to draw in the moderates?

Whether parties win office with a base of the base or a median voter strategy, few readers will be surprised to hear that once political parties win power, they seek to retain it. As "Mr. Dooley," the Chicago saloon-keeper and political sage, once observed, "politics ain't beanbag." The stakes are too high and the fruits of victory are too sweet to treat the rules governing the electoral process as anything but flexible. Officeholders seek to tilt the electoral process in their favor in two principal ways. Both have been on clear display in recent Texas politics. First, the major parties team up to deny potential competitors—third parties, independents, and write-in candidates—access to the fight. And second, if either major party wins control of state government, they seek to shape the electoral districts so that future fights will be conducted to their advantage.

In this chapter, we evaluate the organization, activities, and effectiveness of political parties in Texas. We describe the structure of political parties in Texas, the history of party competition in the state, the rules governing ballot access and redistricting, and the likely balance of power between Democrats and Republicans in the coming decades.

MAJOR PARTY ORGANIZATION IN TEXAS

Q1 How are the Texas Democratic and Republican Parties organized?

The Democratic and Republican parties in Texas spring to life for elections and then fade into the political background between elections. They are composed of full-time officers, part-time activists, and the voters who stand with them on election day. The full-time officers hold official positions in the party bureaucracy. Their job is to lay the groundwork for the successful election of the party's candidates. The temporary party organization is a series of party caucuses and conventions in which the activists choose party leaders and hash out the party platform. Texas has no party registration, so the party's members are those voters who present themselves to vote in the party's primary election.

Precinct-Level Organization

Precinct Geographical area within which voters go to a polling place to cast their ballots on election day.

The precinct level is the foundation of Texas politics. A **precinct** is the geographical area surrounding the local polling place where voters go on election day to cast their ballots. There are 8,595 precincts in Texas.

The major parties hold party primary elections in March of even-numbered years. Voters in the party primary elections select the party's candidates for the general election, as well as party precinct and county chairs. The precinct chair's job is to organize the precinct so that the party carries it on election day. The precinct chair registers new voters, raises money, secures a volunteer workforce for election day, insures that voters get to the polls, and reports the precinct vote totals to the county office when the election is over. The precinct chair draws no salary.

Any voter who voted in the party primary is entitled to participate in the precinct convention (commonly referred to as the precinct caucus) that evening. The precinct caucus begins with the election of a caucus chair (usually the precinct chair, though it may be the outgoing precinct chair if the position is changing hands) and secretary. The caucus then selects delegates, one for every twenty-five votes cast in the precinct earlier that day, to later attend the county or district-level convention. Finally, the floor is opened to resolutions offered by participants. These resolutions are debated and those adopted are forwarded to the county convention for consideration.

Normally, voter turnout in primaries is light, usually between 5 and 10 percent of eligible voters in each party, and precinct caucus turnout is very light, usually attracting only a handful of party activists to each precinct. 2008 was dramatically different, especially on the Democratic side: 4.24 million Texans, 2.87 million Democrats, and 1.36 million Republicans, 33 percent of the registered voters voted in the 2008 primary. The previous record was 2.7 million, set in 1988. Even more remarkably, nearly a million voters, including 750,000 Democrats, returned in the evening to participate in the precinct caucuses. The caucus organization and infrastructure was nearly overwhelmed and talk of reform began almost immediately.

Corbis/Tom Fox

Fired up supporters leaped to their feet when U.S. Senator Ted Cruz took to the stage at the Texas GOP convention in Fort Worth. Just one year later, Cruz had declared for the presidency.

Turnout always falls in non-presidential election years, though the 2010 Texas primaries posted the highest off-year primary election turnout in twenty years. A hotly contested Republican primary, pitting incumbent Governor Rick Perry against the state's senior senator, Kay Bailey Hutchison, brought out 1.5 million GOP voters. Six hundred thousand Democrats nominated former Houston mayor Bill White to oppose Rick Perry, the Republican victor. Overall turnout was about 19 percent of registered voters.

Primary election turnout in 2012 was remarkably similar to 2010 and way down from 2008, particularly among the Democrats. In 2012, with an incumbent Democratic president unchallenged for renomination, Democratic primary turnout fell from 2.87 million in 2008 to 590,000 in 2012, about what it had been in 2010. Though Mitt Romney had locked up the Republican nomination before Texas voted, a hotly contested U.S. Senate nomination, ultimately won by Ted Cruz, brought out nearly 1.5 million Republican primary voters. Still, only about 16 percent of registered voters cast primary election ballots in 2012.

In 2014, Governor Rick Perry's decision not to stand for re-election shook up the Republican primary. Attorney General Greg Abbott was unchallenged for the gubernatorial nomination, but Lieutenant Governor David Dewhurst was challenged by Texas state Senator Dan Patrick and two statewide officeholders, Land Commissioner Jerry Patterson and Agriculture Commissioner Todd Staples. These moves opened up the Attorney General, Land Commissioner, and Agriculture Commissioner spots, and the retirement of Comptroller Susan Combs opened up the final statewide office. Even with exciting races for Lieutenant Governor and Attorney General, Republican primary turnout was just 10 percent of registered voters. The Democrat primary drew just 4 percent for a total Republican and Democrat turnout of 14 percent.

Runoffs are required in races where multiple candidates split the primary vote and no candidate gets a minority. The big primary runoffs in 2014 were on the Republican side; Dewhurst v. Patrick for Lieutenant Governor and state Representative Dan Branch v. state Senator Ken Paxton for Attorney General. The "tea party" candidates, Patrick and Paxton, won going sway over the "establishment" candidates, Dewhurst and Branch, but turnout dropped as it usually does in runoffs. The Republican runoff drew just 5.5 percent of eligible voters, while the Democrat runoff drew just 1.5 percent.

County and District-Level Organization

Parties organize by county in rural areas and by state senatorial districts in the more populous urban areas. The county and district conventions occur three weeks after the primary. The convention process closely mirrors the precinct level, beginning with the election of a convention chair and secretary. The delegates select representatives to the state convention, usually one for every 300 votes cast in the party primary. Precinct resolutions that have been vetted and approved by the county convention's resolutions committee are then

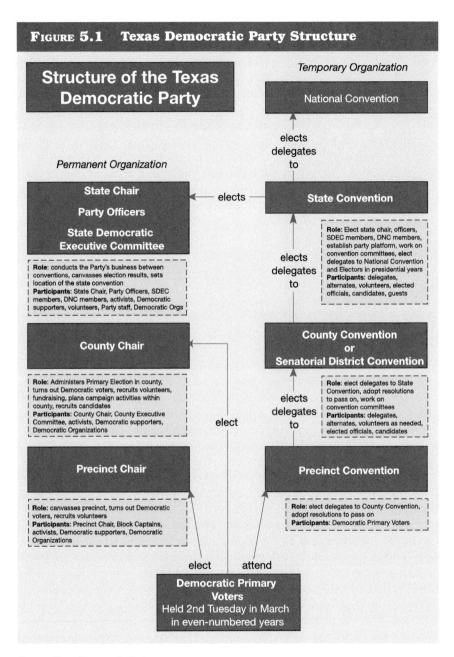

FIGURE 5.1   Texas Democratic Party Structure

Source: Texas Democratic Party.

Boyd Richie and Gilberto Hinojosa, former and current Democratic Party state chairs.

debated and voted upon. Approved resolutions are sent forward to the state convention.

County and district chairs are elected by voters in the party primary. They serve for two years and may be re-elected as often as the party's voters wish. There is no salary. County chairs preside over a county executive committee made up of all of the precinct chairs in the county. The county chair's job is to coordinate the precinct chairs and serve as liaison with statewide candidates that come to campaign and with the state party. County chairs are also spokespersons and fundraisers for the county party.

State-Level Organization

State party conventions are held in June of even-numbered years. The convention selects a chair and secretary to guide the delegates through several critical tasks. First, delegates dis-cuss and approve the party platform. Second, delegates elect a party chair and vice chair. Third, the delegates separate into state senatorial districts and each of the thirty-one groups elect a man and a woman to serve on the state party executive committee. Finally, in presidential election years, they elect delegates to the national party convention and select presidential electors in case their party's presidential candidate carries Texas in November.

In 2014, both party conventions were held in June. Eighteen thousand Republican delegates and alternates gathered in Fort Worth and fourteen thousand Democratic delegates and alternates gathered in Dallas. State party conventions are gatherings of the party's most faithful and, therefore, ideological members. Republicans made news at their convention by reelecting their state party chair, Steve Munisteri, but then back-tracked on the moderate immigration plank in their party platform he had advocated in 2012. Democrats made news by re-electing the first Hispanic party chair, Gilberto Hinojosa, in the state's history.

The party chair, vice chair, and executive committee are unpaid and all serve two-year terms. The party chair serves essentially full-time. He or she is the party's statewide spokesman, organizer, problem solver, and fundraiser. With the vice chair and the executive committee, the party chair organizes the next state convention, prepares the party for the next election, and directs the party's professional staff. Steve Munisteri, a Houston lawyer, resigned as Republican Party chair to join the Rand Paul presidential campaign. Tom Mechler, GOP treasurer, was elected to replace Munisteri. Gilberto Hinojosa, a lawyer and former Cameron County judge from South Texas, has been Democratic Party chair since 2012.

LET'S COMPARE   2014 PETITION REQUIREMENTS FOR BALLOT ACCESS

The major parties, Democrats and Republicans, dominate the politics of all 50 states, including Texas. They use their control of state government to enact and enforce laws that make it very difficult for minor-party, independent, and write-in candidates to get on the ballot. The greater the number of signatures required and the earlier the deadline for submitting the signatures, the greater the difficulty. Texas requires a large, though not extraordinary, number of signatures, but its deadline for turning in the signatures is very early.

Note that four states simply require that minor parties "be organized" to be listed on the ballots, while six states, including Texas, require that a specific number of signatures be gathered. All ten states require that signatures be gathered to permit an individual or independent candidate to be listed on the state ballot for president. In 2014, the two largest and most established third parties, the Libertarians and the Greens, won ballot access in most of the large states listed below. The Green Party failed to achieve ballot access in North Carolina and Georgia.

Finally, the date by which parties must gather the requisite number of signatures or otherwise establish ballot eligibility is important. The earlier the date, the more difficult it is to meet. The Texas deadline for third parties to submit signatures was May 20. Minor parties have 75 days to gather signatures from registered voters that had not voted in the Democratic or Republican primary.

State	Signatures for Minor Party	Signatures for Independent Candidate	Libertarian Success in 2014	Green Party Success in 2014	Deadline for Party Signatures
California	103,004	172,859	Yes	Yes	January 8
Texas	49,729	49,729	Yes	Yes	May 20
New York	No procedure	15,000	Yes	Yes	August 19
Florida	Be organized	112,174	Yes	Yes	September 1
Pennsylvania	No procedure	16,625	Yes	Yes	August 1
Illinois	No procedure	25,000	Yes	Yes	June 23
Ohio	27,905	5,000	Yes	Yes	July 2
Michigan	32,261	30,000	Yes	Yes	July 16
North Carolina	89,366	89,366	Yes	No	June 12
Georgia	50,334	50,334	Yes	No	July 8

Source: Derived from *Ballot Access News*, January 2014. http://www.ballot-access.org/

MINOR PARTIES, INDEPENDENTS, AND WRITE-INS

The Republicans and Democrats see minor-party, independent, and write-in candidates as distractions and irritants. Major parties cannot exclude them completely without insulting constitutional principles and popular expectations,

Q2 How does Texas law treat minor-party and independent candidates?

but they do all they can to make life difficult for them.[2] Minor-party, independent, and write-in candidates almost never win partisan elections, though they occasionally win non-partisan county and local office.

Two minor parties, the Libertarian Party and the Green Party, are particularly active in Texas. The Libertarian Party was founded in Texas in 1971 and stands for maximizing individual autonomy and minimizing the size and cost of government. The Green Party was founded in Texas in 1999 and stands for environmental awareness, corporate regulation, and local democracy. Texas allows minor parties to select their candidates in state conventions, rather than in statewide primary elections like the major parties do.

Texas law requires that minor parties gather signatures equivalent to 1 percent of the votes cast in the last gubernatorial election to gain access to the ballot. These signatures must be gathered in the seventy-five days after the Republican and Democratic primaries, from registered voters who did not participate in the primaries. In 2014, minor parties were required to collect 49,729 valid signatures each. To maintain ballot access from one election to the next, at least one of the party's nominees must win 2 percent of the vote in the last governor's race or 5 percent of the vote in any other statewide race. Libertarians and Greens secured automatic ballot access for 2014 when their candidates won 10.5 percent and 6.3 percent respectively in the 2010 Comptroller race.

The hurdles facing most independent candidates for political office in Texas are even higher than those facing minor parties. Each independent candidate has to gather the same number of signatures as minor-party candidates, 1 percent of the vote in the last governor's race. Moreover, they have to do it in sixty days after the primary, rather than the seventy-five days allowed to minor parties. Independent candidates for statewide office in Texas are rare, though two, Carole Strayhorn and Kinky Friedman, were on the ballot for governor in 2006. Independent candidates for president have to gather signatures equivalent to 1 percent of the votes cast in Texas in the last presidential election, or 79,642 signatures in 2016.

Finally, voters who do not wish to vote for any of the candidates who appear on the ballot for a particular office cannot simply write in another name. To be a certified write-in candidate in Texas, one must file a declaration of intent, along with a filing fee or designated number of signatures, with the appropriate authorities at least seventy days before the general election. If these requirements are met, the candidate's name appears on an approved list of write-in candidates posted in polling places. Write-in votes for persons not on the list are not counted.

THE EVOLUTION OF PARTISAN CONFLICT IN TEXAS

Q3 Why was Texas a one-party Democratic state for so long?

Texas has long been a conservative state, favoring small government, low taxes, and pro-business policies as the best paths to social order and economic growth. Once these commitments drove most Texans to the Democratic Party; now they drive them to the Republican Party.[3] As with most southern states, the evolution of party competition in Texas pivots on two events—the Civil War and the civil rights struggle of the mid-20th century.

In the agricultural economy of the 19th and early 20th centuries, looking after the interests of white men and their families meant a firm commitment to the Democratic Party. No Republican won statewide elective office in Texas between 1874 and 1961. However, as the American society and economy evolved, particularly in the post–World War II period, many Texans came to see the Republican Party as the more dependable vehicle to pursue social conservatism and economic development. The movement of Texas from one-party Democrat to one-party Republican took decades. It is now, at least for a time, complete. No Democrat has held statewide office in Texas since 1998. Though Democrats made gains in 2006 and 2008 they suffered a broad and deep defeat in 2010.[4] In 2012, Democrats rebounded a bit, but just a bit only to suffer another devastating setback in 2014. In 2014, the statewide democratic slate lost by 20 points and Democrats remain at a near two-to-one minority in the legislature. The Democrat's road back to competitiveness will be steep and rocky.

The Democratic Ascendancy

Texas was a Democratic state before it was a state. Most white settlers entered Texas from the American South. Sam Houston, for example, was born in Virginia, went to Tennessee as a young man, and rose through the ranks of the state's Jacksonian Democratic machine to become a general, congressman, senator, and governor. When a new marriage collapsed, Houston fled into the wilderness and eventually ended up in Texas. He and Texas made brilliant use of his military and political skills. Houston commanded the victorious Texans at San Jacinto and then served as Texas's leading political figure for a quarter century.

Still, the fact that Texas was a one-party state for most of its history, first Democrat, now Republican, did nothing to dampen political conflict. One party dominance often invites factionalism within the dominant party as V.O. Key explained in his 1949 classic *Southern Politics*. It was certainly so in early Texas. The politics of the Republic of Texas revolved around San Houston, you were either for him or against him and usually vehemently so. As the Texas presidential election of 1844 approached, Dr. Francis Moore, editor of the *Telegraph and Texas Register*, wrote that, "the party spirit in the United States is tame and mild compared to the bitter, malignant, demoniac zeal which is displayed in many instances by the partisans of our candidates."[5] As we shall see, the same might be said of many periods in Texas history.

When Texas seceded from the Union in February 1861 (over then-Governor Houston's vehement objection), most officeholders were Democrats. Most of those elected to serve in state government and those appointed to high military positions during the Confederacy also were Democrats. In the wake of the Civil War, the U.S. Congress barred senior Confederate political and military officials from voting or holding office. The Republican Party—the party of northern carpetbaggers, southern scalawags, former slaves, Lincoln, the Union Army, and Reconstruction (you get the point)—dominated Texas politics between the end of the war in 1865 and the end of Reconstruction a decade later. By the early 1870s, former Confederates were allowed back into the electorate, and by 1875 they had resumed control of state politics.

For the next seventy-five years, the dominant Democratic Party stood for small government, low taxes, state's rights, local control, and white supremacy. Poll taxes, the white primary, and political and economic intimidation kept minorities from the polls, except where their votes were managed by white power brokers. Agricultural interests and rural issues dominated Texas politics. They controlled the Constitutional Convention of 1875, provided the basis for Governor James Stephen Hogg's influence between 1890 and 1910, and then for Jim and Miriam (Pa and Ma) Ferguson's influence between 1914 and 1935.[6]

Occasionally, however, Texas Democratic leaders and voters had looked at national politics and saw trouble on the horizon. In 1928, when the Democrats nominated Al Smith, the Catholic Governor of New York, for president, Texas's former Governor Oscar Colquitt endorsed the Republican Herbert Hoover and Texas voters agreed. Hoover carried Texas with 52 percent of the vote. Nervous conservatives quickly repented, rushing back to the Democratic fold in 1932 when the national economy crashed on Hoover's watch.

The Democratic ascendancy in Texas really began to crack when the national Democratic Party departed from the traditional orthodoxy. Franklin Roosevelt's "New Deal" signaled an era of bigger, more expensive, intrusive government that concerned many Texans. FDR's Vice President, John Nance "Cactus Jack" Garner, longtime leader of the Texas congressional delegation and former Speaker of the House, ultimately broke with Roosevelt over his desire to stand for a third term. Garner challenged FDR for the Democratic nomination for president in 1940. A few Texans, including a young LBJ, stayed with FDR, but many, led by Speaker Sam Rayburn, went with Garner. That breach in the Texas Democratic Party, between the liberals who sided with FDR and the conservatives who sided with Garner, never fully healed.[7]

When the national Democratic Party approved a strong civil rights plank for the 1948 campaign, the split within the Texas Democratic Party deepened. These divisions hardened into a factional split within the party between the liberals, led by Lyndon Johnson, Ralph Yarborough, Minnie Fisher Cunningham, and former Governor James Allred, who called themselves the **Democrats of Texas**, and conservatives, led by John Garner, former Governor Coke Stevenson, and Governor Allan Shivers, who called themselves the **Texas Regulars**. Governor Shivers led the Texas state Democratic Convention away from Adlai Stevenson and to the Republican presidential candidate, Dwight D. Eisenhower, in both 1952 and 1956. Texas voted for Eisenhower both times. Despite this presidential Republicanism, Democrats retained near total dominance in Texas.[8]

Democrats of Texas Liberal faction of the mid-20th-century Democratic party, led by elected officials like Lyndon Johnson and Ralph Yarborough.

Texas Regulars Conservative faction of the mid-20th-century Democratic party, led by elected officials like Coke Stevenson and Allan Shivers.

If there is a hinge on the political history of Texas in the 20th century, then Lyndon Baines Johnson, universally known as LBJ, is it. LBJ went to Washington as a young man in the 1930s, dominated the city in the 1950s and 1960s, and returned to Texas a broken man. The twin sorrows of his brief post-presidential career were that the Vietnam War had compromised his "Great Society" domestic policy programs and that his civil rights program had sped the decline of the Democratic Party in Texas.

LBJ was born near Stonewall in the Texas hill country on August 27, 1908. He is the only Texas president to have been born and raised in the state. His introduction to politics came through his father, Sam Ealy Johnson, Jr., who served in the Texas House between 1905 and 1909 and from 1918 to 1925. Lyndon often accompanied his father to the legislature and on the campaign trail. Johnson attended Southwest Texas State Teachers' College (now Texas State University), where he dominated the small school's student politics, and graduated in 1930. Within a few months he was on his way to Washington as a congressional secretary. He immediately became a leader among congressional aides, presiding over the "Little Congress," which brought him into contact with the real Congress's senior members. LBJ married Claudia Alta "Lady Bird" Taylor in 1934.

Johnson was appointed by President Roosevelt (FDR) to be Texas National Youth Administrator, overseeing Texas youth work programs during the depths of the Great Depression. He soon developed a statewide network of political contacts and when an Austin-based congressional seat came open in 1937, he jumped at it, won it, and won re-election in 1939. When a U.S. Senate seat came open in 1941, LBJ, a protégé of FDR, was the favorite. To his great dismay and considerable outrage, Texas Governor W. Lee "Pappy" O'Daniel entered the race late and worked his own statewide contacts to finagle a few more votes, legal and illegal, than Johnson. Johnson swore that he would never be out-maneuvered again and he rarely was. When a U.S. Senate seat again came open in 1948, LBJ out-stole former Governor Coke Stevenson to win by 87 votes out of 250,000 cast. This

narrow victory also won him the sneering nickname "Landslide Lyndon." The famous Box 13 from Alice, Texas, provided the margin of victory.

LBJ may have been the most effective U.S. Senator of the 20th century. By 1955 he was the Majority Leader of the Senate and proved himself to be a consummate nose-counter and deal-maker. As the Senate's Democratic Leader, he worked closely and effectively with Republican President Dwight D. Eisenhower. Johnson made a weak run at the Democratic presidential nomination in 1956 and stronger run in 1960, but he fell short both times. After John Kennedy won the Democratic nomination for president in 1960, he asked Johnson to be his vice presidential running mate. Johnson agreed, somewhat reluctantly, because he saw the vice presidency as one step closer to his ultimate goal, the presidency.

Johnson languished as Vice President. When President Kennedy was tragically shot and killed in Dallas in November 1963, LBJ assumed the presidency promising to complete the slain president's agenda. In fact, LBJ turned out to be as good a domestic policy president as he had been a Senate Majority Leader. In 1964 and 1965, LBJ moved beyond the Kennedy program to pass his own "Great Society" program, including the Civil Rights Acts of 1964 and 1965, the Voting Rights Act of 1965, and a major school desegregation and funding bill in 1965, Medicare and Medicaid in 1965, as a series of programs known as the "War on Poverty."

Texas conservatives, of course, were aghast at the scope, cost, and intrusiveness of these programs, but also at their social implications. In the mid-1960s, a full decade after the Supreme Court's 1954 Brown v. Board decision, Texas schools and broader society still were largely segregated. LBJ knew when he signed the Civil Rights Act of 1964 that Texas and the South would be outraged. When he signed the Voting Rights Act of 1965, he is reported to have said to Bill Moyers, his young Texan aide, "We have lost the South for a generation." He was wrong, great politician though he was, because the South took a generation to become majority Republican, has been majority Republican for a generation, and shows no signs of shifting back.

The Rise of the Republican Party

Q4 What led to the rise of the Republican Party in the late 20th century?

The Republican Party had no meaningful presence in Texas between 1875 and 1950. Black votes kept a few Republicans in the state legislature until 1900, by which time most blacks were disenfranchised, and a few wealthy precincts in Houston and Dallas voted defiantly Republican through the first half of the 20th century. Robert B. Hawley served as a Republican congressman from Galveston from 1897 to 1901 and Harry M. Wurzbach of San Antonio served from 1921 to 1929 and then again briefly before his death in 1931. After 1896 there were rarely more than two or three Republicans in the Texas House and one in the Texas Senate. Once the depression hit in 1929, there were literally no Republicans in the Texas House or Senate for more than two decades.[9] As late as 1950, there were no Republicans in the Texas state legislature, in statewide office, or in the state's congressional delegation. The first notable Republican victory in Texas was the election of Bruce Alger of Dallas to the U.S. House in 1954. Alger, a fierce anti-communist and conservative firebrand, was re-elected four more times. The next three decades saw isolated Republican success, but little that suggested permanent change.

One Republican, though not yet the party, got a big break in 1960. Lyndon Johnson campaigned for the Democratic nomination for president in 1960, but John F. Kennedy defeated him. When Kennedy offered LBJ the vice-presidential nomination, he accepted. But Johnson was majority leader of the U.S. Senate and was unwilling to risk this powerful position for the chance of becoming vice president. So he pressured the Texas legislature to pass a bill allowing him to run for vice president on the Democratic ticket with Kennedy and re-election to the Senate at the same time.

In the spring of 1960, Johnson won the Democratic primary for the U.S. Senate and a little known political science professor, John G. Tower, from Midwestern State University in Wichita Falls, won the Republican nomination. In the November general election, LBJ retained his Senate seat with nearly 60 percent of the vote, but he was also elected vice president on the Democratic ticket with Kennedy. Hence, LBJ resigned his Senate seat to become Vice President of the United States. Governor Price Daniel Jr., a conservative Democrat, appointed Dallas's staunchly conservative William Blakley, also a Democrat, to fill Johnson's Senate seat until a special election could be held.

Seventy-one candidates declared for the special election. Several prominent Democrats, including San Antonio's Congressman Henry B. Gonzales, Fort Worth's Congressman Jim Wright, and Senator William Blakley, entered the race. John Tower was the only prominent Republican. In this crowded field, Tower ran first with 31.5 percent, and the conservative Democrat William Blakley edged the more liberal Democrat, Jim Wright, 18.3 percent to 16.4 percent. Texas Democrats were flummoxed; two conservatives, Tower and Blakley, were in the runoff. Liberal Democrats saw little to choose between them. Many liberals simply stayed home while some voted for John Tower to send Blakley and Daniel a message. Tower squeaked through to win the Senate seat by about 10,000 votes out of almost 900,000 votes cast.[10]

TABLE 5.1	Growth of Republican Officeholders in Texas, 1974–2014						
Year	U.S. Senate	Other Statewide Offices	U.S. House	Texas Senate	Texas House	Local Offices	Total
1974	1	0	2	3	16	53	75
1976	1	0	2	3	19	67	92
1978	1	1	4	4	22	87	119
1980	1	1	5	7	35	166	215
1982	1	0	5	5	36	270	317
1984	1	0	10	6	52	377	446
1986	1	1	10	6	56	504	578
1988	1	5	8	8	57	613	692
1990	1	6	8	8	57	722	802
1992	1	8	9	13	58	822	911
1994	2	13	11	14	61	958	1,059
1996	2	18	13	17	68	1,225	1,343
1998	2	27	13	16	72	1,397	1,527
2000	2	27	13	16	72	1,579	1,709
2002	2	27	15	19	88	1,815	1,966
2004	2	27	21	19	87	2,010	2,166
2006	2	27	19	20	82	2,203	2,353
2008	2	27	20	19	76	2,251	2,395
2010	2	27	23	19	101	2,802	2,974
2012	2	27	24	19	95	3,012	3,191
2014	2	27	25	20	98		

Source: Political Department, Republican Party of Texas.

John Tower's stunning victory made him the first Republican to win a state-wide race in Texas since 1870. In fact, though Tower held his U.S. Senate seat with statewide wins in 1966 and 1972, only a few other Republicans were able to join the ranks of Texas officeholders during these years.

To the surprise of most, 1978 was a watershed year for the Republican Party in Texas. Senator Tower held his U.S. Senate seat one more time by just 12,000 votes, and Republican gubernatorial candidate, William P. Clements, defeated the Democratic favorite, John Hill, by 17,000 votes. Though Clements was defeated for re-election in 1982, he came back to win again in 1986.[11] Clements' governorship, far more than Tower's elections to the Senate, marked the arrival of competitive two-party politics in Texas. Clements systematically used his appointment powers to build a Republican presence in the bureaucracy and the courts.

Texas Republicans slowly gathered strength and momentum during the 1980s as lifelong Democrats edged nervously toward and eventually into the Republican Party.[12] Republican President Ronald Reagan helped to draw some high-powered Democrats into the Republican Party, including Congressman Phil Gramm in 1983. Gramm resigned his House seat, won it as a Republican, and then in 1984 won the U.S. Senate seat being vacated by John Tower. Six new Republicans, dubbed the "Texas six-pack," won seats in the U.S. House. Republican strength in the 150-member Texas House grew from thirty-five in 1980 to fifty-two in 1984 and fifty-seven in 1988; a big improvement, but still barely a third of the membership. The Republican presence in the Texas Senate inched ahead from seven to eight from 1980 to 1988.

In 1988, Texas Republican George H.W. Bush, Reagan's vice president during the previous eight years, won the presidency, and Texas Republicans showed deeper strength in statewide races. Republicans won three seats on the Texas Supreme Court and one of the three seats on the Texas Railroad Commission. In 1990, Phil Gramm easily retained his Senate seat, despite Democrat Ann Richards' victory over gaffe-plagued millionaire Clayton Williams for governor. Two new Republican faces, Kay Bailey Hutchison and Rick Perry, a recent convert from Democrat to Republican, won state-wide election to the positions of treasurer and agriculture commissioner, respectively.

The changing shape of Texas politics became even more clear in 1993 when Democratic Senator Lloyd Bentsen resigned to become Secretary of the Treasury in the Clinton administration. Democratic Governor Ann Richards appointed a Democrat, Bob Krueger, to fill the vacant Senate seat until a special election could be held. An even two-dozen candidates, including Krueger, as well as two U.S. congressmen, Republicans Jack Fields and Joe Barton, and Republican State Treasurer Kay Bailey Hutchison, contested the election. Hutchison and Krueger ran first and second and Hutchison prevailed in the runoff with an impressive two-to-one majority.

TABLE 5.2 Partisanship in Texas, 1950–Present			
	% Democrat	% Republican	Ind./Others
1952	66	6	28
1972	57	14	29
1984	35	34	31
1990	34	30	36
2002	35	36	29
2012	37	43	20

Sources: James A. Dyer, Arnold Vedlitz, and David B. Hill, "New Voters, Switchers, and Political Party Realignment in Texas," *Western Political Quarterly*, vol. 41, no. 1, March 1988, pp. 155–167. Harte-Hanke Communications, 1990, American National Election Studies, 2002, and Gallop, 2012.

Texas A&M political scientists James A. Dyer and Arnold Vedlitz and political consultant David B. Hill charted the slow rise of Republican partisan identification in the electorate through the 1970s until the dam broke in the mid-1980s. As late as 1972, 57 percent of voters still considered themselves Democrats compared to 14 percent who considered themselves Republicans. By late 1983, Democrats were down to 40 percent while Republicans had risen to almost 25 percent. By 1984, which was Ronald Reagan's re-election year as president, Texas Democrats slipped to 35 percent while Republicans closed to just a one point deficit. The Republican surge was fueled predominantly by two groups: young voters coming of age in the Reagan years and Republican migrants moving from the North and the Midwest to Texas.[13]

But from the time that Republican strength first began to show itself, its Achilles heel was evident as well. As early as the mid-1960s, University of Texas political science professor Clifton McCleskey, author of one of the leading Texas politics texts of the day, wrote that the Republican Party had "virtually written off that one-fifth of the electorate composed of Negroes and Latin Americans."[14] Democrats, of course, had their problems with blacks and Latinos as well, having stood for white supremacy for the better part of a century, but their image among minorities was rapidly changing as LBJ and the national Democratic Party pushed a strong civil rights agenda.

By the time Ann Richards won her term as governor in 1990, the racial voting lines in Texas were set and, though they were evolving, they favored Republicans. Even Richards' awkward opponent, the rancher and oilman Clayton Williams, won 57 percent of the Anglo vote, but Richards won 89 percent of the black vote and 78 percent of the Hispanic vote.[15] Richards narrowly won with just under 50 percent of the total vote, to Williams's 47 percent, and Libertarian Jeff Daiell's 3 percent. However, in 1994, Republican George W. Bush comfortably beat Ann Richards, 53.5 percent to 45.9 percent, by winning 70 percent of the white vote, though he won only 25 percent of the Hispanic vote and 10 percent of the black vote.[16]

The Republican Ascendancy

In 1994, George W. Bush, son of the former president and managing partner of the Texas Rangers baseball team, challenged the popular Democratic incumbent governor Ann Richards. Initially given little chance of winning, Bush ran a careful, competent, controlled, and, ultimately, convincing campaign to win comfortably. Rick Perry retained his position as commissioner of agriculture and Republicans picked up seats to take majority control of the Supreme Court, the Railroad Commission, and the State Board of Education. Meanwhile five Democratic incumbents, including the powerful lieutenant governor, Bob Bullock, retained their statewide elective offices. In fact, Bullock, the wily Democratic veteran, took Bush under his wing and Bush was smart enough to let him do it.

By 1996, George W. Bush was secure in his role as governor and the Republican Party was ready to assume the majority-party mantle in Texas.

Pro & Con   Campaign Contribution Limits in the States

States vary greatly in the role that they permit money to play in their elections. Laws in all of the states recognize that candidates for public office have to be able to accept contributions to defray the cost of their campaigns. States use laws governing disclosure of campaign contributions, amount of contributions, source of contributions, and some states offer public funds to candidates willing to abide by campaign finance and spending rules. Some states have extensive campaign finance regulations while others set few limits.

Texas law requires candidates and officeholders to file semi-annual reports on January 15 and July 15 of campaign contributions, expenditures, and balances, as well as special reports 15 days after appointing a campaign treasurer, and 30 days and 8 days before an election. Detailed information must be provided on all contributors giving more than $50 in a campaign period. However, Texas law does not limit the amount that an individual, state party, or PAC can give to a candidate's campaign. Texas provides no state funds to candidates.

Below we present a breakdown of contribution limits, if any, allowed each election cycle to candidates for the top statewide office, usually governor. We see that Texas is not alone in allowing unlimited contributions from individuals to candidates. Texas is one of twelve states that allow unlimited contributions in state elections. Another seven states allow large contributions, ranging up to $60,000 in each election cycle, but all of the remaining states set limits at or below $5,000. Fifteen states allow contributions between $2,501 and $5,000, seven allow contributions of $1,001 to $2,500, and nine set maximum contributions below $1,000.

Those who support the right of individuals, parties, PACs, and others to make unlimited contributions to campaigns argue that, like political speech, campaign contributions should not be limited by law. They argue that it is unfair to tell a rich person that they cannot dedicate as much of their money as they want to political purposes. Opponents argue that wealth has its due weight in the marketplace and should not be allowed to overwhelm the equality—one man, one vote—that we expect in elections. The 2010 Supreme Court decision known as Citizens United did not strike down either national or state limits on campaign contributions by individuals, but it did strike down laws in 23 states that had limited or prohibited contributions to campaigns from corporations or unions.

Do you think that money is the equivalent of speech for political purposes, and, therefore, we can no more limit political contributions than political speech? Or do you think setting campaign contribution limits, say at $5,000, assures that every voice is heard in our political discussions? Why do you think Texas sets no limits on campaign contributions?

Under $1,000	$1,000–$2,500	$2,501–$5,000	$5,001–$60,000	Unlimited
Alaska	Arizona	Connecticut	California	Alabama
Colorado	Arkansas	Florida	Georgia	Indiana
Kentucky	Delaware	Idaho	Hawaii	Iowa
Massachusetts	Kansas	Louisiana	Illinois	Mississippi
Montana	Maine	Maryland	New York	Missouri
New Hampshire	Rhode Island	Michigan	Ohio	Nebraska
Vermont	Washington	Minnesota	Wisconsin	North Dakota
West Virginia		Nevada		Oregon
Wyoming		New Jersey		Pennsylvania
		New Mexico		Texas
		North Carolina		Utah
		Oklahoma		Virginia
		South Carolina		
		South Dakota		
		Tennessee		

Source: National Conference of State Legislatures, "State Limits on Contributions to Candidates, 2013–2014 Election Cycle," Individual to Candidate Contributions, http://www.ncsl.org/Portals/1/documents/legismgt/Limits_to_Candidates_2012-2014.pdf

In 1996, Republicans took control of the Texas Senate, seventeen seats to fourteen. In 1998, George W. Bush won re-election as governor with 68 percent of the vote, Rick Perry moved up to lieutenant governor, and Republicans carried all of the statewide executive offices, as well as every seat on the Texas Supreme Court, the Texas Court of Criminal Appeals, and the Railroad Commission.

When George W. Bush resigned as governor in late-2000 to become president of the United States, Lieutenant Governor Rick Perry assumed the governorship and the Republican juggernaut never missed a beat. In 2002, Perry easily retained the governorship and Republicans won every statewide office on the ballot and took majority control of the Texas House, eighty-eight seats to sixty-two. Once the Texas House fell to the Republicans, they turned to address the last bastion of Democratic power, the U.S. House delegation, where Democrats clung to a seventeen to fifteen majority.

> **Who Knew?**
>
> There are 29 offices elected statewide in Texas—two United States senators, six executive officers, including the governor, lieutenant governor (actually more a legislative officer), attorney general, comptroller, agricultural commissioner, land commissioner, three railroad commissioners, and nine judges each on the Texas Supreme Court and Texas Court of Criminal Appeals. The last time Democrats won any of these offices was 1994.

THE GREAT TEXAS REDISTRICTING BATTLE, 2001–2006

The U.S. Constitution gives each state the responsibility to draw the districts within which its state and federal elections will be conducted. Article I, section 2 of the U.S. Constitution requires that a national census be conducted every ten years and that U.S. House seats be allocated among the states based on population. The Constitution says nothing directly about how election districts should be drawn—which opens the process to mischief. **Redistricting** provides the dominant party in a state the opportunity to draw district boundaries that favor them and limit the electoral prospects of their opponents. Partisan redistricting, also known as "gerrymandering," is as old as the republic.[17]

The term "gerrymander" derives from the early 19th century. Elbridge Gerry was a prominent founding father; signer of the Declaration of Independence, delegate to the Constitutional Convention, Governor of Massachusetts, and vice president in the Madison administration. As governor of Massachusetts, Gerry oversaw a particularly creative redistricting process in which one district was said to look like a salamander, hence the term "gerrymander."

From Elbridge Gerry's day until the mid-20th century, state redistricting fights were between political parties and, just as importantly, between rural and urban actors and interests. Partisan redistricting battles are easy enough to understand—parties want to draw electoral boundaries that advantage their candidates. But until the 1960s, rural versus urban redistricting battles were just as important as partisan battles. Early in the 19th century, most states were overwhelmingly rural. As the 19th century gave way to the 20th, states became increasingly urban, some faster than others. In many states, rural legislators

Redistricting The political process by which electoral district boundaries are redrawn to reflect changes in population and party power.

fought the loss of political clout that would come from recognizing urban population growth by refusing to redistrict. New census data would come in every decade showing the loss of rural population and the growth of urban population, but rural legislators would refuse to draw new districts.

The U.S. Supreme Court finally stepped in in the early 1960s with a series of decisions that created the modern redistricting regime. The first and most famous of the redistricting cases was **Baker v. Carr** (1962). The rural majority in the Tennessee legislature had not redrawn state legislative election districts since 1900. *Baker v. Carr* mandated that the lower houses of state legislatures have equal population legislative districts, decisively shifting legislative districts out of rural areas to more populous urban areas. Two related decisions, *Reynolds v. Sims* and *Wesberry v. Sanders*, both from 1964, extended the logic of one-man-one-vote, equal population districts, to state senate electoral districts (*Reynolds*) and to congressional and local electoral districts (*Wesberry*).

The Texas legislature has the initial responsibility for redistricting, but they are at something of a disadvantage. The legislature meets in regular session from January to May of odd-numbered years. The census, carried out at the begin ning of each decade (1950, 1960, and 1970, for example), delivers preliminary data to the states in December and final data in March of the following year. By March, the Texas legislature is halfway through its regular session and little time is left for the complicated and contentious process of redistricting.

In 1950, Texas voters approved a constitutional amendment providing for a new redistricting process. If the legislature fails to approve a plan, a Legislative Redistricting Board (LRB), made up of the Speaker, lieutenant governor, comptroller, land commissioner, and attorney general, is charged to adopt a plan within 150 days of the end of the legislative session.[18] Whether or not the legislature or the LRB passes a plan, state and federal courts inevitably become involved. With so much at stake, the minority party, interest groups, and individuals head to court if they think they have been treated unfairly—and they *always* think they have been treated unfairly.

For most of Texas history, Democrats drew electoral boundaries at will. Texas passed redistricting bills in 1951 and 1961, but neither came close to creating equal population districts. As late as 1963, "42 percent of the Texas population could elect a majority of the house and 30 percent a majority of the senate."[19] Rural and small town Anglo elites maintained substantial advantages, but urban Anglos were careful to protect themselves as well. Their principal tool was "at-large" electoral districts. Whereas single member districts might produce majority minority districts, an at-large electoral district over a whole city would usually allow the Anglo majority to control all of the seats elected in that district. "In 1970, approximately half of the state legislature and nearly all city council members and school board trustees were elected from at-large districts."[20]

Baker v. Carr (1962) U.S. Supreme Court declared in 1963 that equal population state house districts were required by the 14th Amendment promise of equal protection of the laws.

Following the 1970 census, the Texas legislature reapportioned the state's electoral districts. The reapportionment of the Texas House was challenged, in a case called **White v. Regester** (1973), principally over multi-member at-large districts in Dallas and Bexar counties. Mark White, Texas Secretary of State and future Governor of Texas, represented the state, along with Attorney General John Hill and Leon Jaworski. The complainants were represented by David R. Richards, whose wife Ann Richards was another future Governor of Texas. Richards argued that at-large districts were intended to and did dilute minority voting impact. The Supreme Court agreed with Richards and ordered that the at-large districts in Dallas and Bexar counties be dismantled in favor of single member districts. This process was complete in regard to the legislature by 1976 with slower changes coming over subsequent decades in regard to election of city councils and school boards.

White v. Regester (1973) U.S. Supreme Court held that multi-member electoral districts discriminated against minority groups. Single member districts were mandated.

Democrats still controlled state government following the 1990 census, though Republican fortunes were on the rise. Martin Frost, a senior Democratic congressman from the Dallas–Fort Worth area, oversaw the redistricting process. Lines were drawn to protect Democratic incumbents and check the rise of Republican challengers. Though Texas Democrats won just 51 percent of the vote in the 1992 congressional races, Frost's carefully drawn congressional districts helped Democrats win 70 percent (twenty-one of thirty) of House seats. Though the Republican vote share rose to 55 percent by 1998, they won only 43 percent (thirteen of thirty) seats.

The 2000 census recorded population growth in Texas that resulted in two new congressional seats, moving the state's total from thirty to thirty-two. All of the state's congressional districts had to be redrawn to accommodate the two new districts and to insure that each district contained an equal number of residents. But control of the Texas legislature remained split; Republicans controlled the Senate sixteen to fifteen, while Democrats controlled the House seventy-eight to seventy-two. Partisan divisions blocked action in the legislature. The five-member, all-Republican LRB moved quickly to adopt new district lines for the Texas House and Senate, but the proposed congressional-district boundaries were challenged in the federal courts.

A three-judge panel, composed of Judge Patrick Higginbotham of the U.S. Fifth Circuit Court of Appeals, District Judge Lee Rosenthal of Houston, and District Judge T. John Ward of Marshall, produced a congressional map that accommodated the two new districts, preserved eight majority-minority districts as required by the VRA, and protected incumbents wishing to stand for re-election. Democrats were generally pleased with the court's map, Republicans were not. In the 2002 Texas elections, Republicans won 55 percent of the total congressional vote, but only 47 percent (fifteen of thirty-two) seats. On the other hand, Republicans completed their takeover of state government by winning control of the Texas House (eighty-eight to sixty-two) for the first time since Reconstruction.

In 2003, when the 78th Texas legislature convened with Republican majorities in both houses for the first time since the 1870s, redistricting was high on their agenda. Republican leaders believed that previous Democratic maps had treated them unfairly and they meant to redress those grievances. Republicans set out to grieve the Democrats for a change.

Texas Republicans soon began arguing that redistricting was a state legislative responsibility and, while the courts had reasonably stepped in when the legislature was unable to complete the task in 2001, they were now both ready and entitled to revisit the issue. And so a new Republican map was proposed in the 78th regular session of the legislature. Fifty Texas House Democrats fled to Ardmore, Oklahoma, thus denying a quorum and halting business until the session ended. It took three special sessions during the summer of 2003, punctuated by Texas Senate Democrats fleeing to Albuquerque, New Mexico, to push through the Republican congressional map. With the new map in place, Republicans won 60 percent of the 2004 congressional vote and six new Republican seats.[21]

Democrats and minority interest groups remained convinced that at least three aspects of the new plan were unconstitutional or otherwise illegal. They argued that redistricting could only be done once per decade, that it could not be done strictly for partisan gain, and it could not be done to the detriment of minority voters. The Civil Rights Division of the U.S. Justice Department and the three-judge panel headed by Judge Higginbotham upheld the Republican map. Democratic challenges in *LULAC v. Perry* reached the U.S. Supreme Court twice, with the final ruling coming on June 28, 2006.

The Supreme Court generally supported the Republican view of redistricting. First, Democratic claims that redistricting could be done only once a decade were rejected. Texas Solicitor Ted Cruz argued that Democrats had gerrymandered the state's congressional districts for decades and, when the Republicans came to power, they had the right to bend the political and electoral systems to their advantage. Justice Anthony Kennedy, who wrote the lead opinion for the court, said "There is nothing inherently suspect about a legislature's decision to replace mid-decade a court-ordered plan with one of its own."

Second, the court reiterated its earlier findings in *Davis v. Bandemer* (Indiana, 1986) and *Vieth v. Jubilier* (Pennsylvania, 2003) that redistricting is an inherently partisan process. Though they left open the possibility that some future gerrymander might be so harshly partisan as to be unconstitutional, no rules for separating acceptable from unacceptable partisanship currently exist.

Finally, LULAC and the Texas Democratic Party claimed partial vindication when the Supreme Court struck down one part of the Republican map. Republicans had moved about 100,000 Hispanic voters out of Congressman Henry Bonilla's 23rd district to improve his chances of holding his seat. Though Bonilla was the only Hispanic Republican in the Texas congressional delegation, Hispanic voters tend to support Democrats two-thirds of the time. The court held that making Bonilla's district less Hispanic illegally "diluted the voting rights of Latinos who remain in the district." Five districts had to be adjusted to return the 23rd to its previous ethnic make-up.

As the 2006 election approached, Republican gains began to erode. Congressman Tom DeLay's legal problems, some stemming from aggressive fundraising for 2002 state House races, led to his resignation from Congress. In a particularly galling development for Republicans, former Democratic Congressman Nick Lampson, a victim of the 2003 redistricting plan, won DeLay's seat in a special election. In November 2006, scandals and declining support for the Iraq war led to a drop in the Republican Congressional vote to 54.4 percent of votes cast. Lampson held the DeLay seat and Republican Congressman Henry Bonilla was forced into a runoff and was eventually defeated by Democrat Ciro Rodriguez. Republicans retained nineteen of thirty-two seats in the congressional delegation. Democrats also picked up six seats in the Texas House in 2006.

The 2008 elections continued Democratic gains, highlighted by six new seats in the Texas house. Not so 2010. The Republican share of the congressional vote rose to an all-time high of 68.5 percent and Republican challengers defeated three Democratic congressmen—Chet Edwards, Ciro Rodriquez, and Solomon Ortiz. Republicans enjoyed a 23 to 9 advantage in the congressional delegation. Republicans also took 22 Democratic seats in the Texas House to assume an overwhelming 101 to 49 majority. Both were historic highs for the triumphant Republicans.

THE REDISTRICTING DUST-UP OF 2011–2012

Given the successful mid-decade redistricting described immediately above, Texas Republicans were shaken by the electoral results of 2008. In the excitement surrounding Barack Obama's first presidential campaign, Democratic turnout surged and Democrats came within two seats of taking control of the Texas House. The dramatic Republican sweep of 2010, which drove Republican House majorities to all-time high, 101 to 49, only made them more determined to lock-in Republican control.

The 2011 Texas legislature met as the first reports of the 2010 census began to circulate. Early reports in December 2010, confirmed in official figures in March 2011, showed that the population of Texas had grown by 20.6 percent over the previous decade. Because Texas had grown faster than the nation and faster than any other big state, Texas got four new seats in the U.S. House of Representatives, expanding the Texas delegation from 32 to 36 members. Census reports also showed that most of the population growth had been among the state's minority populations. Texas Hispanics accounted for 65 percent of the population growth, and Hispanics, blacks, and Asians together accounted for 90 percent of the growth. Hence, Hispanic leaders called for a redistricting process that would give them most of the new seats, while Republican leaders, noting their complete control of the process, discussed how best to draw the lines in the long-term interest of the party.

FIGURE 5.2   Texas Congressional Districts

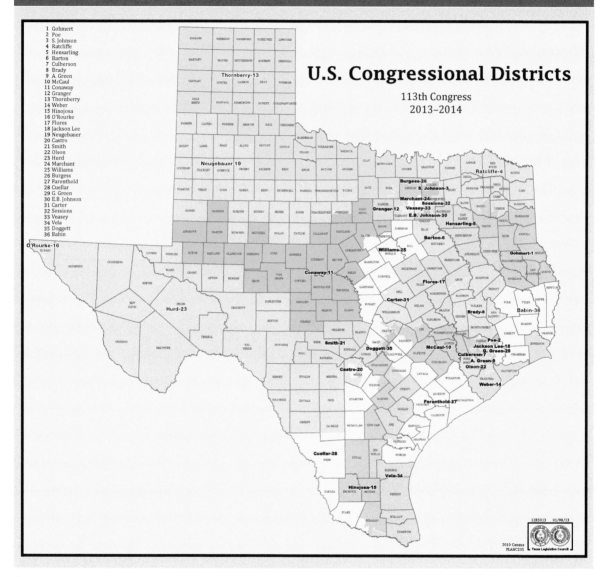

Source: Texas Legislative Council, http://www.tlc.state.tx.us/redist/congress.htm.

Texas Senator Kel Seliger (R-Amarillo), chair of the Senate Redistricting Committee, observed that, "it is going to look Republican. The only question is how Republican."[22]

Smelling trouble, minority leaders and interest groups went to court even before redistricting maps were released, arguing that minority elected officials, mostly Democrats to be sure, had been barred from the map-drawing discussions. In mid-May, 2011, with the regular session of the legislature in its final month, the legislature approved maps for the Texas House and Senate, but maps for the U.S. House were delayed and had to be completed in a June special session. For the next year, battles raged in three federal courts, including the U.S. Supreme Court, the Texas primary had to be delayed from March to May 2012, and final maps remained uncertain into the 2013 legislative session.

Democrat and minority challenges to the Republican legislature's maps were consolidated before a three-judge federal court panel sitting in San Antonio. As the San Antonio court began to work, Republican officials, led by Governor Perry and Attorney General Abbott, moved to secure federal approval of the legislature's maps. The Voting Rights Act of 1965, as amended, required that states with a history of racial and ethnic discrimination, including Texas, get "preclearance" of electoral changes like new voting districts either from the Civil Rights Division of the U.S. Department of Justice or from a three-judge panel of the Washington D.C. Circuit Court of Appeals. State officials were wary of seeking approval of their maps from what they frequently described as "the Obama Justice Department," so they chose to go before the D.C. Circuit Court of Appeals. This proved to be a fateful decision.

In October, 2012, the U.S. Justice Department joined the suit in the D.C. Circuit Court arguing that the Texas Legislature's maps evinced a discriminatory intent in violation of the Voting Rights Act. The appeals court, instead of providing the quick "preclearance" that Texas officials had hoped for, scheduled a hearing and then a full trial on the Justice Department's complaints. In November, the San Antonio court found that the legislature's legislative and congressional maps were discriminatory and replaced them with court drawn maps more favorable to minorities, and, therefore, to Democrats. Attorney General Abbott quickly appealed to the U.S. Supreme Court to block the lower

AP Photo/The Brownsville Herald, Yvette Vela

Eulalia Garcia-Maturey, 101, posing in Brownsville with her naturalization certificate. She arrived in Texas as an infant.

TIMELINE: TEXAS POLITICAL PARTIES

	1840	1850	1860	1870	1880	1890	1900	1910
Majority Party	Democrats			Republicans (1868-74)	Democrats			
Minority Party		Whigs		Democrats	Republicans			
Third Parties			American Party	Farmer's Alliance	Populist Party		Progressive Movement	

court's maps, arguing that the San Antonio federal court had overstepped its judicial bounds by displacing the elected legislature's maps. In mid-December, the Supreme Court agreed to hear the Texas case, but within days the three-judge panel of the D.C. circuit held that there were "genuine issues" of discrimination in the legislature's maps.

On January 20, 2012, the Supreme Court agreed with Attorney General Abbott that the San Antonio court had erred in too easily replacing the legislature's maps with their own. A unanimous high court wrote that redistricting is a political process and federal courts should be careful about intervening absent clear violations of law. The Supreme Court instructed that, "A district court should take guidance from the state's recently enacted plan in drafting an interim plan. . . . That plan reflects the state's policy judgments on where to place new districts and how to shift existing ones in response to massive population growth."[23] Hurried bargaining between the San Antonio court, the plaintiffs, and Attorney General Abbott produced some revisions to the Texas Senate and U.S. House maps, but by early March the San Antonio court had approved interim maps much closer to the legislature's original maps. These maps were to be used for the rapidly approaching 2012 Texas primaries, held on May 29, and the subsequent general election in November, but not for future elections unless again approved by the three-judge panels in San Antonio and Washington, D.C. Texas minority groups, including the NAACP and LULAC, vowed to continue the fight over permanent maps to be used in 2014 and beyond.

In late August, 2012, the three-judge panel in Washington, from whom Texas had sought preclearance, pronounced its trial verdict. The court held that the legislature's original U.S. House and Texas Senate maps, and probably its Texas House maps too, had been drawn with intent to discriminate against minority voters. Attorney General Abbott continued to argue that the legislature's maps had been drawn to advantage Republicans, not to disadvantage minorities. He declared that the court's decision, "extends the Voting Rights Act beyond the limits intended by Congress and beyond the boundaries

1920	1930	1940	1950	1960	1970	1980	1990	2000	2010
					Democrats	Competitive	Republicans		
					Republicans		Democrats		
		Dixiecrats			La Raza Unida		Reform Party		

imposed by the Constitution."[24] Once more, this pushed the case back to the three-judge panel in San Antonio to fix the problems identified by the D.C. court.

Texas rarely takes defeats in the federal courts lying down. When Texas was found guilty of intentional dilution of minority voter influence in violation of the Voting Rights Act, Attorney General Abbott promised not just to appeal but to challenge the constitutionality of the Voting Rights Act itself. Many Texas conservatives argued that even if the Voting Rights Act was initially warranted, now forty years on, it is no longer. They argue that Texas no longer deserved to be singled out for the special scrutiny involved in "preclearance." Democrats countered that Texas had just been found guilty in two federal courts of drawing intentionally discriminatory electoral boundaries, so continued oversight obviously was necessary.

Meanwhile, the interim maps used in the 2012 Texas elections allowed marginal Democratic gains but left Republicans in complete control of the state's government. In 2012, Republican congressional candidates captured 59 percent of the vote to 41 percent for the Democrats, but won 67 percent of the House seats, 24 to the Democrats' 12. While the Texas Senate remained 19 to 12 Republican, the Republican majority in the Texas House declined modestly, from 101–49 to 95–55. Republicans were satisfied that they had defended their maps and held their legislative majorities, but were wary of unresolved redistricting issues still before the courts.

In June 2013 the U.S. Supreme Court delivered victory to Texas Republicans by striking down the "preclearance" provisions of the VRA. The court held that the states subject to preclearance were identified based on outdated data. Texas immediately implemented its districts. While these districts can still be challenged in the courts, by citizens or even by the Justice Department, they can no longer be blocked in a mandatory preclearance process.

Redistricting battles in Texas have gone on for decades. Thirteen of the 50 states have tried to make redistricting less political and even less partisan by taking the process away from elected officials and putting it in the hands of appointed and citizen commissioners. In most cases, political officials do the appointing, but the fact that the process has been taken out of the legislature is some recognition that it has been focused too much on politicians and not enough on citizens and voters.

In Texas, Senator Jeff Wentworth (R-San Antonio) pushed a commission redistricting bill beginning in 1993. Wentworth's bill passed the Senate in 2005, 2007, and 2011 but never passed the House. Wentworth's reward was a Tea Party challenge and electoral defeat in 2012.

THE FUTURE

Q5 Is the power shift from Democrats to Republicans in Texas permanent?

Republican dominance since 1994 has been based on winning at least two-thirds of the Anglo vote, one-third of the Hispanic vote, and one-tenth of the black vote. Texas Democrats must win one-third of the Anglo vote and overwhelming majorities of the black and Hispanic votes just to be competitive.[25] The Democratic formula has not worked in a couple of decades because they have not been able to win even a third of the Anglo vote, but the rapid growth of the Hispanic population suggests to many political analysts that Texas will again be a competitive two-party state, though perhaps not for a decade or more.[26]

Recent elections highlight the racial and ethnic differences between the parties in Texas. In 2008, McCain beat Obama in Texas by almost 12 points, carrying 73 percent of the Anglo vote, but only 35 percent of the Hispanic vote and just 2 percent of the black vote. Similarly, in 2010 Rick Perry beat Bill White by 13 points, winning 69 percent of the Anglo vote, 38 percent of the Hipanic vote, and 11 percent of the black vote. Though no exit polls were conducted in Texas in 2012, the best evidence available suggests that Romney did even better than McCain among Anglos, winning near 80 of the vote, Obama did better among both blacks and Hispanics in 2012 than he had in 2008. Two points seem clear: one is that if Republicans continue to win more than 70, sometimes up toward 80 percent, of the Anglo vote, their majority can be extended for years, but the other is that Anglos are a shrinking share of the Texas population while Hispanics are an increasing share.

In 2013, Battleground Texas, led by Obama campaign veterans Jeremy Bird and Jenn Brown, declared its intention to assist the Democratic Party in turning Texas blue. Battleground Texas launched a long-term, grassroots, effort to mobilize Texas Democrats through volunteer recruitment and training, voter registration, messaging, fundraising, and turnout. So what must Republicans do to extend their majority status and what must Democrats do to cut it short? Texas Republicans must hold their Anglo base and grow their Hispanic vote if they are to maintain their current dominance of state politics. If their Anglo base is to remain intact, Republicans must hold the social conservative and fiscal conservative wings of their party together. **Social conservatives** focus on moral or values issues, such as abortion, marriage, school prayer, and judicial appointments. **Fiscal conservatives** focus on limiting government regulation of business, cutting taxes, and balancing budgets. Social and fiscal

Social conservatives
Conservative faction that focuses on social issues such as abortion, school prayer, and gay marriage.

Fiscal conservatives
Conservative faction that focuses on fiscal and economic issues such as taxation, spending, and business regulation.

conservatives often agree, or at least agree to work together, but when they disagree it is usually because social conservatives want to foreclose options, say on access to abortion services, that fiscal conservatives wish to keep in their own hands.

Complicating this traditional analysis of the Republican vote in Texas is the rise of the Tea Party beginning in 2009. Since 2010, the Tea Party has dominated the Republican primary, defeating prominent Republican incumbents, carrying Ted Cruz to victory in 2012, and Dan Patrick to victory over three-term incumbent David Dewhurst in the 2014 race for lieutenant governor. As the Tea Party pushes the Republican Party further right, some Republicans worry about losing touch with moderate voters.

Republicans must continue to reach out to minority voters. Governor Bush's 1998 re-election, a blowout in which he received 68 percent of the vote, drew high levels of minority support. Governor Perry's election in 2002, while a comfortable win, attracted only about one-quarter of Hispanics and one-tenth of blacks. Perry did better in 2010, attracting 38 percent of the Hispanic vote. With the Hispanic population of Texas growing rapidly, Republicans must hold at least a third of the Hispanic vote to continue to dominate the electoral politics of the state. How Texas Republicans handle the immigration debate will be critical.[27]

Looking at recent Texas elections geographically rather than demographically, though obviously they are connected, also highlights Republican dominance. Republicans still dominate in the state's rural and exurban districts. Democrats increasingly dominate in the state's major metropolitan areas, especially Dallas, San Antonio, Austin, and El Paso. The battleground in future elections will be in the state's midsize cities and in the increasingly diverse inner ring suburbs of the major cities, though Republicans won them handily in recent elections.

Texas Democrats now know that they cannot expect Republicans to fumble away their majority status, they must develop a strategy for taking it from them. Democrats must continue to hold their minority, union, and working-class support. At the same time, they must build new connections to Anglo, middle-class, suburban voters. These voters worry about taxes, but they also worry about good public schools, affordable health care, and skyrocketing college tuition and fees.[28]

Republicans must, of course, resist Democratic inroads on their suburban base and fight to enlarge their share of the Hispanic vote. Republicans contend that Hispanics are less focused on government support than blacks and more conservative on social issues. They point particularly to Hispanic commitment to family and opposition to abortion and gay marriage as shared values to which they can appeal. Democrats contend that Hispanics, particularly new immigrants and members of the working class, are more focused on access to education, health care, and jobs than on social issues. In the coming years, we will see who is right.

Chapter Summary

Political parties in Texas are composed of a few full-time professionals, many unpaid volunteers, and the voters who respond to their calls for support on election day. The Democratic and Republican parties are similarly organized. Elected but unpaid party activists serve as precinct, county, state senate district, and state officers. These officers prepare for party conventions and primary and general elections. Political parties develop party platforms, recruit candidates, and contest elections with the goal of winning majority control over government and controlling public policymaking and implementation. Minor-party, independent, and write-in candidates have all they can do just to get their names on the ballot.

The Democratic Party was the majority party of Texas from the initial Anglo settlement of the state through the 1960s and 70s. Democratic dominance was seldom challenged until tensions over FDR's New Deal agenda and civil rights divided the liberal Democrats of Texas from the more conservative Texas Regulars. As Texas Democrats squabbled among themselves, Texas Republicans began a slow, almost imperceptible, rise to majority status.

By 2002, Republicans held every statewide office and majorities in the Texas House and Senate. With the support of powerful Texas Republicans in Washington, Governor Perry, Texas House Speaker Tom Craddick, and Lt. Governor David Dewhurst pushed redistricting through the Texas legislature. In an extremely tumultuous political battle which featured an unusual mid-decade redistricting process and two occasions on which Democrats fled the state in vain attempts to stop the process, Republicans redrew Texas legislative and U.S. House district lines. Republicans solidified their legislative majorities and gained six congressional seats in 2004. From 2011 through 2014, Texas Republicans successfully fought Democrats, minority interest groups, and the federal courts to protect and extend their gains through another round of redistricting.

Nonetheless, social change in Texas renders Republican dominance insecure. The Anglo proportion of the Texas population, which votes mostly Republican, is declining, while the Hispanic proportion of the population, which votes mostly Democrat, is increasing. Democrats won back six Texas House seats in 2006 and six more in 2008. While big Republican gains in 2010 pushed back any Democratic resurgence, demographic change is on the Democrats' side. By 2030, Hispanics will be a majority of Texans, if not of Texas citizens and voters. Despite these great changes, one thing will not change: Democrats and Republicans will continue to struggle for partisan advantage and political dominance.

Key Terms

Baker v. Carr 124	Redistricting 123
Big tent model 107	Responsible party model 107
Democrats of Texas 116	Social conservatives 130
Fiscal conservatives 130	Texas Regulars 116
Political parties 107	*White v. Regester* 125
Precinct 108	

Review Questions

1. Outline the structure of political parties in Texas and explain the rationale for that structure.
2. Describe the differences between how major party candidates and minor or third party candidates gain access to the ballot.
3. Analyze the issue and policy positions of the national Democratic Party during the second half of the 20th century that undercut Texas Democrats.
4. Assess the likelihood that the Republican Party will be the majority party in Texas in the 2030s.
5. Evaluate the strengths and weaknesses of the campaign finance system in Texas.

Suggested Readings

Steve Bickerstaff, *Lines in the Sand: Congressional Redistricting in Texas and the Downfall of Tom DeLay* (Austin, TX: University of Texas Press, 2007).

Earl Black and Merle Black, *The Rise of Southern Republicanism* (Cambridge, MA: Harvard University Press, 2002).

Kenneth Bridges, *Twilight of the Texas Democrats* (College Station, TX: Texas A&M University Press, 2008).

Thomas M. Carsey and Jeffrey J. Harden, "New Measures of Partisanship, Ideology, and Policy Mood in the American States," *State Politics and Policy Quarterly* (2010), 10: 136–156.

Kimberly H. Conger, "A Matter of Context: Christian Right Influence in U.S. State Republican Politics," *State Politics and Policy Quarterly* (2010), 10: 248–269.

Chandler Davidson, *Race and Class in Texas Politics* (Princeton, NJ: Princeton University Press, 1990).

Ricky F. Dobbs, *Yellow Dogs and Republicans: Allan Shivers and Texas Two-Party Politics* (College Station, TX: Texas A&M University Press, 2005).

John R. Knaggs, *Two-Party Texas: The John Tower Era, 1961–1984* (Austin, TX: Eakin Press, 1986).

Web Resources

1. **http://www.txdemocrats.org/**
   The official website of the Democratic Party of Texas.

2. **http://www.txgreens.org/**
   The official website of the Green Party of Texas.

3. **http://www.tx.lp.org/**
   The official website of the Libertarian Party of Texas.

4. **http://www.texasgop.org/**
   The official website of the Republican Party of Texas.

5. **http://www.tlc.state.tx.us/**
   Explore the Texas Legislative Council's redistricting website.

Chapter 6

THE TEXAS LEGISLATURE

THE DIRTY THIRTY: FIGHTING CORRUPTION IN THE TEXAS LEGISLATURE

Most times in politics, the insiders win and they use their victories to solidify their control of institutions and offices and to reward their benefactors by crafting policies to serve their interests. Usually, the outsiders cannot do much about this because they lack the power to force the insiders out into the sunlight where their "pay-to-play" politics can be seen by all. But sometimes the insiders get both greedy and careless and this gives the outsiders an unexpected opportunity to force change. The most famous instance in Texas politics of the insiders being dragged out into the sunlight was the Sharpstown Scandal of 1969 to 1971. The outsiders that grabbed their opportunity to force change are known in Texas history as the "Dirty Thirty."

In the 1969 regular session of the Texas legislature, the insiders, led by Speaker Gus Mutcher (D-Brenham), his floor leader Tommy Shannon (D-Fort Worth), and others were doing their insider thing. Houston financier Frank Sharp wanted legislation that would benefit his Sharpstown State Bank and National Bankers Life Insurance Corporation. Sharp offered several leading Texas politicians, including Mutcher and Shannon, but also Governor Preston Smith and Democratic State Party Chair Elmer Baum, loans from his bank to buy stock in his insurance company which he conspired to let them quickly sell at a profit in exchange for the legislation he wanted. What could be simpler—the insiders win again.

Following the 1969 regular session of the Texas legislature, Governor Smith called a special session in which two bills that Sharp wanted were quickly passed to little notice. The insiders, including Governor Smith and Speaker Mutcher, had their loans, bought their stock, and made their profits, while Sharp had his desired legislation, at least briefly. Then Governor Smith, following the advice of state banking regulators, vetoed the bills he had called the special session to pass. This, of course, created some tension among the insiders, but, as in most conspiracies, no one, including Sharp, could say anything without implicating themselves.

Texas State Library and Archives Commission

A portrait of power in Texas in 1970: House Speaker Gus Mutscher, Governor Preston Smith, former president Lyndon Johnson, and Lieutenant Governor Ben Barnes. Within two years, the Sharpstown scandal ended the political careers of all but the former president, and his was already over.

Unbeknownst to the insiders, two sets of outsiders were watching and, though neither knew exactly what was happening, both wanted to know more. One group of outsiders was the U.S. Securities and Exchange Commission (SEC). The SEC had been watching Sharp and his financial dealings for some time and in January 1971, just as the new legislative session was getting underway in Texas, they filed criminal and civil charges against Sharp, Texas Attorney General Waggoner Carr, Insurance Commissioner John Osorio, and, before long, Mutcher, Shannon, Smith, and others. The second group of outsiders was actually in the legislature, but outside the good graces of Speaker Mutcher and his "team." The "Dirty Thirty" was a bipartisan group, Democrats and Republicans, liberals and conservatives, who stood against Mutcher and kept the spotlight on the SEC inquiry throughout the 1971 regular session.

One of the acknowledged leaders of the "Dirty Thirty" was Frances "Sissy" Farenthold of Corpus Christi, the only woman in the House. Other members were Zan Holmes of Dallas and Curtis Graves of Houston, the only two blacks in the House. These urban liberal Democrats were joined by urban conservative Republicans like Fred Agnich of Dallas, Sid Bowers of Houston, and Tom Craddick of Midland. The liberals were motivated by ideological distain for Mutcher while the conservatives were motivated by partisan distain. They mostly failed in their legislative challenges to Mutcher until his legal troubles eroded his support. The "Dirty Thirty's" calls for reform entered Texas legend, but not so much Texas law.

Nonetheless, eventually Mutcher fell. He and several co-defendants were tried and convicted in Abilene in 1972. Mutcher, Shannon, and another

Mutcher aide named Rush McGinty, drew five years probation for conspiring to accept bribes. Sharp drew three years probation and a $5,000 fine for violating federal banking laws. Governor Smith and half of the state legislature were turned out of office in the 1972 elections. "Sissy" Farenthold ran for governor, made the runoff, but eventually lost to Dolph Briscoe, a conservative Democrat and rancher. The outsiders sometimes win a battle or two but they rarely take over.

Focus Questions

Q1 Who serves in the Texas legislature?

Q2 How much influence do the leaders of the Texas House and Senate exercise?

Q3 What roles do committees play in the legislative process?

Q4 How does a bill become a law in Texas?

Q5 How does the legislative process differ in the House and Senate?

Democratic theory gives pride of place to the legislative branch of government. Democracy is based on the ideas of **popular sovereignty**, that all legitimate political authority comes from the people, and **legislative supremacy**, that the people's elected representatives should make the laws that bind citizens. But the power to make law might be abused, so bicameralism, **separation of powers**, and **checks and balances** are intended to limit and constrain legislative powers.

At the national level, the House of Representatives and Senate are jointly referred to as the Congress. In fact, when Texas was an independent republic (1836–1845), its legislature was called the Congress; not so today. No state refers to its legislature as Congress. Though there is some variation in how states refer to their legislatures, Massachusetts calls theirs the General Court and Virginia calls theirs the General Assembly, Texas keeps it simple. The Texas state legislature is called—well, the state legislature, the legislature, or, as the iconic Texas humorist Molly Ivins taught us, simply "the lege," but not Congress.

The authors of the Texas Constitution were intently focused on the potential abuse of government power. They limited all government power, especially executive authority (as we shall see in Chapter 7), but legislative authority was limited as well. In this chapter, we describe the members and leaders of the Texas legislature. We then ask how the Texas legislature is organized to do the state's business and how well that business is being done.

Popular sovereignty The idea that all legitimate governmental authority comes from the people.

Legislative supremacy The idea that the law-making power in government is superior to the executive and judicial powers.

Separation of powers The idea that distinctive types of governmental power, legislative, executive, and judicial, should be placed in separate hands.

Checks and balances The idea that government powers should be distributed to permit each branch of government to check and balance the other branches.

SERVICE IN THE TEXAS LEGISLATURE

Q1 Who serves in the Texas legislature?

Article III of the Texas Constitution mandates a bicameral legislature. The Texas Senate has thirty-one members, each elected to a four-year term, while the Texas House of Representatives has 150 members, each elected to a two-year term. Each House district contains about 175,000 residents and each Senate district contains about 850,000. In November of even-numbered years, all 150 House seats and half of the Senate seats are up for election.

Formal Qualifications

Who Knew?

Texans hate to be outdone—so when it came time in the 1880s to erect a new state capitol building, state leaders made sure it was taller than the national capitol. At 308 feet, the Texas state capitol rises 15 feet higher than the U.S. capitol.

Article III of the Texas Constitution also lays out the qualifications for service in the legislature. To sit in the Texas House, one must be at least 21, a U.S. citizen, a registered voter, and a resident of Texas for two years and of the legislative district for one year. To sit in the Texas Senate, one must be at least 26, a U.S. citizen, a registered voter, and a resident of Texas for five years and of the district for one. These qualifications are very general and exclude few Texans from potential service. Nonetheless, some Texans have a much better chance to serve in the Texas legislature than do others.

Member Characteristics

Because the population of Texas is more diverse than the population of the U.S. in general, Texas has a more diverse legislature than most states, but still not as diverse as its population. The U.S. population is about 65 percent Anglo as we say in Texas, 15 percent Hispanic, 13 percent black, and 5 percent Asian. State legislatures are 86 percent Anglo, just 3 percent Hispanic, 9 percent African-American, and 1 percent Asian.[1]

Fifty years ago, the Texas legislature was the preserve of white, middle-aged businessmen, lawyers, and ranchers. Since then, the legislature has become more diverse, but the growth of that diversity has slowed in recent decades. Anglos still hold two-thirds of the legislative seats, though they make up only about 47 percent of the population.

Hispanics make up about 38 percent of the population, but because citizenship rates and voter turnout among Hispanics trail whites and blacks, they hold just 23 percent of the seats in the Texas legislature. Blacks, who have made up a steady 12 percent of the Texas population for decades, hold 10.5 percent of the seats. Asians make up just over 3 percent of the Texas population and hold 1.7 percent of the seats. Women have made gains in the Texas legislature, but they still hold just under 21 percent of the seats.[2]

Nationally, women hold 1,804, or 24.4 percent, of the 7,382 state legislative seats. Sixty percent of female legislators nationally are Democrat while 40 percent are Republican. In Texas, as noted above, women hold just under 21 percent of state legislative seats and getting there has been a struggle. In Texas,

Year	%Anglo	%Hispanic	%Black	%Asian-American	%Women
1987	78.5	13.3	8.3	0	9.9
1989	77.9	14.4	7.7	0	10.5
1991	78.5	13.3	8.3	0	13.3
1993	73.5	17.7	8.8	0	17.1
1995	72.4	18.8	8.8	0	19.3
1997	73.0	18.5	8.4	0	18.2
1999	71.8	19.3	8.8	0	18.2
2001	71.8	19.3	8.8	0	18.8
2003	69.6	21.0	8.8	0.6	19.9
2005	70.2	20.4	8.8	1.1	19.9
2007	70.2	20.4	8.8	0.6	19.9
2009	69.0	21.0	8.8	1.1	23.8
2011	66.3	22.1	10.5	1.1	21.0
2013	65.2	22.1	11.0	1.7	20.6
2015	64.6	23.2	10.5	1.7	20.6

TABLE 6.1 Ethnicity and Gender in the Texas Legislature, 1987–2015

Source: Texas Legislature webpage. www.capitol.state.tx.us. See also National Conference of State Legislatures, "Legislator Demographics."

55 percent of female state legislators are Republican and 45 percent are Democrat. The first woman elected to the Texas House was Edith Wilmans of Dallas in 1922 and the first woman elected to the Texas Senate was Margie Neal of Carthage in 1926. Forty years later there was still just one woman in the Texas Senate, Barbara Jordan elected in 1966, and one in the House, "Sissy" Farenthold elected in 1968. Numbers of women rose in the 1970s and 1980s but have been flat, at about 20 percent, since 1993.[3]

Texas legislators tend to be well-educated. Only about 6 percent hold less than a four-year college degree. Forty-three percent have a B.A., but no advanced degree. Twelve percent have an M.A. and 6 percent have a Ph.D. Just over 30 percent hold a J.D., which means they have graduated from law school. Only Massachusetts and Ohio have more lawyers in their state legislature.[4]

Sessions, Salaries, and Support

Molly Ivins used to quip that the approach of the Texas legislative session meant that "every village is about to lose its idiot."[5] Legislators, somewhat defensively to be sure, take a different view. One veteran legislator noted that,

LET'S COMPARE   LEGISLATIVE COMPENSATION IN THE TEN LARGEST STATES

As we have noted throughout this book, Texas has a traditional political culture that promotes elite rule and social stability. Texas legislative salaries are very low compared to similar states, though its per diem rate is about average, and its legislative retirement system is very generous. Low pay keeps people who have to work for a living, particularly in hourly-wage jobs, out of the legislature. Only those who can afford to serve, or, like lawyers, whose professional status might benefit from the visibility of holding public office, are intended to be in the legislature. Once in the legislature, elites expected to treat themselves and each other well. Hence, low pay, but extremely generous benefit packages.

Nonetheless, legislator compensation is not as ridiculously low as it might seem. A legislator that drew the base pay of $7,200 a year and the $190 per diem for the 140 day regular session and the maximum 12 days per month when the legislature is not in session would draw about $40,000 annually. But it is the retirement package that makes service worthwhile.

Legislators' retirement benefits are pegged, not to their own $7,200 salaries, but to the earnings of Texas district judges, who make 19 times as much, or $140,000 annually. Legislators who choose to participate in the retirement program, and virtually all do, must pay $48 a month into the system. Legislators at age 60 with eight years of service, or 50 years of age with twelve years of service, are eligible for retirement benefits. The formula is $140,000 times years of service times 2.3 percent, meaning that a lawmaker with ten years of service would be eligible for an annual pension of $32,200. Each extra year of service adds $3,220, so a lawmaker with twenty years of service would draw $64,400. Sweet!

States	Salary*	Per Diem**	Retirement***
California	$90,526	$142 per day	None
Texas	**$7,200**	**$190 per day**	**High**
New York	$79,500	$165 per day	Medium
Florida	$29,687	$131 per day	Medium
Pennsylvania	$83,801	$159 per day	Medium
Illinois	$67,836	$111 per day	High
Ohio	$60,584	None	Medium
Michigan	$71,865	$10,800 annually	Medium
North Carolina	$13,951	$104 per day	Low
Georgia	$17,342	$173 per day	Low

*Annual salary
**Daily per diem when the legislature is in session or for intersession workdays.
***Retirement systems are complex. Here we divide them into None, Low, Medium, and High (most generous).

Source: Council of State Governments, *The Book of the States, 2013* (Lexington, KY: 2013) Table 3.9, pp. 70–73; Table 3.13, pp. 86–91. See also National Conference of State Legislatures, http://www.ncsl.org/legislatures-elections/legisdata/2012-ncsl-legislator-compensation.

"if you took all the fools out of the state legislature, it would no longer be a representative body."[6] While both points seem at least partially true, neither seems particularly reassuring.

The Texas legislature meets in **biennial session** for 140 days, beginning on the second Tuesday in January of odd-numbered years. The **regular session** of the Texas legislature comes to a hectic climax around the end of May. Texas is one of only four states, and the only one of the thirty-four most populous states, to retain biennial sessions. The other three states meeting biennially are, absurdly enough, Montana, Nevada, and North Dakota. Between 1949 and 1975, Texas voters rejected no fewer than five constitutional amendments permitting annual sessions. The topic is rarely raised today.

If the legislature does not complete its work during the regular session, the governor may call one or more thirty-day special sessions. After a spate of ten special sessions called by Governors Bill Clements and Ann Richards between 1989 and 1992, there were no special sessions for more than a decade. Then-Governor Rick Perry called seven special sessions between 2003 and 2006 to deal with legislative redistricting and school finance. A very brief special session following the 2009 regular session dealt with transportation issues, and a longer, more contentious, special session was required in 2011 to pass an education funding and reform bill that had failed in the regular session. Three special sessions followed the 2013 regular session, dealing with criminal justice, abortion, and transporation funding.

Texas state legislators receive just $600 a month, or $7,200 a year, for their service. They also receive a *per diem* (daily expenses) of $190 a day during regular and special sessions and for interim service, such as committee work, up to twelve days each month. The Texas Ethics Commission may change the *per diem* rate as it sees fit, but the salary of Texas legislators is set in the constitution. Legislators can, however, increase their retirement benefits, which they did in the 83rd (2013) regular session.[7]

Legislators are allocated support for secretarial, administrative, and research assistance both during and between sessions. Each member receives a staff and office allowance. In recent years, Senators have received $38,000 a month for staff and office expenses, while House members have received $13,250 a month during the session and $11,925 a month between sessions. Members must decide how to allocate these funds across an Austin office and one or more district offices. Members also receive some support from staff assigned to committees on which they serve. Most members also draw on their campaign/officeholder accounts to fund their staff and office expenses.

Turnover and Experience

Nationally, state legislatures experience an average turnover of 20 to 25 percent in each electoral cycle, though redistricting and the occasional voter revolt can increase turnover. The Texas House had twenty-four (16 percent) in 2007, and twenty (13 percent) in 2009 before jumping up to 37 new members (25 percent) in 2011. The Senate, usually more stable than the House, had

Biennial session The Texas legislature meets in regular session every other year, that is biennially, rather than annually.

Regular session The regularly scheduled biennial session of the legislature.

four new members (13 percent) in 2007, but just two new members (6 percent) in 2009, and 2011.[8] Following the 2010 census and subsequent redistricting, the Texas House had 44 new members (29 percent) and the Texas Senate had 5 new members (16 percent) when the 2013 session opened.[9] In 2015, the house had 24 new members (16 percent) and the senate had 8 (26 percent).

The average length of service for members of the Texas House in 2013 was twelve years and fourteen years for the Senate. Some members serve much longer. The longest serving legislator in Texas history was A.M. Aiken, Jr. Aiken served continuously from 1933 through 1979, 1933–1937 in the House and 1937–1979 in the Senate, for a total of 46 years; surpassing Aiken with his service in the 2015 session, Tom Craddick (R-Midland) has served continuously in the House since 1969 and John Whitmire (D-Houston), not far behind, has served continuously in the Texas House and Senate since 1973. New legislators often take a session or two to learn the ropes. Experienced legislators exercise the most influence because they know how the system works.[10]

If a legislator dies, becomes incapacitated, or resigns during his or her term, the office is filled by special election unless the next regular election is near. The governor is responsible for calling the special election. The election must occur at least 36 days after the call and, except under emergency conditions, like a

FIGURE 6.1 Balance of Power: The Republican Rise in the Texas House and Senate

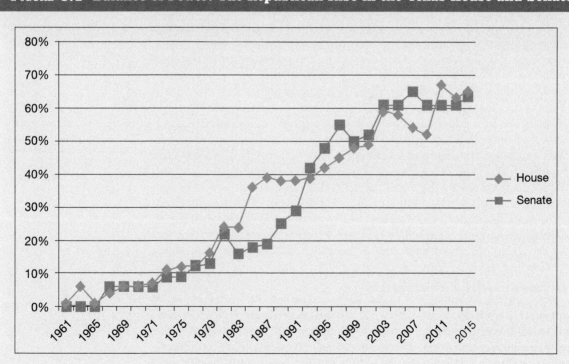

Source: Texas Legislative Council.

TABLE 6.2	Permanent Legislative Staff in the Ten Largest States					
State	**Leg. Type**	**1979**	**1988**	**1996**	**2003**	**2009**
California	Professional	1,760	2,865	2,506	2,334	2,067
Texas	**Hybrid**	**986**	**1,460**	**1,964**	**1,745**	**2,090**
New York	Professional	1,600	3,580	3,461	3,077	2,676
Florida	Professional	1,095	1,581	1,896	1,650	1,457
Illinois	Professional	984	1,066	969	905	980
Pennsylvania	Professional	1,430	1,984	2,682	2,947	2,918
Ohio	Professional	390	524	552	505	465
Michigan	Professional	1,047	1,287	1,359	1,153	973
Georgia	Amateur	275	466	511	603	605
North Carolina	Hybrid	90	118	168	290	321

Source: National Conference of State Legislatures, "Size of State Legislative Staff," http://www.ncsl.org/legislatures-elections/legisdata/staff-change-chart. See also NCSL, "Full and Part-time Legislatures," http://www.ncsl.org/?tabid=16701.

looming legislative session, must occur on uniform election days, either the first Saturday in May or the first Tuesday after the first Monday in November.

Scholars and students of state legislatures often distinguish among professional legislatures, amateur legislatures, and hybrids. **Professional legislatures** look a lot like the U.S. Congress, and their members are full-time politicians. Professional legislatures, like those in California, Michigan, Pennsylvania, and New York, meet nearly year round and are supported by large and well-trained staffs. **Amateur legislatures**, often called citizen legislatures, are not well-paid or supported, meet less frequently, and their members generally have other jobs and professions. Small or lightly populated states, such as Nevada, Wyoming, and the Dakotas, tend to employ amateur or citizen legislatures.

Texas is usually described as having a hybrid legislature. **Hybrid legislatures** have elements common to both professional and amateur legislatures. In Texas's case, a large and well-trained staff is suggestive of professional standards while the biennial session and low pay are characteristic of amateur legislatures. According to the National Council of State Legislatures, Texas is by far the largest state to employ a hybrid legislature.[11]

Professional legislatures State legislatures which pay and support their members well and, in turn, demand nearly full-time service from them.

Amateur legislatures State legislatures which provide low pay and support to their members. Sessions are generally short and members have other jobs.

Hybrid legislatures State legislatures, including the Texas legislature, that share some of the characteristics of professional legislatures, such as long sessions and good staff support, and some of the characteristics of amateur legislatures, such as low pay and biennial sessions.

PARTIES AND LEADERS IN THE
TEXAS LEGISLATURE

In both the U.S. Congress and the Texas legislature, the majority party controls the legislature and the majority party is controlled by its elected leaders. Republicans have enjoyed a majority in the Texas Senate since 1997 and in the Texas House since 2003. In the 84th (2015) legislative session, the Senate is composed of twenty Republicans and eleven Democrats, while the House is composed of 98 Republicans and 52 Democrats. The Republican rise to power in Texas is charted in Figure 6.1.

Q2 How much influence do the leaders of the Texas House and Senate exercise?

Among Texas legends, if Sam Houston ranks first, who ranks second? One could make a very strong argument that another Sam—Sam Rayburn—should have that high place. Sam Rayburn was, first and foremost, a legislator. He was the Speaker of the Texas House and the longest serving ever Speaker of the U.S. House of Representatives.

Samuel Taliaferro Rayburn was born on January 6, 1882, in Roane County, Tennessee. The family moved to Texas when Sam was just five, settling in rural North Texas, near Bonham in Fannin County. One of eleven children in a poor but hardworking family, Sam Rayburn grew up doing his share of the farm work and attending rural schools. Texas politics in Rayburn's youth were dominated by two larger-than-life personalities, Governor Jim Hogg, elected when Sam was eight, and U.S. Senator Joseph Weldon Bailey. Rayburn was turned to politics and the idea of a career in Congress by a speech Senator Bailey gave in Bonham. After high school, Rayburn took a two-year Bachelor of Science degree, taking time-off to make tuition money by teaching, at what is now the University of Texas, Commerce.

Sam Rayburn's first political race was in 1906 for a seat in the Texas House, which he won by 163 votes at age 24. Between his first and second legislative sessions, he attended law school at the University of Texas and read law in the office of an experienced lawyer back home. At the beginning of his third term in the Texas House, Rayburn stood for Speaker and won on the second ballot at age 29. When the U.S. congressman from Rayburn's district chose to run for the U.S. Senate in 1912, Rayburn declared for the open House seat and won narrowly in a crowded field. At 30, Sam Rayburn was going to Congress.

When Rayburn arrived in the House, a fellow Texan, John Nance Garner of Uvalde, was a member of the powerful Ways and Means Committee and, therefore, able to help Rayburn secure his first choice of committee assignments—Interstate and Foreign Commerce. A work horse rather than a show horse, Rayburn gained stature within the Democratic caucus, being named its chairman in 1920, but as the Republicans held the majority from 1919 through 1931, he wielded little real political power. When Democrats retook the House in 1931, Garner became Speaker and Rayburn, his chief lieutenant, became chairman of the Committee on Interstate and Foreign Commerce. When Garner became FDR's vice president in 1933, Rayburn moved up in the Democratic hierarchy but he was not yet ready to bid for the Speakership.

After a failed bid for Speaker in 1934, Rayburn won the office that he had always coveted in 1940. He served as Speaker from September 1940 until illness forced him to step down in 1961, except for two brief periods, 1947–1949 and 1953–1955, when Republicans held the majority—longer than anyone in history. Rayburn was beloved of Democratic members and liked by most Republican members. Most Americans came to know him as the gruff Permanent Chairman of the Democratic National Conventions of 1948, 1952, and 1956. Finally, Rayburn was the guide and mentor to two generations of Texas Democrats in Washington, most famously of Lyndon Johnson. Even after LBJ became Democratic leader in the Senate, Speaker Rayburn was the leading Texan in Washington. Sam Rayburn died of cancer at home in Bonham on November 16, 1961.

Legislative leaders always exercise more influence and control than regular members, but in some legislatures, such as the U.S. Congress, there are many leaders serving to limit, check, and balance each other. Not so in the Texas legislature. In the Texas legislature, the Speaker of the House and the lieutenant governor (who serves as the presiding officer in the Senate) have no peers and few challengers for authority over their respective bodies. The 2007 and 2009 sessions were highly unusual in that there were concerted attempts, ultimately successful, to depose Speaker Tom Craddick. Half-hearted efforts to replace Speaker Joe Straus were made in 2011, 2013, and 2015, but they lacked the pop and sizzle of the assaults on Speaker Craddick.

The Speaker of the House

The Speaker of the House is a constitutional office, though the constitution describes it only in the most general terms. The Texas Constitution simply says: "The House of Representatives shall, when it first assembles, organize temporarily, and thereupon proceed to the election of a Speaker from its own members." The rules of the House determine the Speaker's actual powers.

The Speaker of the Texas House is elected by House members as the first order of business in each regular session. The Secretary of State presides over the balloting, but the outcome of the election is usually known well in advance. Since 1973, candidates for Speaker have been required to keep detailed records of loans, contributions, and expenditures relating to the election. As with most Texas campaign contribution restrictions, these limits proved ineffectual, and then in August 2008 a federal judge, citing the importance of free speech, struck down the law barring third parties from trying to influence the Speaker race. In reality, the business lobby has long played a gate-keeper role for members aspiring to the Speakership.[12]

The fine history of the Texas Speakership, *The House Will Come to Order*, by Patrick Cox and Michael Phillips, describes an office that has changed dramatically over the decades. They argue that, "institutional changes in the Texas House and larger social changes in the state since World War II transformed the Speakership from a rotating, largely honorary position charged mainly with presiding over House debates to an office in which individual Speakers have wielded tremendous power and even control over state policy."[13]

Through the 1940s, Speakers served a single two-year term and then retired or sought higher office. From 1951 to 1975, most Speakers served one or two terms, but no more than two. Since 1975, Speakers have served multiple terms. Billy Clayton served four terms, between 1975 and 1983, followed by five terms each for Gib Lewis (1983–93) and Pete Laney (1993–2003). Laney sought a sixth term, despite the Republican takeover of the House in 2003, but he was pushed aside by Tom Craddick.

Though the Speakership has evolved over time, it has always been the preserve of ambitious men—and they have all been men so far. One does not wield the gavel over 149 other elected politicians unless ambition has driven you to compete for that role. Sam Rayburn, one of Texas's most successful legislators, both in Austin and Washington, said of the Texas Speakership, "The job had real power—that's what a man wants—but power's no good unless you have the guts to use it."[14] One way that Rayburn used his power, as he said quite candidly, was to see "that all my friends got the good appointments and that those who voted against me as Speaker got none."[15]

The powers of the Speaker are grounded in the Texas Constitution and laws, as well as in the rules and traditions of the House. The Speaker: (1) defines the jurisdiction of the standing committees; (2) appoints all committee chairs and vice chairs; (3) appoints most committee members; (4) refers all bills and resolutions to the appropriate committee; (5) serves as presiding officer over all House sessions; and (6) appoints all conference committee members, as well as members of special and interim committees.

Speaker Tom Craddick was a lightning rod. He worked hard in 2002, coordinating Republican-leaning interest groups and channeling campaign contributions to needy members in order to produce the first Republican House majority since the 1870s. He campaigned energetically for Speaker and then used his position to assist then-U.S. House Majority Leader Tom DeLay in pushing a partisan redistricting plan through the 2003 Texas legislature. The new Republican majority was extremely grateful to Craddick for his role in bringing them to power. Craddick ruled the House with an iron hand in 2003 and 2005, but by 2007 the Republican majority effectively exploded.

The 2007 regular session opened on January 9. By late December 2006, Brian McCall (R-Plano) and Jim Pitts (R-Waxahachie), chair of the powerful Appropriations Committee in the previous session, had declared that they would stand against Craddick for the Speakership. McCall withdrew in favor of Pitts and Pitts promised House members to eschew "arm twisting and intimidation" in favor of a new "spirit of cooperation and bipartisanship."[16] The insurgents wanted a secret ballot, while Craddick, with his well-deserved reputation for playing hardball, wanted an open vote. On January 9, when the Pitts forces fell five votes short on a key procedural motion, Pitts withdrew and Craddick was elected to a third term as Speaker.

Craddick told his colleagues that he had heard their criticisms and concerns and would make changes. But Craddick used his power over House committees to reward his supporters and punish his opponents.[17] Pitts not only lost the chairmanship of Appropriations but was bounced completely off the committee. Tensions built throughout the session as Craddick sought to give members somewhat more autonomy and they increasingly gained a taste for it. In early May the House overruled one of Craddick's decisions from the chair, the first such instance since 1973. On May 21, Byron Cook (R-Corcicana) called in a floor speech for Craddick to step down, the first such challenge to a sitting Speaker since 1959, and Jim Pitts and Jim Keffer (R-Eastland), chair of the tax writing Ways and Means Committee, filed to challenge Craddick for the Speakership in any special session or in 2009.

With just three days left in the session, the House descended into chaos. When members sought to offer a motion "to vacate the chair," Craddick recessed the House for more than two hours. When he returned, he declared that there was no such motion in the rules. The House parliamentarian and her assistant disagreed and resigned. Craddick appointed allies to the now vacant parliamentarian positions and proceeded to overrule all attempts to challenge him. Craddick's opponents yelled "dictator" and supporters shouted

AP Photo/Eric Gay

Joe Straus (R-San Antonio) was first elected Speaker of the Texas House in 2009.

"anarchists" back at them. Craddick survived to the end of the session, but a bare knuckled Speaker race was guaranteed for 2009.[18]

Republican losses in the 2008 Texas House elections fed opposition to Speaker Craddick as the 2009 regular session approached. Though Craddick struggled to retain the gavel, he was ultimately forced to relinquish it to San Antonio's Joe Straus. Straus was elected when a dozen mostly moderate Republicans joined with Democrats to oust Craddick. Members believed Straus when he promised a more collegial and open administration of the House. Nonetheless, the House amended its rules for the 2009 session to allow a Speaker to be removed mid-session by a simple majority vote of the House. Though the session got off to a slow start, members seemed not to mind as they felt much freer and more independent than they had under Craddick. It did not take long before conservative Republicans began to complain that Speaker Straus was not conservative enough.

Soon after the end of the 2009 regular session, Straus had already collected enough pledge cards to assure his re-election as Speaker in 2011. Nonetheless, Tea Party-fueled Republican gains in the 2010 elections produced a more conservative House and Straus was challenged by two staunch conservatives—Warren Chisum (R-Pampa) and Ken Paxton (R-McKinney). After intense behind-the-scenes battles, the challengers fell short and Straus survived, though 18 members arranged to be absent or abstained on the final vote. As the session ground on, conservatives demanded that Straus use the 101–49 Republican majority to roll over what they considered Democratic obstructionism. Straus ultimately complied on key votes involving the budget, immigration, and school funding, but conservatives continued to be suspicious of him. As the 2013 legislative session approached, first Bryan Hughes (R-Mineola), and then David Simpson (R-Longview), challenged Straus but both had withdrawn from the Speaker's race on the opening day of the 2013 session. Straus was elected to his third term as Speaker by acclamation. In 2015, Straus was again challenged, this time by Scott Turner (R-Frisco), but again prevailed, 127 to 19. This was the first recorded speaker vote since 1975.

The Lieutenant Governor

The lieutenant governor is a statewide elected official who presides in the Texas Senate by constitutional mandate. Unlike the U.S. vice president, the Lt. Governor of Texas is an independent political figure. The vice president is selected by the president and remains subservient to him while in office. The Lieutenant Governor of Texas is the dominant figure in the Texas Senate. The lieutenant governor: (1) appoints the chairs, vice chairs, and members of all Senate committees, including standing committees, conference committees, and interim committees; (2) assigns all bills and resolutions to the appropriate committee; (3) presides over the Senate and interprets the rules, and (4) chairs or co-chairs the Legislative Budget Board, Legislative Council, and Legislative Audit Committe.[19] The lieutenant governor generally does not vote in the Senate, though he may if doing so makes an important substantive or political point. Not voting allows the lieutenant governor to play the deal-maker or honest-broker role among all the members and groups contesting a given issue.

During the past several decades, two lieutenant governors have become legendary figures, on a par with any governor of the period. Bill Hobby, son of a former governor, served as lieutenant governor for 18 years, between 1972 and 1990. Hobby was a quiet, scholarly man, well-liked by his colleagues in the Senate and very effective. Bob Bullock, as bullying and boisterous as Hobby was quiet and retiring, served as lieutenant governor for eight years, between 1990 and 1998. Bullock knew Texas state government inside out and was credited with helping a newly elected governor—George W. Bush—learn the ropes. The Bob Bullock State History Museum opened in Austin in April 2001 and is well worth a visit.

Rick Perry, longtime Texas Agriculture Commissioner, moved up to lieutenant governor in 1998 as George W. Bush was winning a second term as governor. When Governor Bush won the presidency in 2000, Rick Perry became governor and the members of the Texas Senate elected one of their own, Senator Bill Ratliff (R-Mount Pleasant), to preside in the Senate. Ratliff declined to run for lieutenant governor in 2002 and the position was won by one-term land commissioner and wealthy businessman, David Dewhurst.

Dewhurst, a novice when he approached the 78th (2003) regular session, won high marks for hard work and a willingness to listen and search for common ground. In the 79th (2005) legislative session, Craddick's unwillingness to compromise on the major issue of the session, school finance, made Dewhurst's search for compromise seem ineffectual, perhaps weak, and left both men seeking to blame the other.[20] Craddick and Dewhurst both benefited when the 2006 special session finally succeeded in passing a school finance bill. Dewhurst gained experience and confidence in the 2007 and 2009 legislative sessions and easily won re-election in 2010. In 2012, Dewhurst was trounced in a bid for the U.S. Senate. Though he had little time to lick his wounds before the 2013 legislative session opened, he immediately declared his intention to stand for re-election as lieutenant governor in 2014.

Eric Gay/AP/Corbis

Lt. Gov. Dan Patrick at his inauguration, January 20, 2015. A Republican, Patrick decisively defeated Republican incumbent Lt. Gov. David Dewhurst.

In 2014, Lieutenant Governor Dewhurst was defeated for re-election by Texas Senator Dan Patrick (R-Houston). Patrick, a radio talk show host and a Tea Party favorite, ran first in the Republican primary, taking 41 percent of the vote to Dewhurst's 28 percent. In the runoff, Patrick easily dispatched Dewhurst, 65 percent to 35 percent. Patrick promised a more determinedly conservative Texas Senate and state government than previous Republican administrations—most of whom had thought they were pretty conservative.

The Team

Supporters and close associates of the presiding officers are commonly referred to as "**the team**." While the idea of "the team" applies to both the House and the Senate, it is most clear in the House. Legislators that support the successful candidate for Speaker, particularly if they signed on early and worked to build support, are usually rewarded with important committee assignments. If they are senior members of the House, they are likely to be named committee chairs or vice chairs.

Historically, "the team" has not been a strictly partisan group. While the presiding officer usually draws most heavily on the members of his own party, leaders have always tried to include members of the other party on the team. Drawing support from both sides of the aisle enhances prospects of consistently controlling the body and gives the leader's team an air of bipartisanship. In truth, the willingness of most members of the minority party to join the Speaker's "team" is less a matter of bipartisanship than it is a desire to be close to power and share in some of its benefits.

"The team" The Speaker's closest associates, through whom he attempts to control and direct the House. A similar pattern operates in the Senate.

Legislative Institutions and Leadership Power

The lieutenant governor and Speaker share control over the legislature's research, budgetary, audit, and oversight staff. The lieutenant governor and Speaker serve as joint-chairs of the Legislative Council. The fourteen-member Council is filled out with six House members appointed by the Speaker and six senators appointed by the lieutenant governor. The Legislative Council, established in 1949, has a staff director and a professional staff that assists the leaders, committee chairs, and members with interim research as well as bill-drafting services before and during the session. Between sessions, the Legislative Council conducts studies, inquiries, and investigations as directed by the leaders.

The lieutenant governor and Speaker also jointly control the powerful Legislative Budget Board (LBB), the Legislative Audit Committee (LAC), and the Sunset Advisory Committee (SAC). The ten-member LBB, established in 1949, is composed, in addition to the lieutenant governor and Speaker, of the chairs of the House Appropriations and Ways and Means Committees and the Senate Finance Committee, as well as two more House members appointed by the Speaker and three more Senate members appointed by the lieutenant governor. The LBB oversees the drafting and monitoring of the state budget. The six-member LAC, established in 1943, is composed of the lieutenant governor and Speaker, the chairs of House Appropriations and Ways and Means and Senate Finance, and one additional senator appointed by the lieutenant governor. The LAC oversees spending audits and investigations. The SAC, established in 1977, is composed of five senators and five House members, appointed by the lieutenant governor and Speaker, and two public members, also appointed by the presiding officers. The SAC conducts a review of every state agency, on a twelve-year cycle, to determine whether the agency is still needed. Control of these boards and committees is central to the power of the presiding officers of the Texas legislature.[21]

Limits on Legislative Leadership

The Speaker and the lieutenant governor wield tremendous power, but their power is not unchecked. Obviously, each is in a position to check the other. Moreover, leaders sometimes make demands with which their followers are unwilling to comply. In these contests of will, leaders win some and they lose some.

First, the leaders are well aware that they cannot simply dominate their fellow legislators. Many members have a decade or more of service in the legislature, are skilled legislative tacticians, and have broad contacts in the lobby and the executive branch. The presiding officers tend to communicate closely and continually with senior members of the team to make sure that they are all on the same page.

Second, the leaders know that it is futile to pass something in one house of the legislature, or even in both houses, without insuring that the rest of state government is receptive. Leaders stay in close touch with the governor's office and the elected and appointed officials that run the bureaucracy to be sure that they support and approve legislative actions. Leaders also pay continuous attention to the lobby to get their input and gauge their likely reaction to whatever the legislature might do.

Finally, leaders know that members are more afraid of the voters than they are of them. Members are likely to defect if leaders ask that they take positions or cast votes that might get them defeated in the next election. On the other hand, members that regularly stray from the course set by the leaders often find themselves marooned on a marginal committee and sometimes find themselves opposed for re-election.

THE COMMITTEE SYSTEM

The committee system is a set of working groups into which the members are divided to more efficiently process the business of the legislature. Committees are frequently called "little legislatures" because each one takes responsibility for a particular aspect of the legislature's work. The Texas legislature employs several kinds of committees, including standing committees, conference committees, and special and interim committees.

Q3 What roles do committees play in the legislative process?

Standing Committees

Standing committees are the most important legislative committees. Each standing committee has a designated area of responsibility, and all bills must be considered by the appropriate standing committee before proceeding to the floor for final action. However, standing committees in the Texas legislature are less powerful and independent than are standing committees in the U.S. Congress, or even in many other state legislatures. The Speaker and lieutenant governor regularly change the number, jurisdiction, leadership, and membership of standing committees.

Standing committees
Continuing committees of the legislature appointed at the start of each legislative session unless specific action is taken to revise or discontinue them.

Standing committees come in two varieties, policy committees and power committees. Policy committees, such as the House committees on Agriculture and Livestock, Border and International Affairs, Criminal Jurisprudence, and Natural Resources, have jurisdiction over particular policy areas. Power committees, such as the House committees on Appropriations, Calendars, and Ways and Means, control how bills come to the floor and how much money is to be raised and spent.

In the 84th (2015) legislative session, the Senate had fourteen standing committees and the House had thirty-eight. Lieutenant Governor Patrick named twelve Republicans and two Democrats to chair the Senate's standing committees. In general, the most important committees, including Finance, Education, State Affairs, and Business and Commerce, were not only chaired by Republicans, but Republicans keep two-thirds of the seats. This being Texas, the Natural Resources Committee was given a nine to two Republican

TABLE 6.3   Committees of the 84th Texas Legislature

Senate Committees

Administration	Higher Education
Agriculture, Water & Rural Affairs	Intergovernmental Relations
Business and Commerce	Natural Resources & Economic Development
Criminal Justice	Nominations
Education	State Affairs
Finance	Transportation
Health & Human Services	Vet. Affairs & Mil. Installations

House Committees

Agriculture & Livestock	International Trade
Appropriations	Investments and Financial Services
Business & Industry	Judiciary and Civil Jurisprudence
Calendars	Juvenile Justice & Family Issues
Corrections	Land & Resource Management
County Affairs	Licensing & Admin. Procedure
Criminal Jurisprudence	Local & Consent Calendars
Culture, Rec. & Tourism	Natural Resources
Defense and Veterans Affairs	Pensions
Economic and Small Bus. Development	Public Education
Elections	Public Health
Energy Resources	Redistricting
Environmental Regulation	Rules & Resolutions
General Investigating & Ethics	Special Purpose Districts
Government Transparency & Operation	State Affairs
Higher Education	Transportation
Homeland Security and Pub. Safety House Administration	Urban Affairs
Human Services	Ways & Means
Insurance	

Source: Texas House and Senate websites, http://www.house.state.tx.us/committees/welcome.htm;
http://www.senate.tx.us/75r/Senate/Commit.htm

Pro & Con   Annual v. Biennial Legislative Sessions

Over the course of the last 100 years, most states have moved from holding biennial legislative sessions, every other year, to holding annual legislative sessions. In 1918, only six states met annually and all the rest met biennially. By 1960, 19 states met annually and 31 states biennially. Today, 46 states meet annually and just four—Montana, Nevada, North Dakota, and Texas—meet biennially.

The National Conference of State Legislatures (NCSL) has laid out the arguments in favor of both annual and biennial legislative sessions. The arguments in favor of annual sessions are generally positive, those in favor of biennial sessions generally negative. Proponents of annual sessions argue that modern governance is complex and fast-paced. National initiatives must be addressed, oversight of the state executive must be ongoing, and the legislative process cannot work in fits and starts.

Proponents of biennial sessions argue that there are already too many laws and regulations, government is already too expensive, and legislators constantly in the state capital lose touch with their constituents. Moreover, the time between regular sessions can best be used for constituent service and interim study committees on key issues. Texans, or at least the Texas economic and political elite, has always taken this latter view.

When 46 of 50 states and all of the more populous ones (Nevada ranks 35th in population, Montana 44th, and North Dakota 48th) choose annual sessions, it probably makes sense to ask why. One of the biggest reasons seems to be economic forecasting and budgeting. Biennial budgeting requires economic forecasts going out 30 months, whereas annual budgeting requires forecasts going out 18 months. Moreover, the close connection between the state and federal levels of government, in which states get 35 to 40 percent of their revenue from the federal government, means that changes in federal programs can dramatically impact states.

Texas handles these potential difficulties by leaving the governor and the Legislative Budget Board (LBB), which is co-chaired by the lieutenant governor and the Speaker, with considerable budgetary discretion between regular legislative sessions. The governor can also call 30-day special sessions, and several of them in a row if needed, to manage special circumstances and dramatic changes. Texas citizens seem satisfied with biennial meetings because constitutional amendments calling for annual sessions were defeated five times between 1949 and 1975.

However, there is a middle ground adopted by 20 states. They hold a brief, 60- to 90-day, budget session in even-numbered years, and a longer, 150- to 180-day, regular legislative session in odd-numbered years. Exclusive focus on the budget in even-numbered years, with opportunities to make adjustments in odd-numbered years, might improve the budget process. Taking the budget out of the regular legislative session in odd-years would open the way for important substantive legislation and maybe even limit the end of biennial session logjam so characteristic of the current Texas legislative process.

What do you think? Should Texas follow most other states to annual sessions, stick to its biennial sessions, or look for a middle ground?

majority. The committees chaired by Democrats were generally of lesser importance and had Republican majorities to boot.

Speaker Straus appointed twenty-five Republicans and thirteen Democrats to chair standing committees. As in the Senate, the most important committees were reserved for Republican chairs and Republican majorities. The Democrats tapped to lead committees were either charter members of "the team" or were given marginal committees with light policy agendas.

Special or Temporary Committees

Interim committees
Legislative committees that work
in the interim between regular
legislative sessions to study issues,
prepare reports, and draft legislation.

The Texas legislature also employs various special or temporary committees. Conference committees, which are the most common and important of the special committees, will be discussed in detail later in the chapter. **Interim committees** are appointed to work during the interim between regular sessions or in preparation for a special session. They may be composed of the members of a standing committee or freshly formed to deal with a particular issue.

HOW A BILL BECOMES A LAW

Q4 How does a bill become a law in Texas?

The journey from bill introduction to final passage is long and arduous. In the 81st (2009) regular session, 7,419 bills (bills are proposed laws) were introduced into one or both chambers, and 1,459 passed. This approval rate of about 20 percent is a little lower than the 25 percent approval rate in past legislative sessions. In the 2011 legislative session, with unprecedented budget deficits looming. Just 5,795 bills were filed, and just 1,379 passed and were signed into law, for a pass rate of 24 percent. Filings remained low in 2013, with 5,868 bills filed, 1,437 passing, for a rate of 24.5 percent.[22] In the 84th regular session (2015), 6,276 bills were filed, 1,323 passed, for a pass rate of just 21 percent.

The Texas Constitution requires that a bill be read three times, on three separate days, before it is passed. This three-readings requirement is a centuries-old procedure designed to slow the legislative process and assure time for thoughtful consideration.[23] The Texas legislature's heavy workload, short 140-day regular session, and the general tumult of the legislative process go a long way toward defeating the goals of slow and thoughtful decision-making.

Introduction and Referral

Carrying a bill Carrying a bill
means to take responsibility for
seeing it successfully through the
legislative process.

Though the idea behind a bill can come from anyone, only an elected member can introduce a bill into the Texas legislature. A bill may be introduced into both houses simultaneously, or into either initially, though revenue bills must be introduced into the House first. The legislator that files the bill is called its sponsor and other legislators that sign on to support the bill are called co-sponsors. A bill's sponsor or a leading co-sponsor is often said to "carry" a bill. **Carrying a bill** means to be responsible for monitoring and facilitating the bill's progress through the many stages of the legislative process. To carry a bill requires endless conversations, horse trades, deals, and amendments to nudge the bill over each hurdle to final adoption. Texas allows pre-filing, meaning that a bill can be filed during the interim before a regular session, or during the first 60 days of the 140-day regular session. After the 60th day, only local bills affecting one city or county, emergency appropriations, or matters that the governor declares to be emergencies may be filed.

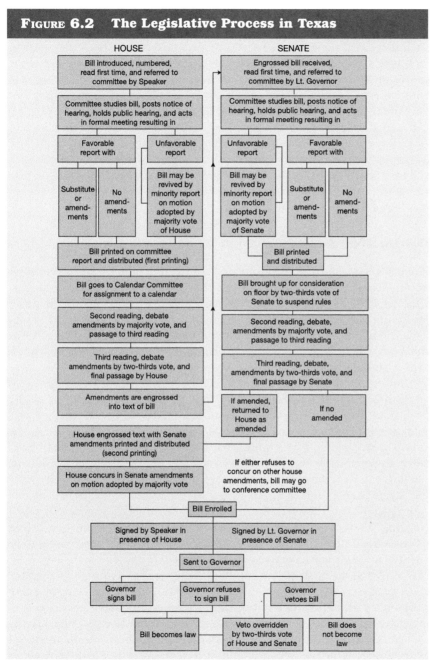

FIGURE 6.2   The Legislative Process in Texas

This diagram displays the sequential flow of a bill from the time it is introduced in the House of Representatives to final passage and transmittal to the governor. A bill introduced in the Senate would follow the same procedure in reverse. Students who have difficulty understanding this fairly complicated chart should pay close attention to the accompanying text.

Source: Texas Legislature Online. www.capitol.state.tx.us

Once a bill is filed, it is assigned a reference or tracking number, such as "H.B.1," or "S.B.1," for House Bill 1 or Senate Bill 1, respectively. Bills are assigned a number in the order in which they are filed, though it has become common for leaders to set aside the first few numbers for the most important bills of the session. After the bill has been filed and a number assigned, the clerk reads the bill (really just author, bill title, and number) for the first time and announces the committee to which the presiding officer has referred the bill.

The presiding officers have great discretion in selecting the committee to which a given bill will be referred. If the presiding officer approves of the bill, he may refer it to a friendly committee, chaired by a member of "the team," and instruct that it be treated positively. If he disapproves of the bill, he may refer it to a committee he knows will "pigeonhole" it. Two-thirds of bills introduced into the Texas legislature die in committee.

Committee Action

When a bill is referred to committee, it comes under the control of the committee chair. The committee chair sets the agenda for his or her committee, allocates the committee's staff resources, and determines to which issues the committee will dedicate its time and attention. If the committee chair buries a bill far down the committee's agenda, that bill is dead. If the chair puts a bill near the top of the committee's agenda, that bill will go through three major stages of committee consideration.[24]

The first stage of committee consideration is public hearings. While public hearings are not mandatory in the House, they are common, especially for major bills. Public hearings are mandatory in the Senate. Public hearings acknowledge the public's right to participate in the legislative process. The Texas Open Meetings Law requires that notice of hearings be posted five calendar days before the meeting in the House and one day before in the Senate. Senators can slow the committee process on a particular bill by requesting of the Senate Secretary or committee chair that they be notified in writing of a committee hearing 48 hours before it is scheduled. Such a request is called **"tagging"** the bill and is especially effective late in the session. Any citizen who wishes to attend the hearings may do so and any citizen who wishes to be heard may fill out a brief witness identification card and wait his or her turn.

Tagging Senators try to slow the legislative process on a particular bill by requesting 48 hours' notice before a committee hearing is held.

The second major stage of committee consideration is committee markup. During mark-up, the chairman leads the committee through a line-by-line consideration of the bill, revising and amending it where necessary. The original bill may have been drafted by an interest group, a bureaucrat, a paid lobbyist, or by the committee staff. The mark-up stage is where the committee members, guided by the wishes of the Speaker and committee chair, make the bill their own.

Following mark-up, the committee votes whether to approve the bill and pass it on to its parent body, or to disapprove it, thereby killing it for the remainder of the session. If the committee vote is favorable, the chair and committee staff draft a report which briefly describes the intent of the bill, the changes it makes in current law, the cost of implvementation, and the comptroller's certification that revenues are available to fund the bill should it become law. Bills that clear committee must then be scheduled for consideration on the floor.

Calendar Assignment

Both the House and Senate employ legislative calendars. **Legislative calendars** determine when and under what "rules" of debate bills come to the floor for final action. The House has the more formal and orderly calendaring process. Bills approved by the policy committees go either to the Calendars Committee or to the Local and Consent Calendars Committee. The Calendars Committee places the major bills of the session on the Emergency, Major State, and General State calendars. The Local and Consent Calendars Committee manages three calendars for local bills and various types of resolutions. The Calendar Committees control and coordinate traffic onto the House floor. The general goal is to move minor legislation onto and off the floor quickly to preserve time for the session's major bills. The Calendars Committee becomes increasingly important as the session winds down. Eighty percent of bills pass in the last ten days of the session, so it is the Calendars Committee's job, working closely with the leaders, to insure that the most important bills get to the floor in time for debate and approval. Every session ends with hundreds of bills waiting in the queue. The Calendars Committee's job is to make sure that that does not happen to the "must pass" bills, like the budget, school finance, or transportation funding.

The Senate employs a single calendar and a process that is quite different from the one used in the House. Formal Senate rules for bringing a bill to the floor, called "the regular order," are similar to the House rules. But for more than half a century, the Senate ignored the regular order to follow intended informal rules to promote collegiality, and consensus. Allan Shivers, lieutenant governor in the late 1940s, and governor for most of the 1950s, refined the Senate's calendar process to enhance his influence.[25] At the beginning of each legislative session, lieutenant governors instructed the Secretary of the Senate to place a minor bill with no meaningful support at the top of the calendar. With this **blocker bill** permanently in place, every subsequent bill had to come to the Senate floor under suspension of the rules, which required a two-thirds vote. A senator wishing to bring a bill to the floor had to consult with the lieutenant governor, secure the support of two-thirds of his or her colleagues, and file a "notice of intent" with the Secretary of the Senate.

Q5 How does the legislative process differ in the House and Senate?

Legislative calendars Lists of bills passed by committees but awaiting final action on the floor.

Blocker bill A minor bill placed at the top of the Senate calendar to block all other bills from coming to the floor before they have achieved broad support.

Eric Gay/AP/Corbis

Senator Kirk Watson, left, D-Austin, and Senator Royce West, right, D-Dallas, vote against starting debate on a contentious abortion measure late in the 2013 legislature session.

Shockingly, the Senate opened its 2009 session with a pitched partisan battle over its decades-old two-thirds rule for bringing a bill to the floor. Republicans had a nineteen to twelve majority in 2009, just short of two-thirds. Tommy Williams (R-Woodlands) proposed a one-time exemption from the two-thirds rule for a voter I.D. bill. Though Democrats howled, the rules were amended by simple majority vote. Senate Republicans then passed their bill but it died in the House. In 2011, Governor Perry declared Voter I.D. to be an emergency issue so it could be dealt with early in the session, the Senate again suspended its two-thirds rule to pass the bill, and the House eventually passed it as well. Many observers worried that the usually decorous Senate was tending toward the kind of partisan bitterness that often erupts in the House. Newly elected Lieutenant Governor Dan Patrick, a senator since 2008, campaigned on a promise to do away with the two-thirds rule. Patrick won in 2015 and won senate approval to change the two-thirds rule to a new three-fifths rule. The new rule, with Republicans in a 20 to 11 majority, allowed Republicans to move their agenda unobstructed.

As the legislature moves toward adjournment and time remaining in the session grows short, the management of the calendars by the presiding officers becomes increasingly important. The key bills, especially the state budget, have to be brought to the floor with enough time remaining to complete action. Bills not brought to the floor at least forty-eight hours prior to final adjournment are doomed.

Floor Action

When a bill reaches the floor of the House, it receives its second reading, and debate begins. The bill's sponsor or floor manager, oftentimes with other senior supporters, stands in the well of the House (down front) to describe the bill, urge support, and answer questions. The bill's manager gets twenty minutes at the beginning and at the close of debate. Other members are restricted to one ten-minute statement in favor of, or opposition to, the bill. Any member can offer an amendment to a bill, but a majority of members present and voting must approve for the amendment to be adopted.

When the debate concludes, the Speaker calls the vote. Proponents walk the aisles holding up one finger, urging a yes vote, while opponents walk the aisles holding up two fingers, urging a no vote. Members unfamiliar with the issue look to see whether their friends, partisans, or highly respected members are urging a yes or a no vote and follow their lead. If the vote is positive, the bill will be laid over to the next day, given a third reading (debate is uncommon on third reading because amendments require a two-thirds vote), and passed for a final time. To an outsider, the House floor often looks chaotic.

For a bill to reach the Senate floor, it requires the support of the lieutenant governor and three-fifths of the senators. During floor debates, senators speak standing at their desks, as frequently and as long as they like, before voting from their desks. Senate floor action has little of the tumult that characterizes floor action in the House.

Texas Senators, like their national counterparts, have the right to **filibuster**, or to speak continuously for as long as they wish, once they gain control of the floor. The filibuster is a devise to gain public attention, but, more importantly, to block action on a bill that the senator opposes vehemently. The Texas Senate record is held by former Senator Bill Meier (R-Hurst) who spoke for 43 hours in 1977 against a workman's compensation bill that he considered to be anti-business.[26] Still, filibusters are fairly uncommon in the Texas Senate, though the threat of a filibuster can get a senator attention they might not otherwise be able to achieve.

More recently, Senator Wendy Davis (D-Fort Worth) ran out the clock on the 2013 regular session with an 11-hour filibuster of a restrictive abortion bill. While Davis's filibuster was successful at least temporarily, Governor Perry and the Republican majorities in the Texas House and Senate had the last laugh, passing the bill in a special session just weeks later. Nonetheless, Senator Davis's filibuster catapulted her to national celebrity and into a 2014 run for governor.

Filibuster Senators can speak as long as they wish once they gain the floor, oftentimes to slow or defeat an objectionable bill.

Conference Committee

Even when bills are introduced simultaneously into both the House and the Senate, they seldom survive committee deliberation and floor action in identical form. In most cases, when differences between the House and Senate versions of the same bill are minor, one house concurs in, or accepts, the version passed by the other. Where differences are too important to ignore, they must be resolved. The **conference committee** is the device that legislatures use to resolve differences between House and Senate bills. All differences must be resolved and accepted by both houses before the bill can be sent to the governor for his or her signature.

In the Texas legislature, the Speaker and lieutenant governor each name five legislators to form a conference committee. These members usually are the bill's sponsors, the chairs of the committees that produced the bill, and other senior members with knowledge of the subject. Once the conference committee has completed its work, a committee report is drafted comparing the original House and Senate language on each point in disagreement to the new language proposed by the committee. At least three of the five conferees from each house must approve the report before it can be returned to the full House and Senate for their consideration.

Conference committees Committees composed of members of the House and Senate charged to resolve differences between the House and Senate versions of a bill.

Conference committees frequently do their work late in the session, as adjournment looms, and under great pressure. Though only 5 to 10 percent of the bills passed in the regular session go through the conference committee process, they are many of the most important bills of the session. When conference committees do reach agreement, those agreements are almost always ratified by both bodies. The 81st legislature (2009) sent 186 bills to conference committee and 159 of them were reported out and approved by the House and Senate. Similarly, the 82nd legislative session (2011) sent 116 bills to conference committee and 98 were reported out and approved by the House and Senate. During the 83rd legislature (2013), 93 bills were sent to conference committee and 87 of those were subsequently passed by both houses and sent to the governor for his signature.

TIMELINE: TEXAS LEGISLATIVE COMPENSATION

	1842	1845–1865	1866–1876	1876–1930	1930–1954
Salary					
Per Diem	$6 per day	$3 per day	$8 per day	$5 per day for 1st 60, $2 thereafter	$10 per day for 1st 120, $5 thereafter
Mileage		12 cents per mile	32 cents per mile		10 cents per mile

The Governor

The governor is involved in the legislative process throughout, though mostly as an adviser, coach, and cheerleader. Legislators know that the governor has a veto and that while he or she normally vetoes only about 1 percent of bills passed, they take his or her views into account to insure that their bill is not among the unfortunate few vetoed at the close of the term.

It should come as no surprise that tensions exist between the governor and the legislature. For eighteen months out of every two years, the governor is cock-of-the-walk in Austin. When the legislature comes into session, governors must struggle to maintain even a modicum of control over events. Governors usually hold their tongue and seek to work with the legislature, but sometimes their exasperation bursts forth. An exasperated President Sam Houston addressed the Texas Congress in early December 1842, saying, "since the commencement of legislation in Texas ... we find the proceedings of Congress characterized by selfishness and partiality. ... Its decline ... has been regular and more rapid than perhaps that of any country."[27] More recently, Governor John Connally, the state's chief executive from 1962 to 1968, described legislators this way:

> Individually, they're all great. I traveled the state. I was in their districts. I bragged on them. I worked with them. But as soon as the legislature convenes, they all come to Austin, where they're surrounded by lobbyists. They're constantly told how important and strong they are, and how valuable their service is. I suppose anybody in public office has more than their share of vanity – but you haven't seen anything until you've seen the combined arrogance and vanity of a legislature.[28]

In Chapter 7, we look at the office and role of governor in some detail.

REFORMING THE TEXAS LEGISLATURE

The Texas Constitution of 1876 was designed to limit and diffuse power. It did so by limiting the legislative session and setting legislative pay low enough to make the office unattractive to those not yet wealthy. In the nearly 140 years

1954–1960	1960–1975	1975–1991	1991–2011	2015
	$4,800 annually	$7,200 annually	No change	No change
$25 per day for 1st 120, none thereafter	$12 per day	$30 per day	Regular increases	$190 per day
				50 cents per mile

since the Constitution was approved, much has changed. Modern Texas is a large, populous, and complicated state facing myriad opportunities and challenges. To face them effectively, Texas needs a modern legislature.

Almost 54 years ago, two prominent political analysts of the day, the newspaperman Sam Kinch, Jr., and TCU historian Ben Proctor, described the difficult task of legislative reform this way:

> There is no simple way to approach reform of the Texas legislature. It is a task that must take into consideration the fact that 181 elected individuals are paid $4,800 a year to run a state government that costs more than $7 billion every two years to serve the needs of more than 11 million Texans. . . . During the regular session of 1971, the legislature introduced a total of 2,731 bills and passed about one-third of them.

Kinch and Proctor concluded that, "the constitution's restriction of a 140-day regular session of the Legislature every two years is patently ridiculous."[29]

Before proceeding to a discussion of potential reforms, let's simply update the quote from Kinch and Proctor to see where what was judged "patently ridiculous" in 1971 stands today. Instead of the $4,800 legislators made in 1971, today they make $7,200, but instead of the two-year cost of state government being $7 billion as it was in 1971, it was $200 billion in 2013. And instead of handling 2,731 bills as they did in 1971, the 2013 legislature handled more than twice as many, 5,868, in the same 140-day period. Clearly, the fact that something is "patently ridiculous" does not mean that it cannot go on for a very long time. Several potential reforms have been under discussion for decades.

First, Texas is the only one of the thirty-four largest states in the U.S. to still employ a biennial legislature. Oftentimes, the Texas legislature is so hard pressed in the closing days and hours of the session that critical business is left undone. The Texas Constitution should be amended to require annual, meaning yearly, rather than biennial sessions. Unlike California and New York, the Texas legislature might not need to meet year around, but it should meet annually and it should be able to stay in session until its most critical business has been completed.

Second, and this comes hard, Texas legislators should be paid more. Historically, southern states paid legislators little so that only "the better sort" could afford to serve. But Texas, at $7,200 a year plus *per diem*, remains among the lowest in the nation. Low pay means legislators must be wealthy, must have jobs that take them away from the public's business, or they must allow themselves to be kept by the lobby. Texas legislators should be paid in the range of $50,000 to $75,000, still well below California's $95,000, but enough to allow full attention to their duties. This, too, would require a constitutional amendment.

The powers of the Speaker and the lieutenant governor, the presiding officers of the Texas House and Senate, should be checked and the individual legislators should be empowered. This could be done simply by changing the House and Senate rules that are adopted at the beginning of each regular legislative session. The key change would be to limit the presiding officer's ability to define the number and jurisdiction of committees and name members to them each session. Rather, as in the U.S. Congress, members should have seniority in their committees. This would allow members to remain on committees from session to session once named to the committee and to grow in expertise and rise in influence. Somewhat weaker leaders and somewhat more secure members would, one hopes, restore a lost civility and balance to the Texas legislature.

And finally, the far too cozy relationship between lobbyists and legislators must be broken.[30] A 2006 study by the Austin-based Center for Public Integrity found that Texas had more legislators turned lobbyists, 70, than any other state. Florida was second with 60, Minnesota and Illinois had 50 each, and it trailed off from there. Moreover, allowing active legislators to mix their campaign and officeholder contributions and to dip into them to defray official expenses is an invitation to corruption. Neither should former members be able to continue spending from their campaign accounts once their final expenses have been cleared. One might also wonder whether members and former members who run afoul of the law should be able to retain their generous public pensions—as they do now.

Chapter Summary

The Texas legislature was once the preserve of white, male professionals. Most were lawyers, businessmen, and ranchers, so they tended to take a fairly conservative view of politics, government, and public policy. Though there are more women and minorities in the legislature than there once were, the low pay, uncertain schedule, and hectic pace keep expertise low and turnover high.

Though the population of Texas is about 45 percent Anglo today, the Texas legislature remains about two-thirds Anglo. Hispanics now comprise about 23 percent of the legislature's members, blacks about 10.5 percent, Asians about 2 percent, and women about 20 percent. Moreover, change has been slow. Since 2001, Anglo numbers are down about 7 percent, Hispanic and black numbers are up about 2 or 3 percent each, and Asian and female numbers have barely budged.

The presiding officers of the Texas legislature wield extraordinary power. The Speaker of the House and lieutenant governor in the Senate set the number of standing committees and their jurisdiction, appoint all of the committee chairs and most of the committee members, interpret and apply the rules, and preside over the conduct of business on the floor. Members seek to be on "the team," meaning to be among the presiding officer's recognized loyalists in order to receive favorable committee assignments and some modicum of influence.

The presiding officer's chief supporters chair the most important standing committees (especially those that handle the major bills), set the schedule for floor debate, and control the appropriations process. The Speaker and the lieutenant governor, working with and through their respective committee chairs and "teams," can usually manage the legislative process to produce the results they desire, or at least those that they find acceptable. Sometimes, however, the presiding officers cannot agree, will not compromise, and have to settle for the lesser satisfactions of blocking each other.

Finally, Texas is one of the few large states to maintain a hybrid legislature and the only state among the 34 largest states to have a legislature that meets only every other year. Over the past half century, several reforms have been advocated, though none have been adopted. Annual meetings of the legislature have been proposed many times, as has the idea of raising legislator pay well above current levels. Some have also suggested limiting the influence of the presiding officers and increasing the influence of members, especially senior members, by giving them seniority rights in their committee assignments.

Key Terms

Amateur legislatures 145	Legislative calendars 159
Biennial session 143	Legislative supremacy 139
Blocker bill 159	Popular sovereignty 139
Carrying a bill 156	Professional legislatures 145
Checks and balances 139	Regular session 143
Conference committees 161	Separation of powers 139
Filibuster 161	Standing committees 153
Hybrid legislatures 145	Tagging 158
Interim committees 156	"The team" 151

Review Questions

1. Assess how the low pay of Texas legislators effects who serves in that body.
2. Evaluate whether or not the powers of the presiding officers of the Texas House and Senate are too strong or too weak.
3. Distinguish between the roles played by the power committees and those played by the policy committees in the Texas House and Senate.
4. Trace the stages that a bill submitted to the Texas House or Senate goes through on the way to final passage.

5. Explain the merits and demerits of the two-thirds rule for bringing a bill to the Senate floor for consideration on final passage.

Suggested Readings

Nancy Baker Jones and Ruthe Winegarten, *Capitol Women: Texas Female Legislators, 1923–1999* (Austin, TX: University of Texas Press, 2000).

Jimmy Banks, *Gavels, Grit & Glory: The Billy Clayton Story* (Burnet, TX: Eakin Press, 1982).

Thomas Carsey, Richard Niemi, William Berry, Lynda Powell, and James Snyder, Jr., "State Legislative Elections, 1967–2003," *State Politics and Policy Quarterly* (2008), 8: 430–443.

Jason Casellas, "The Institutional and Demographic Determinants of Latino Representation," *Legislative Studies Quarterly* (2009), 34: 399–426.

Patrick L. Cox and Michael Phillips, *The House Will Come to Order* (Austin, TX: University of Texas Press, 2010).

Gerald Gamm and Thad Kousser, "Broad Bills or Particularistic Policy? Historical Patterns in American State Legislatures," *American Political Science Review* (2010), 104: 151–170.

Keith E. Hamm and Robert Hogan, "Campaign Finance Laws and Candidacy Decisions in State Legislative Elections," *Political Research Quarterly* (2008), 61: 458–467.

Karen Olsson, *Waterloo: A Novel* (New York: Farrar, Straus, and Giroux, 2005).

Alan Rosenthal, *Engines of Democracy: Politics and Policymaking in State Legislatures* (Washington, D.C.: CQ Press, 2008).

Thomas M. Spencer, *The Legislative Process, Texas Style* (Pasadena, TX: San Jacinto College Press, 1981).

Peverill Squire, *The Evolution of American Legislatures: Colonies, Territories, and States, 1619–2009* (Ann Arbor: University of Michigan Press, 2012).

Web Resources

1. http://www.ncsl.org
   National Conference of State Legislatures.

2. http://www.capitol.state.tx.us
   Texas legislature's website.

3. http://www.house.state.tx.us
   Texas House of Representatives' website.

4. http://www.senate.state.tx.us
   Texas Senate's website.

5. http://www.lrl.state.tx.us
   Texas legislature's Reference Library.

6. http://www.capitol.tx.us/capitol/legproc/summary.htm
   Summary of Texas Legislative precedents.

Chapter 7

THE GOVERNOR AND THE EXECUTIVE BRANCH

ELEANOR KITZMAN AND WHAT CONSUMERS NEED TO KNOW

Oftentimes, it is difficult to get a good sense of what government actually does. Everyone knows that judges decide court cases, legislators pass laws, and governors oversee the administrative activities of government. But what does an insurance commissioner do and what difference is it likely to make to the average citizen and consumer of insurance products. Insurance is pervasive—auto, life, home, health, liability, etc.—and is more important the older you get and more you have to protect.

Between 2011 and 2013, the Texas Commissioner of Insurance was Eleanor Kitzman. A native of Texas and a lawyer, Kitzman worked in the insurance industry for two decades before becoming insurance commissioner in South Carolina, where she lost a race for lieutenant governor in 2010 before accepting the post of insurance commissioner in Texas in July 2011. But what does a Commissioner of Insurance actually do and how does that affect insurance companies on the one hand and consumers of insurance products on the other? Basically, the Texas Department of Insurance, pursuant to laws passed by the legislature and signed by the governor, writes rules and regulations that outline the content and coverage of insurance policies and establishes procedures for setting and reviewing prices for those products.

In what became a highly contentious example of how insurance regulation works and sometimes does not work, the Department of Insurance, under Mike Geeslin, Kitzman's predecessor, drafted rules regarding what the insurance industry calls "balance billing." Balance billing can occur when a consumer with health insurance goes to a hospital that is "in-network," meaning approved by the health insurance company for use by its policy-holders, and ends up seeing a particular doctor who is not "in-network" for the policy-holder. In other words, the doctor is a staff member of the hospital but has not agreed to the payment levels approved by the insurance company. The patient might be surprised to receive a bill for the balance between what the insurance company paid and the doctor charged. What role might the Department of Insurance play here?

Commissioner Geeslin developed rules requiring insurance companies to disclose online which providers are parts of their network so consumers can research them ahead of time and make sure they are staying in-network. When Commissioner Kitzman arrived, she withdrew and proposed to rewrite the balance billing regulations, saying "I just don't believe that consumers, the average consumer, is really going to be able to use that information in a meaningful way." Consumer advocates howled, of course, and Republican Senator Bob Deuell, a physician, said, "There are many senators, Republican and Democratic, that are concerned that she's a little too pro-insurance company."[1] Kitzman left office, after nearly two years, when the Texas Senate declined to confirm her appointment in 2013.

It surely would drive some additional costs into the insurance industry to provide more information to consumers, but how can consumers avoid high out-of-network charges if they have no easy way to know who is in-network and who is not? Do you think state regulators should lean toward protecting insurance companies from additional costs or insuring consumers have all the information they need to make informed decisions?

Focus Questions

Q1 What is the governor's role in Texas politics?

Q2 What are the governor's formal and informal powers?

Q3 What other statewide elected officials share power with the governor?

Q4 What roles do elected and appointed boards and commissions play in Texas?

Q5 What reforms do analysts propose for the executive branch?

The traditional political culture of Texas and the South intends to leave political power and initiative in the hands of the social and economic elites and to make political officials, including governors, their servants. J. David Woodard, a contemporary scholar of southern politics, described the expectations regarding governors and lesser public officials in the South in this way,

> The general populace of the southern states accepted the leadership of their economic and social superiors, and the governor was . . . expected to provide institutional care of the state's businesses in agreement with the ruling elites. . . .

Executives did not expect to be problem-solvers; instead they had more ceremonial and ambassadorial duties.[2]

Only two governors in Texas history wielded great power in office: one rejected it and is a hero in Texas history, the other seized it and is the goat in Texas history. Sam Houston, during the early 1840s in his second term as president of Texas, faced bankruptcy and two Mexican invasions by his old foe, Santa Anna. The Texas Congress, swept by equal measures of panic and patriotism, passed a War Bill putting Houston at the head of the army with dictatorial powers for a retaliatory invasion of Mexico. The bill empowered Houston to conscript one-third of the population for war service and to sell ten million acres of land to pay for the war. Houston calmly considered the War Bill and then vetoed it for awarding him unconstitutional powers.[3] E.J. Davis, the Reconstruction governor of Texas after the Civil War, on the other hand, engineered a constitution that gave him near dictatorial powers and he used them. From his perspective and that of his Republican Party government, his great powers were wielded to insure the freedom, education, and opportunity of former slaves, but conservative white Texans took it as rank oppression and moved to dismantle it as soon as they were able. When whites returned to control of Texas politics in the mid-1870s, they wrote a new constitution dramatically limiting gubernatorial authority.

The Texas Constitution of 1876 limited executive authority and dissipated what remained across a half dozen senior elected officials and dozens, now literally hundreds, of agencies, boards, commissions, and other advisory and consultative bodies. The executive branch of Texas state government is a plural executive in which the governor must share power with an independently elected lieutenant governor, attorney general, comptroller of public accounts, land commissioner, and, since 1907, agriculture commissioner, and scores of independent agencies, boards, and commissions.[4]

Despite the constitutional limitations on the governor's powers, most Texans still assume that the governor is the chief executive and natural leader of Texas state government. In a sense, he is, but he is not the undisputed leader because the tools he has to make his leadership felt are modest. The Texas Constitution and state statutes create a plural executive with power and responsibility spread diffusely through the system. If the Governor of Texas is to lead, it must be by political skill and force of personality.

For most of the last century of Texas history there was at least as much force of personality as political skill on display in the governor's office. Texas governors James Stephen Hogg (1891–95), James Ferguson (1915–17), and W. Lee O'Daniel (1939–41) come easily to mind. Hogg is credited both with political skill and a larger than life personality, but Ferguson and O'Daniel rose and fell, won and lost, on the force of their personalities.

Governor Jim Hogg earned a permanent place in Texas political lore by naming his daughter "Ima" and claiming that he did not see the inevitable result—Ima Hogg—until it was too late. Despite Governor Hogg's unfortunate sense of humor, he was a skilled politician. He created the Texas Railroad

Commission, which we will learn more about below, and otherwise sought to limit the free rein previously enjoyed by the railroads and other corporate interests.

Governor James Ferguson, a small town banker, campaigned as "Farmer Jim" to strengthen his connection to rural voters. Jim Ferguson did try to benefit the common people by providing financial relief to tenant farmers, improving farm-to-market roads, and providing free textbooks to the public schools, but he did not forget to benefit himself along the way. Early in his second term, "Farmer Jim" was accused of embezzling state funds, impeached, convicted, and removed from office. Impeachment made him ineligible to hold state office in the future. Undeterred, Jim convinced his wife, Miriam "Ma" Ferguson, to run for governor on the slogan "two governors for the price of one." With "Pa" at her side, "Ma" Ferguson served two terms, 1925–27 and 1933–35, as Governor of Texas. "Ma" and "Pa" Ferguson kept Texas politics in an entertaining turmoil for two decades, but their political accomplishments were relatively few.

W. Lee "Pappy" O'Daniel had no discernible political agenda and left public life after a decade as governor and U.S. senator with no major and few minor political accomplishments. "Pappy" was a flour salesman, a radio personality, and leader of the "Hillbilly Boys"—his radio and campaign band. "Pappy" campaigned on "the ten commandments and the golden rule." Texans expect little from state government and "Pappy" gave them just what they expected—along with some country wisdom and a song.

The great mid-20th-century political scientist and student of southern politics, V.O. Key, in his 1949 classic, *Southern Politics*, described Hogg as "the greatest governor of modern Texas history." Key was more ambivalent about "Pa" Ferguson and absolutely disdainful of "Pappy" O'Daniel. About O'Daniel, Key wrote, "That by his skill in selling flour over the radio a man could become governor and United States Senator is in itself an eloquent commentary on the one-party system. . . . Attention-getting antics substituted for an organized politics."[5]

Despite the limitations of the office, the title Governor of Texas still has a mesmerizing effect on both Texas politicians and the public. Describing the role of governor in the century following the adoption of the Constitution of 1876, T.R. Fehrenbach, the leading mid-20th-century Texas historian, wrote, "Ironically, the governor continued to be thought of as the leader and the focus of state politics, because most Texans failed to see the true state of affairs. The clearest indication, however, was that in Texas men who preferred power to local prestige went to Washington."[6] Fehrenbach is obviously thinking about John Nance Garner, Sam Rayburn, and Lyndon Johnson. But James Reston, the biographer of Texas Governor John Connally, highlights an equally important point when he writes that, "To be governor of Texas remained the ultimate dream of most true-blooded Texas politicians."[7] For example, in 1956, Price Daniel gave up a seat in the U.S. Senate to run for governor, saying he would "rather be governor of Texas than President of the United States."[8] Daniel got his wish and served as governor from 1957 to 1963. More recently,

U.S. Senator Kay Bailey Hutchison thought about running for governor in 2006 and, when Rick Perry, after serving ten years, did not step aside, she challenged him in 2010. Perry defeated her easily and as her four decades of public service came to an end, she lamented, "I love the Senate, but I always wanted to be governor, and I know I would have been a governor for all Texans."[9]

In this chapter, we analyze both the limitations and the allure of the Office of Governor of Texas and the executive branch that he or she—sort of—leads. The Texas Constitution of 1876 created a plural executive of five statewide elected officials: the governor, lieutenant governor, attorney general (AG), comptroller of public accounts, and land commissioner. Each statewide elected official has independent constitutional powers and responsibilities. Constitutional amendments and statutes also mandate that the agriculture commissioner and the members of the Railroad Commission be elected state-wide. Members of the State Board of Education (SBE) are elected in districts across the state. The governor must work with these elected officials, but he does not control them.[10]

THE GOVERNOR

Now we explore the structure of the Office of Governor, the qualifications required to hold the office, and the formal and informal powers of the office. Despite a paucity of formal powers, the governor is the focal point of public and media attention. He cannot always determine outcomes, but he has formal and informal powers that allow him to set the public agenda of the state, lead the public and political discussion, and nudge the process toward desired outcomes. Finally, we ask what reforms might strengthen and improve the performance of the executive branch of Texas state government. Though being Governor of Texas may be frustrating at times, it is not a bad job. It pays $150,000 a year and the perks include a newly restored mansion in Austin, a fleet of cars and planes (drivers and pilots included), and reimbursement for official travel, business, and entertainment expenses. A staff of 266 serves the governor's personal and political needs.

Q1 What is the governor's role in Texas politics?

Despite the nice salary and perks, until recently, job security had been uncertain.[11] During the first century of Texas statehood, no governor was elected to more than two two-year terms. In the 1950s and 1960s, governors were commonly elected to three two-year terms. But after the term was length-ened to four years in 1974, governors had difficulty being re-elected. George W. Bush was the first Texas governor to be elected to consecutive four-year terms in 1994 and 1998, though he resigned in the middle of his second term to become president.

Lieutenant Governor Rick Perry succeeded Bush as governor on December 21, 2000. Governor Perry was elected to a full four-term of his own in 2002 and re-elected in 2006 and 2010. He was the longest serving governor in Texas history when he declined to stand for re-election in 2014. Rick Perry has led a charmed political life. He switched from Democrat to Republican in 1989,

Texas Attorney General and candidate for governor before an appreciative 2014 Texas GOP convention audience in Fort Worth.

just as the Republicans were coming to majority status. After eight years as Agriculture Commissioner, Perry defeated the well-respected Democrat Comptroller John Sharp in 1998 to become lieutenant governor under George W. Bush. Perry became governor when George W. Bush went to Washington and held the office through three re-election campaigns. Thirty-six states impose term limits on their governors, but Texas does not.[12]

In 2014, Texas Attorney General Greg Abbott had a clear path to the Republican gubernatorial nomination. Abbott's tenure as Attorney General was highlighted by firm opposition to what conservatives call federal government overreach. Defending Texas's interests against the federal government made him a Tea Party favorite, even though, running essentially unopposed in the Republican primary, he ran a careful campaign. Abbott won the governorship easily over Democrat Wendy Davis, a Texas state senator from Fort Worth.

Formal Qualifications

Article IV of the Texas Constitution stipulates that the governor "be at least thirty years of age, a citizen of the United States, and shall have resided in this State at least five years immediately preceding

TABLE 7.1	The Texas Governor and His Peers					
Name	State	Salary	Staff	Term	Consecutive Terms Allowed	Campaign Cost ($ millions)
Jerry Brown	California	$173,987	185	4 yrs	2	$231
Rick Perry	**Texas**	**$150,000**	**266**	**4 yrs**	–	**$103**
Andrew Cuomo	New York	$179,000	180	4 yrs	–	$40
Rick Scott	Florida	$130,273	325	4 yrs	2	$23
Tom Corbett	Pennsylvania	$187, 256	68	4 yrs	2	$71
Patrick Quinn	Illinois	$177,412	130	4 yrs	–	$35
John Kasich	Ohio	$148,886	60	4 yrs	2	$34
Rick Snyder	Michigan	$159,300	62	4 yrs	2	$50
Pat McCrory	North Carolina	$141,265	68	4 yrs	2	$17
Nathan Deal	Georgia	$139,339	56	4 yrs	2	$29

Source: *The Book of the States, 2013*, vol. 45 (Lexington, KY: Council of State Governments, 2013), pp. 148, 154, 157.

Rex C. Curry/AP/Corbis

his election." These, obviously, are minimum qualifications. Voters have more than these minimum qualifications in mind when they think about who truly is qualified to be Governor of Texas.

Informal Qualifications

All but a very few Texas governors have been wealthy, middle-aged, white, protestant, professional men. Most have been wealthy ranchers, businessmen, or lawyers. Even as Texas rapidly evolved from rural and agricultural to urban and industrial after World War II, having ranching roots seemed a prerequisite to being governor of Texas. Allan Shivers in the 1950s, John Connally in the 1960s, Bill Clements in the 1970s and 1980s, and, less convincingly, George W. Bush in the 1990s, all cultivated the rancher image. The real deal was Dolph Briscoe, governor of Texas from 1973 to 1979. The Briscoe family arrived in Texas in 1832 and Andrew Briscoe led a company of men in the Battle of San Jacinto. Dolph Briscoe's father moved the family to Uvalde in South Central Texas in 1910. Eventually, the Briscoe family controlled 600,000 acres, making them one of the largest landowners in the state. Dolph Briscoe served four terms in the Texas House, 1949 to 1957, before returning to business and ranching fulltime. Briscoe was the kind of successful Anglo ranching and business leader that Texans looked to lead the state through most of the 20th century.

Texas has had two female governors, Miriam (Ma) Ferguson (1925–27 and 1933–35) and Ann Richards (1990–94), but no minority governors. All but two Texas governors have been protestant. Our two Catholic governors offer the same interesting story. Frank Lubbock was a Civil War governor of Texas (1861–1863). Long before that, he was a young man in love. At 19, the future governor courted 16-year-old Adele Barron. She was of French Creole ancestry and Catholic. Adele agreed to marry Frank when he agreed to convert to Catholicism so they could be married in the church. Frank Lubbock, being a wise man, remained a Catholic throughout his long marriage. Greg Abbott, like Lubbock, was a marital convert to Catholicism and, we assume, also a young man in love.

Formal Powers

Unlike most other governors, the Governor of Texas does not prepare the state budget for submission to the legislature, nor does he appoint most of the other top administrators. On the other hand, the Texas Constitution and statutes do award the governor some important executive, budgetary, legislative, judicial, and military powers.

Executive Powers. The Texas Constitution describes the governor as the state's "Chief Executive Officer." The governor does have some of the powers of a chief executive. The governor's **appointment power** extends to a number of senior officials, including the secretary of state; the Adjutant General; the

Q2 What are the governor's formal and informal powers?

Appointment power The Texas Constitution and statutes empower the governor, often with the approval of two-thirds of the Senate, to appoint many senior government officials.

commissioners of education, insurance, health and human services; and the executive director of the department of commerce. Texas governors also make nearly 2,500 appointments during each four-year term to fill and keep filled about 1,900 seats on 275 independent agencies, boards, and commissions.[13] Most such appointments are to staggered six-year terms. Most gubernatorial appoints require approval by a two-thirds vote of the Senate, so a wise governor checks with interested senators before making a nomination. Gubernatorial nominees rarely are rejected by the Senate, though Perry did lose two high-profile nominees in each of the 2009 and 2011 legislative sessions and another in 2013. Perry's total appointments reached 8,149 according to the Legislative Reference Library.

Historically, once appointed, members of agencies, boards, and commissions have been highly independent because they are very difficult to remove. Governors can dismiss members of their personal staff at will, but they can remove persons that they appoint to agencies, boards, and commissions only with the approval of two-thirds of the Senate, and they cannot remove the

TABLE 7.2   Recent Governors of Texas

Name	Party/Home	Term	Occupation	Previous Office
Allan Shivers	D-Port Arthur	1949–57	Law	Texas Senate Lt. Governor
Price Daniel	D-Liberty	1957–63	Law/Ranching	Texas House Attorney General U.S. Senate
John Connally	D-Floresville	1963–69	Law/Business	Secretary of the Navy Secretary of the Treasury
Preston Smith	D-Lubbock	1969–73	Business	Texas House Texas Senate Lt. Governor
Dolph Briscoe	D-Uvalde	1973–79	Rancher	Texas House
Bill Clements	R-Dallas	1979–83	Business	Deputy Secretary of Defense
Mark White	D-Houston	1983–87	Law	Secretary of State Attorney General
Bill Clements	R-Dallas	1987–91	Business	See above
Ann Richards	D-Austin	1991–95	Teacher/Politician	Travis County Commissioners Court State Treasurer
George W. Bush	R-Midland	1995–2000	Business	None
Rick Perry	R-Austin	2000–present	Farmer/Politician	Texas House Agriculture Commissioner Lt. Governor
Grey Abbott	R-Houston	2015–present	Law/Politician	Texas Supreme Court Attorney General

Source: Legislative Reference Library of Texas. See http://www.lrl.state.tx.us/lesls/leaders/govbio.html

William P. "Bill" Clements was the first Republican Governor of Texas since Reconstruction. Clements was born on April 13, 1917, in Highland Park, an exclusive enclave within Dallas. But his father lost his job and much of his wealth in the Great Depression of the 1930s, so Clements had to go to work early. He attended Southern Methodist University in Dallas, where he studied petroleum engineering and played football, but did not graduate. Instead, he returned to work in the oil fields and then after serving in the Army Corps of Engineers during World War II, he founded the Southeastern Drilling Company, called SEDCO, in 1947.

SEDCO started with two old rigs, but Clements built it into the world's leading offshore drilling company. Clements took SEDCO into the deep Gulf of Mexico and then around the world, pioneering the technology and technique of deep water drilling. Clements sold SEDCO to Schlumberger in 1984, though his attention had been shifting from business to public service for more than a decade. Despite selling his company, Clements always maintained the persona of the no-nonsense, blunt speaking bottom-line businessman in public service.

Bill Clements entered public service as Deputy Secretary of Defense, the number two man and day-to-day operations manager, in the Nixon and Ford administrations from 1971 to 1977. He brought his businessman's instinct for modernization, analysis, and best practices to the Pentagon. He left the Pentagon determined to return to Texas and run for governor. Most analysts thought the campaign quixotic. Texas had not elected a Republican governor since E.J. Davis in 1869, but Clements brought the same drive and determination to the 1978 gubernatorial campaign as he had earlier brought to SEDCO and the Pentagon.

As the 1978 race got underway, Democrats were confident. Attorney General John Hill, having dispatched three-term Governor Dolph Briscoe in the primary, assumed that the toughest contest was behind him. In fact, Bill Clements, spending more than $7 million of his own money, simply outworked Hill, beating him by just 17,000 votes out of about 2.4 million cast. As governor, Clements faced an overwhelmingly Democratic legislature with which he clashed frequently. In a weak economy, Clements was defeated for re-election in 1982 by Mark White, the Democratic Attorney General, but in an even weaker economy, Clements came back to defeat White in 1986. Clements' second term was plagued by a deep recession, which forced him to accept tax increases demanded by the legislature, and an SMU football scandal in which he had played an important role—but he remains a Texas legend, why?

Not only was Bill Clements the first Republican elected governor of Texas in modern times, he brought his businessman's focus on organization building to state politics. Despite facing large Democratic majorities throughout his governorships, he used his endorsement and appointment powers to create a generation of young Republicans who got their first experience in government under him. Texas governors appoint about 2,500 people to agencies, boards, and commissions each four-year term, as well as hundreds of judges to district and appellate courts. Before Clements, Republicans never had access to these positions, or they had to pose as conservative Democrats if they wanted to win appointments. With a Republican governor, long-time Republicans and conservatives converting to the Republican Party looked to Clements for patronage and promotion. That is why, when Clements died at 94 in 2011, Perry called him "the father of the modern-day Texas Republican Party."

appointees of previous governors at all. This limited removal power makes it difficult for Texas governors to control bureaucrats and guide policymaking and program implementation.

Rick Perry's long tenure in office, fourteen years when he completed his last term, highlighted the importance of the appointment power. As mentioned above, most appointees serve six-year terms, so a governor serving one four-year term has the opportunity to replace most but not all of them. A governor serving two consecutive four-year terms—and Perry is the only one in the state's history—would have the opportunity to fill every appointive position in Texas government. Perry served fourteen years, so he had the opportunity to fill every position twice. More importantly, he had the opportunity to identify, develop, and reward talent—as he saw it—throughout Texas state government. Few serve in high appointed office in Texas today that did not play on team-Perry.[14] Governer Abbott's appointees will only slowly replace the Perry people.

Governors work hard to expand their authority, but others work just as hard to limit and check it. In 2007, Governor Perry argued that the Texas Constitution's declaration that the governor is the "Chief Executive Officer of the State" allowed him to direct state agencies by "executive order." Perry's spokesman, Robert Black, said "it's the governor's job to provide leadership and direction to the executive branch of government . . . . The governor's ability to lead this branch is inherent in the office." Governor Perry issued executive orders requiring that public schools spend at least 65 percent of state funds in the classroom, speeding up administrative review of coal plant permits, and requiring that sixth-grade girls be vaccinated against the human papillomavirus (HPV).

Others read the Texas Constitution differently. Steve Bickerstaff, former director of constitutional research for the Texas Legislative Council, said "an executive order is a statement by the Governor of Texas about what he thinks is in the best interest of the state. But he can't issue an order and tell that agency or hearing examiner that, 'you have to do this.'"[15] Interest groups, the courts, and the legislature all took the same view, arguing that the Constitution denied the governor such sweeping unilateral powers. This is classic American political theory—separation of powers and checks and balances—it is just that the Governor of Texas is easier to check than most other federal and state executives.

Budgetary Powers. In forty-six states, the governor has a major role in drafting the state's budget.[16] Not so in Texas. Article IV, section 9, of the Texas Constitution requires the governor to submit a **budget message** and an estimate of revenue needs to the legislature at the commencement of its regular session. Traditionally, governors followed their estimate of revenue needs with a detailed spending plan. In recent years, governors "have tended to submit either general outlines or no separate budget at all."[17]

While the governor has little power on the front end of the budgetary process, he has some on the back end. Like most U.S. governors, the Governor of Texas has a **line-item veto**. This means that once the budget is adopted by

Budget message The governor is required by law to address the legislature on budget matters in the first thirty days of each regular session.

Line-item veto The power to strike out or veto individual items in the state budget without striking down the whole budget.

LET'S COMPARE   GOVERNOR'S INSTITUTIONAL POWERS

Gubernatorial power flows from a number of sources, including the formal authority of the office, the political environment of the state, and the personal attributes of the governor. In Texas, the formal powers of the governor are among the weakest in the nation, but Rick Perry is seen as a strong governor. How can this be?

First, the data below comes from a comparison of the formal or institutional powers of the 50 U.S. state governors that now retired Professor Thad Beyle of the University of North Carolina, Chapel Hill, has made since the 1970s. In later years, Beyle brought on co-authors, including Margaret Ferguson, who have continued and updated his work. Institutional power is measured on a 5 (high) to 1 (low) scale on six elements—(1) unitary to plural executive, (2) open re-election to limited terms, (3) appointive power, (4) budget power, (5) veto power, and (6) party control. The institutional power rating is an average of the five-point scale ratings across the six dimensions. The Massachusetts governorship, at 4.3, is the strongest in the nation and the Rhode Island governorship, at 2.3, is the weakest.

Texas, at 2.8, ranks among the weaker governorships in the nation on institutional powers. Governors of Texas are weakened by the fact that they work within a plural executive structure, have limited appointment power in relation to high officials, and limited control over the budget process. The Texas governor has somewhat more institutional power through the veto, unlimited re-election opportunities, and the unified party control of the state. Overall, just seven states have weaker governorships than Texas, though five more states are tied with Texas at 2.8.

So what made Rick Perry seem like a strong governor if his formal powers did not support strength? Three things were critical. One was longevity, tenure-potential in the language of Beyle and Ferguson. Perry assumed the governorship when George W. Bush went to Washington and then he won three full terms on his own. You could not look past him. Two was and remains Republican Party domination of the state. No statewide elected official and neither house of the state legislature opposed his agenda. And three was the appointment power. Even though Perry worked within a plural executive system, he appointed 7,000 people to hundreds of agencies, boards, and commissions. As a result, governors of Texas have the opportunity to build more influence than their formal powers would suggest.

Massachusetts 4.3	New York 3.7	Connecticut 3.4	Kentucky 3.2	New Hampshire 2.8
Maryland 4.2	Mississippi 3.7	Maine 3.3	Colorado 3.1	Tennessee 2.8
New Jersey 4.0	Utah 3.6	Montana 3.3	Nebraska 3.1	**Texas 2.8**
Washington 4.0	Alaska 3.5	Wisconsin 3.3	Florida 3.1	Arkansas 2.7
Illinois 3.9	New Mexico 3.5	Delaware 3.3	Georgia 3.0	South Carolina 2.7
Hawaii 3.9	Kansas 3.5	Arizona 3.3	Nevada 3.0	Vermont 2.6
North Dakota 3.8	Wyoming 3.5	Virginia 3.3	California 2.9	Oregon 2.5
Ohio 3.8	West Virginia 3.4	Indiana 3.3	Idaho 2.8	North Carolina 2.5
Michigan 3.8	Pennsylvania 3.4	Alabama 3.3	Louisiana 2.8	Oklahoma 2.4
South Dakota 3.8	Minnesota 3.4	Iowa 3.2	Missouri 2.8	Rhode Island 2.3

Source: **Virginia Gray, Russell L. Hanson, and Thad Kousser,** *Politics in the American States: A Comparative Analysis,*
10th ed. (Washington, D.C.: CQ Press, 2013), pp. 225–226.

the legislature and submitted for approval, the governor can veto individual items in the budget without vetoing the whole budget. Moreover, legislators know that the governor has a line-item veto at the end of the process, so they listen to him throughout the process.[18]

Legislative Powers. The Governor of Texas enjoys four main legislative powers. These are the message power, emergency power, session power, and veto power. First, the Texas Constitution requires the governor to deliver a **State of the State message** at the beginning of each regular legislative session. This message gives the governor an opportunity to lay out an agenda for the session and to focus the attention of the public and the legislators on that agenda.[19] In 2011, as the state faced large budget deficits, Governor Perry used his State of the State message to rally his small government troops, saying "Now the mainstream media and big-government interest groups are doing their best to convince us that we're facing a budget Armageddon. Texans don't believe it, and they shouldn't, because it's not true. Are we facing tough choices? Of course, but we can overcome them by setting priorities."[20] The legislature followed his lead.

Second, the governor is empowered to identify "emergency items" for the legislature's early attention. Emergency items are the only issues that can be brought to a final vote during the first 60 days of the regular session. Other issues can be introduced, committee hearings can be held, and bills amended, but they cannot be passed until after the 60 day mark. By identifying an

Governor	Term	Bills Vetoed	No. of Special Sessions
Allan Shivers (D)	1949–57	89	2
Price Daniel (D)	1957–63	42	8
John Connally (D)	1963–69	104	2
Preston Smith (D)	1969–73	93	6
Dolph Briscoe (D)	1973–79	71	3
Bill Clements (R)	1979–83	78	3
Mark White (D)	1983–87	95	5
Bill Clements (R)	1987–91	113	8
Ann Richards (D)	1991–95	62	4
George W. Bush (R)	1995–2000	97	0
Rick Perry (R)	2000–14	301	12
Abbott (R)	2015–	42	0

TABLE 7.3   BILLS VETOED AND SPECIAL SESSIONS CALLED BY RECENT TEXAS GOVERNORS

Source: Legislative Reference Library of Texas, *Texas Legislative Sessions and Years*. See http://www.lrl.state.tx.us/legis/sessionYears.html. Bills Vetoed 1860–2012. See http://www.lrl.state.tx.us/legis/vetoes/lrlhome.cfm

issue as an "emergency item," the governor can give it publicity and early momentum.

Third, once the biennial regular session is over, the governor can call the legislators back to Austin for a **special session**. The governor controls the timing and the agenda for special sessions. Issues not included in the governor's "call" for the special session cannot be taken up. Hence, the governor usually issues a narrow call, requiring the legislators to deal with his key issues first, before broadening the call to allow other issues to be considered. Special sessions of the legislature can last no more than thirty days, but the governor can call two or three special sessions in a row if need be.

Special session If the legislature does not complete its business in the regular session, the governor can call one or more thirty-day special sessions.

Finally, the governor wields both a regular and a line-item veto, either of which can be threatened or actually employed. During a regular or special session, the governor can try to shape the development of a bill by threatening a **veto**. Governor Dolph Briscoe noted in his autobiography that, "The governor's authority to veto any law passed by the legislature is an extremely strong tool for influencing the direction of a bill while it is being legislated. . . . Of course, the veto is a negative power, but the threat of a veto can be a positive power if the governor uses it to create an opportunity to negotiate with the sponsors."[21]

Veto The governor is empowered to veto or strike down acts of the legislature. A veto can be overridden by a two-thirds vote of both houses of the legislature, but it rarely happens.

Once the legislature passes a bill, the constitution gives the governor ten days to decide whether to sign or veto the bill. He gets an additional twenty days if the legislature adjourns during the initial ten days. Moreover, as we saw above, the governor has a line-item veto that allows him to strike out particular budgetary items without striking down the whole budget. The governor's regular and line-item veto powers are his greatest sources of influence over the legislature.

Formally, a governor's veto can be overridden by a two-thirds vote of both houses of the Texas legislature. But this rarely happens because most major bills are passed so late in the session that the legislature is adjourned and the legislators are gone before the governor announces his vetoes. Governor Abbott vetoed 42 bills in the wake of the 2015 legislative session. Of the 1,947 vetoes cast by Texas governors since 1876, only twenty-six have been overridden by the legislature, none since 1979.

Judicial Powers. Though the Texas Constitution requires that state judges be elected, the governor is empowered to fill judicial vacancies at the level of district judge and above by appointment. Like other gubernatorial appointments, interim judicial appointments require the concurrence of two-thirds of the Texas Senate. Half of Texas judges first reach the bench by appointment. Once the term of their appointment ends, they must stand for election to a new term, but they have the advantage of running as incumbents.

Beyond the initial selection of many of the state's judges, the governor has few judicial powers. Though many state governors have

Who Knew?

Governor Perry rejected two-thirds of the clemency recommendations made by his own appointees on the Texas Board of Pardons and Paroles.

Clemency Some governors have the power to forgive or lessen the punishment for criminal infractions by granting pardons, paroles, or commutations.

an independent **clemency** power, the Governor of Texas does not. In Texas, the governor acts in response to recommendations from the seven-member Texas Board of Pardons and Paroles. Once the board acts, the governor has the power to approve or reject their recommendations on pardons, paroles, and sentence reductions. The governor can grant one thirty-day reprieve in death penalty cases.

Military Powers. The Governor of Texas has modest military powers. In the normal course of events, the governor appoints the Adjutant General to command the Texas Army and Air National Guard and the Texas State Guard. If the Texas Army and Air National Guard is called up for national service, as some units were in the Afghan and Iraq wars, command passes from the governor to the president. In the event of a statewide or local emergency, the governor has the power to declare martial law and to assume command of the National (if not in national service) and State Guard.

The Texas Army and Air National Guard is composed of a headquarters compliment of 663 and 25,600 guardsmen. Since 9/11, thousands of Texas national guard men and women have served in Iraq and Afghanistan each year. The 2,300-member Texas State Guard supports the Army and Air National Guard in the event of local emergencies and natural disasters, and fills in for them when they are called to national service.[22]

Informal Powers

The formal powers of the Texas governor are fewer than those of most other governors, but one must be careful not to dwell exclusively on these limits. Even if the governor has limited powers, so does everyone else in Texas politics and no one has *more* power than the governor. It is common to suggest that the lieutenant governor may be the most powerful figure in Texas politics. But politics is about winning and using power. So ask yourself this: has any governor ever capped off his or her political career by running for lieutenant governor? (Hint: the answer is no.)[23]

Former Governor Dolph Briscoe (1973–79) explained quite well the expectations that Texas governors face and the limits on their ability to meet them. Briscoe wrote,

> Texans perceive the governor to be the head of state government. They look to the governor for leadership, and they hold that person to be responsible for the condition of the state. These are understandable expectations. The reality is, however, that the Texas Constitution does not establish a form of government in which the governor controls the executive branch.[24]

Governors must act as if the public expectations of executive leadership are legitimate and realistic, even while knowing that the bluff can be called at any time. Nonetheless, Texas governors are generally able to establish themselves as the leading figure in the state's politics. There are several important reasons for this. First, the governor is the face of his party; he is expected to develop an agenda for the legislature and to speak to major public issues.

Second, the governor is the only figure who has a finger in every pie. While his powers do not allow him to control most events, he is in a position to influence them. Third, when the legislature is not in session, which is most of the time, the governor dominates the stage in Austin. Finally, most Texans are only vaguely aware of the real limitations on the power of the governor. They assume that, as governor, he is the leader of Texas state government. Governors use this visibility, centrality, and presumption of authority to direct events more authoritatively than their formal powers alone might allow.

THE BUREAUCRACY

To exercise the influence and leadership that most citizens and voters expect, the governor must distinguish himself on a crowded stage. The lieutenant governor, AG, comptroller of public accounts, commissioner of public lands, and agriculture commissioner are also elected statewide, and with the exception of the lieutenant governor, who is principally a legislative official, they are executive department heads. Hence, Texas is often said to have a **plural executive**. The lieutenant governor is paid a legislative salary of $7,200 a year, plus *per diem*, while the others draw a salary between $137,500 and $150,000.

Photo courtesy of Office of the Attorney General of Texas

Greg Abbott, former Texas Supreme Court Justice and Attorney General is the first new governor of Texas in fourteen years.

Plural executive An executive branch featuring several officials with independent constitutional and legal authority.

The executive branch of Texas state government is made up of about 275 separate departments, agencies, boards, and commissions. Each executive branch office is headed in one of four ways: by elected or appointed single administrators, or by elected or appointed multimember boards or commissions. These executives direct the work of about 311,000 state employees; 147,580 are full-time state employees and 163,400 work in public colleges and universities. Some 743,000 Texans work in county and municipal governments.[25]

Single-Elected Administrators

Like the governor, the lieutenant governor, AG, comptroller of public accounts, land commissioner, and agriculture commissioner are elected to renewable four-year terms. Because they are elected independently, they often act independently. Usually governors consult with other statewide elected officials behind the scenes, but sometimes, as we shall see below, differences become public.

Q3 What other statewide elected officials share power with the governor?

Lieutenant Governor. While the lieutenant governor is one of the top officials in Texas government, the office is almost exclusively legislative rather than executive. The lieutenant governor's legislative responsibilities were described in Chapter 6, so here we simply note that the lieutenant governor

Pro & Con   If You're Going to Retire, Then Retire Already

Many public employees, including Texas state government employees, have defined benefit retirement programs, though most of the private sector has moved to defined contribution, 401k style, plans. In the Texas defined benefit plan, employees contribute 6.5 percent of their monthly salary to the retirement program and the state contributes a similar amount on their behalf. Then employees are entitled to a set amount every month after retirement. An employee with twenty years of service would be eligible for 46 percent of full-time salary and an employee with thirty years of service would be eligible for 70 percent. Most private sector workers now have defined contribution plans, in which they and their employers (if they are lucky) contribute as described above, but the employee must invest and manage the retirement account subject to all the risks of the market.

Many Texans and all conservative Texans suspect waste in government and so there has been discussion of whether state employees' defined benefit plans should be transitioned to 401k style defined contribution plans. Recently, attention has been focused on the retired, but not really retired, status of a small "elected class" of state retirees. The financial disclosure reports that Rick Perry filed during his brief 2012 presidential campaign disclosed that he had taken state retirement in 2011, drawing about $92,000 a year, while continuing to receive his $150,000 a year salary as governor. How can this be?

In 1991, the Texas Legislature, directed by then Lieutenant Governor Bob Bullock, enacted a provision allowing non-judicial elected officials, both statewide elected officials and legislators, to retire under elected class or employee class provisions. Before reading on, guess which class is better—elected or employee. OK, if you answered "elected class," read on, if you answered "employee class," go to your professor for some special tutoring.

Accrued years of service can be transferred between classes both before and after retirement. Rick Perry retired in January 2011 as a state employee with more than thirty years of service, drawing $7,700 a month or $92,000 annually, while continuing to work and accrue additional retirement credit as an "elected class" state employee. Perry was not alone. In early 2012, news reports indicated that 189 state employees were making $100,000 or more while also drawing a state pension. Though regular state employees who continue to work or return to work for the state cannot accrue additional retirement benefits, elected officials can.

Knowledgeable people differ on the propriety of this. Former Texas Senator Bob Glascow who carried the bill when it passed in 1991, claimed not to have known that the provision was in there, but also said, "That's just got the tenor of double dipping." Others, including Texas Land Commissioner Jerry Patterson, said, "I don't see anything wrong with it, and I intend to do the same thing." Perry himself said, "it's rather inappropriate if you've earned something if you don't take it and take care of your family."[26] Good government types were bothered by the secrecy and by the starkly obvious instance of politicians taking especially good care of themselves.

In the private sector, a person drawing social security is permitted to keep working as is a person making mandatory withdrawals from retirement accounts. Is it, or should it be, different for public sector employees being paid with taxpayer funds? Should a governor or other elected official actually have to leave office before he or she begins drawing a public-sector pension? What do you think?

serves as acting governor when the governor is out of state or incapacitated. If the governor should resign or die, the lieutenant governor ascends to the governorship for the remainder of the open term. If the lieutenant governor becomes governor, dies, or is forced to resign, the Senate selects one of its own to serve as lieutenant governor until the next general election.

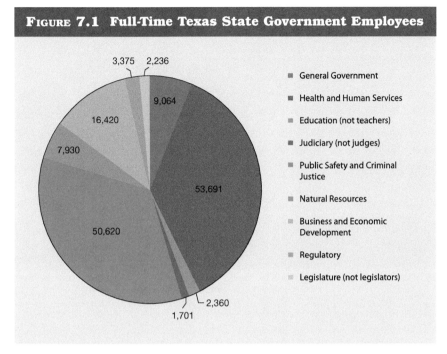

FIGURE 7.1 Full-Time Texas State Government Employees

- General Government
- Health and Human Services
- Education (not teachers)
- Judiciary (not judges)
- Public Safety and Criminal Justice
- Natural Resources
- Business and Economic Development
- Regulatory
- Legislature (not legislators)

3,375 2,236
9,064
16,420
7,930
53,691
50,620
2,360
1,701

Source: State Auditor's Office, "A Summary Report on Full-Time Equivalent State Employees for the Quarter Ending August 31, 2012, October 2012," Report No. 13-703.

Lieutenant Governor Dan Patrick, formerly a Houston radio talk show host and radio station owner, was first elected to the Texas Senate in 2006. In 2014, Patrick was elected lieutenant governor by defeating incumbent Republican Lieutenant Governor David Dewhurst (2002–2014), 63.5 percent to 36.5 percent.

Attorney General. The Office of Attorney General (OAG) is mandated by the Texas Constitution. The AG is one of the state's most visible public officials. Texas Senator Ken Paxton of McKinney was elected Attorney General in 2014. The OAG has 4,200 employees, more than 400 of them lawyers, in seventy offices located throughout the state. Most of the department's responsibilities involve legal representation of state agencies and civil administration. The AG makes $150,000 annually.

The AG is the principal legal advisor and advocate for Texas state government. The AG represents the officers and agencies of Texas state government in court when they are party to a suit. Moreover, the AG's Opinion Committee issues opinions to the legislature and other state agencies concerning whether existing or proposed laws and regulations comply with the requirements of the U.S. and Texas Constitutions. While these opinions are not legally binding, they are seldom challenged or disobeyed.

Most of the thirty-eight divisions in the OAG engage in civil administration; they punish delinquency and enforce compliance with Texas laws and regulations. The OAG investigates and punishes violations of family and tax

New Attorney General Ken Paxton is sworn in by Governor Greg Abbott on January 5, 2015, as his family as well as former Governor Rick Perry and former Lieutenant Governor David Dewhurst, look on.

law, consumer and environmental law, antitrust legislation, and worker's compensation and Medicare fraud. Key divisions of the OAG include the Child Support Enforcement Division, the (Tax) Collections Division, the Consumer Protection Division, and the Cyber Crimes Unit.

Comptroller of Public Accounts. The Texas Constitution has mandated a Comptroller of Public Accounts since 1835. Only a dozen other states have an elected comptroller; the rest have appointed comptrollers or state treasurers. The comptroller is the state's chief accountant, auditor, tax collector, and investment officer. Many credit the legendary Bob Bullock, Texas comptroller from 1975 to 1990 and lieutenant governor from 1990 to 1998, with modernizing the comptroller's office and making it one of the most powerful offices in Texas politics.[27] Carole Strayhorn was elected comptroller in 1998 and 2002. She ran unsuccessfully for governor in 2006. Susan Combs, Texas Agriculture Commissioner from 1998 to 2006, was elected comptroller in 2006 and re-elected in 2010. Texas state Senator Glenn Hegar was elected comptroller in 2014. The comptroller makes $150,000 annually.

Revenue estimate The Texas Comptroller is empowered to make revenue estimates that the Texas state budget must stay within.

The key to the comptroller's political influence lies in his constitutional responsibility to produce a **revenue estimate** at the beginning of each legislative session. The revenue estimate may be updated during the session, but the legislature cannot pass and the governor cannot sign a budget that expends more money than the comptroller predicts will be available. Tensions can build between the governor, legislative leaders, and the comptroller because the comptroller tends to make conservative revenue estimates that other leaders feel make budgetary discussions more difficult than they need to be. In the 2003 and 2005 legislative sessions, these tensions led to open conflict between the governor, legislative leaders, and the comptroller. Tensions have eased, though not completely, when Susan Combs became comptroller.

Corbis

New Land Commissioner George P. Bush, flanked by his famous father and his wife, at his swearing-in ceremony, January 2, 2015.

In 2010, then comptroller Susan Combs, like comptrollers and treasurers in other states, clashed with the on-line retailer Amazon.com over whether they had to pay sales tax on the goods they sold just like bricks and mortar businesses do. When Amazon threatened to close its Texas distribution centers if Combs continued to demand sales taxes be paid to Texas, Perry intervened, saying, "This is a problem, and I would suggest to you that we need to look at that decision that our comptroller made. The comptroller made that decision independently. I would tell you, from my perspective, that's not the decision I would have made." The comptroller's office responded firmly, saying "We regret losing any business in Texas, but our position hasn't changed. If you have a physical presence in the state of Texas, you are responsible for sales tax just like any other business located in the state."[28] Soon, Amazon surrendered, agreeing to create 2,500 jobs and invest $200 million in Texas, and begin collecting and remitting sales taxes. The broad lesson here is that a statewide elected official, operating within her area of constitutional authority, is more than a match for a meddlesome governer. That's why Texas is described as a "plural executive" system.

Land Commissioner. Texas has had an elected land commissioner since independence. The land commissioner oversees the General Land Office. David Dewhurst was land commissioner before he was elected lieutenant governor in 2002. Jerry Patterson, a former state legislator, was elected land commissioner in 2002 and re-elected in 2006 and 2010.[29] In 2014, Patterson declined to run for re-election, instead challenging David Dewhurst for lieutenant governor. Into the breach stepped the intriguing figure of George P. Bush. A first-time candidate, though fortunate enough to bear a famous name, Bush notched a strong victory to become Texas Land Commissioner. The land commissioner oversees 20.3 million acres of land and 2.2 million acres of Texas submerged lands (often called tidelands) extending three leagues (10.3 miles) into the Gulf.

The land commissioner is responsible for leasing state land for oil and gas exploration, mining, and grazing. The commissioner is also responsible for maintaining the environmental quality of Texas lands, waters, wetlands, and coastal areas. Finally, the land commissioner administers the Veteran's Land Board, which provides veterans with loans and other assistance to purchase Texas public lands. The Land Commissioner makes $137,500 annually.

Agriculture Commissioner. The office of agriculture commissioner was established by statute in 1907. Governor Rick Perry first won statewide election as agriculture commissioner in 1990. Susan Combs succeeded Rick Perry in 1998 and was easily re-elected in 2002. Republican Todd Staples, a former member of the Texas House (1995–2001) and Senate (2001–06), was elected agriculture commissioner in 2006 when Combs moved up to comptroller. He was reelected in 2010, but declined to run for re-election in 2014. Former Texas House member Sid Miller was elected Agriculture Commissioner in 2014. The Agriculture Commissioner makes $137,500 annually.

The agriculture commissioner oversees the Texas Department of Agriculture (TDA). The TDA has the dual responsibility of regulating and promoting Texas agricultural interests and products. As a regulator, the TDA enforces laws and regulations regarding land use, pesticide use, product certification, and inspection. The TDA also inspects and certifies measuring devices like gas pumps, electronic scanners, and scales. Finally, the TDA promotes Texas agricultural products through research and public education.

Single-Appointed Administrators

The governor, with the approval of two-thirds of the Texas Senate, is empowered to appoint several key executive branch officials to renewable two-year terms of office. While these are not officials of the first rank, they do oversee and administer important elements of Texas state government.

Secretary of State. The Secretary of State (SOS) is the chief election officer for Texas. The SOS interprets the election code, enforces election laws throughout the state, and maintains the voter rolls. Prior to election day, the SOS trains election officials and distributes election supplies. On election day, the SOS receives, reviews, and officially reports election results. Between elections, the SOS receives reports of campaign contributions and maintains a list of lobbyists registered with the state. Finally, the SOS issues corporate charters and licenses notary publics.

The incumbent SOS, Carlos Cascos, was appointed by Governor Abbott in 2015. In addition to the traditional responsibilities of the office, Secretary Steen will serve as the governor's liaison on border and Mexican affairs and as the state's chief protocol officer on international affairs.

Commissioner of Insurance. The Commissioner of Insurance (COI) monitors and regulates the insurance industry in Texas. Governor Perry named Julia Rathgeber to be insurance commissioner in 2013. Rathgeber had no previous direct experience with the insurance industry before taking office. The commissioner's office educates the public on insurance matters, licenses agents and investigates complaints against them and their companies, and monitors the financial health of insurance companies operating in the state. In recent years, the COI has attempted to roll-back home and auto insurance rates and to reform the Texas Windstorm Insurance Association.[30]

Commissioner of Health and Human Services. Governor Abbott named Senator Chris Taylor to be Executive Commissioner of Health and Human Services (HHSC) in 2015. The executive commissioner has oversight, coordination, and review responsibility over five health and welfare agencies, running 200 programs from 1,300 locations around the state. HHSC employs 56,000 workers. Each agency is administered by its own appointed board or commission. The commissioner's responsibility is to review their activities, identify overlaps and redundancies, and recommend efficiencies.[31]

Adjutant General. The Adjutant General, the top military official in Texas state government, is appointed by and reports to the governor. He oversees and manages the Army and Air National Guard and the Texas State Guard.

Elected Boards and Commissions

Much of Texas state government is administered by multimember boards and commissions. The members of most boards and commissions are appointed by the governor with the consent of the Senate, but a few of the most important win their seats in partisan elections.

Q4 What roles do elected and appointed boards and commissions play in Texas?

The most important elected board is the Texas Railroad Commission (TRC). The TRC was founded in 1891 to regulate the railroads. Early in the 20th century, jurisdiction over railroads was ceded to the federal government and the TRC's regulatory mandate was recast to focus on the oil, natural gas, and pipeline industries. The modern TRC's principal responsibilities involve regulating oil and natural gas exploration, drilling, recovery, storage, and transportation while protecting the state's environment. Critics always contend that the commission leans toward exploiting natural resources rather than environmental protection.

The three members of the TRC are elected statewide to staggered six-year terms. One member is up for election every two years and the member next up for election serves as the commission chair. Each commissioner makes $137,500 annually. When a commissioner resigns before the end of his or her term, the governor appoints someone to fill out the term. The commission oversees a professional staff of 750.

The TRC, often seen as a stepping stone to other statewide offices, has seen a lot of turnover in recent years. In 2012, two longtime commission members, Michael Williams and Elizabeth Ames Jones, sought higher office—both failed. In 2014, commission Chairman Barry Smitherman, appointed by Governor Perry in 2011 and elected to a full term in 2012, ran for Attorney General and lost. State law does not require resigning one office to run for another, so Smitherman continues on the TRC. Commissioner David Porter won his seat by defeating incumbent Victor Carillo in 2010. Commissioner Christi Craddock, daughter of former Texas House Speaker Tom Craddick, won her seat in 2012.

Eric Gay/AP/Corbis

Pro-science supporters rally prior to a State Board of Education public hearing on proposed new science text books in Austin in 2013.

The Texas State Board of Education (SBE), initially composed of nine members appointed by the governor, was established in 1929.[32] The modern SBE is composed of fifteen persons, elected to four-year terms from single-member districts. The partisan composition of the current board is 10 Republicans and 5 Democrats. The governor appoints a member of the SBE, currently Barbara Cargill of The Woodlands, to serve a two-year term as chair. The SBE is responsible for reviewing and adopting textbooks for use in the state's public schools, setting curriculum standards and graduation requirements, as well as promotion criteria and passing standards for achievement tests.

The SBE nominates three persons to be Commissioner of Education, from whom the governor, with the consent of the Senate, picks one to serve a four-year term. Governor Perry appointed Michael Williams in 2012, after he failed to win election to Congress, to be Texas Commissioner of Education. The Commissioner of Education is the chief executive officer of the SBE and head of the 717 employee Texas Education Agency (TEA). The Commissioner, SBE, and TEA set and administer policies and standards for the state's 1,024 school districts and 8,400 individual campuses. Texas public schools employ 590,000 teachers and staff to teach more than 5 million students.[33]

Appointed Boards and Commissions

With the consent of two-thirds of the Senate, the governor appoints members to more than 275 agencies, boards, and commissions. Most gubernatorial appointees serve for a six-year renewable term without pay. The boards and commissions of Texas state government set general policy for their agencies, approve agency budget requests and major personnel decisions, hire the agency's executive director, and oversee agency implementation of state and federal law.

Governors try to appoint people who are accomplished and knowledgeable and who share their partisan and ideological commitments and principles. Surprisingly (or not), governors often find their appointees among their political contributors. One-quarter of Governor Perry's appointees (921 of 3,995 contributed) between December 2001 and February 2010 were contributors. They contributed an average of $18,584 to his campaigns. The more important the board, the more likely the appointee was a contributor, and the more likely that the contribution was large. Appointees to the higher education governing boards gave an average of nearly $100,000 to Governor Perry's campaigns.[34]

To serve on some boards and commissions, generous contributors will also need to have appropriate professional credentials. For example, there are thirty-eight examining boards that license individuals to practice particular professions, from dentistry to home building. Service on these boards allows members of these professions to ensure that state law aids the profession and does it no harm. Finally, all gubernatorial appointments are scrutinized for appropriate regional, racial, ethnic, and gender balance.

While the appointment power gives the governor the opportunity to set the general direction of state policy, as well as to elevate his friends and deny his opponents, dangers lurk. Each appointment makes one person happy, but disappoints several others. And as former Governor John Connally observed, "If you want to talk about real 'in fighting,' try making an appointment to the Board of Cosmetology."[35]

Table 7.4 shows that while white men still fill most seats on state boards and commissions, qualified female and minority candidates are present. Governor Ann Richards, a female Democrat, directed 41 percent of her appointments to women, 13 percent to blacks, and 18 percent

TABLE 7.4	Gubernatorial Appointments: Gender, Race, and Ethnicity			
	Texas Population	Ann Richards Administration	George Bush Admistration	Rick Perry Administration
Male	50%	59%	63%	67%
Female	50%	41%	37%	33%
Anglo	46%	67%	77%	75%
Black	12%	13%	9%	8%
Hispanic	38%	18%	13%	14%

Source: Peggy Fikac, San Antonio Express-News, personal communication, May 30, 2014. Updated from Austin American-Statesman "Perry's Appointment Legacy."

TIMELINE: RICK PERRY IN TEXAS POLITICS

1950	1968	1968–72	1972–77	1982
Born in Paint Creek, Texas	Earned Eagle Scout; graduated from high school	Attended Texas A&M; graduated in animal sciences	Served in the U.S. Air Force	Married Anita Thigpen

to Hispanics. Governors Bush and Perry, both male Republicans, gave three-quarters of their appointments to Anglos and almost two-thirds of them to men. Perry did no better than Bush in regard to black and Hispanic appointments, giving 8 percent of appointments to blacks and 14 percent to Hispanics.

EXECUTIVE BRANCH REFORM

Q5 What reforms do analysts propose for the executive branch?

Texas's plural executive and extensive use of independent boards and commissions has created a weak and diffuse executive branch. Historically, Texans have been wary of executive power. But today's Texas is the second most populous state in the Union, with three of the nation's ten largest cities. Some Texans wonder whether the powers of the governor and the structure of the executive branch are adequate. The most frequently mentioned reforms involve making the executive branch in Texas work more like the executive branch at the national level. The goal of these reforms would be to make Texas state government stronger and more hierarchical.

Advocates of reform contend that the governor's ability to energize and direct the executive branch would be dramatically enhanced by the adoption of several key reforms. First, candidates for governor, like candidates for the presidency, should pick their running mates. A lieutenant governor, selected by and working with the governor, would pull together the executive branch. The Senate would likely reduce the power of the lieutenant governor as a presiding officer, making him more of an executive than a legislative figure, but that would allow him or her to take on major tasks assigned by the governor.

Second, reformers argue that the governor, like the president, should have the power to appoint and remove executive branch department heads. These department heads would then form the governor's cabinet. **Cabinet government** would empower the governor to initiate, coordinate, and implement executive policy. Advocates of reform also propose that many of the state's boards and commissions be rolled into the major departments of the state government.

Cabinet government An executive branch in which the governor has broad appointment and budgetary powers.

1984–89	1989	1990–98	1998–2000	2000–14	2012
Served in the Texas House as a Democrat	Switched to the Republican Party	Served as Commissioner of Agriculture	Served as Lieutenant Governor	Served as Governor	Makes an abortive run for president—Oops

Third, reformers argue that the governor, again like the president, should have the power to initiate and submit an executive budget. Today, the governor just goes through the motions of drafting a budget proposal because the legislature favors the budget drafted by the Legislative Budget Board. Reformers suggest that the Texas legislature must be able to consider and revise the governor's budget proposal, but that proposal should be the basis for the legislature's budget considerations.

Finally, many believe that if the powers of the governor are seriously enhanced, a two-term limit should be set.

Chapter Summary

The Texas Constitution of 1876 established a plural executive and a diffuse executive branch. The Governor of Texas shares leadership of the executive branch with five other statewide elected officials. Each is elected to a four-year term of office, each has his or her own constitutional or legislative authority, and each operates with a great deal of independence.

The Texas governor lacks important powers, including the power to draft the state budget and the power to appoint key executive branch officials, enjoyed by other governors. Nonetheless, many governors have been able to wield the powers they do have, including the veto, the line-item veto, and their general appointment powers, to craft for themselves a leading if not dominant role in the state's politics.

Other statewide elected officials—the lieutenant governor, attorney general, comptroller, land commissioner, and agriculture commissioner—look for ways to cooperate with the governor when they can but they know that they can stand against him when they feel they must. Together, the governor, lieutenant governor, attorney general, comptroller, land commissioner, and agriculture commissioner are described as a "plural executive."

In addition to the major departments of Texas state government, there are approximately 275 agencies, boards, and commissions that administer important aspects of state government. While the governor appoints the members of these agencies, boards, and commissions, with the consent of two-thirds of the Senate, they are difficult to remove and are essentially independent once appointed. These bodies set policy within the area of their responsibility, select the executive directors of their agencies, and monitor the agencies' performance. Finally, 147,580 state employees make Texas work day-to-day.

Critics of Texas state government call for reforms that would strengthen the governor's hand and streamline the executive branch. The strengthened governor and streamlined executive branch is often called cabinet government and employs the presidency as the model for the modern governorship. For some, a stronger governor would require term limits, maybe two four-year terms, to insure against too much power in the hands of one person.

Key Terms

Appointment power 173	Plural executive 181
Budget message 176	Revenue estimate 184
Cabinet government 190	Special session 179
Clemency 180	State of the State message 178
Line-item veto 176	Veto 179

Review Questions

1. Describe several of the main roles played by the governor in Texas politics.
2. Distinguish between the formal and informal powers of the governor and the kinds of influence drawn from both.
3. Assess how the plural executive system employed in Texas both aids and hinders the efficient working of the executive branch.
4. Explain the reasoning behind the extensive use of agencies, boards, and commissions in the regulation and oversight of Texas state government.
5. Analyze the potential costs and benefits of moving from a plural executive design to a cabinet form of executive branch organization.

Suggested Readings

Carolyn Barta, *Bill Clements: Texian to his Toenails* (Austin, TX: Eakin Press, 1996).

Ann O'M Bowman, Neal D. Woods, and Milton R. Stark, II, "Governors Turn Pro: Separation of Powers and the Institutionalization of the American Governorship," *Political Research Quarterly* (2010), 63: 304–315.

Adam R. Brown, "Are Governors Responsible for the State Economy? Partisanship, Blame, and Divided Federalism," *Journal of Politics* (2010), 72: 605–615.

William R. Childs, *The Texas Railroad Commission: Understanding Regulation in America in the Mid-Twentieth Century* (College Station, TX: Texas A&M University Press, 2005).

Margaret R. Ferguson and Cynthia J. Bowling, "Executive Orders and Administrative Control," *Public Administration Review* (2008), 68: 520–528.

Kenneth E. Hendrickson, *The Chief Executives of Texas: From Stephen F. Austin to John B. Connolly, Jr.* (College Station, TX: Texas A&M University, 1995).

Thad Kousser and Justin H. Phillips, "Who Blinks First: Legislative Patience and Bargaining With Governors," *Legislative Studies Quarterly* (2009), 34: 55–86.

Brian McCall, *The Power of the Texas Governor: Connally to Bush* (Austin, TX: University of Texas Press, 2009).

Dave McNeely and Jim Henderson, *Bob Bullock: God Bless Texas* (Austin, TX: University of Texas Press, 2008).

Jan Reid, *Let the People In: The Life and Times of Ann Richards* (Austin, TX: University of Texas Press, 2012).

Web Resources

1. **http://www.nga.org**
   Website of the National Governor's Association.

2. **http://www.governor.state/tx/us**
   Website of the Governor of Texas.

3. **http://www.senate.state.tx.us**
   Website of the Lieutenant Governor of Texas.

4. **http://www.oag.state.tx.us**
   Website of the Attorney General of Texas.

5. **http://www.tsl.state.tx.us/trail/agencies.html**
   List of all Texas stage agency websites.

6. **http://gritsforbreakfast.blogspot.com**
   Top criminal justice blog in Texas.

Chapter 8

THE JUDICIAL SYSTEM IN TEXAS

JUDGE SHARON KELLER AND JUDICIAL FAIRNESS

Texas executes more people than any other state and, in some recent years, almost as many as all of the other states combined. So one would assume that the Texas judicial system has well-established procedures for handling executions and follows those procedures scrupulously—after all, it's an execution. But it is not always so. On September 25, 2007, Chief Judge Sharon Keller (R-Dallas) of the Texas Court of Criminal Appeals received a telephone call from the court's general counsel, Ed Marty, relating that lawyers carrying a death penalty petition on behalf of convicted murderer Michael Wayne Richard, scheduled to be executed that evening, were running late and asked that the court be held open past its regular 5pm closing time. She replied that the court closed at 5pm, the petition arrived after 5pm, the execution took place as scheduled—and then all hell broke loose.

Critically, while Keller was Chief Judge of the court, she was not the duty judge assigned to receive appeals that day. Judge Cheryl Johnson was the duty judge and she and two fellow judges were aware that an appeal was expected and were waiting after five for it to arrive. When Ed Marty called Judge Keller to ask if the court should be held open, she said closing time is 5pm, and Johnson was not informed. Keller later said she was just making an administrative point, the office closes at 5pm, not closing the well-known path of presenting appeals to a duty judge after hours.

The facts of the original 1986 crime in which Michael Richard raped and killed a 53-year-old nurse named Marguerite Dixon were not in dispute, nor were the basic facts surrounding Judge Keller's closing of the court on the day of his execution. What was in dispute was what Judge Keller meant by closing the court at five and, behind that, what it said about the attitude of the Texas justice system toward executions. On the morning of the execution, the U.S. Supreme Court accepted a Kentucky case challenging the constitutionality of the three-drug cocktail then used in executions in many states, including Texas. The claim was that the three-drug cocktail caused enough pain to constitute "cruel and unusual punishment." Most states took the Supreme Court's action as a reason to suspend executions until the high court made its ruling and Richard's lawyers prepared an appeal calling for suspension of his pending execution. The lawyers claimed that computer problems caused them to miss the 5pm court closing. The fact that Texas did not suspend executions in light of the Supreme Court's action and the closing of the court when an appeal was on the way brought Chief Judge Sharon Keller, the highest ranking criminal court judge in Texas, before a judicial panel to defend her actions.

Judge Keller appeared before Judge David Berchelmann, a state district judge named special master in charge of fact-finding in the judicial ethics inquiry into what had happened. Judge Berchelmann heard four days of testimony and then submitted "findings of fact" to a thirteen member commission made up of six judges, two lawyers, and five citizens appointed by the governor. On January 20, 2010, Judge Berchelmann found that, "Although Judge Keller's conduct on that day was not exemplary, she did not engage in conduct so egregious that she should be removed from office." Judge Berchelmann advised no "further reprimand beyond the public humiliation she has surely suffered."

Despite Judge Berchelmann's findings of fact and recommendation, the State Commission on Judicial Conduct in February 2010 levied five charges against Judge Keller, saying, "Judge Keller's willful and persistent failure to follow (her court's) execution-day procedures on September 25, 2007, constitutes incompetence in the performance of duties of office." Nonetheless, on July 16, 2010, the Commission issued a light reprimand, a "public warning," and left her in her position. Judge Keller appealed even this slap on the wrist and on October 11, 2010, a special court of review threw out the charges against Keller and, due to procedural errors, prohibited the refilling of the charges. Shockingly, the court found that the commission had erred in issuing too light a sanction, a "public warning," when state law required a more serious "censure." Don't you love it?

Several questions seem obvious—should courts bend over backwards to assure that the condemned get every chance to have their appeals heard? How should courts assure that their procedures are followed? And, does the process for processing charges of misbehavior of judges seem adequate, does it even make sense?

Focus Questions

Q1 How do we define law?

Q2 What is the difference between trial courts and appellate courts?

Q3 How are judges selected in Texas?

Q4 What role does money play in judicial selection?

Q5 Why are the incarceration and execution rates so high in Texas?

Though Article VI of the U.S. Constitution declares that the federal constitution, laws, and treaties are "the supreme law of the land," most legal activity occurs in state courts. The federal courts have a comparatively narrow jurisdiction, while state courts are responsible for resolving many of the disputes of daily life. The state courts are organized and empowered to resolve disputes that range from disagreements between homeowners and traffic violations to burglary and murder. The Texas courts alone process five times as many cases each year as do the federal courts.

Article III, section 2, of the U.S. Constitution provides that the judicial power of the federal courts "shall extend to all Cases . . . arising under this Constitution, the Laws of the United States, and Treaties made . . . under their Authority." Most cases that arise in the federal courts fall into three categories: "First are the criminal and civil cases that arise under the federal laws, including the Constitution." These include such crimes as bank robbery, counterfeiting, mail fraud, and violations of federal civil rights laws. "Second are cases in which the U.S. government is a party . . . Third are civil cases involving citizens of different states, if the amount in question is more than $75,000."[1] The federal court system, composed of the U.S. Supreme Court, the thirteen federal courts of appeals, and the ninety-four federal district courts, employs about 1,000 judges to apply the U.S. Constitution and federal laws. In 2011, they handled about 1.5 million cases, almost 1.1 million of which were bankruptcy cases.

The Texas judicial system, composed of several types of municipal and county courts, as well as three levels of state courts, employs more than 3,468 judges.[2] In 2013, the Texas courts processed 10.1 million cases. More than 8.8 million cases moved through the justice of the peace and municipal courts and nearly 70 percent of those were traffic cases. County and state courts dealt with most of the serious cases, in which significant fines and even jail time were possible. State courts touch the lives of more citizens than any other level or branch of government. Many of those lives are permanently changed.[3]

In this chapter, we begin by defining law and discussing several key principles and concepts that underlie American legal thought and practice.

Second, we look at the organization and structure of the judicial system in Texas. Third, we ask why Texas incarcerates and executes more people than any other state in the union. Finally, we ask what concerns people have about law, the courts, and justice in Texas and whether reforms might be appropriate.

TEXAS LAW AND JUSTICE

Courts are dispute-resolution mechanisms. Some disputes are minor, squabbles between neighbors or between a homeowner and a contractor, while others involve serious wrongdoing and violence. Courts resolve conflicts by publicly proving criminal and civil wrongdoing and applying relevant law. Judges are expected to be impartial, evenhanded, and fair. In fact, courts are carefully designed to reinforce the idea that justice is being done—think of the black robes, the formalities ("All rise, this honorable court is now in session"), and the liberal use of Latin (*writ of mandamus*—say what?).

Law Defined

Courts apply the law. So before we study courts, we must define **law**. Political scientist Herbert Jacob has offered the best simple definition, saying that laws are "authoritative rules made by government."[4] A slightly more elaborate definition is offered by Henry Abraham, highlighting not just authoritative rulemaking, but enforcement. Abraham defines law as "rules of conduct . . . backed by the organized force of the community."[5]

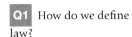 How do we define law?

Law Authoritative rules made by government and backed by the organized force of the community.

Judge Roy Bean was the "Law West of the Pecos" from about 1882 to 1902.

Those civilized definitions even apply in Texas today, though it was not always so. Dispute resolution in 19th-century Texas often dispensed with law and courts. Wilhelm Steinert came to Texas in 1849 to scout settlement sites in central Texas for German immigrants to follow. To ease their transition to Texas, Steinert provided a book of instruction and advice. He advised the immigrants that Texas justice might be swifter than they were used to. He wrote, "In your dealings with Texans of American extraction, you must take care not to provoke them. The consequence might be a bullet in your head, and nobody would take any notice of it."[6]

Though a certain amount of law and order did develop behind the frontier line, beyond the frontier line justice remained rough. One of the iconic figures of late 19th-century Texas was Judge Roy Bean. Judge Bean described himself, accurately for a time, as the only "law west of the Pecos." Today, of course, legislatures make laws and executives enforce them. But when the normal course is breached, when society's authoritative rules of conduct are broken, or when disputes arise between citizens about what the law requires in a particular instance, the courts are charged to restore order and define justice. It is a critical social role and a very tall order.

Civil and Criminal Law

The broadest distinction within both U.S. and Texas law is between civil law and criminal law. They differ in the nature of the disputes that fall under them, the parties involved, and the evidence required for decision. **Civil law** generally covers disputes between individuals, as in tort law (damage claims), family law (divorce and child custody), and contracts. The individual who brings the case is the **plaintiff** (sometimes called the complainant, because this is the person complaining) and the person defending against the plaintiff is the **defendant**. The goal of civil law is to protect individual and property rights and to hold persons to their obligations and responsibilities. Judges and juries resolve civil cases based on "a preponderance of the evidence" and then order the parties to fulfill their obligations, stop engaging in illegal activities, and/or pay a fine. Jail time is unusual in civil cases unless one party resists an initial court order.

Criminal law covers the "Law and Order," "Criminal Minds," "Without a Trace," stuff—murder, rape, assault, theft, and fraud. Under **criminal law** the complaining party is "the state" or "the people." The person charged is still referred to as the defendant. In criminal cases, especially those involving the most heinous crimes, punishments range beyond judgments and fines to long prison terms and even death. Hence, the standard of proof required for conviction is not just a "preponderance of the evidence," but guilt "beyond a reasonable doubt."

Surely the most famous example of the difference between criminal law and civil law and the penalties related to each involves the prosecutions of O.J. Simpson for the deaths of Nicole Brown Simpson

Civil law Deals primarily with relations between individuals and organizations, as in marriage and family law, contracts, and property.

Plaintiff The individual who brings a case before a court is called the plaintiff or complainant.

Defendant The person defending against a charge in court.

Criminal law Criminal law prohibits certain actions and prescribes penalties for those who engage in the prohibited conduct.

Who Knew?

Only about 1 percent of criminal and civil trials are conducted before a jury. The rest are conducted before a judge who both runs the trial, assesses guilt or innocence, and determines penalties.

and Ronald Goldman. In the criminal trial the charge was murder, and the penalties ranged up to imprisonment for life (Simpson was lucky he was tried in California and not in Texas). He was acquitted. He was later convicted on the charge of wrongful death in the civil trial, where the standard of evidence is not as great, and the jury awarded the Brown and Goldman families large monetary awards for damages. These outcomes, acquittal in the criminal case and conviction in the civil case, reflect the differences in standards of proof and punishment between criminal and civil law.

Courts and Jurisdiction

The structure of the Texas judicial system and the broad jurisdiction of the courts are set in the Texas Constitution. The broadest structural distinction among Texas courts is between trial courts and appellate courts. As we shall see more fully below, **trial courts** take evidence, hear testimony, determine guilt or innocence, and apply relevant law. **Appellate courts** do not take testimony or scrutinize facts; rather, they hear appeals from the losing party at the lower-court level claiming that procedures were unfair or the law wrongly interpreted and applied.

The Texas Constitution left it to the state legislature to determine how many courts there would be, how many judges would be assigned to each court, and precisely what kinds of cases the various courts would hear. A court's **jurisdiction** is its constitutional or legal mandate to hear certain kinds of cases. Some courts hear civil cases, some hear criminal cases, and some hear both. Other courts specialize in juvenile, drug, or probate cases.

Q2 What is the difference between trial courts and appellate courts?

Trial courts Trial courts take evidence, hear testimony, determine guilt or evidence, and apply relevant law.

Appellate courts Appellate courts review trial court records to insure that the trial was fair and the law correctly applied.

Jurisdiction The constitutional or legal right of a court to hear certain types of cases.

The Texas Bar

Texas judges and lawyers are required to be members of the Texas bar and to pay annual dues. The Texas bar is an agency of state government, a professional organization that looks out for the interests of the legal community, and a powerful interest group. Both judges and the lawyers that practice before them tend to be white men from comfortable, and often privileged, families. Of the 92,210 members of the Texas bar, about 82 percent are white and 67 percent are male. Still, the Texas bar is more diverse than it once was; today, about 33 percent are female, 8 percent are Hispanic, 5 percent are African American, 3 percent are Asian, and 0.3 percent are Native American.[7]

Texas judges are a good reflection of the broader bar. Texas judges are 65 percent male and 35 percent female. They are 76 percent Anglo, 16 percent Hispanic, 5 percent black, with both Asians and American-Indians registering under 1 percent.[8] Nonetheless, minority judges are moving up through the ranks of the Texas judiciary. Wallace Jefferson was the first black Chief Justice of the Texas Supreme Court from 2004 to 2013 and the court got its first Latina justice, Eva Guzman, in 2009.

THE STRUCTURE OF TEXAS COURTS

Each of the fifty states, including Texas, uses municipal and county courts to handle minor civil and criminal matters. Above the local level, most states use a three-tier system of state courts, much like that of the federal government, with a lower level of district or trial courts, a middle tier of appellate courts, and a high court that is usually called the Supreme Court. Texas and Oklahoma are the only states with dual high courts. Figure 8.1 shows that the top court for civil cases is the Texas Supreme Court, while the top court for criminal cases is the Texas Court of Criminal Appeals.

Trial Courts

Trial courts are the courts of original jurisdiction that actually try cases: they hear witnesses, accept evidence, assess guilt, and declare appropriate remedies and punishments. Texas has several kinds of trial courts, each with a geographic and a substantive jurisdiction. Local government courts are commonly called municipal courts or justice of the peace courts. County courts are either constitutional county courts or statutory county courts at law. District courts are the trial courts of the state system. Finally, there are a number of special courts, dealing with controversies relating to juveniles, domestic relations, and probate. The Texas penal code, summarized in Table 8.1, describes the types of crimes recognized in Texas law.

Municipal Courts. Municipal courts deal with minor criminal matters for which penalties are fines but not jail time. They are authorized to deal with all Class C misdemeanor traffic violations that occur within the city. Class C misdemeanors carry fines of no more than $500. These cases constitute approximately 70 percent of their case load. Municipal courts also try minor violations of state criminal law, such as littering, petty theft, and public intoxication, again with fines of no more than $500. Municipal courts have exclusive jurisdiction over enforcement of city ordinances, such as zoning and code enforcement, with fines up to $2,000. Finally, municipal courts have magistrate functions, including issuing arrest and search warrants and holding preliminary hearings in cases involving serious crimes.

There are about 927 municipal courts in Texas. In 2013, they disposed of just over 6.1 million cases. Most municipal court judges are appointed by city officials to two-year renewable terms. Compensation varies by size of city and court workload. These often are courts of non-record, meaning that no formal transcript is kept and if either party chooses to appeal the result, the case begins anew (de novo) in the district courts.

Justice of the Peace Courts. Justice of the peace courts (also called justice courts or simply JP courts) have exclusive jurisdiction over minor civil matters and share jurisdiction over minor criminal matters, or Class C misdemeanors, with the municipal courts. Texas has 817 JP courts hearing about 2.7 million cases in 2013; 85 percent criminal and 15 percent civil cases. Justices of the peace are elected to four-year terms. The county commissioners court appoints judges to fill the unexpired portion of JP terms that come open.

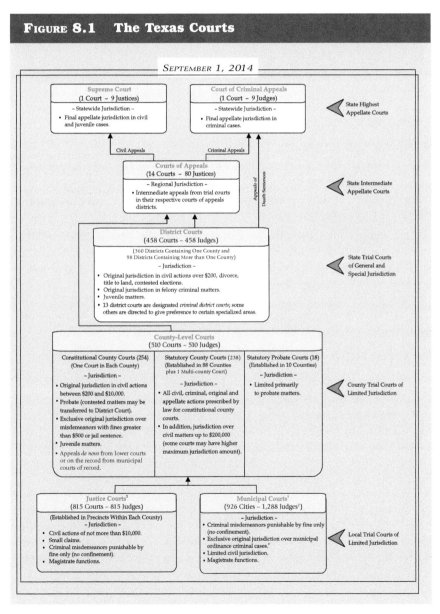

FIGURE 8.1   The Texas Courts

Source: Office of Court Administration, P.O. Box 12066, Austin, TX, 78711. See also Annual Report For the Texas Judiciary, Fiscal Year 2014, p. 3.

TABLE 8.1   Texas Penal Code: Crimes and Punishments

Offenses are designated as misdemeanor or felonies.

Classification	Example	Jail or Prison Term	Maximum Fine
Misdemeanors (classified info three categories, from less to more serious)			
Class C misdemeanor	Theft under $50; Most traffic violations; Public intoxication; Simple assault	None	$500
Class B misdemeanor	Theft over $500; Prostitution; 1st offense DWI	180 days	$2,000 or both
Class A misdemeanor	Theft over $500; Assault with injury; Resisting arrest	1 year	$4,000 or both
Felonies (classified info five categories, from less to more serious)			
State Jail Felony	Theft over $1,500; Auto theft; Forgery	180 days to 2 years	$10,000 or both
Third Degree Felony	Involuntary manslaughter; Kidnapping; Escape	2–10 years	$10,000 or both
Second Degree Felony	Theft over $100,000; Burglary of a home; Sexual assault	2–20 years	$10,000 or both
First Degree Felony	Theft over $200,000; Murder; Aggravated sexual assault	5–99 years	$10,000 or both
Capital Felony	Murder of a police officer; Murder of a child; Serial murder	Life without parole or death	

Source: Texas Penal Code, Title 3, Chapter 12, "Punishments." http://tlo2.tlc.tx.us/statutes/statutes.htm

Traffic cases account for two-thirds of the criminal caseload of the justice courts. Justice courts also serve as small claims courts in Texas with exclusive jurisdiction over cases in which $200 or less is at issue and concurrent jurisdiction with county and district courts in cases involving up to $10,000. Like municipal courts, justice courts also issue arrest and search warrants and handle preliminary hearings. Finally, JPs can act as coroners.

County Courts. Texas has two types of county courts: constitutional county courts, about which we will hear more in Chapter 9, and statutory county courts at law. The Texas Constitution mandates a county court that is presided over by a county judge in each of the state's 254 counties. In the state's rural counties, these constitutional county courts have administrative responsibilities as well as judicial responsibilities for criminal and civil matters. In criminal matters, county courts have original jurisdiction over Class A and B misdemeanors punishable by more than a $500 fine and/or imprisonment. They also have appellate jurisdiction over cases initially tried in the municipal and JP courts. Their civil jurisdiction extends to cases involving up to $10,000 and probate (verifying wills).

In 88 of the state's most populous counties, where the county courts perform almost exclusively administrative responsibilities, the state legislature has created 256 statutory county courts at law. The jurisdiction of county courts at law varies depending upon the initiating statute. Some have broad criminal and civil jurisdiction, while others specialize in civil, criminal, probate, or juvenile matters. Judges of the constitutional county courts need only be well-informed in the law, while judges of the statutory county courts at law must be lawyers. Both are elected to four-year terms by the voters of the county. County courts and county courts at law handled 862,000 cases in 2013; 65 percent of their cases are criminal, 15 percent are civil, while the remaining 20 percent are juvenile, probate, and mental health cases.

District Courts. District courts are the top trial courts in Texas. They have both civil and criminal jurisdiction, though their case loads are two-thirds civil and one-third criminal. Their civil case load leans heavily to family law, especially divorce and child custody, as well as state tax matters, land disputes, workers' compensation claims, and personal injury suits. Criminal cases include all felonies for which jail time might be assessed.

The state legislature creates new district courts as the judicial workload requires. Today there are 459 district courts in Texas and each district court has one judge. Some populous counties have several dozen district courts while several lightly populated counties may share one district court. District court judges run in partisan elections for four-year terms. Vacancies that occur between elections are filled by gubernatorial appointment. Salaries of district court judges now stand at $140,000. Texas district courts handled more than 861,000 cases in 2013.

Appellate Courts

Appellate courts review the work of trial courts to insure that legal rules were followed and the law correctly applied. Appellate courts do not hear witnesses or review evidence; they review the written record of lower-court deliberations and decisions and the written briefs and recorded oral arguments of lawyers challenging and defending the decisions of the lower court. The Texas appellate courts hear all civil and criminal cases, except those criminal cases in which the death penalty has been levied, which go directly to the Court of Criminal Appeals.

Texas has fourteen appellate court districts served by eighty judges. Each court has from three to thirteen judges, elected to staggered six-year terms, in partisan elections. Court of Appeals judges are paid $154,000 annually. The judges in each court hear cases in three-judge panels or en banc (all together). Appellate court decisions are made by a simple majority of the judges hearing the case. Texas appellate courts hear about 11,200 cases each year; evenly divided between criminal and civil cases.

LET'S COMPARE	WHAT THE TEN MOST POPULOUS STATES PAY THEIR JUDGES

No one is more interested in legal salaries than lawyers and judges and perhaps political science majors thinking about law school. The Bureau of Labor Statistics reports that the median annual income for U.S. lawyers was $131,990 in 2013. Naturally, big law firms in big cities pay more than single practitioners earn or small town firms pay. The average starting salary nationally in 2013 was $60,000, though those starting in top firms drew down $160,000. The average salary of lawyers practicing in Houston, the highest paid major city in Texas, was $158,430, while Dallas was $136,730, and El Paso was $133,390. However, partners in major downtown laws firms in the state's major cities can earn beyond a million dollars annually. Top "rainmakers" can make between $5 and 10 million, perhaps more.

So how do judges salaries compare to lawyers' salaries in general. U.S. Supreme Court Justices make $213,900 (the Chief Justice makes $10,000 more), while federal district court judges make $174,000. California judges are the only state judges that keep up with the salaries of federal judges, though Illinois judges come close. Texas state judges make near the national average for state judges, though not as much as judges in comparably large and complex states. Of the ten largest states, only Ohio and North Carolina consistently pay their judges less than Texas. Clearly, California and Illinois are the pace-setters on judicial compensation, paying their judges an average of 40 percent more than Texas.

	Highest Court	Appellate Court	District Court
California	$218,000	$205,000	$179,000
Texas	**$168,000**	**$154,000**	**$140,000**
New York	$177,000	$168,000	$160,000
Florida	$158,000	$150,000	$142,000
Pennsylvania	$200,000	$188,000	$173,000
Illinois	$211,000	$199,000	$182,000
Ohio	$142,000	$132,000	$121,000
Michigan	$165,000	$151,000	$140,000
North Carolina	$139,000	$133,000	$126,000
Georgia	$167,000	$166,000	$150,000
50 State Average	$155,143	$148,843	$139,166

Source: National Center for State Courts, "*Survey of Judicial Salaries*," vol. 38, no. 1, as of January 1, 2013, pp. 2, 5–11.

Dual High Courts

The Federal Government and forty-eight of the fifty states cap their judicial systems with a single high court, usually called the Supreme Court. Texas and Oklahoma employ dual high courts. In Texas, the Supreme Court

Sarah Tilghman Hughes (1896–1985), at five foot one-half inch tall, was a giant and a legend of Texas law and politics. Born into a prominent Baltimore family, the Tilghmans, with pre-revolutionary roots in Maryland politics and society, Sarah attended the girls only Western High School in Baltimore and then the girls only Goucher College, also in Baltimore, graduating in 1917 with a degree in Biology. After teaching science for two years at Salem Academy in North Carolina, she enrolled in law school at George Washington University in Washington, D.C.

While attending law school, she worked full-time as a Washington, D.C. police officer. Without the standard uniform and gun, she worked mostly on crimes against vulnerable women and girls, including runaways and prostitutes, to keep them safe and get them back on track. While in law school, Sarah met and married George Hughes, a Texan, and together they moved to Texas after graduation. One of only two women in her law school graduation class, Sarah Hughes faced gender discrimination common to the first three-quarters of the 20th century, but before long she had Texas by the throat.

Upon arriving in Dallas in 1922, George Hughes quickly found a legal job working with the Veteran's Bureau, which he held until shortly before his death in 1964. Like many of the relatively few female law school graduates of her era, Sarah Hughes could not find a law firm that would hire her. Finally, the small firm of Priest, Herndon, and Ledbetter agreed to hire her in 1923 as a receptionist, in exchange for allowing her to do legal work on the side and directing a few small cases her way. As her practice grew, her role in the firm evolved, and she practiced law with the firm until 1935. Rather than just keeping her foot in the door, she worked hard to push it wide open for herself and others.

In addition to practicing law, Sarah Hughes was active in the community and, soon, in politics. In 1930, she was elected to the first of three terms in the Texas House and, in 1935, Governor Jimmy Allred appointed her the first female state district judge in Texas history. She was subsequently elected district judge six times, serving in that role until President John F. Kennedy nominated her to be a federal district judge for the Northern District of Texas in 1961. Tragically, her iconic moment as a federal judge came aboard Air Force One when she swore Lyndon Johnson in as president in the immediate wake of John Kennedy's assassination in Dallas.

Though she rose high, Sarah Hughes's ascent was not smooth. She lost a few fights along the way, but she was not deterred. In 1946, she was defeated in the Democratic primary for a seat in the U.S. House and in 1958 she lost a race for a seat on the Texas Supreme Court. And in 1961, she had to fight for her nomination to the federal judiciary. Because she was 65 at the time, neither the ABA nor Attorney General Robert Kennedy wanted to nominate her, but her close friend, U.S. House Speaker Sam Rayburn, pressured President Kennedy to make the nomination.

Sarah Hughes left a memorable judicial trail behind her. She was a member of the three-judge panel that heard *Roe v. Wade*, striking down Texas's restrictive abortion laws, thereby establishing a woman's "right to choose" abortion services. She also presided over the main cases in the Sharpstown Scandal in 1972. Other key cases involved women's service on juries, equal pay for equal work, juvenile justice, and prison reform. Judge Hughes assumed senior judge status in 1975, retired in 1982, and died in 1985. Though she notched a lot of firsts in her life, she said, "I never wanted to be a woman lawyer. I wanted to be a lawyer." And she was.

(created in 1845) is the highest appellate court for civil matters, while the Court of Criminal Appeals (created in 1891) is the top court for criminal matters. The Supreme Court is composed of a chief justice and eight associate justices, while the Court of Criminal Appeals is composed of a presiding judge

Courtesy of the Supreme Court of Texas

Texas Supreme Court

and eight serving judges. All are elected statewide in partisan elections to six-year staggered terms. Vacancies are filled by gubernatorial appointment. Most cases are heard by all nine justices or judges, though some cases are heard by three-judge panels. High court judges are paid $168,000 annually.

Texas Supreme Court. The Texas Supreme Court hears only civil cases and issues formal opinions in about 125 cases each year. While these formal opinions receive most of the attention, the Supreme Court is also empowered to issue writs of mandamus or orders to corporations, persons, and public officials (except the governor) to take certain actions. The court takes formal action on 800 to 1,000 matters each year. In 2007 the Supreme Court began offering live video webcasts of oral arguments on its website.[9]

The Supreme Court also has important administrative responsibilities. It sets judicial rules and policies for all Texas courts, including the criminal courts, and it has the exclusive right to approve new law schools in the state. It appoints the Board of Legal Examiners whose responsibility it is to develop, administer, and score the bar examination by which aspiring lawyers earn the right to practice law in Texas. The Texas Supreme Court issues law licenses and oversees the Texas bar.

Texas Court of Criminal Appeals. The Court of Criminal Appeals hears only criminal cases. These cases, except death penalty cases that come directly from the district courts, come on appeal from the fourteen appellate courts. Convictions in death penalty cases must be reviewed by the Court of Criminal Appeals. Lawyers for convicted defendants argue that the trial and appeals court judges erred in the way the cases were handled or in the application of Texas law.

In 2013, the Court of Criminal Appeals disposed of about 6,000 cases, of which about 60 percent were writs of *habeas corpus* challenging felony convictions in trial courts. Eighty-five percent of writs are denied or dismissed. The court affirmed all eleven of the death penalty cases that came before it in 2013. Judges of the court issued 441 opinions in 2013; about half were brief, unsigned, *per curium* opinions, 28 percent were signed opinions, and the remainder were concurring and dissenting opinions.

SELECTION OF TEXAS JUDGES AND JURIES

Q3 How are judges selected in Texas?

How are judges and juries selected to play their critical roles in the judicial system? Federal judges are nominated by the president, with the advice and consent of the Senate, for lifetime appointments. Lifetime appointments are thought to allow federal judges to ignore partisanship and to apply their unbiased judgment. Texas judges are viewed somewhat differently; they are expected to be competent legal practitioners, independent and fair-minded, but also responsive to political and social expectations.

Different states seek to balance judicial competence, independence, and responsiveness in different ways. Some states use gubernatorial appointment of state judges, like presidential appointment of federal judges, to assure judicial competence. Others seek to balance competence and independence with responsiveness through non-partisan elections. Others, including Texas, focus on responsiveness by subjecting most judges to partisan elections and all of the public speaking, campaigning, and fundraising that go along with it. Still others seek to balance competence, independence, and responsiveness through a system of initial appointment of judges followed by retention elections.[10]

Texas's elected judges are expected to be part of the state's elite-run, business-friendly, political system. Elected executives, legislators, and judges work hand-in-hand. For example, tort reform legislation passed in 1996 and 2003 moved issues that used to be questions of fact for juries to issues of law for judges to decide. Moreover, two studies by lawyers from the prominent Dallas firm Haynes and Boone looked at all of the decisions made by the state's 14 courts of appeals in 2000–2001 and 2010–2011 and found that the proportion of civil jury verdicts overturned on appeal had risen from 25 percent to 34 percent. They also found that jury verdicts for plaintiffs were overturned on appeal 49 percent of the time compared to 25 percent for cases in which defendants initially prevailed. A separate study by Texas Watch, a consumer watchdog group, found that the state's highest civil court, the Texas Supreme Court, sided with defendants in overturning pro-plaintiff decisions 74 percent of the time.[11]

Texas Judges

Texas has 3,468 judges, more than any other state. Though municipal judges are usually appointed by city officials, every other Texas judge is elected. Texas is one of only four states to elect all of its state judges in partisan elections. Over the past decade, Texas legislators have introduced several bills calling for non-partisan election of trial court judges and merit selection of appellate court judges. All of these bills have failed, but the debate is sure to continue.

Partisan Elections. Partisan election of judges puts a heavy burden on Texas voters. Voters have a difficult time assessing the credentials, relevant experience, and personal qualities of judicial candidates. It is quite common for voters to confront a ballot that asks them to decide more judicial races than executive or legislative races. Voters frequently respond either by declining to vote for the lesser judicial offices or by voting a straight partisan ticket. Advocates of partisan election of judges contend that even when voters do not know much about the particular candidates, they usually know whether they prefer

Pro & Con   The Governor's Judicial Appointments

Texas elects all of its state judges on a partisan ballot to 4-year terms for district judges and 6-year terms for appeals court and high court judges. The Texas Constitution of 1876, written and approved in the wake of the Civil War and Reconstruction, mandated elected judges so that Texas voters could elect judges that shared their values and remove judges that did not. This populist document also set the qualifications for judges quite low. To run for district judge, one had to be 25, a resident of the judicial district for two years, and a practicing lawyer for four years. To run for the appellate or high courts, one had to be 35, a citizen of the U.S. and Texas, and a licensed lawyer for ten years.

Texas voters tend to know much less about judicial candidates, whether they are sitting judges or challengers, than they do about candidates for executive and legislative offices, especially the top races like governor, state representative, or mayor. As a result, more than half of Texas voters simplify their task by voting a straight party ticket. Many more ignore the races in which they do not know the candidates. The *San Antonio Express-News* editorial page complained that straight-ticket voting produced almost all Democratic judges in 2008 and almost all Republican judges in 2010. They concluded that, "Some excellent judges were ousted and replaced with far less qualified jurists in these elections."[12]

Judges know that there is little they can do, short of messing up badly, to garner public attention and name recognition. As a result, though judges must woo voters, they do not trust them. Hence, a conspiracy of sorts, well known to insiders but not to average citizens, has arisen between judges and governors. The Texas Constitution mandates that state level judicial vacancies that occur as a result of death, disability, or resignation, be filled by gubernatorial appointment for the remainder of the term or until the next scheduled state election. Half of Texas state judges come to the bench for the first time by appointment, not election.

The September 2012 resignation of Justice Dale Wainwright from the Texas Supreme Court raised a number of issues. Justice Wainwright was elected to a second six-year term on the Supreme Court in 2008. If Wainwright had resigned any time prior to August 24, 2012, voters would have elected someone to the remainder of his term. Because he waited until after August 24, Governor Perry was entitled to appoint a replacement. He did; in fact he selected his chief-of-staff, Jeffrey Boyd, to the open seat. Boyd served as Deputy Attorney General beginning in 2000 before becoming Perry's general counsel and then chief-of-staff in 2011.

So here's the dilemma—it is highly likely that Jeffrey Boyd is an accomplished and talented lawyer, probably better than whoever might have been chosen by the voters, given that most voters don't know much about judicial candidates, but the Texas Constitution says judges are to be elected. What do you think—should we take what judicial elections give us, ignore the little conspiracy between the governor and his judges, or look for a better way to select our judges?

Missouri plan To balance competence and accountability, governors appoint judges who later stand in retention elections.

Democrat or Republican judges. Opponents argue that it would be far better to have a well-informed panel screen potential judges and make recommendations to the governor or some other responsible appointing authority.

The Missouri Plan. The **Missouri plan** or merit system for selecting judges tries to balance judicial qualifications with judicial independence and accountability. Fifteen states use the Missouri plan for selecting trial judges and twenty-one use it for selecting appellate judges. The Missouri plan begins with a panel of eminent legislators, judges, law professors, and citizens reviewing judicial candidates and nominating the best among them to the governor. The governor makes an initial appointment, usually for four years, after which the judge must stand in a retention election. If retained by majority vote, the judge serves a six- or seven-year term. Under the Missouri plan, qualifications determine the initial appointment of judges, but voters are allowed to remove judges of whom they disapprove.

Texas's Mixed Appointive/Elective System. The Texas Constitution and laws call for election of most judges, but, in fact, nearly 50 percent of judges first come to the bench by appointment. Judges often resign before the end of their terms, others become ill, and some die. County commissioners courts are allowed to fill vacancies in JP and county courts while the governor is allowed to fill vacancies in the district, appellate, and high courts. Since coming to power late in 2000, Governor Perry had by the end of 2014 appointed 267 Texans to the state's 554 judgeships. Seven of the current nine members of the Texas Supreme Court initially were Perry appointees.[13] These appointed judges serve to the end of the term they are appointed to and then they must stand for election if they wish to continue in office. A sitting judge is rarely defeated for re-election; in fact, about 80 percent of Texas judges are unopposed for re-election.

Texas Juries

Judges are half of the judicial system, juries are the other half (assuming you do not count the lawyers and the crooks). The place of juries in the American judicial system is highlighted by the phrase "a jury of your peers." The idea is that a citizen's liberty is more secure if it rests in the hands of other citizens than if it rests in the hands of government officials. While lofty rhetoric has its place, we should always keep in mind that Texas has a traditional political culture that privileges elite-control over the participation of average citizens. Citizens participate in two kinds of juries: grand juries and petit (or trial) juries. We should not be surprised to find that grand juries are dominated by elites and trial juries are rarely empaneled.

Grand Juries. Grand juries are charged with deciding whether enough evidence exists against a person to charge him with a serious crime and to proceed to trial. The **grand jury** hears the evidence relating to a particular crime presented by the district attorney and then votes on whether it is sufficient to proceed to trial. If at least nine of twelve grand jurors vote yes, an indictment (criminal charge) is issued and a trial is scheduled.

Grand jury A grand jury assesses a prosecutor's evidence against a potential defendant to be sure it is sufficient to proceed to trial.

In most states, grand jurors are selected by a random process that gives all citizens a chance of being called upon to serve. Texas uses what is called a "Key-Man" system that is more elite driven. District judges appoint three to five jury commissioners, key-men, familiar with local government, due process, and legal procedure to vet and nominate 15 to 40 potential grand jurors. One study of the key-man system as it operated in Harris County (Houston and environs) found that half of the grand jury commissioners or key-men worked in government, law enforcement, law, the courts, and related fields.[14] From the list of grand juror nominees, the district judge selects twelve grand jurors and two alternates to serve a 3- to 6-month term. The key-man system may work well, but, again it leans toward elites and away from common citizens.

Jury trial A trial conducted before a jury of citizens who hear testimony, weigh evidence, and assess guilt.

Trial Juries. Texans have the right to a **jury trial** in all felony cases and in most major civil cases. As a practical matter, most legal disputes are resolved through mediation or plea bargaining, and those that do go to trial are usually, by agreement of the parties, conducted before a judge without a jury. At both the county-court and the district-court levels, less than 1 percent of trials are conducted before a jury. When juries are present, they are responsible for weighing evidence and determining guilt. Texas jurors are selected from driver's license and voter registration rolls; they must be at least 18, a U.S. citizen, and not an indicted or convicted felon.

Texas instituted reforms intended to improve jury participation and jury selection. First, juror pay was increased in 2006, the first increase in fifty-two years, from $6 a day to $40 a day. Juror participation had fallen below 20 percent in both Dallas and Houston. The hope was that the improved pay would encourage more people to show up for jury duty when they are called.[15] It has not worked. Three-quarters of people continue to ignore jury summons. Second, the U.S. Supreme Court ruled in 2005 that Texas prosecutors had illegally excused black jurors in the 1986 murder trial of Thomas Miller-El. The Texas Supreme Court is considering changes to jury selection procedures to insure that juries are unbiased.[16] Again, thinking of Texas's traditional political culture, do you think it is possible that setting very low juror pay is intended to keep the poor off juries?

ARE THE TEXAS COURTS JUST?

Most Texans believe that judges should be competent, independent, and accountable. Yet many close observers of the Texas judiciary believe that judges are too accountable, especially to those who fund their campaigns, to be truly independent. Texas lawyers and judges laugh nervously at the jibe that Texas offers "all the justice you can afford."[17]

Money in Judicial Elections

Q4 What role does money play in judicial selection?

Citizens and voters know that governors and legislators are partisan politicians. They represent political parties and organized interests and they raise money from those interests to conduct their campaigns. Politicians, once elected, are expected, within limits, to serve the partisan and special interests that helped them win office. Texas judges are expected to stand for election in partisan contests, to raise campaign cash from friendly interests, and to treat everyone who comes before them in court fairly and equally. While there are always concerns about the undue influence of money in politics, those concerns are simply much greater in regard to judges.[18]

The Texas legislature attempted, ineffectually, to address the role of money in judicial elections in the 1995 Judicial Campaign Fairness Act (JCFA). The JCFA limits the amount that individuals, law firms, and PACs can contribute to judicial candidates. Individuals are allowed to give up to $5,000 to state-wide judicial candidates, and law firms are allowed to give up to $30,000. Candidates are restricted to accepting no more than $300,000 from PACs. Candidates who accept the JCFA guidelines also accept spending limits tied to the population of the district in which they are running. The spending limits range from $100,000 for trial courts in districts of less than 250,000 people; to $500,000 for court of appeals candidates in districts of more than a million; to $2 million for candidates in statewide races for seats on the Texas Supreme Court and Court of Criminal Appeals. The JCFA guidelines are voluntary and a candidate can opt out by a simple public declaration (if you are not laughing, you do not yet understand Texas politics). One study by the public interest group, Texans for Public Justice, entitled "Lowering the Bar: Lawyers Keep Texas Appeals Judges on Retainer," reported that 72 percent of the campaign contributions to the judges of the fourteen appeals courts came from lawyers and law firms with interests before the courts.[19]

Voters, lawyers, and judges all believe that money affects the openness and fairness of the courts. A ten-year legal battle between Bob Perry Homes, owned by Bob Perry, the top Republican contributor ($28 million in Texas since 2000) in Texas until his death in 2013, and a Mansfield, Texas, couple named Bob and Jane Cull highlight the issues. The Culls, believing that their Perry-built home was defective, initially thought to sue Perry, but changed their mind and sought arbitration. The arbitrator awarded the Culls $800,000, which was upheld in district and appellate courts. Perry appealed to the Texas Supreme Court. Perry had made $340,000 in political contributions to the nine Republican judges of the Supreme Court. (Question to students—if you were the Culls, how would you like your chances?) In May 2008, the Texas Supreme Court ruled in favor of Mr. Perry, overturning the Culls' $800,000 award. The Culls went back to court and in 2010 a Fort Worth jury, apparently outraged by the way the Culls had been treated, awarded the couple $58 million. When representatives of Perry Homes threatened to appeal, the judge ordered the two sides into arbitration. A settlement of the 10-year-old dispute was announced in 2011. No terms were disclosed. Does this suggest that money controls Texas politics or not?[20]

More than a decade ago, University of Virginia law professor Paul D. Carrington published an article, entitled "Big Money in Texas Judicial Elections," in the *SMU Law Review*. Carrington concluded that a "genuine crisis is presented when an election is for a judicial office and the sums spent are so large as to dwarf the fifty or hundred dollar contributions that most citizens

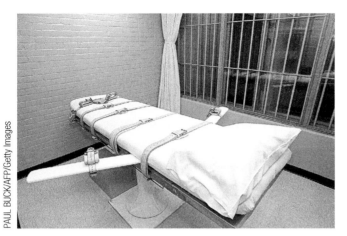

The death chamber in Huntsvllle, Texas is the most active in the nation.

might consider making." He concluded that, "The legal system in Texas, whatever the reality, appears to belong to rich folks or groups."[21]

A June 2009 ruling by the U.S. Supreme Court raised directly the issue of conflicts of interest in judges deciding cases involving their top campaign contributors. Justice Anthony Kennedy, writing for a slim five–four majority, held that the Constitution's "due process" clause required that a judge recuse him or herself in cases involving large donors.[22] Texas judges rarely recuse themselves in cases where their major donors are involved, though top Texas jurists have called both for tighter recusal standards and, more importantly, for changes in how judges reach the bench.

Over the past quarter century, three Chief Justices of the Texas Supreme Court, Democrat John Hill and Republicans Tom Phillips and Wallace Jefferson, have called for dramatically limiting the role of money in judicial elections. Former Chief Justice Wallace Jefferson used his "State of the Judiciary in Texas" address to a joint session of the legislature in February 2009 to declare that, true or not, polls showed that 80 percent of Texans believed that money affected the dispensation of justice in the state. Following his 2014 retirement, Jefferson continued to advise that Texas move to a system of judicial appointment rather than election.[23]

Judicial appointment bills passed the Texas Senate three times in recent years but each failed in the House. Speakers Pete Laney and Tom Craddick opposed reform, as do both political parties, and most of the major stakeholders, including corporations and law firms. Supporters of the current system like keeping judges dependent upon them for campaign contributions. No change is likely soon.

While there seems to be plenty of money, perhaps too much, in Texas judicial elections, there is far too little money in Texas legal aid and indigent criminal defense accounts. Around 5.6 million Texans qualify for free legal aid, but only about one-fifth of those eligible actually get aid. Texas ranks dead last in funding for legal services for the poor. Remarkably, indigent legal aid in Texas is funded by revenue from interest on lawyers' trust accounts. During the financial crisis, that revenue fell from $20 million in 2007 to $4.4 million in 2012. The 2013 legislature allocated $17.6 million to keep the fund afloat, but no permanent solution was offered.

Q5 Why are the incarceration and execution rates so high in Texas?

Incarceration and Execution in Texas

We do not have the time or the space to explore Texas incarceration and execution rates in detail, but we can demonstrate that both are higher, a lot higher, than any other state in the nation. Table 8.2 compares the total population,

TABLE 8.2	The Ten States with the Largest Prison Populations		
State	State Population	Prison Population	Inmates/100,000
California	38,041,000	134,534	351
Texas	26,059,000	166,372	601
New York	19,570,000	54,210	276
Florida	19,318,000	101,930	524
Illinois	12,875,000	48,427	376
Pennsylvania	12,764,000	51,125	398
Ohio	11,544,000	50,876	440
Georgia	9,920,000	55,457	542
Michigan	9,883,000	43,636	441
North Carolina	9,752,000	37,136	357
National	313,914,000	1,571,013	480

Sources: U.S. Census Bureau, *Statistical Abstract of the United States, 2014,* Table No. 14, "Resident Population—States, 2012," p. 17. Bureau of Justice Statistics, "Prisoners in 2012," Appendix, Table 1, p. 21, and Table 3, p. 23.

prison population, and the number of inmates per 100,000 people in the nation's ten most populous states. The national average is 480 prisoners per 100,000. Incarceration rates vary a great deal by state, but Texas is far higher than most other states.

Though California has 38 million citizens to 26 million for Texas, Texas has more people in prison than does California. The Texas incarceration rate is 601 persons per 100,000 of population; the California rate is 351 per 100,000. Even more strikingly, New York, the third most populous state, with 19.5 million people to 26 million for Texas, has a prison population only about one-third the size of Texas's prison population. Several of the nation's largest states, including Pennsylvania (398), Illinois (376), and New York (276) incarcerate people at half to two-thirds the Texas (601) rate.

What explains these high incarceration rates? Does it make sense to believe that Texans are much more disorderly and violent than, say, the good people of California, New York, and Pennsylvania? OK, maybe so, but twice as disorderly and violent! A better explanation is that Texas legislators have made more things illegal and attached more jail time to more of them than have legislators in other states. This not only involves more Texans in the criminal justice system, but it is extremely expensive. The average cost of holding a prisoner for one year in a Texas prison is about $20,000, though some point out that the cost of having them on the street might be higher.[24]

In addition to its state prisons, Texas has 245 county jails and 370 city and town jails. While the county jails are regulated by the Texas Commission on Jail Standards, the city and town jails are completely unregulated. Local police departments fear the costs of changes that might be required if state over-sight was imposed and, as Chairman John Whitmire (D-Houston) of the Texas Senate's Criminal Justice Committee, said, "There's just no support of money for changing the status quo."[25]

Texas does not just put people in prison; it uses capital punishment more frequently than any other state in the nation. In the early 1970s, the U.S. Supreme Court suspended capital punishment and required the states to clarify the procedures and circumstances for its use. Since the death penalty was reinstated in 1976 and executions resumed in 1982, 1,379 people have been executed in the U.S. Well over one-third of those executions—515—have occurred in Texas. No other state employs the death penalty with anything like the frequency that Texas does: Oklahoma is second (111), followed by Virginia (110), Florida (86), and Missouri (74).

Eighteen states do not employ the death penalty, thirty-two do. Ten states declared a moratorium on the death penalty in 2006, most of the rest declared a moratorium in 2007 as the Supreme Court reviewed whether lethal injections constituted cruel and unusual punishment. Texas did not pause. From 2010 through 2014, Texas executed 72 persons, fully one-third of the 206 persons executed in the U.S.

During his brief 2012 presidential campaign, Governor Rick Perry was asked about Texas's commitment to the death penalty. He responded, "If you come into our state and you kill one of our children, you kill a police officer, you're involved with another crime and you kill one of our citizens, you will face the ultimate justice in the state of Texas, and that is you will be executed."[26] Many Texans agree with the governor. A May 2012 poll by the University of Texas and the Texas Tribune found that 73 percent of Texans either strongly or somewhat favored the death penalty, while only 21 percent did not.[27] Others, including Rick Halperin, the Amnesty International state death penalty abolition coordinator, said, "Someday we will look back and shake our heads that we thought this was the best we could do—kill people."[28]

TABLE 8.3 The States That Use the Death Penalty Most Frequently, 1976 to Present			
State	Executions	State	Executions
Texas	515	Alabama	56
Oklahoma	111	Georgia	53
Virginia	110	Ohio	53
Florida	86	North Carolina	43
Missouri	74	South Carolina	43

Source: Death Penalty Information Center, "*Number of Executions by State and Region Since 1976*," last updated May 6, 2014. http://www.deathpenaltyinfo.org

What explains the high execution rates in Texas? Jeff Blackburn, chief counsel of the Texas Innocence Project, says "The death penalty is part of our fine state's religion, it's somewhere up there with football."[29] Nonetheless, while Texas stands apart, it does not stand alone. High execution rates are a southern phenomenon. Of the 1,379 executions carried out in the U.S. since 1976, 1,126 have been carried out in the South, compared to 165 in the Midwest, 84 in the West, and just four in the Northeast. Second, southern judiciaries reflect the traditionalistic political culture of the region, with its focus on elite control, law and order, and security for persons and property.

JUDICIAL REFORM IN TEXAS

Three aspects of the judicial culture in Texas seem to cry out for reconsideration and reform. The first two, judicial selection and money, are closely related and potential reform should take both into account. The third, capital punishment, sees Texas strikingly, even radically, outside the national mainstream.

Most states elect at least some of their judges.[30] Texas elects all of its judges, above the level of municipal judge, and fundraising rules are essentially discretionary. Hence, Texas judicial races are funded, not by regular citizens generally, but by interested parties—mostly lawyers and PACs. Moderate reform might entail movement in the direction of the Missouri system for judicial selection and real limits to campaign contributions in judicial races. Perhaps the governor might make initial judicial appointments based on an expert panel's professional assessment of credentials. Sitting judges might then stand in retention elections. Removing judges from the partisan electoral process would also allow strict limits on campaigning and advertising since they would be running in retention elections rather than against other candidates.

Texas must also take a serious look at its use of capital punishment. Texas has executed more than one-third of all persons executed in the U.S. since 1976. In fact, some change is already under way. In 2005, the Texas legislature approved the sentence of "life without parole." Since then, more than 400 people have been sentenced to life without parole while the number of new death sentences has fallen by about half. Many jurors, aware of the recent string of DNA exonerations of convicts, some on death row, have become less willing to award the death penalty. In 2013, while Texas executed sixteen, only nine new death sentences were handed down.

In 2010, Governor Perry signed a posthumous pardon, the first of its kind, for Tim Cole. Cole was convicted of rape in 1985 and sentenced to twenty-five years. He died of an asthma attack in prison in 1999. A 2008 DNA test exonerated Cole and implicated a convicted rapist named Jerry Wayne Johnson in his place. While the exoneration came too late for Tim Cole, his family is eligible for $1 million in compensation for his thirteen years of wrongful incarceration. Such mistakes make jurors wary of handing out irrevocable—death—sentences.

TIMELINE: A CRIMINAL PROSECUTION IN TEXAS

1	2	3	4	5	6	7	8
A crime occurs	Police respond, investigate, and (hopefully) make an arrest	The accused is informed of the charges and his or her rights in an initial court appearance	In a preliminary hearing, the judge must decide whether probable cause exists to believe a crime has occurred, the defendant may have committed it, and whether bail should be permitted	If probable cause is found, the defendant is bound over to a grand jury. A majority of the grand jury must agree that an indictment is warranted and issue a "true bill"	If the defendant does not plead guilty, a trial is held to determine guilt or innocence. The trial may be a "bench" trial before a judge or a "jury" trial before a jury of citizens	If a jury trial, a process called "voir dire" leads to selection of a jury	In opening statements, the prosecutor lays out the broad case for conviction and the defense lays out reasons to doubt guilt

Chapter Summary

The U.S. Constitution declares federal law to be "supreme" over state law, but, as a practical matter, most legal activity takes place in state courts and under state law. Federal courts deal with violations of the U.S. Constitution, federal laws and treaties, and disputes between citizens of different states. State courts deal with violations of their constitutions and laws. These cover most of the legal requirements and controversies of daily life, including tort law, family law, contracts, zoning, and traffic.

Texas has organized its judicial system in seven types of local, county, and state courts. Local government courts are municipal courts and JP courts. Municipal and JP courts deal with minor criminal and civil matters for which penalties involve fines rather than jail time. Municipal judges are appointed by city officials while justices of the peace are elected to four-year terms. About three-quarters of their caseload are minor criminal—traffic and code—violations. County courts are constitutional county courts and legislative county courts at law. The Texas Constitution mandates that each of the state's 254 counties have a constitutional county court, headed by a county judge and filled out with four county commissioners. In the more populous counties, these courts pursue executive and legislative functions, governing the county, while in lightly populated counties they also have judicial functions. In the more populous counties, county courts at law take over the judicial responsibilities of the constitutional county courts. The state trial courts are called district courts. District courts call witnesses, hear evidence, deliberate on guilt or innocence, and declare sentences and punishments. Above the district courts are fourteen courts of appeals and two high courts. The Texas Supreme Court

9	10	11	12	13	14	15
The prosecution presents its case first, calling and questioning its own witnesses who are then subject to cross-examination by the defense	The defense then calls and questions its witnesses who are subject to cross-examination by the prosecution	The judge issues a charge to the jury laying out the law that the jury must consider in reaching its verdict	In closing arguments, the prosecutor and defense summarize the evidence from their perspective and argue why it calls for conviction or acquittal	In jury deliberation, the jury considers and discusses the evidence and agree or disagree that the crimes charged have been proven	Once the jury has reached a verdict, it returns to the courtroom and announces its verdict to the judge	If the defendant has been found guilty, the punishment phase of deliberations begins. The stages of the punishment phase are the same as those in the guilt of innocence phase—opening statements, evidence from both sides, a jury charge, closing arguments, and decision

hears civil matters and the Texas Court of Criminal Appeals hears criminal matters.

Three questions are frequently raised about Texas courts, judges, and justice. One is whether partisan elections are the best way to select judges. Another is whether the amount of money circulating in Texas judicial elections biases the judicial system in favor of contributors. And the third is whether Texas incarcerates and executes more people than is either advisable or just. All of these questions remain open and will be disputed for years to come.

Key Terms

Appellate courts 199

Civil law 198

Criminal law 198

Defendant 198

Grand jury 209

Jurisdiction 199

Jury trial 210

Law 197

Missouri plan 208

Plaintiff 198

Trial courts 199

Review Questions

1. Define law and describe the role that law plays in our society.
2. Describe the Texas judicial system and the role that each type of court plays in resolving legal disputes in the state.
3. Compare the way Texas selects its judges to the way judges are selected at the federal level and in other U.S. states.

4. Assess the argument that money should play the same role in judicial elections as it does in the election of other public officials.

5. Outline several key historical and cultural factors that have led to Texas's high rates of incarceration and capital punishment.

Suggested Readings

Katharine Beckett and Bruce Western, "Governing Social Marginality: Welfare, Incarceration, and the Transformation of State Policy," *Punishment and Society* (2001), 3: 43–59.

Kyle Cheek and Anthony Champagne, *Judicial Politics in Texas: Politics, Money, and Partisanship in State Courts* (New York: Peter Lang, 2005).

Dale Carpenter, *Flagrant Conduct: The Story of Lawrence v. Texas* (New York: Norton, 2012).

Melinda Gann Hall, "State Supreme Courts in American Democracy: Probing the Myths of Judicial Reform," *American Political Science Review* (2001), 92: 315–330.

John Hubner, *Last Chance in Texas: The Redemption of Criminal Youth* (New York: Random House, 2005).

Garrick Percival, "Ideology, Diversity, and Imprisonment: Considering the Influence of Local Politics on Racial and Ethnic Incarceration Rates," *Social Science Quarterly* (2010), 91: 1063–1082.

Robert Perkinson, *Texas Tough: The Rise of America's Prison Empire* (New York: Metropolitan Books, 2010).

Jack K. Selden, *Texas Justice: The Life and Times of the Third District Court of Texas* (Palestine, TX: Clacton Press, 1997).

Robert M. Utley, *Lone Star Justice: The First Century of the Texas Rangers* (New York: Oxford University Press, 2002).

Web Resources

1. http://www.courts.state.tx.us
   Organization of the Texas judiciary.

2. http://www.texlaw.com
   Information on recent Texas court cases.

3. http://www.Texasbar.com
   Texas Bar Association.

4. http://www.deathpenaltyinfo.org
   Death Penalty Information Center.

5. http://www.cjpc.state.tx.us
   Texas Criminal Justice Policy Center.

6. http://www.ajs.org
   American Judicature Society.

7. http://www.ojp.us.doj/bjs.htm
   U.S. Department of Justice Office of Justice Program and Bureau of Justice Statistics.

Chapter 9

LOCAL GOVERNMENT IN TEXAS

HOUSTON MAYOR ANNISE PARKER

Texas is a red state, with conservative, Anglo, male leaders in the most visible leadership roles. Rick Perry served as governor from late 2000 through 2014; Governor Greg Abbott has served in statewide office since 1995. David Dewhurst has been lieutenant governor since 2003, John Cornyn has been U.S. senator since 2003, and Ted Cruz took a seat in the U.S. Senate in 2013. All are boots-with-suits Anglo conservatives in the Texas tradition. Cruz is Cuban-American, so the Texas tradition is expanding a bit, but not nearly as dramatically as it is expanding at the local level.

The major cities of Texas are mostly blue and have elected a rainbow's array of diverse mayors. Henry Cisneros was the first Hispanic mayor of San Antonia to be elected in the modern era. Cisneros was first elected mayor in 1981 and served four two-year terms. Houston elected Kathy Whitmire to five two-year terms from 1982 to 1992. She appointed Lee P. Brown to be Houston's first black police chief and Brown served as the city's first black major from 1998 to 2004. Dallas elected Annette Strauss its first female mayor in 1987 (Adlene Harrison served as acting major in 1976) and Ron Kirk its first black mayor in 1995. The difference between urban politics in Texas and statewide politics was on stark display when Ron Kirk, an easy winner in his mayoral races, sought the U.S. Senate in 2002. He lost by twelve points.

Despite at least three decades of electing Hispanic, black, and female mayors in Texas's big cities, the election of Annise Parker as Mayor of Houston in 2009 created a stir. Parker is the first openly gay mayor of a large Texas city. Sexual preference was an undercurrent in the mayor's race, but did not become a major issue and she won re-election in 2011 and 2013. Houston is the largest U.S. city ever to have had an openly gay mayor. Let's first ask how Mayor Parker won her first race for mayor and then ask what it is about major cities, even major Texas cities, that make them open to diverse candidates for office.

Annise Parker was a familiar figure in Houston before she ran for mayor. Parker was born in Houston, went to school there, graduated from Rice, and worked as a software analyst for almost twenty years for Mosbacher Energy. Rice and Mosbacher are conservative old-school names in Houston and they assuaged some doubts that might otherwise have existed about Parker. In addition, she paid her political dues before running for mayor. She lost two city council races before winning one in 1997. She held her seat in 1999 and 2001. She then won three two-year terms as Houston Comptroller, a conservative green-eyeshade position, beginning in 2003. When she ran for mayor in 2009, what was familiar about Annise Parker overcame what might, for some, have been unfamiliar.

Houston, San Antonio, and Dallas are three of the ten largest cities in the U.S. Big cities tend to be more diverse, with more different kinds of people living among each other, and, to some extent at least, getting to know each other. Big cities also need more governing—think for a moment about the garbage collection, sewage, water, and electrical systems, as well as roads, from back streets to freeway interchanges, that it takes to keep a big city going. Big cities also have a leadership elite, people who run big corporations, hospital systems, and universities that, one hopes, are thinking not just about what the city needs to run smoothly today, but decades out. Ideally, they ask what needs to be done today about education, health care, roads, and the rest to insure that when the future arrives we are ready to meet it. Thinking ahead makes an "all hands on deck" strategy seem best.

---◆━✕━◆---

Focus Questions

Q1 What is the legal relationship between state and local governments?

Q2 How important are counties in contemporary Texas government?

Q3 What are the key differences between general-law and home rule cities?

Q4 Why do most Texas cities conduct elections within single-member districts?

Q5 Why are there so many special district governments in Texas?

Q1 What is the legal relationship between state and local governments?

Only recently have social scientists, urban planners, and the best public officials begun to think more clearly and systematically about the importance of local communities and their governments. Each of us lives in the United States and in the state of Texas. We all live under the national security umbrella of the U.S. and within the open entrepreneurial culture of Texas. Still, there are vast differences between and among Texas communities. Some Texans live in the impoverished *colonias* of the lower Rio

Grande Valley while others live in the beauty and security of gated communities. Locality, place, and community provide the contexts for our lives.

Of course, wealthy communities have an easier time creating a highly desirable local environment than do poor and rural communities. Wright Patman represented the 1st congressional district in northeast Texas from 1929 to 1976. Patman campaigned, decade after decade, by assuring his hard-scrabble rural constituents that their needs were greater than their more privileged urban cousins. Patman swore that, "Down in Houston there are some neighborhoods so rich that every flea has its own dog."[1] Patman had in mind the exclusive River Oaks neighborhood of Houston, but he might as well have been thinking of other wealthy enclaves, such as Highland Park in Dallas, Westover Hills in Fort Worth, or Alamo Heights in San Antonio. Char Miller and Heywood T. Sanders explain in *Urban Texas: Politics and Development* that, "These exclusive enclaves offered the security of racial, ethnic, and class homogeneity (enforced by restrictive covenants) and minimal taxes. Thus the new urban elite was able to escape the social problems and needs of the city, as well as the vagaries of its politics, even as it directed and profited from urban growth and expansion."[2] Only a few cities are so privileged. Most cities and towns have to make hard choices between streets, parks, libraries, public safety, and the salaries and benefits of public employees.

Think for a moment about the myriad ways in which the most attractive community you know differs from an average community, let alone the least attractive community you've seen. The most attractive communities are not just clean and safe, they are interesting and vibrant, offering good schools, good jobs, and all the amenities that add up to a good quality of life. They are places you want to be. [3]

Cities are municipal corporations and, in some ways, they act more like private sector corporations than one might think. Municipalities complete with each other on service delivery and, like private corporations, they compete to offer the most attractive mix of quality and price. How much does it cost in terms of taxes and fees to live in a given community and what mix of tangible and intangible benefits derive from living in that community? Ask yourself, what kinds of services would a city offer to attract a desirable set of residents and a skilled workforce?

Harvard political scientist Paul Peterson pursued these questions to their uncomfortable conclusions in his path-breaking book, *City Limits*. Soothingly, Peterson began by assuming that "cities select those policies which are in the interest of the city as a whole."[4] But it soon became clear that what was in the best interest of the city was to have a uniformly prosperous and accomplished citizenry. Peterson explained that,

> cities develop a set of policies that will attract the more skilled and white collar workers without at the same time attracting unemployables.... They can provide parks, recreation areas, and good quality schools in areas where the most economically productive live. They can keep the cost of social services, little utilized by the middle class, to a minimum, thereby keeping local taxes relatively low.[5]

Municipalities do this by pursuing a distinctive approach to aligning taxes paid to services delivered at the individual level. Before reading on, think for a moment about the smooth sidewalks and bricked medians in wealthy neighborhoods and the crumbling sidewalks and potholed roads in poor neighborhoods. Peterson explains these neighborhood differences with what he calls the "the benefits received principle; . . . A city concerned about its economic interests does not consider each taxpayers' benefit/tax ratio equally but in proportion to his contributions to the local coffers." The benefits received principle "specifies that individuals should be taxed in accordance with the level of services they receive. In this way, each individual consumes no more services that he pays for . . ."[6] But it also means that those who pay few taxes—the poor—have few claims on services.

In fact, municipalities regularly strive to benefit their most well-off and dissuade the least well-off from staying. From one town to the next, both the wealthy and the poor are mobile. Generous social services provided by a wealthy community might attract the needy, detracting from the community's quality of life, and leading the wealthy to consider moving. Moreover, the high taxes needed to fund social services might also produce an adverse comparison for the wealthy with other attractive but less generous communities. Hence, as Patterson explains, communities "try to insure that the benefits of public services outweigh their cost to those highly skilled workers, managers, and professionals who are vital to sustaining the community's economic growth."[7]

To get a better idea of how this works, consider the 28 separate municipalities in Dallas County. The property tax rates in these 28 cities ranged from just under 2 percent to just over 3 percent of the assessed value of property, homes, and businesses in each. The lowest property tax rate of the 28 was in the very wealthy city of Highland Park at 1.98 percent, while the much more modest cities of Cedar Hill (2.78 percent), DeSoto (2.82 percent), Lancaster (2.9 percent), and Wylie (3.16 percent) struggled under higher rates. Wealthy cities can have lower tax rates and still raise enough revenue to support an upscale environment, while poor cities must set higher tax rates and still generate too few funds to deliver necessary services.

We close this discussion with a little multiplication exercise. In 2014, the Zillow property value website reported that the average value of homes in Highland Park was $1.25 million while in DeSoto the average home value was $125,700. Multiplying the average home value in Highland Park times their property tax rates (1.98 percent) shows they raise $24,750 per home. Multiplying the average home value in DeSoto time their higher property tax rate (2.82 percent) shows they raise $3,544 per home. Everyone knows it's good to be rich, but these quick back of the envelop calculations show why cities with wealthy residents are so attractive.

Local officials and the governments in which they serve are responsible for the streets that you drive on every day, the schools that most of you went to as children, and the parks where you walk your dog. And if you want to shake your fist at government, you can easily do so—at the local school board meeting, at the planning commission, or at city hall. Local governments are open to citizen input and influence in ways that state and national government simply are not and cannot be.

Despite the importance of local governments and all that they do, they have less independence and authority than most people think. Most Americans assume that there are three levels of government in American federalism—national, state, and local—each with its own powers and responsibilities. But this common assumption is wrong. State governments define and limit the structure, resources, and responsibilities of local governments. Not surprisingly, local governments spend a lot of time and money trying to influence what state government demands, allows, and forbids them to do.

In this chapter we begin by asking how Texas organizes and empowers its county and municipal governments. We will see that while the structure and powers of county governments are explicitly defined in the Texas Constitution, municipalities, depending upon their size, have some flexibility in choosing their form of government. Finally, we will describe the special district governments that operate in Texas and ask what reforms might make Texas local governments more effective and responsive.

TEXAS AS A FEDERAL SYSTEM

The U.S. and each of the fifty states, including Texas, are sovereign governments. The U.S. and Texas have their own constitutions and their own chief executives, legislatures, and high courts, all making critical decisions. Texas local governments do not have their own constitutions; they have only those powers granted to them by the state's constitution and laws. In fact, according to a long-standing legal principle known as **Dillon's Rule**, local governments are "creatures of state government."

John Dillon, for whom Dillon's Rule was named, was a member of the Iowa Supreme Court (1862–69) and the nation's leading jurist on municipal law. President Grant named Dillon to the federal appeals court bench, where he served for nearly a decade. While on the federal bench, he wrote Municipal Corporations (1872). After resigning the federal bench in 1879, Dillon taught at the Columbia and Yale University law schools and served as president of the American Bar Association. He died in 1914 but his writing on municipal law and government is still influential. Dillon's formal expression of the relationship of cities to the sovereign states was:

> It is a general and understood proposition of law that a municipal corporation possesses and can exercise the following powers, and no others: First, those

MEI-CHUN JAU/Staff Photographer/The Dallas Morning News

Claudia Fowler, a former school board member in the Wilmer Hutchins ISD south of Dallas took the current board to task, saying: "I think Wilmer-Hutchins is being picked on."

Dillon's Rule A legal concept holding that local governments are the creatures or creations of state governments.

granted in express words; second, those necessarily and fairly implied in or incident to the powers expressly granted; third, those essential to the declared objects and purposes of the corporation—not simply convenient, but indispensable. Any fair, reasonable, substantial doubt concerning the existence of power is resolved by the courts against the corporation, and the power is denied.[8]

Mercifully, Stephen L. Elkins, in *City and Regime in the American Republic*, summarized Dillon's rule as follows: "The contemporary city is not a sovereign body, and in law its limited powers are understood to be the powers that are specifically granted to it by state governments."[9]

The Texas Constitution gives the state the power to create, revise, and reform its county and municipal governments. In the 19th century, Texas state government authorized the creation of new cities, revised their charters, increased the number of counties, and redrew their boundaries as population growth and economic development required. In the 20th century, as the number of counties stabilized and cities grew in size and complexity, the political relationship between the state and its cities and counties evolved and matured.

While local governments are constitutionally and legally dependent on state government, they enjoy considerable political influence over it. While governors and legislative leaders often take a statewide view, the average state legislator thinks of him or herself much more as a local official than as a state official. In Austin full-time only five months every other year, state legislators tend to work closely with the local officials from their area.

Perhaps the most interesting recent example of local governments and officials working to thwart state action that they believed would be detrimental to them involved property tax appraisal caps. Property tax revenues are critical to local governments, so state attempts to limit these revenues met with broad opposition from local governments. The Texas Constitution limits property tax appraisal increases to no more than 10 percent a year. Since 1997, Governors Bush and Perry, taxcutters both, have urged legislation to limit the maximum annual increase in property tax appraisals to 3 to 5 percent, unless more was approved by a vote of the affected public. The legislature has taken up a series of bills over more than a decade, but all were opposed by the Texas Association of Counties (TAC) and the Texas Municipal League (TML) and none have passed.

In an attempt to break through this impasse, Governor Perry appointed a fifteen-member Texas Task Force on Appraisal Reform in 2006. The task force was chaired by Tom Pauken, a former chair of the Texas Republican Party and an anti-tax hawk. In charging the task force, Perry argued that "if people are going to pay higher taxes at the local level, it ought to come with a public vote and not by . . . the appraiser's pen."[10] Local government officials argued that lowering the cap would limit their ability to fund construction and services, particularly in fast-growing areas.

Knowing the sentiment in the legislature, Perry's task force declined to recommend reducing the cap to 5 percent, but they did advocate limiting local government spending growth and allowing counties a half cent sales tax increase if they used the money to reduce property taxes. Neither idea passed and Pauken knew why. He blamed "the vigorous opposition of the Texas Municipal League and the Texas Association of Counties; . . . and unfortunately they had support from a number of legislators, including some Republicans."[11]

Still, the fight is not over. Perry continued to support appraisal reform. Moreover, newly elected state officials, led by Lieutenant Governor Dan Patrick and Comptroller Glenn Hegar, the state's top tax official, argued for getting rid of the property tax entirely in favor of expanded sales taxes. State officials messing with local government revenue sources make local officials very nervous. Who should decide issues of local government taxing and spending? Should it be local officials or state officials? The Texas Constitution and law say state officials, but so far shrewd politics has allowed local governments to fight off tighter caps, let alone a wholesale revision of county and municipal government revenue sources. Let's see what local government officials in Texas actually do.

THE COUNTIES

Texas has more counties—254—than any other state (see Figure 9.1). Texas counties were originally intended to serve an overwhelmingly rural population that needed only occasional access to government services.[12] As the settlement line moved west, county lines were drawn and redrawn to insure that county government was accessible to most citizens. The Texas Constitution mandates the structure and powers of county government, firmly limiting both.

Origins and Purposes

Prior to its independence from Mexico, Texas was part of the province of Coahuila y Tejas. The province was divided into seven administrative departments, three of which, Bexar, Brazos, and Nacogdoches, were in Texas. Within the three Texas departments by 1835 were 23 municipio. Unlike modern cities, municipio, or municipalities, in the Mexican system were regional governments administered by an elected alcalde (executive) and ayuntamiento (council).

Following independence, the Republic of Texas converted the 23 Mexican municipio into counties and instituted the Anglo-American common law system. The alcalde and ayuntamiento were replaced by new county officials. Citizens of each county elected a sheriff, coroner, constables, clerks, and justices of the peace. The justices of the peace elected a chief justice and two associate justices to preside in the county court. New counties could be formed upon the request of at least 100 adult white men in an unorganized area of 900 square miles. Modest reform of the Republic of Texas's county institutions in the Texas statehood Constitution of 1845 gave us the county commissioners court system we know today.[13]

In early Texas, county governments brought state law and services to a widely scattered rural population. Texans went to the county courthouse to file birth and death certificates; apply for a marriage license; register deeds, contracts, and wills; pay taxes; and register to vote. The county built and

Who Knew?

At independence, Texas identified 23 counties. As the settlement line moved north and west, new counties were laid out until the current number of 254 was reached early in the 20th century.

Q2 How important are counties in contemporary Texas government?

LET'S COMPARE   LOCAL GOVERNMENTS IN TEXAS AND BEYOND

Texas is the second most populous state, behind only California, and the second largest, behind only Alaska (not shown here). Texas is organized into far more counties (254) than any other state, and more cities than any state but Illinois. Texas also has more school districts than any other state, though that number has been declining slowly as smaller districts combine with larger districts. Texas also makes extensive use of special districts. For a small government state, Texas has a lot of governments, though this may also mean that they are closer to the people.

On the other hand, it never hurts to ask how elites benefit from a given state of affairs. What does it mean, for example, that Texas has three times as many cities and ten times as many school districts as Florida, another large, populous, sun-belt state? First, it has to mean that Texas cities and school districts are smaller than Florida cities and school districts. Dividing the Florida population by the number of cities and school districts gives you 45,744 per city and 197,905 per school district. For Texas, the same

calculation gives you 20,799 per city and 23,261 per school district. Even acknowledging that Texas is bigger geographically and younger demographically, it is clear that Texas's large number of cities and school districts means that each is smaller and probably more homogeneous than Florida's.

Texas's larger number of more homogenous political jurisdictions means greater variations in wealth. Wealthy enclaves, especially in Texas's major metropolitan areas—River Oaks in Houston, Highland Park in Dallas, and Alamo Heights in San Antonio—are their own upscale cities and school districts. Alternatively, poorer cities and school districts must struggle along on their own or with modest state help. A smaller number of larger cities and school districts would likely include a wider range of rich, middle class, and poor in the same jurisdiction and be able to spread revenues more evenly across cities and school districts—if that were what Texas elites wanted. Do you think it is?

State	Population	Area in Square Miles	Counties	Cities	School Districts	Special Districts	Total Governments
California	38,041,000	163,696	57	478	1,044	2,765	4,344
Texas	26,051,000	268,581	254	1,209	1,081	2,291	4,835
New York	19,570,000	54,556	57	618	680	1,119	2,474
Florida	19,318,000	65,755	66	411	95	1,051	1,623
Illinois	12,875,000	57,914	102	1,299	912	3,249	5,562
Pennsylvania	12,769,000	46,055	66	1,016	515	1,728	3,325
Ohio	11,544,000	44,825	88	938	668	700	2,394
Georgia	9,920,000	59,425	154	535	180	570	1,439
Michigan	9,883,000	96,716	83	533	579	456	1,651
New Jersey	8,865,000	8,721	21	324	549	247	1,141

Source: U.S. Census Bureau, *Statistical Abstract of the United States, 2014* (Washington D.C.: Government Printing Office, 2012), Tables 11 and 448. New York, Illinois, Pennsylvania, Ohio, Michigan, and New Jersey organize very small communities as townships. Townships are not included in the totals above.

repaired roads and provided law enforcement through the county sheriff. As modern Texas emerged over the course of the 20th century, rural counties changed little, but some urban counties added services like libraries, parks, hospitals, and community colleges. Every Texas county, whether its services are few or many, has the same structure and powers mandated by the Texas Constitution of 1876.

Structure of County Government

Today, each Texas county is governed by a commissioners court made up of a county judge and four county commissioners. These officials are elected to four-year terms on a partisan ballot. The county judge is elected countywide and the commissioners are elected within geographical districts called precincts. In addition to the commissioners court, several key officials, including a county sheriff, county clerk, county or district attorney, county tax assessor/collector, county treasurer, and county surveyor are elected countywide and act as independent administrators.[14]

As we shall see below, the commissioners court has broad management responsibility for county government. But other countywide elected officials, such as the county sheriff and county clerk, have a great deal of discretion in running their own departments. They have the authority to set policy, let contracts, and hire and fire within their own departments. Ultimately, each countywide elected official is responsible to the voters and removable only by the voters. County government, like state government, features a plural executive in which no single official is "in charge."

Commissioners Court

Commissioners court, despite the name, is not simply, or sometimes even mainly, a court. In all Texas counties, it is the chief policymaking (legislative) and administrative (executive) institution of county government. In the smaller, rural counties the commissioners court still has judicial duties. While the commissioners court does not have direct authority over most other county officials, it does derive significant influence from its control of the county budget. However, once county officials get their annual appropriation, they generally seek to re-assert their independence.

The commissioners court passes ordinances; sets the property tax rate; adopts the budget; appoints senior administrators; awards contracts for building, road construction, and repair; and generally monitors county government. In most Texas counties the budget for road and bridge construction and repair is divided among the four commissioners and administered independently by each. This encourages overlap, inefficiency, and, at least occasionally, corruption, but it is the basis for commissioners' job and contract patronage.[15] In the rural counties, road building and maintenance is the chief role of county government. In fact, in many rural counties, the county commissioners are simply called "road commissioners." Counties are also responsible for law enforcement outside of cities and towns.

Commissioners court
The chief policymaking and administrative institution of Texas county government.

The state's urban counties often do more than offer basic county services, Some administer a county hospital, parks, libraries, airports, and sports authorities, as well as a range of welfare, health, and education programs. The average annual salary of county commissioners in 2014 was about $80,000, with the largest counties paying about $140,000.[16] Montogomery County, north of Austin, was the high at $154,500.

County Judge

County judge The county judge is elected countywide and presides over the county commissioners court.

The **county judge** is elected on a partisan ballot, to a four-year term, by the eligible voters of the county. Though the office is called county judge, the incumbent does not have to be a lawyer, just "well-informed in the law." Only in the state's rural counties, where the workload is light, do county judges still have judicial responsibilities. The county judge is the county's chief legislator and executive.

The county judge presides over the commissioners court, sets the agenda, and participates in all of the debates. In some counties, the tradition has developed that the county judge votes only in case of ties, but the judge is entitled to vote on all issues that come before the court. As the only member of the court elected countywide, the judge is often in a position to resolve

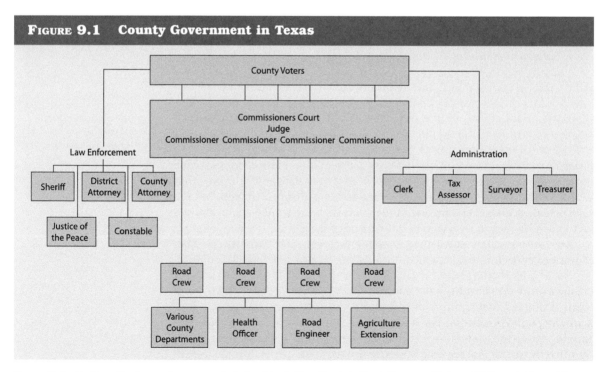

FIGURE 9.1   County Government in Texas

Source: Derived by the author from various sources, including John A. Gilmartin, et al., *County Government in Texas*, V.G. Young Institute of County Government, Texas A&M University System. See also George D. Braden, "Citizens' Guide to the Texas Constitution," prepared for the Texas Advisory Commission on Intergovernmental Relations by the Institute of Urban Studies, University of Houston, 1972.

disputes and broker compromises between the four commissioners that represent individual districts.

The county judge's executive and administrative responsibilities also create opportunities for influence. The judge has the power to fill vacancies on the court, to appoint commissioners to important boards and commissions, and to draft the county budget for the consideration and approval of the full commissioners court. The county judge's legislative and executive powers generally allow him or her to emerge as the county's leading public official. The average salary for county judges in 2014 was $100,000, with the most populous counties paying their county judges about $150,000. Dallas County, at $163,200, was the top.

Other County Administrators

The county clerk, county tax assessor/collector, county treasurer, and county surveyor are each elected countywide to a four-year term. These offices vary somewhat in their structure and responsibilities, depending upon the size and complexity of the county. Salaries in 2012 averaged about $75,000, with offices requiring legal expertise paying about $110,000.

County Clerk. The county clerk maintains the county's legal files, official records, and vital statistics. Some county clerks oversee the work of a few assistants while others oversee a staff of hundreds. The county clerk's office is responsible for maintaining the records of the commissioners court as well as the justice of the peace and county courts. The county clerk maintains records of births, deaths, marriages, deeds, wills, and contracts. The county clerk also serves on the county elections board and is responsible for conducting elections.

In counties with a population of over 8,000, the workload of the district court justifies the election of a district clerk. The district clerk is elected to maintain the records of the district court. The district clerk manages all court filings, schedules cases, and sends out the feared jury summons for the district court.

County Tax Assessor/Collector. Until 1978, tax assessors actually set the value of property for tax purposes with little oversight. Since 1978, the state has established uniform assessment procedures and criteria to streamline and rationalize the assessment process. Today's tax assessor/collector collects state and county taxes as well as vehicle license and title fees and, in some counties, operates as the registrar of voters. Counties of under 10,000 may leave the office of assessor/collector unfilled and devolve its duties onto the county sheriff.

County Treasurer/Auditor. County treasurers receive, deposit, and expend county funds. State law requires counties over 35,000 to supplement the treasurer with an appointed auditor. The district judge with jurisdiction in the county appoints an auditor to a two-year term to monitor the financial practices of the county to insure that they comply with state law.

County Surveyor. The office of county surveyor dates back to the Republic of Texas. Throughout the 19th century, county surveyor was an influential and often lucrative position. Surveyors record and verify land boundaries for individuals, developers, and municipalities. Today, most Texas counties no longer elect a surveyor. Survey work is still required, but it is contracted for on a fee-for-service basis.

County Law Enforcement

The county sheriff and the county attorney are elected at-large to four-year terms. They are the principal non-judicial law enforcement officials of Texas county government.

County Sheriff. The county sheriff is a powerful figure in county government, often second only to the county judge. He or she is the county's chief law enforcement officer, responsible for enforcing state laws and county ordinances within the county and for administering the county jail. Oftentimes, the sheriff's office patrols the unincorporated parts of the county, leaving urban law enforcement to city police forces. Constables are law enforcement officers attached to the JP courts. They perform many of the same duties as deputy sheriffs.

District/County Attorney. Texas counties may have a county attorney, a district attorney, or both. County and district attorneys serve as legal advisers to county government and represent the county in court. Urban counties usually divide the workload between a county attorney and a district attorney. County attorneys usually handle minor criminal matters and juvenile cases in the JP and county courts. District attorneys handle the major criminal cases in the district courts.

CITIES AND MUNICIPALITIES

As noted above, when Texas achieved its independence, population was so thinly distributed that Article IV, section 11, of the constitution required new counties to have at least 100 free male inhabitants in an area of 900 square miles. No constitutional provisions described how cities should be incorporated and early travelers thought that towns were founded by settlers virtually at will. N. Doran Maillard, a South Carolina newspaper editor touring Texas for his health in 1840, wrote that to "incorporate cities . . . in Texas, . . . nothing more is required of a man, woman, or child, than to possess a piece of land, and with a few pegs to section a portion of it, and to tack 'ville' or 'burgh' to the end of their name, and the city town or hamlet is complete."[17] In early Texas, cities worked directly with the legislature to craft city charters specially designed to their purposes. As the state grew, legislators sought to simplify and regularize the process of organizing municipal governments.

Though the needs of larger cities continued to be addressed by special charters, by 1858 the legislature had devised general-law charters that cities meeting particular criteria could adopt. **Incorporation** is the legal process by which cities are born. Today, once an area reaches 200 residents, those residents

Incorporation The legal process by which cities are established.

can petition the county judge to authorize and conduct an incorporation election. The ballot proposes one of the general-law forms of government for adoption. If a majority of voters approve incorporation, the state issues the appropriate municipal charter. In 1912, a series of constitutional amendments were adopted that permitted municipalities of more than 5,000 residents to design and adopt "home rule" charters so long as they met certain criteria and did not violate other state laws. A municipal charter, like a constitution, lays out the basic structure and powers of government. Each of Texas's 1,200 municipalities is organized as a general-law or home rule city.

General-Law and Home Rule Cities

Article XI of the Texas Constitution declares that all cities and towns of under 5,000 residents must adopt a general-law charter. State law authorizes three general-law charters (the mayor–council, the council–manager, and the commission form) with multiple options for structure and powers within each. About 900 small Texas cities operate under a general-law charter. Most of Texas's 300 larger cities operate under a home rule charter of their own design.

Q3 What are the key differences between general-law and home rule cities?

Each year three or four Texas cities replace general-law charters with home rule charters. As a city's population grows past 5,000, the issues that confront them seem to demand more time and attention. Home rule charters allow cities to replace part-time mayors with full-time city administrators, increase their property tax rate from $1.50 per $100 of assessed value to as much as $2.50, and to exercise more control over their growth.

Annexation and the Growth of Cities

State law recognizes that cities, once founded, need the power and authority to manage their growth. Cities have the right to pass ordinances, deliver services, and levy taxes within their borders. They also have certain rights, called **extraterritorial jurisdiction** (ETJ), outside their immediate borders. A city of under 5,000 has ETJ over zoning and building for half a mile beyond its formal boundaries. Big cities, over 100,000 residents, have ETJ up to five miles beyond their borders.

Extraterritorial jurisdiction (ETJ) ETJ describes the limited power that cities exercise over territory just beyond their boundaries.

Annexation is one of the processes by which cities grow. Existing cities can annex land within their ETJ in amounts no greater than 10 percent of their existing territory per year. Home rule cities can annex territory by a simple majority vote of the city council. They do not require the approval of the residents of the area to be annexed. General-law cities must get majority approval of a referendum among the people living in the area to be annexed. No new cities can be incorporated within an existing city's ETJ without the approval of the existing city.

Annexation A legal and political process by which cities absorb adjacent territory.

As the population of a city grows, it tends to spread out across a wider geographical area and eventually population spills beyond the city limits. Residents within the city limits are subject to laws, ordinances, and taxes to provide order, security, and services, such as police and fire protection, roads and bridges, schools, and, eventually, hospitals, parks, and the arts. Persons

TIMELINE: THE GROWTH OF TEXAS'S MAJOR CITIES

		1850	1860	1870	1880	1890	1900	1910	1920
Houston	Population	2,396	4,845	9,332	16,513	27,557	44,633	78,800	138,276
	Sq. Miles	9	25	9	9	9	9	15.8	38.6
San Antonio	Population	3,488	8,235	12,256	20,550	37,653	53,321	96,614	161,379
	Sq. Miles	36	36	36	36	36	36	36	36
Dallas	Population		678	3,000	10,358	38,067	42,638	92,104	158,976
	Sq. Miles	.5							23
Austin	Population	854	3,546	4,428	11,013	14,888	21,736	30,791	34,876
	Sq. Miles	1				4.5	16.5	16.5	16.5

Source: ProQuest LLC, *Statistical Abstract of the United States, 2013*, 1st ed., Bethesda, Maryland, 2012. "Population Section," Table 27, "Incorporated Places with 175,000 or More," pp. 33–34. Various previous years.

outside the city limits often call for extension of city services, especially streets, water, and sewer, and they use city parks, libraries, and civic centers, all while paying the lower taxes common to unincorporated areas.

During the 19th century, Texas's larger cities could not revise their city charters or expand their boundaries without going back to the legislature for a law authorizing the changes. Annexation is always a particularly controversial process. Until the legislature approved "home rule" provisions in 1912, residents desiring annexation to a nearby city had to petition for it; cities could not expand of their own initiative. Notice in the Timeline above, that Houston grew 20-fold in population, from 2,396 in 1850 to 44,633 in 1900, while its 9 square mile geographical footprint did not change at all. In fact, it did expand briefly, from 9 to 25 square miles between 1850 and 1860, only to be beaten back to its original 9 square miles by opponents of expansion. Similarly, San Antonio maintained its 36 square mile area from 1850 to 1940.

Home rule provided that cities over 5,000 had the right, within limits established by the state constitution and laws, to design their own government structures and powers, and to annex territory unilaterally, meaning by vote of the city council and without petition or approval by the effected property owners. Most major Texas cities used their powers of unilateral annexation to keep population growth, city services, and geographical scope in balance. Houston expanded from just less than 16 square miles in 1910 to 160 square miles in 1950 and almost 620 square miles in 2000. Dallas and Austin also took early advantage of their new annexation powers. Only San Antonio waited until mid-century before beginning its expansion.[18]

The near unlimited powers of annexation enjoyed by Texas home rule cities after 1912 were part of a distinctly Texan balance, or imbalance, between the state and its municipalities. Unlike most states, Texas provides no state revenue sharing to its cities and towns for roads, hospitals, and other social services. To compensate for the lack of state support, home rule cities have been allowed

1930	1940	1950	1960	1970	1980	1990	2000	2010
292,352	384,514	596,163	938,219	1,234,000	1,595,000	1,631,000	1,954,000	2,099,000
72.1	73.0	160.0	349.3	446.9	557.7	578.5	618.9	662.3
231,542	253,854	408,442	587,718	654,289	786,000	935,000	1,145,000	1,328,000
36	36	70	160.5	184.0	262.7	333.0	407.6	412.1
260,475	294,734	434,462	679,684	844,189	905,000	1,008,000	1,189,000	1,198,000
42	41	112	279.9	265.6	333.0	342.4	342.5	385.8
53,120	87,930	132,459	186,545	251,817	346,000	466,000	657,000	790,000
20.4	30.9	37.5	55.8	80.1	128.9	225.6	257.9	307.8

unilateral power of annexation to expand services with population growth and to draw those outlying areas enjoying the services into the city's tax base.[19]

Historically, Texas governors and legislators protected the understanding that cities would be responsible for their own funding, by resisting the calls by opponents of annexation that property-owners be permitted to vote proposed annexations up or down. Local officials, arguing that unilateral annexation was the only way to keep the tax base aligned with the expansion of services and costs, prevailed into the 1990s. In 1996, the city of Houston annexed the wealthy subdivision of Kingwood against the determined resistance of many residents. Twenty years earlier, Kingwood's developer had agreed with Houston to permit annexation when the city's expansion reached Kingwood in exchange for extension of Houston water and sewer services. Services were extended, but when Houston initiated annexation, residents of Kingwood mounted an organized resistance that found support in the state legislature.[20]

General law cities always had to take annexation plans to effected property owners for approval and now home rule cities do too. In 1999, the Texas legislature approved Senate Bill 89, which does not prohibit unilateral annexation, but does make it a more contentious, time-consuming, and difficult process. Requirements for posting notification of annexation intent, public hearings, and arbitration expand public input to the process. There are two broad paths to annexation remaining in current law. The first is a three-year path, including a vote, for more populated areas of 100 or more rooftops. The second path, and this is the more commonly travelled path, is still largely unilateral in areas of fewer than 100 rooftops.

The 2015 legislative session put on display new tensions between Texas, its cities, and their residents. Tensions rose in November 2014 when the residents of Denton, a town of about 125,000 near Dallas, voted 59 percent to 41 percent to institute a "fracking ban" within the city limits. Fracking, as most Texans know, is a drilling technique that frees oil and gas trapped in tight

shale formations by pumping fluids under high pressure into those formations deep underground to crack them so the product can flow out. Critics in
Denton and elsewhere claim that fracking may produce air, water, and noise
pollution and some scientists have linked fracking operations, especially deep
well disposal of wastewater, to an increase in as yet minor earthquakes. The
powerful oil and gas industry disputes all of this, claiming that state regulation makes energy exploration and extraction in Texas safe and clean. So
when the residents of Denton passed their fracking ban, the industry took
notice—and action. The Texas Legislature passed and Governor Abbott signed
House Bill 40, a state law overriding local bans on hydraulic fracturing. Local
control has always been an important Texas value, but so has making sure
that the interests of the state's iconic oil and gas industries are not unduly
inconvenienced by occasionally misguided locals.

Forms of City Government

The Texas Constitution and laws permit three general forms of municipal government: the mayor–council form of government, which is often discussed
in terms of strong mayor and weak mayor forms; the council–manager form;
and the commission form. Though the commission form was instrumental in
helping Galveston recover from the devastating hurricane and flood of 1901, it
is rarely used today. There are many variations on both the mayor–council and
council–manager systems and several of Texas's larger home rule cities have
sought to combine mayoral leadership, council representation of neighborhoods, and professional city management.

The great hurricane that destroyed Galveston in 1900 led that city to adopt
a commission form of government in 1901. The commission form was
described as bringing business-like efficiency and expertise to government
and so fit nicely with the traditional political culture of elite leadership. A
mayor and four to six commissioners, elected citywide on a non-partisan
ballot, formed the city council for the purposes of setting tax rates, adopting
the budget, and passing general ordinances. Each commissioner also oversees a major element of city government—administration, finance, public
safety, water and sewer, street, parks, and public improvements. Galveston's
recovery convinced many urban reformers throughout Texas and around the
country that the non-partisan, business efficiency, of the commission form of
government outweighed the loss of popular participation and neighborhood
control.

Most large cities in Texas followed Galveston's example. Houston adopted
the commission form in 1905, Dallas and El Paso did so in 1907, Austin in 1909,
and San Antonio followed suit in 1914. Few cities adopted the commission
form after World War I and over the next several decades most commission
cities revised their charters to adopt council–manager forms of government.
Austin moved to the council–manager form in two stages, 1924 and 1926,
Dallas moved in 1931, Houston in 1942, San Antonio in 1951, and in 1960

Pro & Con   Strong Mayors

The Texas Constitution mandates a plural executive at the state and county levels. At the state level, the governor shares executive authority with the lieutenant governor, attorney general, comptroller, the commissioners of agriculture and land, as well as the railroad and education commissions. At the county level, the county judge and commissioners share executive authority with the sheriff, county clerk, and others. The constitution's authors were intent upon limiting government power and spreading the power that was given across a number of officials.

Municipal governments in Texas, once the city's population exceeds 5,000, have more flexibility in designing and organizing their political institutions. "Home rule" authority means that cities over 5,000 can select a mayor–council system, a council–manager system, or a commission system. Few of Texas's 300 home rule cities use the commission form today. About 90 percent of them use the council–manager system in which the elected council sets policy and the professionally trained city manager administers the city on a day-to-day basis. Council members are elected in single-member districts and a mayor may be elected citywide, but it is the city manager that hires and fires bureau chiefs, like the police and fire chiefs, and drafts the city budget for council consideration.

Though most major cities in the U.S., including New York, Boston, Philadelphia, Chicago, and Los Angeles, have a strong mayor–council system of government, only Houston among the major Texas cities does. Houston's strong mayor has an appointed chief-of-staff to handle day-to-day affairs so that the mayor can focus on policy-making, coalition-building, and the big picture. The mayor hires and fires top city officials, drafts the budget, presides over council meetings, and wields a veto. However, even in Houston's strong mayor system there is an elected Controller with broad responsibility for seeing that city funds are accounted for, invested appropriately, and expended according to standard procedures and best practices.

Why do most major Texas cities avoid the strong mayor form of government while most major cities in the rest of the country use it? One important reason is that the Texas commitment to weak government with powers spread diffusely through the executive branch is influential even where it is not constitutionally mandated. Proponents of the weak mayor and council–manager systems contend that municipal government works best under consensus, when a number of officials need to be convinced before moving forward.

Proponents of strong mayor systems contend that big cities, with all of their problems and opportunities, need strong leadership. Strong mayors can lay out a plan, hire the senior administrators to carry it out, and craft a budget to provide the necessary resources. Do you think that Texas's big cities should be led by strong figures like New York's Bill DeBlasio and Chicago's Rahm Emanuel, or by weak mayors that must cajole and convince their city council colleagues before moving forward?

Galveston abandoned the commission form for the council–manager form. In most cities, business elites, including Houston's Citizens Charter Committee, Dallas's Citizens Charter Association, and San Antonio's Good Government League, led the movement to council–manager government.

In 1947, Houston alone among the state's major cities abandoned the council–manager form of government for the strong mayor form that most big cities around the nation use. Mayor Oscar Holcombe was the moving force behind the initiative for a strong mayor in Houston. Holcombe was one of the most prominent and successful mayors in Texas history.

Annise Parker is sworn in as mayor of Houston as her partner Kathy Hubbard looks on.

Mayor–Council. Most large American cities operate under the mayor–council form of government. In Texas, many small towns employ the mayor–council structure, but among the state's largest cities, only Houston does. The mayor–council form of government reflects, in varying degrees, the classic separation of powers between the executive (mayor) and legislative (council) branches of government. It also reflects the feeling that cities should be led by elected officials rather than appointed managers.

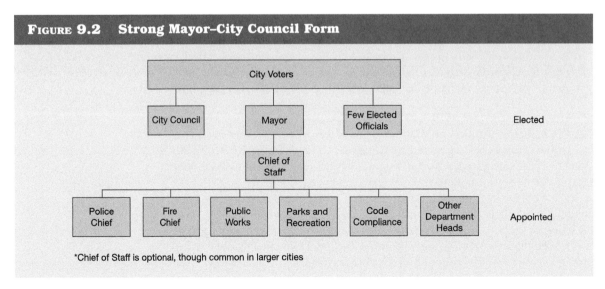

FIGURE 9.2   **Strong Mayor–City Council Form**

*Chief of Staff is optional, though common in larger cities

Source: Produced by the author.

In the mayor–council system, the council ranges from five to fifteen members, elected at-large or in single-member districts. The council makes policy and passes ordinances for the city. It authorizes city programs and services, sets tax rates, and adopts the city budget. Council committees engage in planning, community outreach, investigations, and oversight.

A **strong mayor** is elected citywide and has the classic powers of an American chief executive. Like the president or a strong governor, a strong mayor hires, manages, and, if necessary, fires the principal department heads and prepares the city budget and submits it to the council for adoption. A strong mayor may also preside over council meetings, participate in their debates, and wield a veto over their actions. A strong mayor is the acknowledged representative and leader of his or her city. Houston is the only large Texas city to adopt the strong-mayor form of government.[21] The mayor of Houston makes $209,000 annually.

Strong mayor An elected city executive with strong appointment, budgetary, and council management powers.

The difference between a strong mayor and a weak mayor is often a matter of degrees. Every power that a strong mayor has can be checked a little or a lot to produce a weaker mayor. Most small Texas towns employ a weak-mayor form of government. A **weak mayor** might require council approval, perhaps by a two-thirds vote, for their hires. A weak mayor might be checked in the budgetary process by an appointed or elected treasurer or comptroller. A weak mayor might not have a veto over council action, or might have a veto that is easily overridden. Politically though, a poor politician can struggle to achieve his or her goals in a strong mayor's office, and a good politician can achieve great things even though the mayoral tools are weak.

Weak mayor An elected city executive with few meaningful appointment, budgetary, and council management powers.

Council–Manager. The council–manager form of municipal government is composed of an elected city council of five to fifteen members, of which one will be a weak mayor, and a professional city manager appointed by the council. The council–manager form of government arose early in the 20th century, during the Progressive Era, in an attempt to clean up city government by separating the politics of council policymaking from the non-partisan administration of city services by a professional city manager. The council-manager form

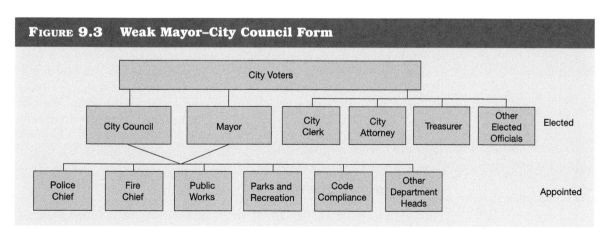

FIGURE 9.3   Weak Mayor–City Council Form

Source: Produced by the author.

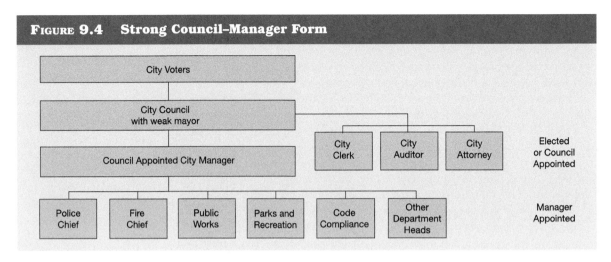

FIGURE 9.4   Strong Council–Manager Form

Source: Produced by the author.

of government is popular with medium-sized cities (50,000 to 250,000) throughout the U.S., but in Texas it is preferred even by the state's larger cities. San Antonio, Dallas, and El Paso all use council–manager governments.[22]

City managers are full-time professional administrators, usually with suitable education and experience. Salaries run from $239,000 in El Paso to $400,000 in Dallas. Mayors, on the other hand, are seen as part-time officials even in large, complex cities. The San Antonio mayor, absurdly enough, is paid only $3,000 a year and $20 per meeting. In El Paso and Dallas, the mayor makes $45,000 and $60,000 respectively.

City council The policymaking or legislative branch of city government.

In the council–manager system, the **city council** is the policymaking branch of city government. Council members are elected at-large in some small Texas cities and in single-member districts in most large cities. The city council hires the city manager, adopts ordinances, approves the budget, and oversees city government, holding inquiries and hearings as problems and issues arise. A mayor may be appointed by the council or elected citywide, but his or her powers are limited to presiding over council meetings, managing the agenda, and otherwise exercising the powers of a council member.

City manager A city manager is an appointed professional executive hired, usually by the city council, to manage or administer city government.

The **city manager** is responsible for hiring and firing department heads, including the police and fire chiefs; preparing the city budget for council approval; and administering the city on a day-to-day basis. The city manager usually holds a degree in public administration or urban studies and has experience in the law and practice of personnel management, budgeting, and finance.

Q4 Why do most Texas cities conduct elections within single-member districts?

Municipal Elections

Unlike county and state elections, which are partisan, municipal elections in Texas are non-partisan. Parties and partisanship are not absent from municipal

TEXAS LEGENDS　　AUSTIN'S MAYOR TOM MILLER: SHAPING A CITY

Most Texas mayors serve one or two, sometimes three or four, two, or more recently four-year, terms as weak mayors in a city council or city manager led systems. These men, and until recently they were almost always men, rarely made a distinctive mark on their cities. Some did, of course. Oscar Holcombe served as mayor of Houston for eleven non-consecutive terms, totaling 22 years between 1921 and 1958. Mayor Holcombe led Houston from a council–manager system into a strong mayor system while he expanded the city's boundaries and improved its services. J. Erik Jonsson, a co-founder and president of Texas Instruments, became mayor of Dallas in 1964, in the immediate wake of the Kennedy assassination, and brought the city back over the next eight years. Jonsson led a city planning process that produced a new convention center, Dallas Central Library, and the DFW International Airport. Similarly, Henry Cisneros served eight years as San Antonio's first Hispanic mayor of modern times. Between 1981 and 1989, Cisneros led development efforts highlighted by the Alamodome sports complex.

One Texas city—Austin—was molded decisively by its long-time mayor Tom Miller. Austin had, and still has, a weak mayor system, but Miller, a charismatic personality, dominated the city and its government anyway. Miller was first elected to the Austin city council in 1933 and immediately chosen mayor by his council colleagues. Tom Miller served continuously as mayor from 1933 to 1949, when he declined to run for re-election, before returning to serve from 1955 to 1961. Miller's influence waned during his second stint in office, but during his first stint he dominated the city and its course of development.

Throughout its history, Austin had been plagued by flooding on the Colorado River. The Colorado originates south of Lubbock on the Llana Escatado and flows southeast through the Hill County emptying into Matagorda Bay. Heavy rain in the Hill Country regularly inundated Austin, most memorably in 1900 and 1917. City leaders had long wanted to control the Colorado with a series of dams, but the cost seemed prohibitive. Tom Miller made flood control his first priority, getting state approval for the Lower Colorado River Authority and federal approval of $20 million in construction funds. Though many others were involved, when the dam was completed in 1940, it bore the name of Tom Miller. The Tom Miller Dam brought cheap power as well as flood control to the Hill Country, Austin, and the lower Colorado.

Mayor Miller focused on other major economic development projects including Mueller Airport, Bergstrom Air Force Base, and a series of parks and public entertainment venues that added to the area's quality of life. Miller ushered Austin from its past as a small university and state government town to a major urban center known nationally as a destination city. Mayor Miller achieved his goals with modest formal powers, but with more charm, influence, and determination than anyone else in the room. Though he served without pay, he spent endless hours building relationships from the White House, to the Austin Chamber of Commerce, to the minority neighborhoods of the city. Few mayors shape their cities the way Tom Miller shaped Austin.

elections, but they tend to be a shadowy, behind-the-scenes presence. Candidates do not run as nominees of their party and there are no partisan symbols on the ballot, but voters often know the candidates' background and candidates sometimes wink at voters and suggest their party background if they think it will help.

Most Texas cities hold their elections in the spring of odd-numbered years, separate from county, state, and national elections. They do this to insulate their local elections from the more glamorous and better funded issues and candidates at the state and national levels. The hope is that voters will focus on local issues and candidates if there are no distractions, but usually voters simply ignore local elections.

At-Large Elections. During the first quarter of the 20th century, Progressive Era reformers sought to clean up the partisan corruption that plagued many American cities. Non-partisan elections were thought to be an obvious part of the solution. So were **at-large elections** of city council members. When city council members are elected at-large, meaning citywide, voters cast a ballot for as many candidates as there are open seats, and the top vote-getters win the seats. The benefit of at-large elections was thought to be that persons of citywide reputation and expertise would be elected. The weakness was that the (usually) white majority elected all of the city council seats and minority candidates were closed out.

At-large elections Elections held throughout a jurisdiction, such as a city or county, rather than in wards or single-member districts within the jurisdiction.

Place or Ward System. Two variations on at-large elections have been common in Texas. In the place system, city council seats are designated as Place 1, Place 2, Place 3, and so on. Candidates file for a particular place and run only against those who file for that place, but candidates can live anywhere in the city and voters from throughout the city elect all of the places. Under the ward system, the city is divided into geographical wards and candidates are required to live in the ward in which they stand for election, but voters throughout the city still vote for candidates in each of the wards. The ward system tries to balance the sense that all parts of the city should be represented on the city council with the sense that voters should elect persons they believe will serve the broad interests of the city.

Single-Member District Elections. Over the past several decades, most Texas cities over 50,000 adopted **single-member district elections**. The move to single-member districts in Texas occurred both because cities were growing larger and more complex and because the courts were demanding that minorities have a better chance to elect their own representatives. Some have moved voluntarily while others needed a judicial push. Austin, the state capital and a city of 850,000, voted single-member districts down six times over the course of several decades. Voters considered the issue again in 2012 and this time adopted a ten-seat single-member district plan.[23] Farmers Branch, a Dallas suburb, was ordered by the federal courts to develop a single-member district plan to end a long and contentious voting rights case brought by Hispanic activists. To create single-member districts, the city council divides the city into equal population wards or districts. Candidates must live within the district they seek to represent, and voters cast ballots for candidates only in the district in which they live.

Single-member district elections Elections held within geographical districts, with one candidate elected in each district.

    The move to single-member districts has changed the balance in local politics. In many cities, neighborhoods are segregated (not legally any more, but practically) by race, and people generally tend to vote for a member of their own race when that option is available to them. Single-member districts, therefore, enhance the prospects that minority districts will send a minority person to the council. On the other hand, some argue that single-member districts encourage council members to focus on their districts to the detriment of the city itself.

Citizen Participation and Voter Turnout

Municipal elections do not generate the interest and excitement of statewide, let alone national, elections. That is not accidental. Holding municipal elections off the cycle of more exciting elections and holding them as non-partisan elections keeps turnout low. In a low-turnout election, a few well-organized interests and activists can have a decisive influence on the outcome. Municipal elections are usually controlled by business groups, municipal unions, neighborhood associations, and social group activists.

Occasionally, the presence of a particularly compelling candidate, match-up, or issue will draw voters to the polls in unusual numbers. When Henry Cisneros, an immensely popular Hispanic, first ran for mayor of San Antonio in 1981, 43 percent of registered voters turned out. When Bob Lanier challenged Kathy Whitmire, the incumbent mayor of Houston in 1991, 40 percent of voters turned out. But more frequently, with just average candidates and no compelling issues, turnout falls into the teens and below. Mayoral elections in 2005 produced turnout levels of 18 percent in Houston and 19 percent in San Antonio. Austin's 2006 mayoral race produced a turnout of 11 percent, and Dallas's 2007 mayoral election produced 15 percent. In 2009, Houston produced a turnout rate of 17 percent, Austin 13 percent, San Antonio 12 percent, El Paso under 10 percent, while Fort Worth mustered just 6 percent. In 2011, turnout in the Dallas mayor's race was 13.7 percent,

Dallas Mayor Mike Rawlings discusses poverty before the annual meeting of the U.S. conference of Mayors, June 20, 2014, in Dallas.

while in 2013 Houston's mayoral turnout was 13 percent and San Antonio's turnout was just 7 percent. In 2015, San Antonio turnout almost reached 12 percent while Dallas reelected Mike Rawlings with turnout under 7 percent.

SPECIAL DISTRICTS

Texas has more than 3,300 special district governments. These are special-purpose local governments set up to deliver a particular service within a defined geographical area. The geographical areas served by special districts range from multi-county regional planning districts to small town water districts. **Special districts** are established by general-purpose governments, usually counties and municipalities, to deliver a service that the general-purpose government cannot or does not wish to deliver. School and water districts are common examples of special district governments.[24]

Special districts are usually administered by an appointed or elected multi-member board. The board hires an executive director or professional manager to run the day-to-day operations of the district. Funding may come as transfers from general-purpose governments, fees charged for services, or taxes that the board is authorized to levy, collect, and spend.

Special districts Special-purpose local governments, established by cities and counties, to deliver a particular service within a limited geographical area.

Types of Special Districts

Special districts are employed for dozens of purposes, but several general types predominate. Texas has more than 1,000 independent school districts, 500 economic development and redevelopment districts, and 500 flood control and water sanitation and delivery districts. Fifty Texas counties run community college districts. Metropolitan areas are often served by regional transportation districts, as well as utility, hospital, and airport districts. Rural Texans depend upon fire, soil conservation, and flood control districts.

School Districts

Q5 Why are there so many special district governments in Texas?

The most common special districts in Texas are the state's independent school districts (ISD). Each ISD is administered by an elected school board. School boards usually have five to nine members, depending on the size and population of the district. Board members are selected, usually for four-year terms, in non-partisan elections. Rural districts may conduct their elections at-large, but urban districts usually conduct their elections within single-member districts.

School boards are responsible for setting tax rates and budgets, building and maintaining facilities, hiring senior administrators, selecting textbooks and curricula, and setting general policy for the district, all within guidelines set by the Texas Education Agency. Perhaps the most important decision that the board makes is the selection of the district's educational leader, the superintendent of schools. School superintendents, especially in the state's largest urban districts, are visible public figures and often work in an intensely political environment.

Councils of Governments

The proliferation of special districts and the increasing complexity of issues facing Texas municipalities have highlighted the need for regional planning and coordination. Texas is divided into twenty-four regional planning districts, called **councils of governments** (COGs), to facilitate voluntary cooperation between local governments. COGs provide training to local officials; coordinate regional land use, transportation, economic development, and environmental protection programs; and assist in the preparation of grant applications to state and federal governments.[25] Effective COGs can facilitate the spread of best practices, avoid duplication of effort across local governments and special districts, and improve regional planning.

Councils of governments COGs are voluntary planning districts that provide training, planning, and coordination services to member local governments.

COUNTY AND MUNICIPAL REFORM

As with Texas state government, critics complain that Texas county government is outmoded and in serious need of reform. There are several common criticisms. First, the Texas Constitution requires the same single, rigid structure of government for both Loving county with its several dozen residents and Harris county with its several million residents. More flexibility, perhaps even county home rule, is frequently recommended.

Second, the election of plural executives leaves no one in charge of county government. Empowering the county judge to appoint some of the officials who are now elected would focus authority and promote unity in county government. Third, patronage thrives in county government. Savings and efficiencies that might be achieved are sacrificed to politics and personal agendas, especially in county road building and maintenance. Modernizing county personnel and contracting systems and implementing a unified road maintenance and building budget are pressing needs.

Local governments in Texas have more flexibility in their organizational design and powers. Nonetheless, unlike large cities in most of the country, most large Texas cities still use a council–manager form of government. In most of the country, council–manager governments are employed by medium-sized cities, from 50,000 to 250,000 while large cities use the mayor–council form of government. The mayor–council form of government, especially in its strong mayor variant, is seen as more capable of forcefully leading large and complex cities in dealing with their many problems and opportunities. Houston has a strong mayor, Dallas, San Antonio, and Austin should probably consider it.

Chapter Summary

Local government lacks some of the distant majesty of state and national government. Yet, most government, most of the time, for most people, is local. But as we have seen, local government is a "creature" of state government. State constitutions and laws determine what form local governments will take, what powers they will enjoy, and what resources they will have to meet their responsibilities. Texas has more counties, at 254, than any other state (Georgia is second with a measly 154) and more municipalities, at 1,209, than every state but Illinois (1,299).

The Texas Constitution mandates that counties be governed by a five-member commissioners court, composed of a county judge and four county commissioners. Other countywide elected officials include the sheriff, district attorney, clerk, tax assessor/collector, and treasurer/auditor. Urban counties offer more programs and services than rural counties and rural counties are permitted to consolidate some county offices, but the key deficiency of county government is a lack of flexibility.

Texas municipal governments have more flexibility. Towns under 5,000 residents select some variation on the mayor–council, council–manager, or commission forms of government. But larger cities may design their own home-rule charters and most do. Texas also employs more than 3,300 special district governments to deliver particular services. Twenty-four regional planning districts, called COGs, seek to coordinate this welter of local government activity.

The reforms most frequently advocated in regard to local governments in Texas are three. First, each of the 254 Texas counties is required to have the same county commission form of government. Some advocate county home rule so that large, complex, urban counties could, within limits set by the state legislature, design their own governing structures. Second, only Houston among Texas's great cities has a strong mayor system. Some argue that big cities like Dallas, San Antonio, Fort Worth, and Austin would be more effectively governed by a strong mayor. And third, since Texas does not provide revenues to its cities, as most other states do, Texas cities should be given more flexibility to raise the revenues they need to keep up with growth.

Key Terms

Annexation 231	Dillon's Rule 223
At-large elections 240	Extraterritorial jurisdiction (ETJ) 231
City council 238	Incorporation 230
City manager 238	Single-member district elections 240
Commissioners court 227	Special districts 242
Councils of governments 243	Strong mayor 237
County judge 228	Weak mayor 237

Review Questions

1. Summarize the importance of Dillon's Rule for understanding the legal relationship between state governments and their municipalities.

2. Describe the political organization mandated for counties in the Texas Constitution.
3. Outline the main differences between general law and home rule cities in Texas.
4. Explain why most major Texas cities adopt council–manager governments when most major cities in the U.S. adopt strong mayor governments.
5. Evaluate the arguments for at-large election of city councils as opposed to election within single-member districts.

Suggested Readings

Amy Bridges, *Morning Glories: Municipal Reform in the Southwest* (Princeton, NJ: Princeton University Press, 1997).

Stephen L. Elkin, *City and Regime in American Politics* (Chicago, IL: University of Chicago Press, 1987).

Richard L. Florida, *The Rise of the Creative Class: And How It's Transforming Work, Leisure, Community, and Everyday Life* (New York: Basic Books, 2002).

Mario T. Garcia, *The Making of a Mexican-American Mayor: Raymond L. Telles of El Paso* (El Paso, TX: Texas Western Press, 1998).

Char Miller and Heywood T. Sanders, ed., *Urban Texas: Politics and Development* (College Station, TX: Texas A&M University Press, 1990).

Paul Peterson, *City Limits* (Chicago: University of Chicago Press, 1981).

Michael Phillips, *White Metropolis: Race, Ethnicity, and Religion in Dallas, 1841–2001* (Austin, TX: University of Texas Press, 2006).

Jesse M. Shapiro, "Smart Cities: Quality of Life, Productivity, and the Growth Effects of Human Capital," *Review of Economics and Statistics* (2006), 88: 324–335.

Web Resources

1 **http://www.nlc.org/**
National League of Cities.

2 **http://www.ci.dallas.tx.us/**
Instead of Dallas, type in any Texas city you want.

3 **http://www.co.harris.tx.us/**
Instead of Harris, type in any Texas county you want.

4 **http://www.tml.org/**
Texas Municipal League.

5 **http://www.tac.orp/**
Texas Association of Counties.

Chapter 10

FINANCING STATE GOVERNMENT: BUDGETS, REVENUES, AND EXPENSES

TAX RESISTANCE AND THE COMING OF THE TEXAS REVOLUTION

Texas has always been and today remains one of the lowest of the low tax states. In fact, like the United States, Texas was born in a tax revolt. British attempts to tax stamps, tea, and other imported goods in the colonies sparked resistance behind the cry, "no taxation without representation." The Texas revolution was sparked by the Mexican authority's attempts to tax imports into Texas. Adding to the interest in this first Texas tax revolt is the fact that it was led by Jim Bowie and William B. Travis, later to be co-commanders at the Alamo.

Just like modern real estate developers or CEO's looking for a location to build a new factory, "empresarios" like Stephen F. Austin sought tax breaks to help their new enterprises get off the ground. Austin's empresario contract with the Mexican government included a suspension of import taxes for the first six years, ten years in some of his subsequent contracts. This agreement was to allow colonists to import, tax free, all of the supplies and goods they needed to get farms and businesses up and running. Once the new colony and early colonists were established, regular Mexican import taxes and fees would be levied. Not surprisingly, when the initial period of tax exemption expired, the imposition of taxes was unwelcome by most and resisted by some.

In April 1830, the Mexican government passed laws restricting American immigration into Texas, cancelling all unfulfilled empresario contracts, and establishing six customs ports along the Texas coast. Anglo Texans bristled at the prospect of new taxes. Texan tax resistance centered

Jay Root/Texas Tribune

Former Governor Rick Perry was a staunch fiscal conservative throughout his political career. Here he campaigned for budget discipline prior to the 2013 legislative session.

on a new town and fort at Anahuac. The fort, commanded by Juan Davis Bradburn, a Mexican officer and former U.S. citizen, was on the east bank of the Trinity River where it entered Galveston Bay. Just south of the Austin colony, Anahuac would control commerce into the Anglo Texas heartland.

Two newcomers, Jim Bowie and William Barrett Travis, both hot-heads committed to the "code duello" and other equally violent approaches to dispute resolution, led the fight. Jim Bowie, the most famous knife fighter of his day and one of the designers of the ubiquitous "Bowie knife," arrived in Texas in 1830. Travis arrived in Texas from South Carolina by way of Alabama in 1831. Like many early Texans, they arrived looking over their shoulder—Bowie had killed the sheriff of Rapides Parish, Louisiana, in the "Sandbar Fight" and Travis left a new wife, young son, and extensive debts in South Carolina.

Two disturbances in Anahuac, both precipitated by conflicts over tax collection, left Mexican and Texan dead on the ground and the province sliding toward revolution. The first conflict, in the spring of 1832, saw Travis raise a militia in response to Bradburn's arrest of his law partner, Patrick Jack. By July, Travis's militia had forced Bradburn to release Jack, abandon the fort, and flee. Though tensions remained high, Mexican authorities soon reoccupied the fort and reopened the customs house. In the spring of 1835, Bowie, then living in Nacogdoches, heard about a packet of dispatches on their way to the Mexican Consul in New Orleans. He arranged for their capture and spread the word that the packet contained reports of more troops bound for Texas and another order for Travis's arrest. Travis, then living in San Felipe de Austin, commandeered a ship and with two dozen comrades sailed into Galveston Bay to attack Anahuac from the sea. The Mexican garrison of 40 surrendered without a fight. By the end of the year the Texas fight for independence was at hand. Texans to this day keep a wary eye on the tax collector.

Focus Questions

Q1 What role do budgets play in the political process?

Q2 Who are the leading participants in the budgetary process?

Q3 What key revenue sources support Texas state government?

Q4 What are the principal expenses of Texas state government?

Q5 Where do issues of fairness fit into discussions of taxing and spending?

Budgets Moral and political documents that seek to balance a community's revenue sources with its spending obligations.

Q1 What role do budgets play in the political process?

Much of politics is clashing ideologies, contrasting campaign promises, and conflicting partisan agendas. **Budgets**, on the other hand, force concrete decisions about who pays and who benefits. Officials in Texas state government make critical decisions about how much revenue to raise, through what kinds of taxes and fees, levied against whom. It makes other decisions, just as critical, about how to spend those revenues, on what services, and for whose benefit.

Because budgets declare what government will do, who will pay, and who will benefit, they are often said to be moral documents. They are. But honorable people can differ fundamentally about what morality requires. Moreover, people are motivated not just by what they think is right, but by what they think is best for them. Hence, the budgetary process is both a moral debate about what the political community should do and a political struggle over who benefits and who pays.

In states with moralistic political cultures (states like Massachusetts, Minnesota, and Washington) the moral requirements of budgetary decision-making are often thought to demand more—more spending for education, health care, and parks. But in states with traditionalistic political cultures (states like Georgia, Florida, and Texas) the moral injunction to keep government's hands out of people's pockets is thought to be equally compelling. Texas politicians frequently make the case that low taxes expand opportunity and encourage personal responsibility. Texas politicians rarely acknowledge that low taxes severely limit the state's ability to aid its most vulnerable citizens.

In this chapter, we describe how budgets are drafted in Texas, how revenues are raised, and how the money is spent. In general, the legislature dominates the budgetary process, taxes are kept low, and revenues are directed to basic, no-frills programs in education, health and human services, and transportation. The 2015 regular session of the Texas legislature approved a 2016–17 biennial state budget totaling $209.4 billion. The numbers are large and the struggle over them is intense.

THE BUDGETARY PROCESS

The Texas Constitution and laws establish what taxes can be levied, what services can be delivered, and who has the power and responsibility to create the budget.[1] For example, the Texas Constitution and related laws prohibit a state income tax and a statewide property tax, permit a state sales tax and user fees, and require that the state provide basic services, including an "efficient system of public free schools"—all within a balanced budget.

Prior to 1949, Texas had no systematic budgetary process and no single, unified, coherent budget document. Each state agency was funded by a separate appropriations bill and the only budgeting was done by the Board of Control which recorded requisitions but had no power to limit or reject them. During the 1940s, first to reflect the priority setting demanded by war and then to better track and manage postwar spending increases, Texas undertook major budgetary reforms.

Coke Stevenson and Allan Shivers, both of whom served as lieutenant governor before becoming governor, and both of whom were fiscal conservatives, drove these reforms. In 1941, the Texas legislature passed the "pay-as-you-go amendment," approved by voters in 1942, requiring a balanced budget. The pay-as-you-go amendment, now Article III, section 49a, of the Texas Constitution, requires the Comptroller of Public Accounts to submit to the legislature and governor at the beginning of each legislative session a "revenue estimate" of funds anticipated in the coming biennium. The legislature may not pass a budget higher than the revenue estimate without a four-fifths vote of each house.[2]

The legislature also began building the expertise required to do serious budgeting. In 1943, the Office of the State Auditor was transferred from the executive branch to the legislative branch. Soon the Auditor recommended that the legislature create more institutional memory and staff expertise. In 1949, the legislature established the Legislative Budget Board (LBB) to provide continuous support for budgetary drafting, implementation, and oversight and a Legislative Council to serve as a research and bill-drafting agency. By 1951, the legislature had a modern budgeting process in place.[3]

In the late 1970s, Texas politicians and voters again sought to limit government spending. In 1977, the legislature approved the "Texas Tax Relief Act" and in 1978 voters approved it with 84 percent of the vote. Article VIII, section 22a, of the Texas Constitution declares that Texas general fund

TEXAS LEGENDS   JOHN BOWDEN CONNALLY: A BIG MAN IN TEXAS

John Connally was a major force in Texas politics for half a century. A close associate of Lyndon Johnson until the latter's death in 1973, Connally served as the 39th governor of Texas (1963–69), before serving as Secretary of the U.S. Treasury in the Nixon Administration (1971–72), switching from the Democratic to the Republican Party in 1973, and running unsuccessfully for the Republican presidential nomination in 1980. His high-flying post-politics business career ended in personal bankruptcy in the mid-1980s. An iconic Texas both in success and failure, Connally died on June 15, 1993.

Connally was one of seven children born to John and Lela Connally in the small Wilson County town of Floresville, Texas, southeast of San Antonio. Though from a poor family, Connally earned Bachelor's (1939) and law (1941) degrees from UT. In 1940 he married Nellie Brill, also a UT undergraduate. Connally joined the navy in 1941, where he served on the staffs of Undersecretary of the Navy James V. Forrestal and then on the staff of General Dwight D. Eisenhower. Late in the war he was a flight director on aircraft carriers involved in some of the key naval battles of World War II.

Both before and after the war, Connally was a close confidant and junior partner to LBJ. Connally managed five of LBJ's campaigns, including his losing 1941 Senate campaign, his winning 1948 Senate campaign, his losing 1960 presidential campaign, after which John Kennedy picked LBJ to be his vice presidential running mate, and his winning 1964 presidential campaign. LBJ's most famous (or infamous) campaign, in which he earned the nickname "Landslide Lyndon," was the 1948 Senate campaign, won by 87 votes when 200 late votes mysteriously appeared in Jim Wells County Box 13. Jim Wells County is less than 100 miles due south of Connally's home county of Wilson.

In 1951, Connally left LBJ's staff to become general counsel to Fort Worth oilman Sid Richardson. Like Richardson, Connally, always more conservative than LBJ, quietly supported Eisenhower over the Democrat Adlai Stevenson for president in 1952 and 1956. He left Richardson's employ in 1959 to run LBJ's 1960 presidential campaign. Though the campaign failed, Kennedy chose LBJ as his running mate to shore up the south and LBJ later prevailed on Kennedy to appoint Connally Secretary of the Navy. Connally served in the Kennedy administration just over a year before returning to Texas to run for governor.

At just 4 percent in the early polls, Connally proved to be a smart, articulate, and dogged campaigner. Though three-term incumbent Democratic Governor Price Daniel was in the field, Connally made the runoff against a liberal Houston lawyer named Don Yarborough. Connally won narrowly and then went on to defeat Republican Jack Cox, 54 percent to 46 percent. During his first term as governor, Connally was riding in an open limousine with President John Kennedy in Dallas when Lee Harvey Oswald shot and killed Kennedy and badly wounded Connally. Connally won two more terms as governor with 74 percent of the vote in 1964 and 73 percent in 1966. As governor, Connally was an economic progressive, investing heavily in higher education and economic development, but a social conservative.

Soon after leaving the governorship, Connally began moving toward the Republican Party. In 1971, President Nixon appointed Connally Secretary of the Treasury, where he performed impressively, before resigning to head "Democrats for Nixon" in 1972. Connally formally left the Democratic Party for the Republican Party in 1973. Connally ran for the Republican presidential nomination in 1980. Though he raised $11 million and spent lavishly, he won just a single delegate. Though his last race ended in defeat, he had been a national leader for more than forty years.

revenues may not be expended at a growth rate faster than that of the state's economy. The amendment does not limit spending of federal funds or dedicated funds like state gas taxes, licenses, or fees. The growth limit on spending can be overridden by a majority vote of both houses of the state legislature, though this has happened just once, in 2007, to fund school property tax relief.

The responsibility for navigating the budgetary process is distributed across the legislative and executive branches of Texas state government. The state legislature has the dominant role, but the governor's line-item veto gives him important leverage late in the process. Occasionally, as with the troublesome school finance issues, the Texas courts become involved as well. There are two broad stages to the budgetary process: preparation and consideration for approval.

Budgetary Preparation

The Texas state legislature meets in regular session for 140 days, from January to May, in odd-numbered years. The most important bill to move through the legislative process in each regular session is the state budget. Budget planning occurs during the even-numbered year prior to the legislative session. The actors driving the process are the governor, lieutenant governor, Speaker, and comptroller.

The Texas Constitution identifies the governor as the state's chief budget officer, but, in fact, the legislature crafts the budget. Specifically, the ten-member **Legislative Budget Board** (LBB), co-chaired by the lieutenant governor and Speaker, prepare a budget for submission to the legislature. The lieutenant governor and Speaker each appoint four additional members to complete the LBB, usually including the chairs of the key revenue and spending committees. While the governor also submits a budget, or at least a budget outline, to the legislature, the legislature concentrates on the work of its own leaders and generally ignores the governor's budget.

The governor and legislative leaders set the strategic planning and budgeting process in motion in the spring of even-numbered years by defining the goals and priorities for the coming biennium (see Figure 10.1). Each agency then embarks on a review of their role in meeting those goals and priorities. Agencies update their strategic plans, request adjustments in their broad budget structures, and develop new budget requests. Agencies are usually instructed to develop alternative budget scenarios. For example, in a normal budget year, they might be required to plan for a 3 percent increase, no increase, a 5 percent cut, and a 10 percent cut. In spring 2010, facing a dire fiscal situation in the 2011 regular session, the governor, lieutenant governor, and Speaker ordered an immediate 5 percent cut, with some exceptions, and preparation for an additional 10 percent cut in the coming biennium. In the end, cuts totalled 8.1 percent. As the 2013 legislative session approached, agencies were ordered to plan for spending cuts of 5 percent, with contingency plans for an additional 10 percent cut. As the national and Texas economic recoveries continued through 2014, the 2015 legislative session faced a brighter fiscal picture.

Q2 Who are the leading participants in the budgetary process?

Legislative Budget Board The ten-member LBB, co-chaired by the lieutenant governor and the Speaker, drafts the state's biennial budget.

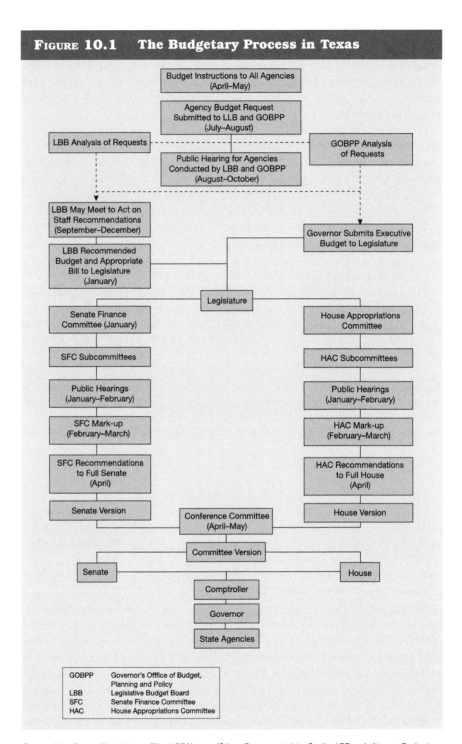

FIGURE 10.1   The Budgetary Process in Texas

Source: http://www.llb.state.tx.us/The_LBB/Access/Other_Documents.htm On the LBB website, see Budget
101: A Guide to the Budget Process in Texas Courtesy of the Senate Research Center, p. 5.

Agency budget requests are submitted to the LBB and the Governor's Office of Budget, Planning, and Policy (GOBPP) in July and August of even-numbered years. From August through October, the LBB and GOBPP hold joint hearings in which the agencies are required to explain, justify, and defend their budgetary priorities and funding requests. Agencies respond to the LBB and GOBPP with additional information and, often, with revised priorities and requests. Between September and December, both the LBB and GOBPP develop budget proposals for submission to the legislature.

Before the legislative session begins in January of each odd-numbered year, the comptroller is constitutionally required to issue a revenue estimate. On January 12, 2015, the comptroller Glenn Hegar estimated that state revenues for the 2014–15 biennium would total $220.9 billion. Historically, the comptroller made a conservative estimate at the beginning of the session so that legislative leaders wishing to spend more have to include her preferences in their plans. Unless the comptroller raised her initial revenue estimate, the governor and legislature could not spend more without a 4/5th vote of the House and the Senate. In the last few legislative sessions, as the legislature moved increasingly to the right, legislators chose to spend less than the comptroller told them was available.

In addition to the comptroller's budget estimate, three more limitations on taxing and spending are anchored in the Texas Constitution. First, as noted above, spending growth from general revenues may not exceed the growth rate of the state's economy. Second, no more than 1 percent of general funds can be spent on welfare. And third, annual debt service cannot exceed 5 percent of general revenues. Texas keeps a tight lid on taxing and spending.

Budget Consideration and Approval

The 84th regular session of the Texas legislature opened on January 13, 2015. The LBB is required by law to submit a budget bill during the first week of the session.[4] The LBB's budget bill was submitted to both the Appropriations Committee in the House and the Finance Committee in the Senate on January 14. The chairs of the Appropriations and Finance committees, together with the presiding officers in each chamber, are members of the LBB, so, in a critical sense, they submit the budget to themselves.

If the governor chooses to submit a budget proposal to the legislature, he is required to do so in the first week of the session and he delivers his "State of the State" message at that time. Like Governor Perry, Governor Abbott chose to submit a full budget, so he has delivered his state of the state speech several weeks into the session, once things have calmed down a bit. The governor's State of the State message, delivered to a joint session of the legislature, is his opportunity to outline goals for the state, set priorities, and argue for his funding preferences. The legislators know and the governor subtly reminds them that, while they control the process during the session, he must ultimately approve the budget they produce.

In the 83rd and 84th regular sessions of the Texas legislature, the House Appropriations Committee included twenty-seven members, all appointed by Speaker Straus. The Speaker named John Otto (R-Dayton) to chair the committee and Sylvester Turner (D-Houston) to serve as vice chair. Each of the twenty-five regular members of the Appropriations Committee was liaison to another standing committee of the House where he or she chaired a subcommittee on budget and oversight. Speaker Straus's goal was to formalize and tighten the relationship between the Appropriations Committee and the substantive committees of the House. Chairman Otto divided the Appropriations Committee into five subcommittees: education, health and human services, criminal justice, business and economic development, and current fiscal conditions.

The Senate Finance Committee included fifteen members, all appointed by Lieutenant Governor Patrick. In the 83rd legislative session Tommy Williams (R-Woodlands) chaired the committee and in the 84th session Jane Nelson (R-Flower Mound) was the chair. Juan "Chuy" Hinojosa (D-McAllen) served as vice chair in both sessions. Chairman Nelson generally held hearings before the full Finance Committee, though four working groups were named to hear testimony on specific areas of the budget. The legislative phase of the budgetary process involves four stages: committee hearings, mark-up, floor debate, and conference committee deliberations.

By the time the 2015 legislative session approached, only Speaker Straus remained in place. Lieutenant Governor Dewhurst was denied re-nomination in the 2014 Republican primary, defeated by Senator Dan Patrick (R-Houston), and Chairmen Pitts and Merritt had left the legislature. Pitts retired and Merritt was defeated in the Republican primary for Agriculture commissioner. Budgeting, particularly during tight fiscal circumstances, is hard work for which no gratitude is to be expected.

Hearings. The House Appropriations and Senate Finance Committees began hearings on the LBB's budget bill in late January, 2015. Some hearings were held before the committees' subcommittees and working groups, some before the full committees. Hearings provide an opportunity for citizens, lobbyists, interest groups, agency representatives, and spokesmen for the governor's office to voice their concerns to the committee before it takes any action.

Mark–Up. In many legislatures, mark-up is the stage in the budget writing process where the committees get to place their mark on the document. But in Texas, the budget is drafted by the legislative leaders serving on the LBB. Hence, the presiding officers and committee chairs work hard to defend their handiwork from tampering by committee members. Mark-up in the Texas legislature takes place before the full Appropriations and Finance committees, under the watchful eyes of the presiding officers and committee chairs.

Floor Debate. When the committees finish their work, the House version of the budget goes to the House Calendars Committee and the Senate version

New Comptroller Glenn Hegar presented his "reverse estimate" on January 2, 2015, in advance of the 2015 legislative session.

is placed on the daily calendar to await floor action. The Calendars Committee writes a special rule scheduling floor action on the budget and limiting amendments to changes that do not affect the "bottom line." Amendments that propose to add money somewhere in the budget must propose cuts somewhere else in the budget. Floor action in the House involves consideration of many amendments, but little real change. Senate rules require approval of the presiding officer and two-thirds of the senators before any bill, including the budget, can come to the floor, so most member concerns are argued out before floor consideration even begins. The Senate usually passes the budget with no amendments from the floor.

Conference Committee Deliberations. Once a budget bill has cleared both the House and the Senate, the differences between the two versions of the bill, and there are always differences, must be resolved. A House–Senate conference committee is the vehicle for resolving the differences between the two bills. The lieutenant governor and Speaker each appoint five members to the conference committee, usually senior members including the Appropriations and Finance chairs. The conference committee works under great pressure, in the closing days of the session, so the resolutions hammered out in the conference committee are usually approved by the full House and Senate just prior to adjournment.

Even after the legislature has completed its work, two hurdles remain before approval of the budget is final. First, the comptroller has 10 days to certify, based on the latest information available, that the revenues required to fully fund the budget will be available in the coming biennium. In the closing days of the 2015 regular session, the comptroller declared that anticipated revenue would cover the $209.4 billion for 2016–17.

Second, the budget goes to the governor for his consideration. The governor can sign the budget, putting it into immediate effect, which governors sometimes do, or they can veto the whole budget, which they rarely do. Generally, governors exercise their line-item veto by striking out those appropriations that they think ill-advised. It is the line-item veto, and the legislators fear of it, that give Texas governors their influence, modest, but still appreciable, over the state budget. Governor Abbott signed the 2016–17 budget after vetoing $300 million in proposed spending.

REVENUES: WHERE THE MONEY COMES FROM

Q3 What key revenue sources support Texas state government?

Most state constitutions carefully define the general kinds of taxes that may be levied by state and local governments. Broadly, there are four kinds of taxes: taxes on income, sales, property, and special fines and fees. Most states employ them all. Seven states (Alaska, Florida, Nevada, South Dakota, Texas, Washington, and Wyoming) do not levy a state income tax and five (Alaska, Delaware, Montana, New Hampshire, and Oregon) do not use a general sales tax. Most local and special district governments depend heavily on property tax revenues.

Texans and their elected representatives have acted to keep taxes low and to restrict their growth. The Texas Constitution prohibits a state income tax and a state property tax. Texans are nothing if not wary of taxes.

Tax Revenues

Texas has long derived the bulk of its tax revenues from a general sales tax and several specialized sales taxes. It derived lesser amounts from a corporate franchise fee, oil and gas severance taxes, motor fuels taxes, and taxes on alcohol and tobacco, often called sin taxes. The spring 2006 special session of the Texas legislature, called under court order to address school funding issues, replaced the corporate franchise fee with a general business tax usually called the margins tax. State taxes provide about half the money that flows into Texas coffers. Texas revenues for the 2014–15 biennium were $208.2 billion.

Sales tax Taxes charged on the sale of designated goods. In Texas the general sales tax is 6.25 percent, with localities permitted to charge up to an additional 2 percent.

General Sales Tax. The largest source of tax revenue is the general **sales tax**. During the 2014–15 biennium, Texas collected $54.6 billion, or 26.2 percent of its total revenues, from the general sales tax. Texas has one of the highest general sales taxes in the U.S., at 6.25 percent. Moreover, local governments are permitted to add up to 2 percent to the state sales tax, which most urban areas do. To ease the burden on the poor, most groceries, prescription drugs, medical services, housing, and utilities are excluded from the sales tax.

Specialized Sales Taxes. Texas also taxes the sale, rental, and operation of motor vehicles. Though Texas records it separately, it levies the same 6.25 percent sales tax on the purchase of motor vehicles as it does on other purchases. It charges a higher tax, 10 percent, on motor vehicle rentals of less than 30 days. Motor vehicle sales and rental taxes brought in $8.2 billion, or 3.9 percent of total revenues, during the 2014–15 biennium. Motor fuel taxes provided another $6.5 billion, or 3.1 percent. The state receives 20 cents a gallon on gas and diesel purchases (on top of 14.5 cents in federal tax) and 15 cents on liquefied gas.

Business Taxes. Through 2006, Texas corporations paid a **corporate franchise fee** of 0.25 percent of taxable capital (value of the corporation) or 4.5 percent of earned income (corporate taxable profits). Limited partnerships and professional associations, including most legal, accounting, and financial management firms, were not subject to the franchise tax. Many businesses that were initially subject to the fee avoided paying by converting to limited partnerships or incorporating out of state. In 2006, only about one in six Texas businesses paid the franchise fee.

The spring 2006 special session of the Texas legislature revised the way business is taxed in the state. It replaced the franchise fee with a broad new business tax. The new tax, commonly called the **margins tax**, is 1 percent on

Corporate franchise fee A business activity tax that in 2005 impacted one in six Texas businesses, mostly corporations and sole proprietorships.

Margins tax A business tax, adopted in 2006 to replace the corporate franchise fee. The margins tax is 1 percent of gross receipts minus costs.

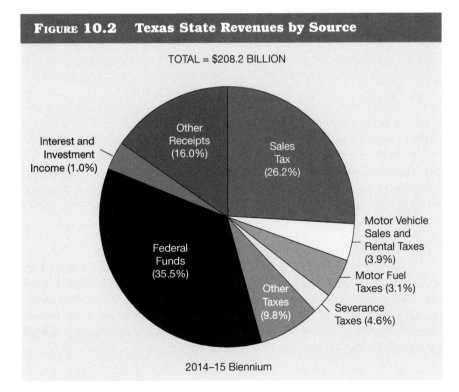

FIGURE 10.2   Texas State Revenues by Source

TOTAL = $208.2 BILLION

- Sales Tax (26.2%)
- Motor Vehicle Sales and Rental Taxes (3.9%)
- Motor Fuel Taxes (3.1%)
- Severance Taxes (4.6%)
- Other Taxes (9.8%)
- Federal Funds (35.5%)
- Interest and Investment Income (1.0%)
- Other Receipts (16.0%)

2014–15 Biennium

Source: Legislative Budget Board, *Fiscal Size-Up, 2014–2015 Biennium*, "Estimated State Revenue Collections," Figure 41, p. 29.

gross receipts, minus either the cost of employee compensation or the cost of goods sold, whichever is greater. Retailers and wholesalers pay 0.5 percent. Sole proprietors, general partnerships, and businesses grossing less than $1,000,000 annually are exempt. The margins tax provided $9.3 billion in 2014–15, about 4.5 percent of total revenues.

Who Knew?

As late as the 1970s and early 1980s, severance taxes provided about one-quarter of total revenue in the Texas budget. Today, severance taxes provide only about 5 percent of the budget.

Sin tax Sales taxes on activities, like smoking and drinking, that society wishes to discourage.

Oil and Gas Severance Taxes. As late as the 1970s, oil and gas severance taxes provided one-quarter of state tax revenue. Texas taxes oil production at 4.6 percent of market value and natural gas at 7.5 percent, though there are several exclusions and exemptions that reduce the tax bite by about half. Oil and gas production in Texas are both on the upswing. The 2014–15 biennium saw oil and gas contribute $9.5 billion, or 4.6 percent, to Texas revenues.

Other Tax Revenues. Another 9.6 percent of revenues come from taxes on several types of economic and business activity. Sales taxes on tobacco and alcohol, often called **sin taxes**, provided about $5 billion, or 2.4 percent of total revenues, during the 2014–15 biennium. Business activity taxes on insurance companies, utility companies, and hotel occupancy, accounted for about $5.3 billion, or 2.5 percent, of revenues.

Non-Tax Revenues

Fully half of the revenues taken in by Texas state government are listed in the state budget as non-tax revenues. The largest streams of non-tax revenues are federal transfer payments. Recall that Texans pay federal income and other taxes, so this is just some of that money coming home. These revenues still come out of the pockets of Texans, just less directly than the sales or business activity taxes. However, after decades in which Texas politicians complained that more money flowed from Texas to Washington than ever returned as federal transfer payments, for the last decade Texas has sent less money to Washington than it has gotten back. The other sources of non-tax revenues are licenses, fees, fines, profits from the Texas state lottery, interest income, and borrowing.

Federal transfer payments Funds provided by the federal government to state and local governments to support key services such as health care, education, and transportation.

Federal Transfers. The federal government provides funds to the states to support key state services, including health care, education, and transportation. **Federal transfer payments** provided about 20 percent of state funds during the 1980s and 30 percent during the 1990s. During the 2010–11 biennium, Texas received $73.9 billion, or 35.5 percent of its total revenues from federal transfer payments. As the federal government struggles with big deficits, its future transfers to the states are likely to decrease.

Fines, Fees, Licenses, and Penalties. If you have ever paid a fee to camp in a Texas state park, bought a hunting license, or seen a state trooper's light flashing in your rear view mirror, you have helped fund Texas state government. Assorted fines, fees, licenses, and penalties accounted for $16.5 billion, or 7.9 percent of total revenues, during the 2014–15 biennium.

Interest, Investment and Lottery Income. Interest and investment income on state funds and accounts totaled $2.2 billion, or about 1 percent, of total revenues during the 2014–15 biennium. The Texas state lottery raised $2.1 billion, or about 1 percent, of total revenues.

Borrowing. State governments, like individuals, sometimes find it convenient to borrow rather than to spend from savings or current income. States borrow by issuing bonds. Texas issues bonds to finance construction, usually of roads, prisons, or university buildings, and to assist veterans to buy land and students to afford college. Not surprisingly though, the Texas Constitution and laws limit state borrowing quite stringently (no more than 5 percent of state budget). At the close of the 2011 fiscal year, Texas had a per capita indebtedness of just $1,479, compared to the average per capita state indebtedness of $3,635.[5]

EXPENDITURES: WHERE THE MONEY GOES

Like most Americans, Texans demand low taxes and high-quality public services. When push comes to shove, as it always does in government finance, Texans demand low taxes more insistently than they demand high-quality public services. As a result, Texas spends much less per person ($4,916) than the average ($6,423) state government.[6] Nearly 85 percent of spending is directed at three broad areas—education, social services, and transportation.

Q4 What are the principal expenses of Texas state government?

Education

Texas spent almost $74.2 billion, or 37 percent of its total budget of $200.4 billion for 2014–15, on education. Just under 76 percent of education funding went to elementary and secondary schools ($56.3 billion) and just over 24 percent ($17.9 billion) went to colleges and universities. The education funding reforms passed in 2006 involved a tax swap of increased state taxes for decreased local property taxes. Because revenues from the new taxes were less than expected, Texas public schools had less money for the 2014–15 biennium than they had in 2008–09 or 2010–11.

As we shall see, these latest reforms did not resolve issues of educational access, quality, and funding that Texas has been wrestling with for more than half a century. Because these issues have been at the top of the political agenda for so long and are so consistently in the news, we will give them special attention here.

Elementary and Secondary Education. The Texas Constitution of 1876 mandated an "efficient system of public free schools" in which whites and blacks would attend separate schools. Hispanic students, not mentioned in the constitution, were

Pro & Con   When to Use the "Rainy Day" Fund

The legislature proposed in 1987 and the voters approved in 1988 the Economic Stabilization Fund, commonly known as the state's "rainy day" fund. The rainy day fund receives 75 percent of oil and natural gas severance tax revenues beyond the level of those taxes in 1987. The Comptroller is also mandated to transfer to the rainy day fund half of any balances remaining in the General Revenue Fund at the end of any biennium, but this has produced only modest amounts twice and, given the state's tight budgets, is unlikely to do so again anytime soon. The rainy day fund is capped at 10 percent of general revenue funds in the previous biennium. The 2014–15 cap was $14.4 billion and the Comptroller projected that the rainy day fund would reach approximately $11.8 billion by the end of fiscal 2015.

Whether to draw on the rainy day fund, how much, and for what purposes, sparked major battles in the 2011 legislative session. When the legislature convened in January 2011, they faced a $4.3 billion deficit in the 2010–11 budget, and a prospective deficit of at least $15 billion in the 2012–13 budget that they were just beginning to draft. Governor Perry favored drawing on the rainy day fund to balance the 2010–11 budget, but not for closing the anticipated budget gap in 2012–13. In the 2013 legislative session, legislators tapped the rainy day fund for $1.75 billion to undo some of the cuts made in 2011, especially in education. They approved a further $2 billion to fund water projects, subject to voter approval, which was granted in November 2013. Generally, liberals argued that the recession of 2008–10 had created emergencies, rainy days, that needed to be addressed. Conservatives resisted using rainy day funds for recurring needs like roads and education.

The table opposite, drawn from the Texas Comptroller of Public Accounts website, shows the growth and use of the rainy day fund since its inception. The fund grows as oil and natural gas revenues are deposited, but drawing from the fund requires political action. To draw from the rainy day fund to fill a hole in an existing budget requires a 60 percent majority, while to draw from it to balance a proposed budget requires a 67 percent majority in both houses. The governor can, of course, exercise his line-item veto if he opposes the use of rainy day funds. The legislature, in turn, can override a gubernatorial veto by a two-thirds vote in each house, but this rarely happens because the legislature is usually adjourned by the time the veto is exercised.

treated differently in different districts; sometimes they were allowed to attend the white schools and sometimes not. Many rural counties had no schools at all until the early 20th century. Free school text-books were made available by the state in 1918. In 1920, Texas made its first concerted attempt to improve public schools. Typically, the Better Schools Amendment of 1920 sought to relieve the financial burden on the state by allowing more local funding. Financial disparities between rich and poor districts soon emerged as an issue.

Rural and minority Texans spent the next half century working to insure that their children got the same educational opportunities as more privileged children. In 1930, Jesus Salvatierra, in *Del Rio ISD v. Salvatierra*, claimed that segregation and inadequate school funding denied Mexican-American children an adequate education. Salvatierra lost in the Texas courts. Not until 1948, in the case of *Delgado v. Bastrop ISD*, did the federal courts rule that segregation of Mexican-American students was illegal. Six years later, the landmark case of *Brown v. Board of Education* declared that racial segregation

Fiscal Year	Deposits*	Withdrawals*	Ending Balance*
1990	$19.3	–	$19.3
1991	$9.7	–$29.0	–
1992	$163.4	–	$163.4
1993	$7.4	–$119.0	$51.7
1994	$34.0	–$56.6	$29.1
1995	$0.6	–$21.5	$8.1
1996	$0.4	–$0.5	$8.0
1997	$0.4	–	$8.5
1998	$49.8	–	$8.5
1999	$21.7	–	$80.0
2000	$4.7	–	$84.7
2001	$111.8	–	$196.5
2002	$707.4	–	$903.9
2003	$103.0	–$446.5	$560.5
2004	$358.1	–$553.0	$365.6
2005	$611.8	–$970.5	$6.9
2006	$926.5	–$528.3	$405.2
2007	$1,617.7	–$691.5	$1,331.4
2008	$3,114.5	–$90.5	$4,355.4
2009	$2,370.7	–$0.4	$6,725.7
2010	$966.9	–	$7,692.6
2011	$492.5	–$3,198.7	$5,012.4
2012	$1,076.0	–	$6,133.4
2013	$1,908.6	–$1,871.8	$6,170.2
2014	$2,941.8	–$2,056.0	$6,656.0
2015	$1,414.5	–	$8,070.5 est.

* in millions

Source: http://www.window.state.tx.us/comptrol/fnotes/fn1102/ See also *Fiscal Size-Up*, 2014–15, Figure 43, p.37.

was an unconstitutional violation of the equal protection clause of the 14th Amendment to the U.S. Constitution.

Meanwhile, though many Texas public officials and school districts would continue to resist integration for decades, the state did undertake major educational reforms. The Gilmer-Aikin Laws of 1949, named for Representative Claud Gilmer and Senator A.M. Aikin, reduced the number of independent school districts in Texas from 4,500 to 2,900, equalized school funding, increased teacher pay, reorganized the State Board of Education (SBE), and established the Texas Education Agency (TEA).

The state of Texas, through the SBE and the TEA, sets the standards and expectations for elementary and secondary education in the state. But

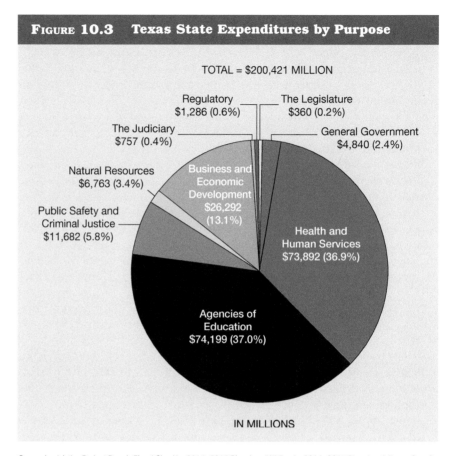

FIGURE 10.3   Texas State Expenditures by Purpose

TOTAL = $200,421 MILLION

Regulatory $1,286 (0.6%)

The Legislature $360 (0.2%)

The Judiciary $757 (0.4%)

General Government $4,840 (2.4%)

Natural Resources $6,763 (3.4%)

Business and Economic Development $26,292 (13.1%)

Public Safety and Criminal Justice $11,682 (5.8%)

Health and Human Services $73,892 (36.9%)

Agencies of Education $74,199 (37.0%)

IN MILLIONS

Source: Legislative Budget Board, *Fiscal Size-Up, 2014–2015 Biennium,* "All Funds, 2014–2015 Biennium," Figure 2, p. 2.

education is expensive, so battles over funding barely slowed, especially after the U.S. Supreme Court, in the landmark *Plyler v. Doe* (1982) case, declared that school districts must provide the children of illegal immigrants with free public education. As the proportion of school funding provided by the state continued to decline, local school boards were forced to increase property taxes to maintain adequate resources. Wealthy districts managed to cope while poor districts struggled.

In the early 1980s, Texas parents, teachers, school administrators, and public officials brought a new focus to issues of education quality and funding. Dallas billionaire H. Ross Perot was appointed to lead a blue ribbon committee on education reform. In 1984, the legislature passed a number of the Perot reforms, including teacher competency testing, student achievement testing, stricter attendance standards linked to school funding, and "no pass-no play."

Equal funding for rich and poor districts was again raised in 1984. The Mexican-American Legal Defense and Education Fund (MALDEF) filed suit in

Edgewood ISD v. Kirby claiming discrimination against children in poor school districts. In 1986, the Texas Supreme Court declared that large differences between rich and poor districts violated the state constitution's mandate of an "efficient" education for all Texas school children. In 1993, Senator Bill Ratliff (R-Mount Pleasant) guided Senate Bill 7 through the legislature. SB 7, known as the "Robin Hood Bill," required wealthy school districts to share some of their money with the poorer districts in the state. Some wealthy districts, such as the Highland Park ISD near Dallas, sent fully 70 percent of their property tax revenues to the state for redistribution to poor districts.

By 2004, two-thirds of the state's school districts were at or near the state-mandated local property tax cap of $1.50 per $100 of assessed property value. Poor districts were at the cap and still unable to raise adequate resources, while wealthy districts were at the cap because they had to fund their schools and send Robin Hood contributions to the state. The Texas Supreme Court again intervened, holding that the state had violated the constitution's prohibition on a statewide property tax by forcing most of the state's school districts to the property tax cap. The Court ordered the legislature to reform the school funding system to give local school boards more flexibility.

In 2006, Governor Perry and the Texas legislature responded to the Court's demand for funding reform by lowering local property taxes by one-third, enacting a broad new business tax, increasing the state cigarette tax from $0.41 to $1.41 a pack, adjusting a couple of other minor tax streams, and drawing on the state surplus. In the 2014–15 school year, Texas spent $9,559 per student while the national average was $12,040.[7] Texas ranked 38th in the nation for per capita spending per student. The state provided 46 percent of school funding while Texas's 1,025 local school districts provided 44 percent. The federal government provided a little over 10 percent of school funds. While these reforms do represent progress, school funding has remained a flashpoint of Texas politics.

The 2006 legislation also allowed local school districts to raise taxes from $1 per $100 of assessed value to $1.04 as needed and to as much as $1.17 with voter approval. Nearly all school districts have raised their rate to $1.04. About 40 percent of districts asked voters to approve higher rates and most of them asked to go to the max—$1.17. School districts won approval a little more than 70 percent of the time. Texas parents, far more than Texas legislators, are focused on their children's need for a high-quality education.[8]

Nonetheless, for the eighth time in the past 40 years, Texas is back in state court charged with unconstitutionally underfunding its public schools. A diverse group of rich and poor school districts, charter schools, and citizen groups have sued the state claiming that the current school funding system provides inadequate funding for schools and distributes funds inequitably among districts. The cases were heard by State District Judge John Dietz in Austin. Judge Dietz opened the trial in October 2012, declaring his intention to finish the trial and release a preliminary decision during the 2013 regular session of the legislature. Dietz issued preliminary findings in favor of the school districts, but delayed a final decision to give the legislature time to act. The 2013 legislature restored more than half of the school funding cut in 2011 and loosened some testing requirements. Judge Dietz took new testimony on the implications of these changes and then withdrew to consider his final decision. In June 2014, the State of Texas petitioned Judge Dietz to recuse himself, suggesting that he was biased in favor of the school districts. The state's move also suggested that they expected to lose and that they were already laying the groundwork for an appeal. Judge Dietz remained on the case and, just as the state feared, decided in favor of the schools. As a result, the 2015 regular session of the legislature and one or more special sessions will focus on education spending and equality.[9]

Higher Education. About 1.56 million students attend 150 public and private colleges and universities in Texas. Ninety percent of these students attend public colleges and universities and half of these attend one of the fifty community college districts in the state.[10] Two issues have roiled Texas higher education in recent years. One is how to divide the cost of higher education between the state and the student. Should the state appropriation to colleges be high and tuition charged to students low, or should the appropriation be low and tuition high?

Historically, Texas had among the lowest college tuition and fees in the country. As late as the 1994–95 academic year, average tuition and fees at Texas state universities was only 60 percent of the national average ($1,608 in Texas versus $2,689 nationally). In 2003, the legislature reduced state funding and allowed the colleges and universities to set their own tuition and fees. Texas tuition and fees still compare favorably with many other states, but they have been rising fast, doubling since 2003. Students attending Texas public four-year universities during the 2014–15 academic year paid slightly below the national average ($8,830 versus $9,139 nationally). Under pressure from students, parents, and legislature, the UT system scrapped anticipated tuition increases of 15 percent over the 2008–09 and 2009–10 school years, and instituted a 5 percent per year cap. Texas community colleges are still a bargain at $2,222 compared to a national average of $3,264.[11]

A second major issue in higher education, both nationally and in Texas, is affirmative action. Admissions criteria are always sensitive, especially when issues of race, ethnicity, and gender are in play. Beginning in the 1970s, Texas universities managed admissions to insure that the student body reflected the diversity of the state. In 1992, Cheryl Hopwood charged in *Hopwood v. Texas* that the University of Texas Law School discriminated against her by rejecting her and admitting minority students with lower grades and test scores. The U.S. Fifth Circuit Court of Appeals found for Hopwood, saying that race should not be a factor in law school or undergraduate admission.

Fearing too great a drop in minority enrollment in Texas colleges and universities, the legislature adopted a program by which the top 10 percent of each high school graduating class in the state would be eligible for admission

Hopwood v. Texas (1992) The U.S. Fifth Circuit Court of Appeals agreed with Cheryl Hopwood and others that the affirmative action program run by the University of Texas gave race too dominant a role in the admissions process.

Charles Dharapak/AP/Corbis

Abigail Fisher, flanked by her parents and her attorney, Edward Blum (left center), share a light moment during a news conference, June 24, 2013, related to her case before the U.S. Supreme Court.

to the state's top universities. Because many of the state's high schools have a clear ethnic or racial identity, some overwhelmingly Anglo, others overwhelmingly Hispanic or black, admitting the top 10 percent of each graduating class assured some diversity.

The U.S. Supreme Court's 2003 *Grutter v. Bollinger* decision, better known as the Michigan decision, overturned Hopwood and restored the right of colleges and universities to consider race in admissions decisions, so long as it was just one of a list of factors considered. Public colleges and universities in Texas employ the top 10 percent rule but they also consider race as a criterion in admission. Some contend that Texas universities should simply take the very best students without regard to non-academic criteria like race or ethnicity. Others point out that non-academic criteria are used in admissions all the time—think of that not so bright quarterback with the great arm and that talented dancer that does not test so well. In 2008, fully 83 percent of UT freshmen were admitted under the top 10 percent rule. The 2009 legislature amended the law to say that no more than 75 percent of UT's incoming class needed to be admitted under the rule. The top 10 percent rule remained in effect for the other thirty-seven public colleges and universities in Texas.

2008 marked the beginning of the latest high profile affirmative action case in the federal courts—*Fisher v. Texas*. The plaintiff, Abigail Fisher, sued UT, claiming that she had been denied admission while less qualified minority students had been admitted. The federal district court and the Fifth Circuit Court of Appeals held for UT, finding, following *Grutter*, that universities were

Grutter v. Bollinger (2003) Also known as the Michigan case, the U.S. Supreme Court upheld affirmative action programs taking race into account as one factor among many.

Fisher v. University of Texas State courts upheld UT's right to use race if "narrowly tailored," as "part of a holistic admissions program."

entitled to use race as one factor among many in its admissions decisions. But in mid-2013, the U.S. Supreme Court sent the case back to the Fifth Circuit to be sure that "available, workable, race-neutral alternatives do not exist."[12] Though this new ruling will likely return to the Supreme Court, most people believe the case is effectively over and "narrowly tailored" affirmative action has survived.

Health and Human Services

Health and human services programs include Medicaid, child health care, mental health and retardation programs, welfare, unemployment compensation, and workmen's compensation for those injured on the job. These programs are among the fastest growing elements of the state budget.

About $73.9 billion, 36.9 percent of the state budget, goes to health and human services. The cost of these programs is usually shared between the federal and state governments, with the federal government setting the basic rules and providing base funding and the states adding to the federal funding and administering the program. Federal funds account for about 60 percent of Texas spending for health and human services. In fact, Texas frequently leaves federal money on the table so that it will not have to raise and allocate additional state revenues.

In the most recent data, Texas ranked 42nd on the percentage of low-income children on Medicaid, 44th on health care expenditures per capita, and 49th on the percentage of the eligible population enrolled in Medicaid. Not surprisingly then, Texas is 1st in the percentage of the total population (25.5) and the percentage of children (21.8) without health insurance coverage. Texas is 6th in the percentage of the total population (16.5) and of children (24.4) living in poverty.

Medicaid is the largest and most expensive health care program run by Texas state government. Medicaid is a state-federal program that provides health care, mostly to low-income children, pregnant women, and the poor and disabled elderly. Medicaid serves 4 million Texans at a biennial cost of $56.2 billion. The federal government provides 60 percent of the funds but Texas sets the rules on eligibility and benefit levels. Two-thirds of Medicaid payments go to support the elderly and disabled, yet Texas sets tighter rules than do most states. Texas ranks 49th in reimbursement for nursing home care, paying $112.79 per day compared to a national average of $163.27 per day.

CHIP stands for Children's Health Insurance Program. CHIP serves about 630,000 children from families that make less than $44,700 (200 percent of the poverty line). Texas spent about $2 billion on CHIP in 2014–15, 70 percent of which were federal dollars. Despite the fact that federal funds pay most CHIP expenses, Texas sets tight eligibility and low benefit rules to limit the number of eligible children served.

Business, Transportation, and Economic Development

During the 2014–15 biennium, Texas spent $26.3 billion, about 13.1 percent of its total budget, on business and economic development. This spending category includes the Texas Department of Transportation (TxDOT), the Department of Economic Development, and the Department of Housing and Community Affairs. About 42 percent of the funds spent in this category come to Texas as federal grants.

Eighty-five percent of the money spent in the business and economic development category of the state budget goes to TxDOT. While TxDOT is responsible for planning, maintenance, and development of the state road, rail, and air transportation infrastructure, most of its resources go to maintain and extend the state's nearly 80,000 miles of roads and highways.[13] Texas's $22 billion roads budget for 2014–15 comes principally from federal and state gas taxes. In recent years, these funds have barely sufficed for road repairs, let alone new construction.

In 2002, Governor Perry developed a plan for the state's future transportation needs that generated great controversy. Perry unveiled plans for the Trans-Texas Corridor, a 4,000 mile corridor, a quarter-mile wide including six lanes for cars, four lanes for trucks, as well as railroad tracks, oil and gas pipelines, and utility lines, running from the Mexican border to the Red River and from El Paso to Houston. Construction of the Trans-Texas Corridor was envisioned to begin in 2010, take many years to complete, and cost $184 billion.

As always, Governor Perry sought to deliver this major project without raising taxes. Initial contracts were awarded to a Spanish-led consortium, Cintra-Zachry, which promised to fund the project in exchange for the right to charge tolls later. Critics complain about lost farmland, foreign contractors, and the prospect of paying tolls far into the future. The 2007 legislative session overwhelmingly, 139–1 in the House and 30–1 in the Senate, passed a bill declaring a two-year moratorium on toll roads. The Trans-Texas Corridor is dead, but Texas needs to invest in transportation improvements to stimulate growth. Conservative legislators, unwilling to raise taxes, face the unpalatable choice of increasingly crowded roads or more toll roads and public–private construction and operating agreements that will put Texas drivers on the hook for decades.[14]

Prisons and Public Safety

Texas spent about $11.7 billion, or 5.8 percent of its 2014–15 budget on criminal justice and public safety. About $5 billion went directly to house nearly 152,700 inmates in the state's 106 prisons and jails. Texas ranks 39th among the states in spending per prisoner, laying out an average of $21,390 annually.[15] The Department of Criminal Justice is responsible for the prisons while the Department of Public Safety (DPS) provides police services throughout the state. Within the DPS, the Texas Highway Patrol (3,400) and the Texas Rangers (134) field about 3,540 uniformed officers.

Parks and Recreation

Finally, the decade-long struggle to fund Texas's 95 state parks highlights the state's budgetary practices. Texas officials try to limit the pressure on state general funds by identifying dedicated funds for particular programs. In 1993, the legislature dedicated a tax on sporting goods to fund Texas parks. In 1995, though the tax produced more than $200 million biennially, the legislature capped park funding at $64 million and directed the rest into the general fund. Park fees bring in an additional $65 million biennially, but the parks continue to lay off workers and defer maintenance.

Public protests over the condition of the parks brought a statewide vote approving $44 million in general obligation bonds for park renovations and improvements. Legislative appropriations rose in 2009, but 2011 was devastating for Texas parks and those who keep them.[16] Drought, the Bastrop fires that destroyed Bastrop State Park around Labor Day, and an 18 percent cut to the department's budget, left the Parks Department in extreme difficulty. The department eliminated 169 of their 1,300 employees and reduced hours and services at state parks. By late 2011, they were reduced to begging the public for $4.6 million to help avoid further layoffs and in 2012 they sought corporate sponsorships to fund the parks.[17]

The legislature has tried to do better in recent budgets. The 2012–13 budget allocated $82 million to state parks, the 2014–15 increased that to $139 million. Nonetheless, nearly $200 million in sporting good tax revenues were diverted to the state general fund over the past five years. Texas ranks 49th among the fifty states in spending on parks.

EXPLORING THE TAX BURDEN IN TEXAS

Q5 Where do issues of fairness fit into discussions of taxing and spending?

Texas ranks among the lowest of the low tax states. Our state takes just 4.7 percent of personal income in state taxes (compared to a national average of 6.2 percent), placing Texas 46th among the fifty states. The per capita tax burden, $1,955 in 2013 (compared to the national average of $2,682) places Texas 42nd.[18] In a sense, all taxes are paid out of income. But, as discussed earlier in this chapter, Texas does not have a classic income tax whereby employers withhold taxes from paychecks. Rather, Texas state and local governments at least let you get your income home before they charge you sales taxes, property taxes, and other fines and fees.

Clearly, governments need to claim revenue, but how they choose to do so raises issues of fairness. As a result, taxes are often described in terms of who pays them. **Progressive taxes** take a larger percentage share of the income of the wealthy than they do of the poor. Nationally, the most common progressive tax is the income tax, but Texas does not employ an income tax. **Regressive taxes**, which are common in Texas, draw a higher proportion of the income of the poor than they do of the wealthy. A 2013 study by the Center for Public Policy Priorities, based on the Texas Comptroller's Tax Exemptions

Progressive taxes Taxes that take a higher proportion of the income of the wealthy than of the poor.

Regressive taxes Taxes that take a higher proportion of the income of the poor than of the wealthy.

LET'S COMPARE   TAX BURDEN IN THE TEN LARGEST STATES

One hears frequently about American jobs being "exported" to low wage countries like Mexico, China, and Vietnam. But not all jobs are equally easy to export. Any job that is done face-to-face, like hair stylist or dentist, must be done locally and many high value jobs, like those in Silicon Valley and around Austin, are less likely to be exported. States also worry that they must be attractive to both employers and employees, ideally high wage employers and workers. How do states try to position themselves to be attractive? Two ways basically—

Some states, generally those in the north and west with a moralistic or communitarian political culture, take a high tax, high service, path to making themselves attractive. California, New York, and Pennsylvania, for example, spend between $2,500 and $3,750 per citizen, mostly on education, health and human services, and transportation infrastructure. The goal is to assure a well-trained workforce and an infrastructure—roads, rail, airports, but also electricity, broadband, water, and sewer—to allow businesses and employees to get where they need to go, get their work done, and move the goods and services

they produce to market. These states take from 6 to 8 percent of personal income in taxes to fund the full range of services they deem necessary to a healthy state economy and society.

Southern states, like North Carolina, Florida, and Georgia, favor low taxes, fewer services, and a focus on personal responsibility as the best way to attract entrepreneurs and those who are willing to work. Both businesses and workers might be attracted to a state in which low taxes allow you to keep more of what you earn. But low taxes also mean less money spent on public education, health care, and infrastructure. This suggests at least the possibility that the workforce will be less well-educated, healthy, and productive than in states that spend more.

Throughout this book, we have argued that Texas has a traditional political culture that has worked to keep taxes low, regulations light, and elites in social and political control. Not surprisingly, Texas ranks 47th among the states in proportion of income taken in state taxes. Texans differ as to whether this is a source of pride or shame.

State	State Tax Per Capita	Rank Among 50 States	% of Personal Income	Rank Among 50 States
California	$3,474	11	7.5%	9
New York	$3,749	8	7.1%	14
Michigan	$2,535	26	6.6%	21
Pennsylvania	$2,659	22	5.9%	33
Illinois	$3,005	14	6.6%	22
Ohio	$2,362	33	5.9%	32
North Carolina	$2,414	32	6.4%	24
Florida	$1,769	50	4.4%	48
Georgia	$1,781	49	4.8%	44
Texas	$1,955	42	4.7%	47
U.S. Total	$2,556		6.3%	

Source: See http://www.taxadmin.org/fta/rate/13taxbur.html. Data is drawn from the U.S. Bureau of the Census and the Bureau of Economic Analysis.

TIMELINE: TEXAS SCHOOL FINANCE AND REFORM

1894	1865	1875	1883	1903	1915	1949
Common School Law of 1854—first state public school system	Freedman's Bureau establishes black schools	Independent school districts established	University of Texas opens	State textbook selection board created	First mandatory attendance law passed	Gilmer-Aiken education reform law passed

and Tax Incidence, found that poor Texans pay 15.6 percent of their income in state and local taxes while the wealthy pay about 4.2 percent.[19]

The reason that the poor in Texas pay a higher proportion of their income in taxes than the wealthy is that our state depends so heavily on the general and special sales taxes. Poor Texans must spend all of their money on consumption, for food, gasoline, and clothing, and hence pay the sales tax on most of their total income. Wealthy Texans can shield some of their income by saving and investing rather than spending it. Saving and investing are good things to be sure, they drive economic growth, but they do allow the wealthy to shield their income while the poor cannot.

Chapter Summary

Some of the most critical decisions made in politics, whether in Washington or Austin, concern taxing and spending. These are decisions about who pays taxes, what kinds of taxes they pay, and how much they pay. Closely related decisions involve what services will be funded and who will benefit from them.

Texas budgets on a biennial, two-year, basis. Planning for the 2016–2017 biennial budget began in April 2014. By the time the 2015 regular session of the Texas Legislature convened in January, eight months of planning in the Legislative Budget Board and the governor's office had produced a draft budget. By the end of the legislative session in June 2015, the budget had been debated, refined, and approved so that it could go into effect in October 2015, the beginning of the 2016–2017 biennium. It is often said that the budget is the only "must pass" bill of the legislative session.

Texas is a low tax state. To keep taxes low, Texans have used the constitution and laws to prohibit a state income tax and a state property tax. Even following the recent increase in business taxes, they remain modest by national standards. On the other hand, Texas has some of the highest sales taxes in the country. Texas deploys its limited resources, supplemented by federal transfers that comprise nearly 36 percent of the Texas budget, to fund basic programs in education, social services, highways, and prisons.

1954	1970	1984	1989	1993	2002	2012
Brown v. Board declares segregated schools violate the U.S. Constitution	*United States v. Texas* mandates Texas Education Agency to oversee desegregation	Texas legislature adopts Perot Committee education reforms	Texas Supreme Court strikes down school finance system	Texas Legislature adopts "Robin Hood" funding system	Congress passes No Child Left Behind education reforms	School districts again sue Texas over adequacy of education funding

Taxes are often discussed and judged in terms of who pays them, how much they pay, and how capable they are of making those payments. Progressive taxes, like the income tax, levy higher rates on the wealthy than the poor on the argument that the wealthy have more ability to pay. Regressive taxes, like the sales tax, gas tax, and lottery, hit the poor harder than the wealthy. Texas has generally favored regressive taxes, arguing that progressive taxes are a tax on entrepreneurs and job creators.

Texans have long favored small government and low taxes. Most Texans applaud careful spending. But the taxes that Texas does levy, especially the general sales tax and the gas tax, bear hard on those who have little. Tight budgets leave many Texans with less education, health care, and job training than a healthy and productive life requires.

Key Terms

Budgets   248

Corporate franchise fee   257

Federal transfer payments   258

Fisher v. Texas   265

Grutter v. Bollinger   265

Hopwood v. Texas   264

Legislative Budget Board   251

Margins tax   257

Progressive taxes   268

Regressive taxes   268

Sales tax   256

Sin tax   258

Review Questions

1. Describe the role that budgets play in state politics and policy-making.
2. Assess the respective roles played by the governor and the presiding officers of the Texas legislature in the drafting and approval of the state budget.
3. Compare the revenue sources supporting the Texas state budget to the revenue sources drawn on by other state governments.

4. Trace the legal battles between Texas public schools and the state government in regard to funding levels and funding equity.
5. Explain whether the state tax system in Texas is progressive or regressive and what difference it makes.

Suggested Readings

Council of State Governments, *Book of the States, 2012 Edition*, vol. 44 (Lexington, KY, 2012).

J. Steven Farr and Mark Trachtenberg, "The Edgewood Drama: An Epic Quest for Educational Equity," *Yale Law and Policy Review* (1999), 17, 2: 607–727.

House Research Organization, Texas House of Representatives, *Writing the State Budget*, State Finance Report, No. 82-1, February 3, 2011. See the LBB website.

Legislative Budget Board, 82nd Texas Legislature, *Fiscal Size-Up, 2012–2013 Biennium*. See the LBB website.

Neil Malhutra, "Disentangling the Relationship Between Legislative Professionalism and Government Spending," *Legislative Studies Quarterly* (2008), 33: 387–414.

Abby Rapoport, "Will Proposed Education Cuts Lead to Lawsuits," *Texas Observer* (2011), February 10.

Robert W. Reed, "Democrats, Republicans, and Taxes: Evidence that Political Parties Matter," *Journal of Public Economics* (2006), 90: 725–750.

Web Resources

1. http://www.window.state.tx.us/revenue.html
   Historical view of state revenue by source.

2. http://www.window.state.tx.us/expend.html
   Historical view of state expenditures by category.

3. http://www.lbb.state.tx.us
   LBB website.

4. http://www.cbpp.org
   Center on Budget and Policy Priorities. Comparing state budgets.

5. http://www.taxadmin.org and http://www.taxfoundation.org
   More good comparative data.

6. http://www.pewcenteronthestates.org
   Highly respected, non-partisan research on state issues.

Appendix A

William Barret Travis's Letter from the Alamo

Commandancy of the Alamo
Bejar, Feby. 24, 1836

To the People of Texas & All Americans in the World

Fellow citizens & compatriots

I am besieged, by a thousand or more of the Mexicans under Santa Anna. I have sustained a continual Bombardment & cannonade for 24 hours & have not lost a man. The enemy has demanded a surrender at discretion, otherwise, the garrison are to be put to the sword, if the fort is taken. I have answered the demand with a cannon shot, & our flag still waves proudly from the walls. I shall never surrender or retreat. Then, I call on you in the name of Liberty, of patriotism & everything dear to the American character, to come to our aid, with all dispatch. The enemy is receiving reinforcements daily & will no doubt increase to three or four thousand in four or five days. If this call is neglected, I am determined to sustain myself as long as possible & die like a soldier who never forgets what is due to his own honor and to that of this country. VICTORY OR DEATH.

William Barret Travis,
Lt. Col. Comdt.

Appendix B

The Texas Declaration of Independence, Washington-on-the-Brazos, March 2, 1836

The Unanimous Declaration of Independence made by the Delegates of the People of Texas in General Convention at the town of Washington on the 2nd day of March 1836.

When a government has ceased to protect the lives, liberty and property of the people, from whom its legitimate powers are derived, and for the advancement of whose happiness it was instituted, and so far from being a guarantee for the enjoyment of those inestimable and inalienable rights, becomes an instrument in the hands of evil rulers for their oppression.

When the Federal Republican Constitution of their country, which they have sworn to support, no longer has a substantial existence, and the whole nature of their government has been forcibly changed, without their consent, from a restricted federative republic, composed of sovereign states, to a consolidated central military despotism, in which every interest is disregarded but that of the army and the priesthood, both the eternal enemies of civil liberty, the everready minions of power, and the usual instruments of tyrants.

When, long after the spirit of the constitution has departed, moderation is at length so far lost by those in power, that even the semblance of freedom is removed, and the forms themselves of the constitution discontinued, and so far from their petitions and remonstrances being regarded, the agents who bear them are thrown into dungeons, and mercenary armies sent forth to force a new government upon them at the point of the bayonet.

When, in consequence of such acts of malfeasance and abdication on the part of the government, anarchy prevails, and civil society is dissolved into its original elements. In such a crisis, the first law of nature, the right of self-preservation, the inherent and inalienable rights of the people to appeal to first principles, and take their political affairs into their own hands in extreme cases, enjoins it as a right toward themselves, and a sacred obligation to their posterity, to abolish such government, and create another in its stead, calculated to rescue them from impending dangers, and to secure their future welfare and happiness.

Nations, as well as individuals, are amenable for their acts to the public opinion of mankind. A statement of a part of our grievances is therefore submitted to an impartial world, in justification of the hazardous but unavoidable step now taken, of severing our political connection with the Mexican people, and assuming an independent attitude among the nations of the earth.

The Mexican government, by its colonization laws, invited and induced the Anglo-American population of Texas to colonize its wilderness under the pledged faith of a written constitution, that they should continue to enjoy that constitutional liberty and republican government to which they had been habituated in the land of their birth, the United States of America.

In this expectation they have been cruelly disappointed, inasmuch as the Mexican nation has acquiesced in the late changes made in the government by General Antonio Lopez de Santa Anna, who having overturned the constitution of his country, now offers us the cruel alternative, either to abandon our homes, acquired by so many privations, or submit to the most intolerable of all tyranny, the combined despotism of the sword and the priesthood.

It has sacrificed our welfare to the state of Coahuila, by which our interests have been continually depressed through a jealous and partial course of legislation, carried on at a far distant seat of government, by a hostile majority, in an unknown tongue, and this too, notwithstanding we have petitioned in the humblest terms for the establishment of a separate state government, and have, in accordance with the provisions of the national constitution, presented to the general Congress a republican constitution, which was, without just cause, contemptuously rejected.

It incarcerated in a dungeon, for a long time, one of our citizens, for no other cause but a zealous endeavor to procure the acceptance of our constitution, and the establishment of a state government.

It has failed and refused to secure, on a firm basis, the right of trial by jury, that palladium of civil liberty, and only safeguard for the life, liberty, and property of the citizen.

It has failed to establish any public system of education, although possessed of almost boundless resources, (the public domain,) and although it is an axiom in political science, that unless a people are educated and enlightened, it is idle to expect the continuance of civil liberty, or the capacity for self-government.

It has suffered the military commandants, stationed among us, to exercise arbitrary acts of oppression and tyranny, thus trampling on the most sacred rights of the citizens, and rendering the military superior to the civil power.

It has dissolved, by force of arms, the state Congress of Coahuila and Texas, and obliged our representatives to fly for their lives from the seat of government, thus depriving us of the fundamental political right of representation.

It has demanded the surrender of a number of our citizens, and ordered military detachments to seize and carry them into the Interior for trial, in contempt of the civil authorities, and in defiance of the laws and the constitution.

It has made piratical attacks upon our commerce, by commissioning foreign desperadoes, and authorizing them to seize our vessels, and convey the property of our citizens to far distant ports for confiscation.

It denies us the right of worshipping the Almighty according to the dictates of our own conscience, by the support of a national religion, calculated to promote the temporal interest of it human functionaries, rather than the glory of the true and living God.

It has demanded us to deliver up our arms, which are essential to our defence, the rightful property of freemen, and formidable only to tyrannical governments.

It has invaded our country both by sea and by land, with intent to lay waste our territory, and drive us from our homes; and has now a large mercenary army advancing, to carry on against us a war of extermination.

It has, through its emissaries, incited the merciless savage, with the tomahawk and scalping knife, to massacre the inhabitants of our defenseless frontiers.

It hath been, during the whole time of our connection with it, the contemptible sport and victim of successive military revolutions, and hath continually exhibited every characteristic of a weak, corrupt, and tyrranical government.

These, and other grievances, were patiently born by the people of Texas, until they reached that point at which forbearance ceases to be a virtue. We then took up arms in defence of the national constitution. We appealed to our Mexican brethren for assistance. Our appeal has been made in vain. Though months have elapsed, no sympathetic response has yet been heard from the Interior. We are, therefore, forced to the melancholy conclusion, that the Mexican people have acquiesced in the destruction of their liberty, and the substitution therfor of a military government; that they are unfit to be free, and incapable of self-government.

The necessity of self-preservation, therefore, now decrees our eternal political separation.

We, therefore, the delegates with plenary powers of the people of Texas, in solemn convention assembled, appealing to a candid world for the necessities of our condition, do hereby resolve and declare, that our political connection with the Mexican nation has forever ended, and that the people of Texas do now constitute a free, Sovereign, and independent republic, and are fully invested with all the rights and attributes which properly belong to independent nations; and, conscious of the rectitude of our intentions, we fearlessly and confidently commit the issue to the decision of the Supreme arbiter of the destinies of nations.

Richard Ellis, President of the Convention and Delegate from Red River

Charles B. Stewart	Tho. Barnett	James Collinsworth	Edwin Waller
Asa Brigham	John S. D. Byrom	Geo. C. Childress	Francis Ruis
Bailey Hardeman	J. Antonio Navarro	Rob. Potter	Jesse B. Badgett
Thomas Jefferson Rusk	Wm D. Lacy	Chas. S. Taylor	William Menifee
John S. Roberts	Jn. Fisher	Robert Hamilton	Matthew Caldwell
Collin McKinney	William Motley	Albert H. Latimer	Lorenzo de Zavala
James Power	Stephen H. Everett	Sam Houston	George W. Smyth
David Thomas	Elijah Stapp	Edwd. Conrad	Claiborne West
Martin Parmer	Wm. B. Scates	Edwin O. Legrande	M. B. Menard
Stephen W. Blount	A. B. Hardin	Jms. Gaines	J. W. Burton
Wm. Clark, Jr.	Thos. J. Gazley	Sydney O. Pennington	R. M. Coleman
Wm. Carrol Crawford	Sterling H. Robertson	Jno. Turner	Benj. Briggs Goodrich
G. W. Barnett	James G. Swisher	Jesse Grimes	S. Rhoads Fisher
John W. Moore	John W. Bower	Saml. A Maverick	Sam P. Carson
A. Briscoe	J. B. Woods	H. S. Kimble, Secretary	

Appendix C

Selections from The Texas Constitution

Preamble

Humbly invoking the blessings of Almighty God, the people of the state of Texas, do ordain and establish this Constitution.

Article 1: Bill of Rights

That the general, great and essential principles of liberty and free government may be recognized and established, we declare:

Sec. 1. FREEDOM AND SOVEREIGNTY OF STATE. Texas is a free and independent State, subject only to the Constitution of the United States, and the maintenance of our free institutions and the perpetuity of the Union depend upon the preservation of the right of local self-government, unimpaired to all the States.

Sec. 2. INHERENT POLITICAL POWER; REPUBLICAN FORM OF GOVERNMENT. All political power is inherent in the people, and all free governments are founded on their authority, and instituted for their benefit. The faith of the people of Texas stands pledged to the preservation of a republican form of government, and subject to this limitation only, they have at all times the inalienable right to alter, reform or abolish their government in such manner as they may think expedient.

Sec. 3. EQUAL RIGHTS. All free men, when they form a social compact, have equal rights, and no man, or set of men, is entitled to exclusive separate public emoluments, or privileges, but in consideration of public services.

Sec. 3a. EQUALITY UNDER THE LAW. Equality under the law shall not be denied or abridged because of sex, race, color, creed, or national origin . . . . (Added Nov. 7, 1972.)

Sec. 4. RELIGIOUS TESTS. No religious test shall ever be required as a qualification to any office, or public trust, in this State; nor shall anyone be excluded from holding office on account of his religious sentiments, provided he acknowledge the existence of a Supreme Being.

Sec. 8. FREEDOM OF SPEECH AND PRESS; LIBEL. Every person shall be at liberty to speak, write or publish his opinions on any subject, being responsible for the abuse of that privilege; and no law shall ever be passed curtailing the liberty of speech or of the press. . . .

Sec. 9. SEARCHES AND SEIZURES. The people shall be secure in their person, houses, papers and possessions, from all unreasonable searches and seizures, and no warrant to search any place, or to seize any person or thing, shall issue without describing them as near as may be, nor without probable cause, supported by oath or affirmation.

Sec. 10. RIGHTS OF THE ACCUSED IN CRIMINAL PROSECUTIONS. In all criminal prosecutions the accused shall have a speedy public trial by an impartial jury. He shall have the right to demand the nature and cause of the accusation against him, and to have a copy thereof. He shall not be compelled to give evidence against himself, and shall have the right of being heard by himself or counsel, or both, shall be confronted by the witnesses against him and shall have compulsory process for obtaining witnesses in his favor, . . .

Sec. 13. EXCESSIVE BAIL OR FINES; CRUEL AND UNUSUAL PUNISHMENT; REMEDY BY DUE COURSE OF LAW. Excessive bail shall not be required, nor excessive fines imposed, nor cruel or unusual punishment inflicted. All courts shall be open, and every person for an injury done him, in his lands, goods, person or reputation, shall have remedy by due course of law.

Sec. 14. DOUBLE JEOPARDY. No person, for the same offense, shall be twice put in jeopardy of life or liberty; nor shall a person be again put upon trial for the same offense after a verdict of not guilty in a court of competent jurisdiction.

Sec. 15a. COMMITMENT OF PERSONS OF UNSOUND MIND. No person shall be committed as a person of unsound mind except on competent medical or psychiatric testimony . . . .

Sec. 18. IMPRISONMENT FOR DEBT. No person shall ever be imprisoned for debt . . . .

Sec. 20. OUTLAWRY . . . . No citizen shall be outlawed . . . .

Sec. 23. RIGHT TO KEEP AND BEAR ARMS. Every citizen shall have the right to keep and bear arms in the lawful defense of himself or the State; but the Legislature shall have power, by law, to regulate the wearing of arms, with a view to prevent crime . . . .

Sec. 27. RIGHT OF ASSEMBLY, PETITION FOR REDRESS OF GRIEVANCES. The citizens shall have the right, in a peaceable manner, to assemble together for their common good; and to apply to those invested with the powers of government for redress of grievances or other purposes, by petition, address or remonstrance . . . .

Sec. 32. MARRIAGE. (a) Marriage in this state shall consist only of the union of one man and one woman. (b) The state or a political subdivision of this state may not create or recognize any legal status identical or similar to marriage. (Added Nov. 8, 2005.)

Article 2: The Powers of Government

Sec. 1. DIVISION OF POWERS; THREE SEPARATE DEPARTMENTS; EXERCISE OF POWER PROPERLY ATTACHED TO OTHER DEPARTMENTS. The powers of the Government of the State of Texas shall be divided into three distinct departments, each of which shall be confided to a separate body of magistracy, to wit: Those which are Legislative to one; those which are Executive to another, and those which are Judicial to another; and no person, or collection of persons, being of one of these departments, shall exercise any power properly attached to either of the others, except in the instances herein expressly permitted.

Article 3: Legislative Department

Sec. 1. SENATE AND HOUSE OF REPRESENTATIVES. The Legislative power of this State shall be vested in a Senate and House of Representatives, which together shall be styled "The Legislature of the State of Texas."

Sec. 2. MEMBERSHIP OF SENATE AND HOUSE OF REPRESENTATIVES. The Senate shall consist of thirty-one members. The House of Representatives shall consist of 150 members.

Sec. 3. ELECTION AND TERM OF OFFICE OF SENATORS. The Senators shall be chosen by the qualified voters for the term of four years; . . .

Sec. 4. ELECTION AND TERM OF MEMBERS OF HOUSE OF REPRESENTATIVES. The members of the House of Representatives shall be chosen by the qualified voters for the term of two years . . . .

Sec. 5. MEETINGS; ORDER OF BUSINESS. (a) The Legislature shall meet every two years at such time as may be provided by law and at other times when convened by the Governor. (b) When convened in regular Session, the first thirty days thereof shall be devoted to the introduction of bills and resolutions, acting upon emergency appropriations, passing upon the confirmation of recess appointees of the Governor and such emergency matters as may be submitted by the Governor in special messages to the Legislature. During the succeeding thirty days of the regular session of the Legislature the various committees of each House shall hold hearings to consider all bills and resolutions and other matters then pending; and such emergency matters as may be submitted by the Governor. During the remainder of the session the Legislature shall act upon such bills and resolutions as may be then pending and upon such emergency matters as may be submitted by the Governor in special messages to the Legislature . . . .

Sec. 6. QUALIFICATIONS OF SENATORS. No person shall be a Senator, unless he be a citizen of the United States, and, at the time of his election a qualified voter of this State, and shall have been a resident of this State five years next preceding his election, and the last year thereof a resident of the district for which he shall be chosen, and shall have attained the age of twenty-six years.

Sec. 7. QUALIFICATIONS OF REPRESENTATIVES. No person shall be a Representative, unless he be a citizen of the United States, and, at the time of his election, a qualified voter of this State, and shall have been a resident of this State two years next preceding his election, the last year thereof a resident of the district for which he shall be chosen, and shall have attained the age of twenty-one years . . . .

Sec. 9. PRESDIENT PRO TEMPORE OF SENATE; LIEUTENANT GOVERNOR OFFICE VACANCY; SPEAKER OF HOUSE OF REPRESENTATIVES. (a) The Senate shall, at the beginning and close of each session, and at such other times as may be necessary, elect one of its members President pro tempore, who shall perform the duties of the Lieutenant Governor in any case of absence or temporary disability of that officer. If the office of Lieutenant Governor becomes vacant, the President pro tempore of the Senate shall convene the Committee of the Whole Senate within 30 days after the vacancy occurs. The Committee of the Whole shall elect one of its members to perform the duties of the Lieutenant Governor in addition to the member's duties as Senator until the next general election . . . . (b) The House of Representatives shall, when it first assembles, organize temporarily, and thereupon proceed to the election of a Speaker from its own members . . . .

Sec. 10. QUORUM; ADJOURNMENT FROM DAY TO DAY; COMPELLING ATTENDANCE. Two-thirds of each House shall constitute a quorum to do business, but a smaller number may adjourn from day to day, and compel the attendance of absent members, in such manner and under such penalties as each House may provide . . . .

Sec. 24. COMPENSATION AND EXPENSES OF MEMBERS OF THE LEGISLATURE; DURATION OF SESSIONS. (a) Members of the Legislature shall receive from the Public Treasury a salary of Six Hundred Dollars ($600) per month, . . . Each member shall also receive a per diem set by the Texas Ethics Commission for each day during each Regular and Special Session of the Legislature. (b) No Regular Session shall be of longer duration than one hundred and forty (140) days . . . .

Sec. 40. SPECIAL SESSIONS; SUBJECTS OF LEGISLATION; DURATION. When the Legislature shall be convened in special session, there shall be no legislation upon subjects other than those designated in the proclamation of the Governor calling such session, or presented to them by the Governor; and no such session shall be of longer duration than thirty days . . . .

Sec. 49a. FINANCIAL STATEMENT AND ESTIMATE BY COMPTROLLER OF PUBLIC ACCOUNTS; LIMITATION OF APPROPRIATIONS. (a) It shall be the duty of the Comptroller of Public Accounts in advance of each Regular Session of the Legislature to prepare and submit to the Governor and to the Legislature upon its convening a statement under oath showing fully the financial condition of the State Treasury . . . . (b) Except in case of emergency and imperative public necessity and with a four-fifths vote of the total membership of each House, no appropriation in excess of the cash and anticipated revenue of the funds from which such appropriations is to be made shall be valid . . . . (Added Nov. 3, 1942; amended Nov. 2, 1999.)

Article 4: Executive Department

Sec. 1. OFFICERS CONSTITUTING THE EXECUTIVE BRANCH. The Executive Department of the State shall consist of a Governor, who shall be the Chief Executive Officer of the State, a Lieutenant Governor, Secretary of State, Comptroller of Public Accounts, Commissioner of the General Land Office, and Attorney General. (Amended Nov. 7, 1995.)

Sec. 2. ELECTION OF OFFICERS OF THE EXECUTIVE DEPARTMENT. All the above officers of the Executive Department (except Secretary of State) shall be elected by the qualified voters of the State at the time and places of election for members of the Legislature . . . .

Sec. 4. INSTALLATION OF GOVERNOR; TERM; ELIGIBILITY. The Governor . . . shall hold his office for a term of four years, or until his successor shall be duly installed. He shall be at least thirty years of age, a citizen of the United States, and shall have resided in this State at least five years immediately preceding his election. (Amended Nov. 7, 1972.) . . . .

Sec. 7. COMMANDER-IN-CHIEF OF MILITARY FORCES; CALLING FORTH MILITIA. He shall be Commander-in-Chief of the military forces of the State, except when they are called into actual service of the United States. He shall have power to call forth the militia to execute the laws of the State, to suppress insurrections, and to repel invasions. (Amended Nov. 2, 1999.) . . . .

Sec. 9. GOVERNOR'S MESSAGE AND RECOMMEN-DATIONS; . . . ESTIMATES OF MONEY REQUIRED. The Governor shall, at the commencement of each session of the Legislature, and at the close of his term of office, give to the Legislature information, by message of the condition of the State; and he shall recommend to the Legislature such measures as he may deem expedient . . . . And at the commencement of each regular session, he shall present estimates of the amount of money required by taxation for all purposes.

Sec. 10. EXECUTION OF LAWS; CONDUCT OF BUSINESS WITH OTHER STATES AND UNITED STATES. He shall cause the laws to be faithfully executed and shall conduct, in person, or in such manner as shall be prescribed by law, all intercourse and business of the State with other States and with the United States . . . .

Sec. 12. VACANCIES IN STATE OR DISTRICT OFFICES. (a) All vacancies in State or district offices, except members of the Legislature, shall be filled unless otherwise provided by law by appointment of the Governor. (b) An appointment of the Governor made during a session of the Senate shall be with the advice and consent of two-thirds of the Senate present. (c) . . . If an appointment of the Governor is made during the recess of the Senate, the Governor shall nominate the appointee, or some other person to fill the vacancy, to the Senate during the first ten days of its next session following the appointment . . . .

Sec. 14. APPROVAL OR DISAPPROVAL OF BILLS; . . . DISAPPROVAL OF ITEMS OF APPROPRIATION. Every bill which shall have passed both houses of the Legislature shall be presented to the Governor for his approval. If he approve he shall sign it, but if he disapprove it, he shall return it, with his objections, to the House in which it originated . . . . If any bill presented to the Governor contain several items of appropriation he may object to one or more of such items, and approve the other portion of the bill . . . . and no item so objected to shall take effect . . . .

Article 5: Judicial Department

Sec. 1. JUDICIAL POWER; COURTS IN WHICH VESTED. The judicial power of this State shall be vested in one Supreme Court, in one Court of Criminal Appeals, in Courts of Appeals, in District Courts, in County Courts, in Commissioners Courts, in Courts of Justices of the Peace, and in such other courts as may be provided by law . . . .

Sec. 2. SUPREME COURT; JUSTICES; SECTIONS; ELIGIBILITY; ELECTION; VACANCIES. (a) The Supreme Court shall consist of the Chief Justice and eight Justices, any five of whom shall constitute a quorum, and the concurrence of five shall be necessary to a decision of a case, . . . (b) No person shall be eligible to serve in the office of Chief Justice or Justice of the Supreme Court unless the person is licensed to practice law in this state and is, at the time of election, a citizen of the United States and this state, and has attained the age of thirty-five years, or a lawyer and judge of a court of record together at least ten years. (c) Said Justices shall be elected (three of them each two years) by the qualified voters of the state at a general election; shall hold their offices six years; . . . [Very similar provisions pertain to the Texas Court of Criminal Appeals.]

Sec. 6. COURTS OF APPEALS; TERMS OF JUSTICES; . . . (a) The state shall be divided into courts of appeals districts, with each district having a Chief Justice, two or more other Justices, and such other officials as may be provided by law. The Justices shall have the qualifications prescribed for Justices of the Supreme Court . . . . (b) . . . Said justices shall be elected by the qualified voters of their respective districts at a general election, for a term of six years . . .

Sec. 7. JUDICIAL DISTRICTS; DISTRICT JUDGES; TERMS OR SESSIONS . . . The State shall be divided into judicial districts, with each district having one or more Judges . . . . Each district judge shall be elected by the qualified voters at a General Election and shall be a citizen of the United States and of this State, who is licensed to practice law in this State and has been a practicing lawyer or a Judge of a Court in this State, or both combined, for four (4) years next preceding his election, who has resided in the district in which he was elected for two (2) years . . . and hold his office for a period of four (4) years . . . .

Article 7: Education

Sec. 1. SUPPORT AND MAINTENANCE OF SYSTEM OF PUBLIC FREE SCHOOLS. A general diffusion of knowledge being essential to the preservation of the liberties and rights of the people, it shall be the duty of the Legislature of the State to establish and make suitable provision for the support and maintenance of an efficient system of public free schools.

Sec. 2. PERMANENT SCHOOL FUND. All funds, lands and other property heretofore set apart and appropriated for the support of public schools; all the alternate sections of land reserved by the State out of grants heretofore made or that may hereafter by made to railroads or other corporations of any nature whatsoever; one half of the public domain of the State; and all sums of money that may come to the State from the sale of any portion of the same, shall constitute a permanent school fund . . . .

Sec. 3. TAXES FOR BENEFIT OF SCHOOLS; SCHOOL DISTRICTS. (a) One-fourth of the revenue derived from the State occupation taxes shall be set apart annually for the benefit of the public free schools. (b) It shall be the duty of the State Board of Education to set aside a sufficient amount of available funds to provide free text books for the use of children attending the public free schools of this State. (c) Should the taxation herein named be insufficient the deficit may be met by appropriation from the general funds of the State. (d) The Legislature may provide for the formation of school districts by general laws, . . .

Sec. 8. STATE BOARD OF EDUCATION. The Legislature shall provide by law for a State Board of Education, whose members shall be appointed or elected in such manner and by such authority and shall serve for such terms as the Legislature shall prescribe not to exceed six years . . . .

Sec. 10. ESTABLISHMENT OF A UNIVERSITY; AGRICULTURAL AND MECHANICAL DEPARTMENT. The legislature shall as soon as practicable establish, organize and provide for the maintenance, support and direction of a University of the first class, to be located by a vote of the people of this State, and styled, "The University of Texas," for the promotion of literature, and the arts and sciences, including an Agricultural, and Mechanicial department . . . .

Article 8: Taxation and Revenue

Sec. 1. EQUALITY AND UNIFORMITY; TAX IN PROPORTION TO VALUE; . . . (a) Taxation shall be equal and uniform. (b) All real property and tangible personal property in this State, unless exempt as required or permitted by this Constitution, whether owned by natural persons or corporations, other than municipal, shall be taxed in proportion to its value, which shall be ascertained as may be provided by law. (c) The Legislature may provide for the taxation of intangible property and may also impose occupational taxes, both upon natural persons and upon corporations, other than municipal, doing any business in this State . . . .

Sec. 1-a. NO STATE AD VALOREM TAX LEVY; . . . The several counties of the State are authorized to levy ad valorem taxes upon all property within their respective boundaries for county purposes, . . . not to exceed thirty cents on each One Hundred Dollars ($100) valuation, . . . Sec. 1-e. No State ad valorem taxes shall be levied upon any property within this State.

Sec. 24. PERSONAL INCOME TAX; DEDICATION OF PROCEEDS. (a) A general law enacted by the legislature that imposes a tax on the net incomes of natural persons, . . . must provide that the portion of the law imposing the tax not take effect until approved by a majority of the registered voters in a statewide referendum held on the question of imposing the tax . . . . (f) In the first year in which a tax described in Subsection (a) is imposed . . . not less than two-thirds of all net revenues . . . shall be used to reduce the rate of ad valorem [county property] . . . taxes levied for the support of primary and secondary education . . . . (g) The net revenues remaining . . . shall be used for support of education, . . .

Article 17. Mode of Amending The Constitution of This State

Sec. 1. PROPOSED AMENDMENTS; . . . SUBMISSION TO VOTERS; ADOPTION. (a) The Legislature, at any regular session, or at any special session when the matter is included within the purposes for which the session is convened, may propose amendments revising the Constitution, to be voted upon by the qualified voters . . . The proposal for submission must be approved by a vote of two-thirds of all the members elected to each House, entered by yeas and nays on the journals . . . . (c) The election shall be held in accordance with procedures prescribed by the Legislature, . . . If it appears from the returns that a majority of the votes cast have been cast in favor of the amendment, it shall become a part of this Constitution, and proclamation thereof shall be made by the Governor.

NOTES

Chapter 1   Texas and the Texans

1. The mildly curious phrase, "Texas and the Texans," was first used as the title of a book by Henry Stuart Foote in 1841. It also appears in the first sentence of the Preface (p. iii) to N. Doran Maillard's *The History of the Republic of Texas* (1842) and in the Englishman William Boellert's diary on February 20, 1842, the day of his arrival in Texas. More recently, it appeared as the subtitle of T.R. Fehrenbach's classic history of Texas, *Lone Star: A History of Texas and the Texans* (New York: Macmillan, 1968).

2. Randolph C. Campbell's fine history of Texas, entitled *Gone to Texas: A History of the Lone Star State* (New York: Oxford University Press, 2005), plays with the Gone to Texas theme throughout.

3. David J. Meltzer, *First Peoples in a New World: Colonizing Ice Age America* (Berkeley, CA: University of California Press, 2009). John Noble Wilford, "Arrowheads Found in Texas Dial Back Arrival of Humans in America," *New York Times*, March 25, 2011, A14; and Andrew Curry, "Finding the First Americans," *New York Times*, May 20, 2012, SR12.

4. Texas Almanac, 2012–2013, Elizabeth Cruz Alvarez, ed. (College Station, TX: Texas A&M University Press, 2012). For a brief history of Texas as well as the size and physical regions of the state, see pp. 17–78, 80–84.

5. Kelly F. Himmel, *The Conquest of the Karankawas and Tonkawas*, 1821–1859 (College Station, TX: Texas A&M University Press, 1999).

6. W.W. Newcomb, *The Indians of Texas: From Prehistoric Times to Modern Times* (Austin, TX: University of Texas Press, 1961), pp. 346–362. See also David La Vere, *The Texas Indians* (College Station, TX: Texas A&M University Press, 2004).

7. Manuel G. Gonzales, *Mexicanos: A History of Mexicans in the United States* (Bloomington: Indiana University Press, 1999), pp. 29–31.

8. Carey McWilliams, *North from Mexico: The Spanish Speaking People of the United States* (New York: Greenwood Press, 1990), p. 84. See also David J. Weber, *The Spanish Frontier in North America* (New Haven, CT: Yale University Press, 2009).

9. Gregg Cantrell, *Stephen F. Austin: Empresario of Texas* (New Haven, CT: Yale University Press, 1999), pp. 297–328.

10. PBS Video, "U.S. Mexican War, 1846–1848" (Alexandria, VA: PBS Video, 1998).

11. Daniel J. Elazar, *American Federalism: A View From the States*, 2nd ed. (New York: Harper and Row, 1972), pp. 84–113.

12. J. David Woodard, *The New Southern Politics* (Boulder, CO: Lynne Rienner Publishers, 2006), p. 6.

13. Saul Elben, "Fehrenbach's Texas," *The Texas Observer*, October 2012, pp. 34–36.

14. Virginia Gray and Russell L. Hanson, *Politics in the American States: A Comparative Analysis*, 10th ed. (Washington, D.C.: CQ Press, 2012), p. 4.

15. C. Allan Jones, *Texas Roots: Agriculture and Rural Life Before the Civil War* (College Station, TX: Texas A&M University Press, 2005).

16. Dave Doolittle, "Longhorns' Texas Roots Run Deep," *Dallas Morning News*, March 29, 3013, p. 314.

17. S.C. Gwynne, "The Next Frontier," *Texas Monthly*, August 2007, pp. 118–125, 178–181, 193–196.

18. Char Miller, *Deep in the Heart of San Antonio* (San Antonio, TX: Trinity University Press, 2004), pp. 4–9.

19. David G. McComb, *Texas: A Modern History* (Austin, TX: University of Texas Press, 2010), pp. 68, 126. See also Robert A. Calvert, Arnoldo De Leon, and Gregg Cantrell, *The History of Texas*, 4th ed. (Wheeling, IL: Harlan Davidson, Inc., 2007), p. 9; Char Miller and Heywood T. Sanders, *Urban Texas: Politics and Development* (College Station, TX: Texas A&M University Press, 1990), pp. 21–22.

20. McComb, pp. 69, 104, 147; Calvert et al., 94, 191; Miller and Sanders, pp. 12, 18–19, 27–28. See also Numan V. Bartley, *The New South, 1945–1980* (Baton Rouge, LA: Louisiana State University Press, 1995), pp. 137, 139.

21. Roscoe Martin, The People's Party in Texas (Austin, TX) University of Texas Press, 1933, pp. 16–17. See also Ninth Census of the United States, I, p. 671 and Twelfth Census, XI, Part II, p. 541.

22. Texas Labor Market Information, http://tracer2.com. See Data Link, Projections-Occupation, December 2012.

23. U.S. Census Bureau, *American Community Survey, State Ranking Tables*, 2011. See http://factfinder.census.gov/.

24. R. G. Ratcliffe, "A Warning Signaled for Hispanics and Texas," *Houston Chronicle*, May 17, 2010.

Chapter 2   The Texas Constitution and American Federalism

1. T.R. Fehrenbach, *Lone Star* (New York: Macmillan Publishing Company, 1968), p. 346.

2. Randolph B. Campbell, *Sam Houston and the American Southwest* (New York: Pearson Longman, 2007), p. 179.

3. Joseph F. Zimmerman, *Contemporary American Federalism: The Growth of National Power*, 2nd ed. (New York: State University of New York Press, 2008), p. 92.

4. Daniel J. Elazar, *American Federalism: A View From the States*, 3rd ed. (New York: Harper & Row, 1984). See also Thomas R. Dye, *American Federalism: Competition Among Governments* (Lexington, MA: Lexington Books, 1990).

5. Virginia Gray, Russell L. Hanson, and Thad Kousser, eds., *Politics in the American States: A Comparative Analysis*, 10th ed. (Washington, D.C.: CQ Press, 2013), pp. 31–36.

6. Joseph E. Zimmerman, *Contemporary American Federalism: The Growth of National Power* (New York: Praeger, 1992), p. 35.

7. All of the Texas constitutions can be found at: http://tarleton.law.utexas.edu/constitutions/text/.

8. Margaret Sweet Henson, *Lorenzo de Zavala: the Pragmatic Idealist* (Fort Worth, TX: Texas Christian University Press, 1996), pp. 7–20.

9. Harold H. Bruff, "Separation of Powers under the Texas Constitution," *Texas Law Review*, vol. 68, no. 7, June 1990, pp. 1337–1367.

10. Randolph B. Campbell, *Grass-Roots Reconstruction in Texas: 1865–1880* (Baton Rouge, LA: Louisiana State University Press, 1997), p. 10.

11. Steve Blow, "Statesman Deserves Greater Fame," *Dallas Morning News*, May 5, 2013, 1B.

12. Carl H. Moneyhon, *Texas After the Civil War: The Struggle of Reconstruction* (College Station, TX: Texas A&M University Press, 2004).

13. John Walker Mauer, "State Constitutions in a Time of Crisis: The Case of the Texas Constitution of 1876," *Texas Law Review*, vol. 68, no. 7, June 1990, p. 1623.

14. *The Book of the States 2013*, vol. 45 (Lexington, KY: Council of State Governments, 2012), Table 1.1, p. 12.

15. Dorothy E. McBride and Janine A. Perry, *Women's Rights in the U.S.A.*, 4th ed. (New York: Routledge, 2011), p. 41.

16. Robert A. Calvert, Arnoldo De Leon, and Gregg Cantrell, *The History of Texas*, 4th ed. (Wheeling, IL: Harlan Davidson, Inc., 2007), p. 307.

Chapter 3   Political Participation in Texas

1. Robert D. Brown, Robert A. Jackson, and Gerald C. Wright, "Registration, Turnout, and State Party Systems," *Political Research Quarterly*, 1999, 52: 463–479.

2. Randolph B. Campbell, *Gone To Texas* (New York: Oxford University Press, 2003), pp. 325–329. See also Anthony Champagne and Edward J. Harpham, *Texas at the Crossroads: People, Politics, and Policy* (College Station, TX: Texas A&M University Press, 1987), p. 70.

3. Roscoe Martin, *The People's Party in Texas: A Study in Third Party Politics* (Austin, TX: University of Texas Press, 1933), p. 180.

4. Martin, *The People's Party in Texas*, p. 102. See also, David Montejano, *Anglos and Mexicans in the Making of Texas* (Austin, TX: University of Texas Press, 1987), p. 130.

5. T.R. Fehrenbach, *Lone Star* (New York: Macmillan Publishing Co., 1968), p. 441.

6. Alwyn Barr, *Black Texans: A History of African-Americans in Texas, 1528–1995*, 2nd ed. (Norman, OK: University of Oklahoma Press, 1996), p. 80. See also, Robert Perkinson, *Texas Tough: The Rise of America's Prison Empire* (New York: Metropolitan Books, 2010), p. 141.

7. Robert A. Calvert, Arnoldo De Leon, and Gregg Cantrell, *The History of Texas*, 4th ed. (Wheeling, Illinois: Harlan Davidson, Inc., 2007), p. 224.

8. Amy Bridges, "Boss Tweed and V.O. Key in Texas," in Char Miller and Heywood T. Sanders, ed., *Urban Texas: Politics and Development in Texas* (College Station, TX: Texas A&M University Press, 1990), p. 62.

9. Donald S. Strong, "The Poll Tax: The Case of Texas," *American Political Science Review*, August 1944, vol. 38, no. 4, pp. 693–709.

10. *Texas Almanac, 1949–50*, Book, 1949, p. 370; digital images, http://texashistory.unt.edu/ark:/67531/metapth117167.

11. V.O. Key, *Southern Politics* (New York: Vintage Books, 1949), p. 273.

12. Darlene Clark Hine, *The Rise and Fall of the White Primary in Texas* (Millwood, NY: KTO Press, 1979). Alexander Keyssar, *The Right to Vote: The Contested History of Democracy in the United States* (New York: Basic Books, 2000), pp. 247–249.

13. Robert A. Caro, *The Years of Lyndon Johnson: The Path to Power*, vol. 1 (New York: Alfred A. Knopf, 1982), p. 277.

14. John Morgan and Felix Vardy, "Negative Vote Buying and the Secret Ballot," *Journal of Law, Economics, and Organization*, November 2010, pp. 1–2.

15. Edna Ferber, *Giant* (Garden City, NY: Doubleday & Company, 1952), pp. 309–310.

16. Charles L. Zelden, *The Battle for the Black Ballot: Smith v. Allwright and the Defeat of the Texas All-White Primary* (Lawrence, KS: University of Kansas Press, 2004).

17. T.R. Fehrenbach, *Seven Keys to Texas* (El Paso, TX: Texas Western Press, 1983), p. 117.

18. Jan Reid, *Let The People In: The Life and Times of Ann Richards* (Austin, TX: University of Texas Press, 2012), p. 84.

19. Todd Gillman, "Voting Law is Dealt A Blow," *Dallas Morning News*, June 26, 2013, pp. A1, A14.

20. Virginia Gray and Russell L. Hanson, eds., *Politics in the American States: A Comparative Analysis*, 10th ed. (Washington, D.C.: CQ Press, 2013), pp. 82–85.

21. See the Texas Secretary of State's website at http://www.sos.state.tx.us/elections/historical/70-92.shtml.

22. Lise Olsen, "Motor Voters' Missing On Rolls," *Houston Chronicle*, October 28, 2012.

23. See the Texas Secretary of State's HAVA website. http://www.sos.state. texas.us/elections/hava/index.shtml.

24. In Stephen K. Medvic, ed., *New Directions in Campaigns and Elections* (New York: Routledge, 2011), p. 11.

25. Eric W. Dolan, "More Than 1.5 Million Texas Voters Could Have Registration Suspended," *Houston Chronicle*, June 4, 2012.

26. See http://www.census.gov/population/socdemo/voting/cps2006/table04b.xls. This is the website of the U.S. Census Bureau.

27. Paul Burka, "Minority Report," *Texas Monthly*, January 2007, pp. 10–14.

28. Dave Mann, "Voto Por Voto: Will Hispanic Voters Stand and Be Counted?" *The Texas Observer*, February 22, 2008.

29. http://elections.gmu.edu/turnout%20 1980-2008.xls. This is Professor Michael McDonald's website.

30. *Seaman v. Upham*, 456 U.S. 37, 40–44 (1982). See also Frank R. Kemerer, *William Wayne Justice: A Judicial Biography* (Austin, TX: University of Texas Press, first paperback printing 2008), pp. 230–231.

31. Michael Ennis, "The Poll Truth," *Texas Monthly*, October 2012, pp. 45–46. See also Saul Elbein, "No Shows: Why So Few Texans Bother to Vote," *The Texas Observer*, October 2012, pp. 9–14.

32. Rutherford B. Hayes, *Diary and Letters of Rutherford B. Hayes, the Nineteenth President of the United States* (Columbus, OH: The Ohio State Archaeological and Historical Society, 1922–26), 1: 252.

33. Martin, *The People's Party*, p. 26.

34. Dolph Briscoe, *Dolph Briscoe: My Life in Texas Ranching and Politics* (Austin, TX: University of Texas Press, 2008), p. 73.

35. Ben Barnes, *Barn Burning, Barn Building* (Albany, TX: Bright Sky Press, 2006), pp. 35, 32.

36. John Spong, "You're Rick Noriega, Do You Approve This Message?" *Texas Monthly*, July 2008, pp. 132–137, 166–171.

37. Christy Hoppe, "Getting to Know You: Perry Camp Studying Up on Voters," *Dallas Morning News*, July 26, 2006, A1, A4.

38. O. Douglas Weeks, "The Texas-Mexican and the Politics of South Texas," *American Political Science Review*, vol. 24, no. 3, August 1930, pp. 606–627. See also Manny Fernandez, "Texas Vote—Buying Case Casts Glare on Tradition of Election Day Goads," *New York Times*, January 31, 2014, A12.

39. Texans for Public Justice, "Money in PoliTex: A Guide to Money in the 2006 Texas Elections," September 2007. http://www.tpj.org/reports/politex2006. See also *Texas Almanac 2008–2009*, pp. 444–450.

40. W. Gardner Selby, "Final Governor's Race Tally," *Austin American-Statesman*, January 19, 2007, 3A.

41. Wayne Slater, "$10M From Perry's Elite: Number of Big Donors Tops Rivals, Predecessors," *Dallas Morning News*, August 17, 2006, 1A, 15A.

42. Paul Burka, "Capture the Flag," *Texas Monthly*, July 2006, pp. 95–101, 172–175.

43. Texans for Public Justice, "Rick Perry and Bill White's Megadonors Tallied," October 2010 and "Money in PoliTex 2010," December 2010. See http://www.tpj.org.

44. Christine Ayala and Bobby Blanchard, "In Airtime, a Candidate Looks Invincible," New York Times, October 24, 2014, A2SA.

45. Gail Collins, *As Texas Goes: How the Lone Star State Hijacked the American Agenda* (New York: W.W. Norton, 2012), p. 50.

46. Alexandra Duszak and Reity O'Brien, "SuperPACs Help Tea Party Candidate Win

Senate Runoff in Texas," The Center for Public Integrity, August 1, 2012.

47. Kelley Shannon, AP, "Unusual Texas Governor's Race Accelerates on Labor Day," *Austin American-Statesman*, September 6, 2006.

48. Editorial Board, "Legislature should close TAB's loophole," *Austin American-Statesman*, July 1, 2006.

49. Mike Ward, "Top Court Agrees to Review Overturned DeLay Conviction," *Houston Chronicle*, March 19, 2014.

50. Richard S. Dunham, "Texas Political Cash Engulfs National Political Scene," *Houston Chronicle*, November 3, 2012. See also Amy Chozick, "For Democrats, Texas Push Gets an Early Shove," *New York Times*, May 17, 2014, A1, A12.

51. Noah Smithwick, *The Evolution of a State, or, Recollections of Old Texas Days* (Austin, TX: University of Texas Press, 1983), p. 185. See also Stanley Siegel, *A Political History of the Republic of Texas, 1836–1845* (Austin, TX: University of Texas Press, 1956), p. 182.

52. Texas Secretary of State website, Election Results, 2014 General Election. http://elections.sos.state.tx.us/elchist175_state.htm

53. Brandi Grissom, "Tea Party Conservatives Win Top GOP Runoff Contests," *Texas Tribune*, May 28, 2014.

54. Texans for Public Justice, http://info.tpj.org/reports/PerryJuly2011update/Perry100kContributorsJuly2011.html.

Chapter 4   Interest Groups in Texas

1. Tim Eaton, "Lobbyist Spent $200,000 in Leftover Campaign Cash on Travel, Restaurants," *Austin American-Statesman*, June 7, 2012.

2. James Madison, *The Federalist* (New York: Modern College Library Edition, 1937), no. 10, 54.

3. James L. Haley, *Passionate Nation: The Epic History of Texas* (New York: Free Press, 2006), p. 289.

4. David B. Truman, *The Governmental Process: Political Interests and Public Opinion* (New York: Knopf, 1958), p. 33.

5. Graham Wilson, *Interest Groups* (Cambridge, MA: Blackwell, 1990), p. 1.

6. L.M. Sixel, "Unions Vie for Health Care Workers," *Houston Chronicle*, July 18, 2007, A1.

7. Robert A. Caro, *The Path to Power: The Years of Lyndon Johnson* (New York: Alfred A. Knopf, 1982), p. 375.

8. Robert T. Garrett, "Business Leaders Try to Derail 'Sanctuary Cities' Bill," *Dallas Morning News*, June 24, 2011, 5A.

9. Robert T. Garrett, "Lobbyists Revision Would Help Client," *Dallas Morning News*, April 30, 2007, A1, A8.

10. Susan Smith Richardson, "Union Defender," *The Texas Observer*, December 2011, pp. 30–31.

11. Lisa Garcia Bedolla, *Latino Politics* (Malden, MA: Polity Press, 2009), pp. 65–67.

12. See Texas Lyceum poll on religion, ethics, and public morality. http://www.texaslyceum.org/pollpage.aspx.

13. Adam Clymer, "Gore Assails Bush on Texas Law that Permits Guns in Church," *New York Times*, September 18, 1999.

14. Ana Campoy, "Texas Duels over Guns," *Wall Street Journal*, February 8, 2010, A8.

15. Arlette Saenz, "Rick Perry Slams Mitt Romney, Talks Gun Control and Church on Sunday," ABC News, *The Note*, September 5, 2011.

16. W. Gardiner Selby, "Dewhurst, Hutchison Speak Out on Immigration," *Austin American-Statesman*, July 26, 2006.

17. Wayne Slater, "Tea Party's Enforcer Makes Waves," *Dallas Morning News*, May 30, 2011, A2.

18. Aman Batheja, "A Big Spender Aims to Push State Politics Further Right," *New York Times*, May 11, 2014, A27, A28.

19. Texas Ethics Commission, http://www.ethics.state.us.tx/tedd/2013_Lobby_List_Lobbyist_Only.pdf. 2007 figure supplied by TEC.

20. Texans for Public Justice, "Texas' Top Lobbyists," 2013 edition, p. 4. http://www.tpj.org/reports/Top%20Lobbyists%202013.pdf.

21. Claudia Grisales, "Phone Industry Outlobbied, Outspent Cable Rivals in Legislative Fight," *Austin American Statesman*, August 18, 2005; and Grisales, "Former State Rep Becomes Top Cable Industry Lobbyist," *Austin American Statesman*, November 15, 2005.

22. Robert T. Garrett, "Liquor Wholesalers Ply Legislator with Cash," *Dallas Morning News*, January 24, 2007, A1, A2.

23. Mike Ward, "Flores Gets Five Years Probation in Ethics Case," *Austin American-Statesman*, December 13, 2010.

24. Ross Ramsey, "An Expensive Celebration, Courtesy of the Lobby," *Texas Tribune*, May 22, 2013.

25. Matt Stiles, "Lobbyists Reach Out to State Employees Too," *Houston Chronicle*, March 31, 2009.

26. Richard S. Dunham and Kathrine Schmidt, "Texas' Top Corporations Stay Loyal to GOP," *Houston Chronicle*, November 26, 2007.

27. See National Conference of State Legislatures at http://www.ncsl.org/programs/legismgt/about/IndCond.htm.

28. Wayne Slater, "Texas Was Largest Donor to Campaigns," *Dallas Morning News*, December 6, 2006, 3A.

29. Paul Burka, "Court Attack," *Texas Monthly*, April 2010, pp. 12–18.

30. "Bob Perry, GOP ATM," Texans for Public Justice, October 2012. http://info.tpj.org/reports/pdf/BobPerryGOPATM.pdf.

31. Dave Mann and Abby Rapoport, "Lifestyles of the Corrupt and Elected," *The Texas Observer*, January 6, 2011.

32. Karen Brooks, "Revolving Door Likely to Stay Open For Lawmakers," *Dallas Morning News*, May 9, 2011, A1.

33. Patrick L. Cox and Michael Phillips, *The House Will Come to Order* (Austin, TX: University of Texas Press, 2010), p. 146.

34. Christy Hoppe, "Cash Gift Sums Can Stay Secret," *Dallas Morning News*, November 28, 2006, 3A.

Chapter 5   Political Parties in Texas

1. Marjorie R. Hershey, *Party Politics in America*, 13th ed. (New York: Longman, 2008).

2. John F. Bibby and L. Sandy Maisel, *Two Parties—Or More*, 2nd ed. (Boulder, CO: Westview Press, 2003).

3. Sean P. Cunningham, *Cowboy Conservatism: Texas and the Rise of the Modern Right* (Lexington, KY: University of Kentucky Press, 2010), p. 210.

4. Virginia Gray and Russell L. Hanson, eds., *Politics in the American States: A Comparative Analysis*, 9th ed. (Washington, D.C.: CQ Press, 2008), p. 84.

5. Stanley Siegel, *A Political History of the Texas Republic, 1836–1845* (Austin, TX: University of Texas Press, 1956), pp. 240–241.

6. Roscoe Martin, *The People's Party in Texas: A Study in Third Party Politics* (Austin, TX: University of Texas Press, 1933).

7. D.B. Hardeman and Donald C. Bacon, *Rayburn: A Biography* (New York: Madison Books, 1987).

8. Ricky F. Dobbs, *Yellow Dogs and Republicans: Allan Shivers and Texas Two-Party Politics* (College Station, TX: Texas A&M University Press, 2005).

9. Sean P. Cunningham, *Cowboy Conservatism* (Lexington, KY: University of Kentucky Press, 2010), pp. 41–42. See also, Patrick L. Cox and Michael Phillips, *The House Will Come to Order* (Austin, TX: University of Texas Press, 2010), p. 86.

10. John R. Knaggs, *Two-Party Texas: The John Tower Era, 1961–1984* (Austin, TX: Eakin Press, 1986).

11. Carolyn Barta, *Bill Clements: Texian to His Toenails* (Austin, TX: Eakin Press, 1996).

12. Earl Black and Merle Black, *The Rise of Southern Republicanism* (Cambridge, MA: Harvard University Press, 2002), pp. 88–93.

13. James A. Dyer, Arnold Vedlitz, and David B. Hill, "New Voters, Switchers, and Political

Party Realignment in Texas," *The Western Political Quarterly*, vol. 41, no. 1 (March 1988), pp. 158–159.

14. Clifton McCleskey, *The Government and Politics of Texas*, 2nd ed. (New York: Little, Brown and Company, 1966), pp. 102–103.

15. Sue Tolleson-Rinehart and Jeanie R. Stanley, *Claytie and the Lady: Ann Richards, Gender, and Politics in Texas* (Austin, TX: University of Texas Press, 1994), p. 109.

16. Cox and Phillips, *The House Will Come to Order*, p. 153. See also Randolph B. Campbell, *Gone to Texas: A History of the Lone Star State* (New York: Oxford University Press, 2003), p. 461.

17. Danny Hayes and Seth C. McKee, "The Participatory Effects of Redistricting," *American Journal of Political Science*, 53, 4, October 2009, pp. 1006–1023.

18. Cox and Phillips, *The House Will Come to Order*, p. 67.

19. Robert A. Calvert, Arnoldo DeLeon, and Gregg Cantrell, *The History of Texas*, 4th ed. (Wheeling, IL: Harlan Davidson, Inc., 2007), p. 403.

20. F. Chris Garcia and Gabriel Sanchez, *Hispanics and the U.S. Political System* (New York: Pearson, 2007), p. 212.

21. Steve Bickerstaff, *Lines in the Sand: Congressional Redistricting in Texas and the Downfall of Tom DeLay* (Austin, TX: University of Texas Press, 2007).

22. Todd J. Gillman, "Texas's Growth Surge to Add 4 House Seats," *Dallas Morning News*, December 22, 2010, A1, A15.

23. Adam Liptak, "Justices Reject Election Maps by U.S. Court," *New York Times*, January 21, 2012, A1, A13.

24. Chuck Lindell, "Texas Redistricting Plan Denied Preclearance: Abbott Will Appeal," *Austin American-Statesman*, August 28, 2012.

25. Chandler Davidson, *Race and Class in Texas Politics* (Princeton, NJ: Princeton University Press, 1990).

26. Paul Burka, "Almost Blue," *Texas Monthly*, May 2008, pp. 18–22.

27. Christy Hoppe, "Abbott Sees Future Tied to Hispanic Vote," *Dallas Morning News*, March 27, 2014.

28. Christy Hoppe, "Suburbs Key For Davis Bid," *Dallas Morning News*, October 6, 2013, pp. A1, A10–11.

Chapter 6   The Texas Legislature

1. Dennis L. Dresang and James J. Gosling, *Politics and Policy in American States and Communities*, 8th ed. (New York: Pearson, 2013), pp. 255–256.

2. See Texas legislation web page, www.capitol.state.tx.us.

3. Judith N. McArthur and Harold L. Smith, *Texas Through Women's Eyes: The Twentieth Century Experience* (Austin, TX: University of Texas Press, 2010), pp. 224–226.

4. National Conference of State Legislatures, "2009 State Legislator Education Levels," http://www.ncsl.org/default.aspx?tabid=19823.

5. Katherine Q. Seelye, "Obituaries: Molly Ivins is Dead at 62; Writer Skewered Politicians," *New York Times*, February 1, 2007, A20.

6. Patrick L. Cox and Michael Phillips, *The House Will Come to Order* (Austin, TX: University of Texas Press, 2010), p. 118.

7. Robert T. Garrett, "Officials Act to Raise Own Pensions," *Dallas Morning News*, May 14, 2013, p. 3A.

8. For the national numbers, see Virginia Gray, Russell L. Hanson, and Thad Kousser, eds., *Politics in the American States: A Comparative Analysis*, 10th ed. (Washington, D.C.: CQ Press, 2013), p. 181.

9. Claire Cardena, "Lawmakers in Largest Freshman Class in 40 Years," *Dallas Morning News*, January 9, 2013, 6A.

10. Ross Ramsey, "In Legislature, Fresh Faces and an Experience Deficit," *Texas Tribune*, April 27, 2012.

11. See http://www.ncsl.org/programs/press/2004/backgrounder fulland part.htm. Updated June 2009.

12. Sam Kinch, Jr., and Ben Proctor, *Texas Under a Cloud* (Austin, TX: Jenkins Publishing Co., 1972), p. 142. See also Cox and Phillips, *The House Will Come to Order*, p. 78.

13. Cox and Phillips, *The House Will Come to Order*, p. 2.

14. D.B. Hardeman and Donald C. Bacon, *Rayburn: A Biography* (New York: Madison Books, 1987), p. 54.

15. Alfred Steinberg, *Sam Rayburn: A Biography* (New York: Hawthorne Books, 1975), p. 23.

16. Christy Hoppe, "Another Joins Fray for House Speaker," *Dallas Morning News*, December 29, 2006, A1.

17. Laylan Copelin, "Craddick Rewards Loyalists," *Austin American-Statesman*, January 27, 2007, A1.

18. Paul Burka, "Speaker for Life," *Texas Monthly*, September 2007, pp. 14–18.

19. Bill Hobby, *How Things Really Work: Lessons from a Life in Politics* (Austin, TX: University of Texas Press, 2010), p. 77.

20. American Statesman Staff, "In the End, Key Goals Unreached," *Austin American-Statesman*, May 31, 2005.

21. Karl T. Kurtz, "Strong Staff, Strong Institution: Custodians of American Democracy," *State Legislatures*, July/August, 2006, pp. 28–32.

22. Texas Reference Library, at http://www.lrl.state.tx.us/legis/profile83.html.

23. Calvin Jillson and Rick K. Wilson, *Congressional Dynamics: Structure, Coordination, and Choice in the First American Congress, 1774–1789* (Stanford, CA: Stanford University Press, 1994), p. 23.

24. House Research Organization, "House Committee Procedures in the 83rd Legislature," February 22, 2013.

25. Sam Kinch and Stuart Long, *Allan Shivers: The Pied Piper of Texas Politics* (Austin, TX: Shoal Creek Publishers, 1973), pp. 46–47.

26. Manny Fernandez, "You Call That A Filibuster," *New York Times*, July 4, 2013, A14.

27. Stanley Siegel, *A Political History of the Texas Republic, 1836–1845* (Austin, TX: University of Texas Press, 1956), p. 212.

28. James Reston, Jr., *The Lone Star: The Life of John Connally* (New York: Harper & Row, 1989), p. 309.

29. Kinch and Proctor, *Texas Under a Cloud*, pp. 141, 145.

30. Cox and Phillips, *The House Will Come to Order*, p. 152.

Chapter 7   The Governor and the Executive Branch

1. Becca Aaronson, "Insurance Chief Answers Industry Bias Charge," *New York Times*, September 7, 2012, pp. A25A, A26A.

2. J. David Woodard, *The New Southern Politics* (Boulder, CO: Lynne Reinner Publishers, 2006), p. 368.

3. Marquis James, *The Raven: A Biography of Sam Houston* (Austin, TX: University of Texas Press, 1929), pp. 325–327.

4. James Reston, Jr., *The Lone Star: The Life of John Connally* (New York: Harper and Row, 1989), pp. 288–289.

5. V.O. Key, Jr., *Southern Politics* (New York: Random House, 1949), pp. 266–267.

6. T.R. Fehrenbach, *Lone Star: A History of Texas and the Texans* (New York: Macmillan Publishing Company, 1968), p. 437.

7. Reston, *The Lone Star*, p. 209.

8. Patrick L. Cox and Michael Phillips, *The House Will Come to Order* (Austin, TX: University of Texas Press, 2010), p. 78.

9. Brad Watson, "Accomplished Sen. Hutchison Proud of Senate Term, Regretful of Failed Gubernatorial Primary," *WFAA*, December 12, 2012.

10. For a full list of Texas governors, lieutenant governors, statewide elected officials, and a description of key agencies, see the *Texas Almanac, 2012–2013*, pp. 474–480.

11. Elizabeth C. Alvarez, *Texas Almanac: 2012–2013* (Dallas, TX: Texas State Historical Association, 2012), pp. 474–475.

12. John J. Harrigan and David C. Nice, *Politics and Policy in States and Communities*, 9th ed. (New York: Pearson Longman, 2006), p. 222.

13. The governor's office provides a list of all the agencies, boards, and commissions to which the governor makes appointments and the number of appointments made to each. See http://www.governor.state.tx.us/divisions/appointments/positions.

14. Emily Ramshaw, "Perry Helps Advisers Take a Big Next Step," *New York Times*, December 9, 2012, p. 39A.

15. Christy Hoppe, "Does Perry Really Have the Power?" *Dallas Morning News*, February 23, 2007, A1, A6. See also Corrie MacLaggan, "Abbott: Perry's HPV Mandate Does Not Carry the Weight of Law," *Austin American-Statesman*, March 13, 2007, A1.

16. Dennis L. Dresang and James L. Gosling, *Politics and Policy in American States and Communities*, 8th ed. (New York: Pearson Longman, 2013), p. 225.

17. House Research Organization, "Writing the State Budget," 82nd Legislature, State Finance Report, no. 82-1, p. 5.

18. Bill Hobby, *How Things Really Work: Lessons from a Life in Politics* (Austin, TX: University of Texas Press, 2010), p. 71.

19. Jason Embry, "Perry Seeks to Hold the Line This Session: Speech Offers Few Bold Initiatives," *Austin American-Statesman*, January 28, 2009, A1.

20. James C. McKinley, Jr., "Gap Aside, Texas Governor Offers Optimism on Budget," *New York Times*, February 9, 2011, A15.

21. Dolph Briscoe, *Dolph Briscoe: My Life in Texas Ranching and Politics* (Austin, TX: University of Texas Press, 2008), pp. 205–206.

22. Legislative Budget Board, *Fiscal Size-Up, 2012–13 Biennium*, "Adjutant General's Department," pp. 332–333.

23. T.R. Fehrenback, *Lone Star: A History of Texas and the Texans* (New York: Macmillan Publishing Company, 1968), p. 437. See also George Norris Green, *The Establishment in Texas Politics: The Primitive Years, 1938-1957* (Norman, OK: University of Oklahoma Press, 1979), pp. 16–17.

24. Dolph Briscoe, *Dolph Briscoe: My Life in Texas Ranching and Politics* (Austin, TX: University of Texas Press, 2008), pp. 203–204.

25. State Auditor's Office, "A Summary Report on Full-Time Equivalent State Employees for the Quarter Ending August 31, 2012," October 2012, Report No. 13-703.

26. Jay Root, "Perry's On-the-Job Retirement Lifts Obscure Pension Perk From the Shadows," *New York Times*, February 26, 2012, pp. 23A–24A.

27. Dave McNeely and Jim Henderson, *Bob Bullock: God Bless Texas* (Austin, TX: University of Texas Press, 2008), p. 89.

28. Robert T. Garrett, "Perry Criticizes Combs' Handling of Amazon," *Dallas Morning News*, February 11, 2011.

29. S.C. Gwynne, "This Land Is His Land," *Texas Monthly*, pp. 146–151, 254–259.

30. Dave Lieber, "New Boss Urges Transparency," *Dallas Morning News*, June 23, 2013, B1, B8.

31. Robert T. Garrett, "Ex-Senator Named Social Services Czar," *Dallas Morning News*, July 31, 2012, 3A.

32. Robert A. Calvert, Alberto DeLeon, and Gregg Cantrell, *The History of Texas*, 4th ed. (Wheeling, IL: Harlan Davidson, Inc., 2007), p. 288.

33. http://www.tea.state.tx.us/sboe_history_duties.html.

34. Texans for Public Justice, "Governor Perry's Patronage," September 2010, pp. 2–5.

35. James Reston, Jr., *The Lone Star: The Life of John Connally* (New York: Harper & Row, 1989), p. 309.

Chapter 8 The Judical System in Texas

1. Lawrence Baum, *The Supreme Court*, 11th ed. (Washington, D.C.: Congressional Quarterly Press, 2013), pp. 5–6.

2. Annual Statistical Report for the Texas Judiciary, Fiscal Year 2013, Office of Court Administration, January 2014, p. 3. See http://www. courts.state.tx.us/pubs/AR2013/published-annual-report-2013.pdf.

3. Vesla M. Weaver and Amy E. Lerman, "Political Consequences of the Carceral State," *American Political Science Review*, vol. 104, no. 4, November 2010, pp. 817–833.

4. Herbert Jacob, *Law and Politics in the United States* (Boston: Little, Brown, 1986), pp. 6–7.

5. Henry J. Abraham, *The Judicial Process*, 7th ed. (New York: Oxford University Press, 1998), p. 147.

6. Wilhelm Steinert, *North America, Particularly Texas, in the Year 1849: A Travel Account* (Dallas, TX: DeGolyer Library and William P. Clements Center for Southwestern Studies, 2003), p. 121.

7. State Bar of Texas, Department of Research and Analysis, "State Bar of Texas: Attorney Statistical Profile," 2012–2013, p. 1.

8. Annual Statistical Report of the Texas Judiciary, 2013, p. 14.

9. Mark Trachtenberg, "Webcasts Open a Window to the Texas Supreme Court," *Houston Chronicle*, March 30, 2007, B11. See http://www. supreme.courts.state.tx.us/.

10. Former Supreme Court Justice Sandra Day O'Connor, "Justice Off the Ballot," *New York Times*, May 23, 2010, p. Wk 9.

11. Mark Currigan, The Texas Lawbook, "Day in Court Vanishing," *Dallas Morning News*, April 3, 2012, 8D. See also Janet Elliott, The Texas Lawbook, "Reversals of Civil Jury Verdicts Rise in Texas," *Dallas Morning News*, May 1, 2012, 8D. Anna Whitney, "Consumer Group: Supreme Court Favors Business," *The Texas Tribune*, January 26, 2012.

12. Editorial Board, "Experience Matters in Judicial Races," *San Antonio Express News*, September 9, 2012.

13. Ross Ramsey, "Make It One More Supreme Court Justice From the Perry Camp," *New York Times*, December 2, 2012, p. A39A.

14. Larry Karson, "The Implications of a Key-Man System for Selecting a Grand Jury: An Exploratory Study," *Southwest Journal of Criminal Justice*, vol. 3, no. 1 (2006), pp. 3–16.

15. Michael Grabell, "Majority Called for Jury Duty Aren't Showing Up," *Dallas Morning News*, December 27, 2006, 9B.

16. Warren Richey, "Court Hits Jury Race Bias," *Christian Science Monitor*, January 14, 2005.

17. Ralph Blumenthal, "DeLay Case Turns Spotlight on Texas Judicial System," *New York Times*, November 8, 2005, A19.

18. Randy Lee Loftis and Ryan McNeill, "Is Justice For Sale in Texas Courts?," *Dallas Morning News*, March 2, 2009, A1, A10.

19. See Texans for Public Justice website at http://www.tjp.org/press_releases/.

20. Wayne Slater, "Home Owners Battle Finally Over," *Dallas Morning News*, January 29, 2011, 3A.

21. Paul D. Carrington, "Big Money in Texas Judicial Elections: The Sickness and Its Remedies," *SMU Law Review* (2000), vol. 53, pp. 263–276, see especially pp. 266, 268.

22. Adam Liptak, "Justices Issue Recusal Rule for Judiciary," *New York Times*, June 9, 2009, A1, A3.

23. Chuck Liddell, "Chief Justice Seeks to Abolish Judicial Elections," *Austin American-Statesman*, February 12, 2009. See also Brian W. Sweany, "The Verdict: Wallace Jefferson Sizes Up His Historic Tenure," *Texas Monthly*, December 2013, pp. 72–78.

24. Virginia Gray and Russell L. Hanson, eds., *Politics in the American States: A Comparative*

Analysis, 9th ed. (Washington, D.C.: CQ Press, 2008), p. 273.

25. Mike Ward, "Hundreds of City Jails Have No Oversight," *Austin American-Statesman*, October 2, 2010.

26. Anna Tinsley, "Texas Still Top State for Death Penalty," *Fort Worth Star Telegram*, January 1, 2012.

27. Ross Ramsey, "Texans Stand Behind Death Penalty," *The Texas Tribune*, May 24, 2012.

28. Tinsley, "Texas Still Top State for Death Penalty," January 1, 2012.

29. Deborah Sontag, "Perry Displays Varied Stance Toward Crime," *New York Times*, November 31, 2011, A1, A2.

30. Erwin Chemerinsky and James J. Sample, "You Get the Judges You Pay For," opinion piece, *New York Times*, April 18, 2011, A21.

Chapter 9   Local Government in Texas

1.   Chandler Davidson, *Race and Class in Texas Politics* (Princeton, NJ: Princeton University Press, 1990), p. 89.

2.   Char Miller and Heywood T. Sanders, ed., *Urban Texas: Politics and Development* (College Station, TX: Texas A&M University Press, 1990), p. xiii.

3.   Peter Engardio, "Slicker Cities: The Real Contest Is Among Cities, Not Nations," *Business Week*, August 21–28, 2006, pp. 108–110.

4.   Paul Peterson, *City Limits* (Chicago: University of Chicago Press, 1981), p. 4.

5.   Peterson, *City Limits*, p. 27.

6.   Peterson, *City Limits*, pp. 36, 71.

7.   Peterson, *City Limits*, p. 27.

8.   John Dillon, *Commentaries on the Law of Municipal Corporations*, 5th ed. (Boston: Little, Brown, 1911), 1: 237.

9.   Stephen L. Elkins, *City and Regime in the American Republic* (Chicago: University of Chicago Press, 1987), p. 19.

10. Clay Robison, "Panel to Study Law Appraisal Caps," *San Antonio Express News*, August 21, 2006, A1.

11. Will Lutz, "Tom Pauken on Appraisal Reform," Dallasblog.com, September 4, 2007.

12. Ralph Blumenthal, "1 Cafe, 1 Gas Station, 2 Roads: It's America's Emptiest County," *New York Times*, February 25, 2006, A1, A11.

13. Seymour V. Connor, "The Evolution of County Government in the Republic of Texas," *Southwestern Historical Quarterly*, October 1951, 55: 163–200. See also, Robert A. Calvert, Arnoldo DeLeon, and Gregg Cantrell, *The History of Texas*, 4th ed. (Wheeling, IL: Harlan Davidson, Inc. 2007), p. 35; and David G. McComb, *Texas: A Modern History*, revised edition (Austin, TX: University of Texas Press, 2010), p. 55.

14. John A. Gilmartin, Richard O. Avery, and Eric S. Cartrite, *County Government in Texas: A Summary of Major Offices and Officials* (V.G. Young Institute of County Government, Texas A&M University System, 2000).

15. Molly Bloom, "New Accusations Against Bastrop Commissioner," *Austin American-Statesman*, December 18, 2007.

16. Texas Association of Counties Salary Survey, 2014.

17. N. Doran Maillard, *The History of the Republic of Texas* (London: Smith, Elder, and Co, 1842), p. 205.

18. Char Miller and Heywood T. Sanders, ed., *Urban Texas: Politics and Development* (College Station, TX: Texas A&M University Press, 1990), pp. 131, 148.

19. Amy Bridges, *Morning Glories: Municipal Reform in the Southwest* (Princeton, NJ: Princeton University Press, 1997), pp. 152–154.

20. Scott Houston, "Municipal Annexation in Texas," *Texas Municipal League*, March 2012, http://www.tml.org/legal-pdf/ANNEXATION.pdf.

21. Jonathan Martin and Ben Smith, "Houston Election Signals Key Trend," *Politico*, December 16, 2009.

22. David Crowder, "Mayoral Race Is for a Different City Role," *El Paso Times*, March 7, 2005, A1. See also Paul Burka, "Fed Up," *Texas Monthly*, April 2008, pp. 12–16.

23. Mike Kanin, "What's Left: For Nearly Four Decades, White Liberals Have Dominated Austin Politics," *Texas Observer*, December 2013, pp. 20–27.

24. Susan Berfield, "There Will Be Water," *Business Week*, June 23, 2008, pp. 40–45.

25. Kevin Krause, "County Roadwork: Responsive Service or Separate Fiefdoms?" *Dallas Morning News*, August 22, 2006, A1, A2.

Chapter 10 Financing State Government

1. House Research Organization, Texas House of Representatives, *Writing the State Budget*, State Finance Report, No. 83-2, February 8, 2013. See the LBB website.

2. Richard Morehead, *50 Years in Texas Politics* (Burnet, TX: Eakin Press, 1982), p. 37.

3. Patrick L. Cox and Michael Phillips, *The House Will Come to Order* (Austin, TX: University of Texas Press, 2010), pp. 49–50.

4. See LBB website at: http://www.lbb.state.tx.us/ under Budget Bills and Reports, 2012–13 biennium.

5. Legislative Budget Board, *Fiscal Size-Up, 2014–2015 Biennium*, "State Indebtedness" p. 22. See LBB website as noted above.

6. *Fiscal Size-Up, 2014–2015*, "Per Capita State Government Expenditures," Figure 69, p. 58.

7. *Fiscal Size-Up, 2014–2015*, Public School Expenditures Per Enrolled Pupil," Figure 202, p. 250.

8. Eva-Marie Ayala, "McKinney, Plano ISDs Seek Tax Hike," *Dallas Morning News*, September 8, 2013, 1B, 6B.

9. Chuck Liddell, "School Finance Trial Could Spill Into January," *Austin American-Statesman*, July 11, 2012.

10. *Fiscal Size-Up, 2012–2013*, "Higher Education Enrollment," Table 212, p. 255.

11. College Board, "Trends in College Pricing, 2013–2014," http://trends.collegeboard.org.

12. Manny Fernandez, "College: Race Admissions Policy is Debated." *New York Times*, November 14, 2013, A17.

13. *Fiscal Size-Up, 2012–2013*, "DOT Funding sources," Figure 336, p. 457.

14. Aman Batheja, "Tolling Texans: Impact of Trans-Texas Corridor Lingers," *The Texas Tribune*, December 3, 2012.

15. Center on Sentencing and Corrections, VERA Institute of Justice, http://www.vera.org/priceofprisons.

16. Steve Campbell, "Cleburne Park One of Dozens on Mend," *Fort Worth Star-Telegram*, April 28, 2010, B1.

17. Asher Price, "State Parks and Wildlife Department Turns to Corporate Sponsorship to Raise Money," *Austin American-Statesman*, July 29, 2012.

18. See http://www.taxadmin.org/fta/rate/13taxbur. See also, *Fiscal Size-Up, 2014–2015*, Figure 66, p. 53.

19. Center for Public Policy Priorities, "Updated: Who Pays Texas Taxes," March 28, 2013. See also http://www.window.state.tx.us/taxinfo/incidence/incidence13.

GLOSSARY

Amateur legislatures State legislatures which provide low pay and support to their members. Sessions are generally short and members have other jobs.

Anglo A Spanish term referring to non-Hispanic whites.

Annexation A legal and political process by which cities absorb adjacent territory.

Appellate courts Appellate courts review trial court records to insure that the trial was fair and the law correctly applied.

Appointment power The Texas Constitution and statutes empower the governor, often with the approval of two-thirds of the Senate, to appoint many senior government officials.

At-large elections Elections held throughout a jurisdiction, such as a city or county, rather than in wards or single-member districts within the jurisdiction.

Baker v. Carr (1962) U.S. Supreme Court declared that equal population state house districts were required by the 14th Amendment promise of equal protection of the laws.

Balcones Escarpment A geological faultline that separates the lowlands of East Texas from the prairies and plains of West Texas.

Biennial session The Texas legislature meets in regular session every other year, that is biennially, rather than annually.

Big tent model Sees political parties as organizations that appeal to the broadest range of potential voters rather than seeking to implement a coherent ideological program.

Blocker bill A minor bill placed at the top of the Senate calendar to block all other bills from coming to the floor before they have achieved broad support.

Budget message The governor is required by law to address the legislature on budget matters in the first thirty days of each regular session.

Budgets Moral and political documents that seek to balance a community's revenue sources with its spending obligations.

Cabinet government An executive branch in which the governor has broad appointment and budgetary powers.

Carrying a bill Carrying a bill means to take responsibility for seeing it successfully through the legislative process.

Checks and balances The idea that governmental powers should be distributed to permit each branch of government to check and balance the other branches.

City council The policymaking or legislative branch of city government.

City manager A city manager is an appointed professional executive hired, usually by the city council, to manage or administer city government.

Civil law Deals primarily with relations between individuals and organizations, as in marriage and family law, contracts, and property.

Civil War The U.S. Civil War, pitting the northern states against the southern states, occurred between 1861 and 1865.

Clemency Some governors have the power to forgive or lessen the punishment for criminal infractions by granting pardons, paroles, or commutations.

Closed primary A primary election that is open only to registered members of the sponsoring political party.

Commissioners court The chief policymaking and administrative institution of Texas county government.

Conference committees Committees composed of members of the House and Senate charged to resolve differences between the House and Senate versions of a bill.

Constitution Basic or fundamental law that lays out the structure of government, the powers of each office, the process by which officials are elected or appointed, and the rights and liberties of citizens.

Corporate franchise fee A business activity tax that in 2005 impacted one in six Texas businesses, mostly corporations and sole proprietorships.

Councils of governments COGs are voluntary planning districts that provide training, planning, and coordination services to member local governments.

County judge The county judge is elected countywide and presides over the county commissioners court.

Criminal law Criminal law prohibits certain actions and prescribes penalties for those who engage in the prohibited conduct.

Defendant The person defending against a charge in court.

Democrats of Texas Liberal faction of the mid-20th-century Democratic party, led by elected officials like Lyndon Johnson and Ralph Yarborough.

Devolution The return of political authority from the national government to the states.

Dillon's Rule A legal concept holding that local governments are the creatures or creations of state governments.

Electioneering To take an active part in working for the election of a particular candidate or party.

Elitism The belief that the interest group system is skewed toward the interests of the wealthy.

Enumerated powers The specifically listed, or enumerated, powers of the Congress and president found in Article I, section 8, and Article II, section 2, of the U.S. Constitution.

Extraterritorial jurisdiction (ETJ) ETJ describes the limited power that cities exercise over territory just beyond their boundaries.

Federal transfer payments Funds provided by the federal government to state and local governments to support key services such as health care, education, and transportation.

Federalism A form of government in which some powers are assigned to the national government, some to the states, and some, such as the power to tax, are shared.

Filibuster Senators can spend as long as they wish once they gain the floor, oftentimes to slow or defeat an objectionable bill.

Fiscal conservatives Conservative faction that focuses on fiscal and economic issues such as taxation, spending, and business regulation.

Fisher v. University of Texas (2013) Texas state courts upheld UT's right to use race, if "narrowly tailored," as "part of a holistic admissions program."

General election A final or definitive election in which candidates representing their respective parties contend for election to office.

Grand jury A grand jury assesses a prosecutor's evidence against a potential defendant to be sure it is sufficient to proceed to trial.

Grovey v. Townsend (1935) U.S. Supreme Court found that the Democratic Party in Texas was a private organization and could exclude blacks from its primary elections.

Grutter v. Bollinger (2003) Also known as the Michigan case, the U.S. Supreme Court upheld affirmative action programs taking race into account as one factor among many.

Hopwood v. Texas (1992) The U.S. Fifth Circuit Court of Appeals agreed with Cheryl Hopwood and others that the affirmative action program run by the University of Texas gave race too dominant a role in the admissions process.

Hybrid legislatures State legislatures, including the Texas legislature, that share some of the characteristics of professional legislatures, such as long sessions and good staff support, and some of the characteristics of amateur legislatures, such as low pay and biennial sessions.

Incorporation The legal process by which cities are established.

Interest groups Organizations that attempt to influence society and government to act in ways consonant with their interests.

Interim committees Legislative committees that work in the interim between regular legislative sessions to study issues, prepare reports, and draft legislation.

Jurisdiction The constitutional or legal right of a court to hear certain types of cases.

Jury trial A trial conducted before a jury of citizens who hear testimony, weigh evidence, and assess guilt.

King Ranch Founded in 1853 by Captain Richard King, the 825,000 acre King Ranch south of Corpus Christi epitomizes the huge dry land cattle ranches of Texas.

Law Authoritative rules made by government and backed by the organized force of the community.

Legislative Budget Board The ten-member LBB, co-chaired by the lieutenant governor and the Speaker, drafts the state's biennial budget.

Legislative calendars Lists of bills passed by committees but awaiting final action on the floor.

Legislative supremacy The idea that the law-making power in government is superior to the executive and judicial powers.

Line-item veto The power to strike out or veto individual items in the state budget without striking down the whole budget.

Lobby Registration Act A 1973 Texas law requiring groups and individuals attempting to influence state government to register and report on certain of their activities.

Lobbying To attempt, often on behalf of an organized group, to influence the making or implementation of public policy in ways favorable to the group's interests.

Lobbyists Hired agents who seek to influence government decision making in ways that benefit or limit harm to their clients.

Margins tax A business tax, adopted in 2006 to replace the corporate franchise fee. The margins tax is 1 percent of gross receipts minus costs.

Missouri plan To balance competence and accountability, governors appoint judges who later stand in retention elections.

Motor Voter A 1995 law, also known as the National Voter Registration Act, that permits persons to register to vote at motor vehicle and other state government offices.

Necessary and proper clause The last paragraph of Article I, section 8, of the U.S. Constitution states that Congress may make all laws deemed necessary and proper for carrying into execution the powers specifically enumerated in Article I, section 8.

Nixon v. Herndon (1927) U.S. Supreme Court held that Texas could not exclude blacks from voting in state sanctioned primary elections.

Open primary A primary election that is open to the participation of any registered voter, irrespective of party affiliation.

Peak associations Peak associations, such as the U.S. Chamber of Commerce, represent the general interests of business.

Permian Basin A geological formation in West Texas, around Midland, where oil discoveries were made in the 1920s that remain productive today.

Plaintiff The individual who brings a case before a court is called the plaintiff or complainant.

Plural executive An executive branch featuring several officials with independent constitutional and legal authority.

Pluralism The belief that the interest group system produces a reasonable policy balance.

Political action committee Legal entity, often associated with interest groups, through which campaign contributions and other forms of support can be given to parties and candidates.

Political culture Widely held ideas concerning the relationship of citizens to their government and to each other in matters affecting politics and public affairs.

Political participation All of those activities, from attending campaign events, to voting, and even running for office, by which individuals and groups undertake to affect politics.

Political parties Organizations designed to elect government officeholders under a given label.

Political subcultures Distinct regional variations produced when some elements of the national political culture are emphasized and others deemphasized.

Poll tax In 1902 Texas adopted a poll tax of $1.50 to discourage the poor and minorities from voting.

Popular sovereignty The idea that all legitimate governmental authority comes from the people.

Precinct Geographical area within which voters go to a polling place to cast their ballots on election day.

Preclearance The Voting Rights Act requires states and communities with a history of racial discrimination in voting to seek prior approval from the Justice Department for changes to their election codes to insure against dilution of minority electoral impact. The Supreme Court struck down preclearance in 2013.

Primary elections A preliminary election in which voters select candidates to stand under their party label in a later general election.

Professional associations Organizations formed to represent the interests of professionals in occupations like medicine, law, accounting, and cosmetology.

Professional legislatures State legislatures which pay and support their members well and, in turn, demand nearly full-time service from them.

Progressive taxes Taxes that take a higher proportion of the income of the wealthy than of the poor.

Reconstruction The period of post–Civil War (1867 to 1872) military occupation of the South during which the North attempted to reconstruct southern social, political, and economic life.

Redistricting The political process by which electoral district boundaries are redrawn to reflect changes in population and party power.

Regressive taxes Taxes that take a higher proportion of the income of the poor than of the wealthy.

Regular session The regularly scheduled biennial session of the legislature.

Republic of Texas Texas was an independent nation from 1836 until it became a U.S. state on December 29, 1845.

Reserved powers The 10th Amendment to the U.S. Constitution declares that powers not granted to the national government by the Constitution are reserved to the states or their citizens.

Responsible party model Sees political parties as organizations that campaign on coherent ideological platforms and then seek to implement their policies if elected.

Revenue estimate The Texas Comptroller is empowered to make revenue estimates that the Texas state budget must stay within.

Right-to-work Legal principle prohibiting mandatory union membership.

Rio Grande Spanish for Grand River, the Rio Grande forms Texas's southern border with Mexico from El Paso to Brownsville.

Rio Grande Valley Texas's four southernmost counties, often referred to simply as "the valley," are heavily Hispanic. The phrase is sometimes used more expansively to refer to all of South Texas.

Sales tax Taxes charged on the sale of designated goods. In Texas the general sales tax is 6.25 percent, with localities permitted to charge up to an additional 2 percent.

Separation of powers The idea that distinctive types of governmental power, legislative, executive, and judicial, should be placed in separate hands.

Sharpstown scandal 1972 scandal in which Houston financier Frank Sharp and a number of prominent Texas politicians were accused of trading political for financial favors.

Sin tax Sales taxes on activities, like smoking and drinking, that society wishes to discourage.

Single-member district elections Elections held within geographical districts, with one candidate elected in each district.

Smith v. Allwright (1944) U.S. Supreme Court overturned *Grovey*, declaring that political parties are "agencies of the state" and must abide by the 15th Amendment's prohibition on racial discrimination in voting.

Social conservatives Conservative faction that focuses on social issues such as abortion, school prayer, and gay marriage.

Sovereign immunity The 11th Amendment to the U.S. Constitution declares that states cannot be sued in their own courts, the courts of other states, federal courts, or the courts of other nations, except as their own state laws or federal law explicitly allows.

Special districts Special-purpose local governments, established by cities and counties, to deliver a particular service within a limited geographical area.

Special election Special elections are held to decide constitutional amendments, local bond proposals, and other non-recurring issues.

Special session If the legislature does not complete its business in the regular session, the governor can call one or more thirty-day special sessions.

Spindletop A.F. Lucas's Spindletop well near Beaumont came in on January 10, 1901, kicking off the 20th-century Texas oil boom.

Standing committees Continuing committees of the legislature appointed at the start of each legislative session unless specific action is taken to revise or discontinue them.

State of the State message At the beginning of each regular legislative session, the governor lays out his agenda for the session in a speech to a joint session of the legislature.

Straight-ticket voting Voting for all of the candidates of one party, often by marking a box at the top of the ballot designating the favored party.

Strong mayor An elected city executive with strong appointment, budgetary, and council management powers.

Suffrage Another term for the legal right to vote.

Supremacy clause Article VI of the U.S. Constitution declares the U.S. Constitution, federal laws, and treaties to be the supreme law of the land.

Tagging Senators try to slow the legislative process on a particular bill by requesting 48 hours' notice before a committee hearing is held.

Texas Ethics Commission Created in 1991, the TEC administers the state's ethics, campaign finance, and lobbying laws.

Texas Regulars Conservative faction of the mid-20th-century Democratic party, led by elected officials like Coke Stevenson and Allan Shivers.

Texas two-step Name popularly given to the primary election process where voters cast ballots during the day and return during the evening to conduct other party business.

"The team" The Speaker's closest associates, through whom he attempts to control and direct the House. A similar pattern operates in the Senate.

Trade associations Associations formed by businesses and related interests involved in the same commercial, trade, or industrial sector.

Trial courts Trial courts take evidence, hear testimony, determine guilt or evidence, and apply relevant law.

Unfunded mandates States frequently complain that the federal government mandates actions, such as improving education, without providing sufficient funds to fulfill the mandate.

U.S. v. Texas (1966) U.S. Supreme Court struck down the poll tax in state elections.

Veto The governor is empowered to veto or strike down acts of the legislature. A veto can be overridden by a two-thirds vote of both houses of the legislature, but it rarely happens.

Voter turnout That portion of the eligible electorate that actually turns up to cast a vote on election day.

Voting Rights Act Law requiring federal officials to facilitate minority voter registration and participation in states with a history of voter discrimination.

Weak mayor An elected city executive with few meaningful appointment, budgetary, and council management powers.

White primary In 1906 Texas Democrats held their first white primary, meaning that only whites were permitted to vote in the Democratic primary.

White v. Regester (1973) U.S. Supreme Court held that multi-member electoral districts discriminated against minority groups. Single member districts were mandated.

INDEX

Page numbers in italics refer to figures. Page numbers in bold refer to tables.

elections 69, 79–80; reserved powers 31; special districts 242–3; state control of 223–4; Texas Constitution 43; *see also* cities and municipalities
Long, Jane 78
lottery income 259
Lower Rio Grande Valley *see* South Texas
Lubbock, Frank 173
Lucas, A.F. 14
LULAC v. Perry 126
Lynch, Mike 74
McCain, John 132
McCall, Brian 148
McCleskey, Clifton 121
McCrory, Pat **172**
McCulloch v. Maryland 31, 46
McDaniel, Demetrius 94
McDonald, Michael 67
McGarry, Mignon 94
McGinty, Rush 138–9
McWilliams, Andrea 94
McWilliams, Dean R. 94
Madison, James 83
Mann, Dave 101
Mann, Pamelia 1–2
manufacturing 15
margins tax 257–8
marijuana laws 32
mark-up of bills 158
mark-up of the budget 254
Marty, Ed 194
Mattox, Jim 44
Maverick, Maury 56
Mayfield, Earle B. 57
mayor-council city government 235, 236, *236*, 243
mayors 235, *236*, 237, 239, 243
media 71, 74, 98
Medicaid 266
Medina, Debra 72
Meier, Bill 161
Menard, Michael 13
Meredith, Tom and Lynn 75
merit system for selecting judges 208–9
Messer, Bill 94
Mexican American Legal Defense and Education Fund 88, 99, 262–3
Mexican independence 5
Mexican settlers 4–5
Mexico: Anglo settlers 5; Coahuila y Tejas Constitution 35; municipal government 225; tax resistance 246–7
Middle Atlantic states 8
Middle Western states 8
Midwesterners 9

mileage compensation for legislators 162–3
military powers 180
Miller, Robert D. 94
Miller, Tom 239
Miller-El, Thomas 210
minorities: affirmative action 264–6; Democratic Party 116; education 260–1; interest groups 88; political participation 79; redistricting 125, 127, 129–32; Republican Party 121; single-member district elections 240–1; voting and voting rights 53, 54, 68
minority parties 130–1
misdemeanors 200, 201, 202
missions 4, 5, 11
Missouri plan 208–9, 215
modern Texas 15–16
Montfort, John 46
Moore, Francis 115
Moore, Kathleen 61
moralistic political culture 8, 248
Morgan, James 75
Mostyn, Steve 75
Motor Voter 62
Moyers, Bill 117
mudslinging 75–6
multi-member electoral districts 125
municipal courts 200
Munisteri, Steve 112
Murrah, Pendleton 29
Mutcher, Gus 93, 137–8

National Abortion Rights Action League 90
National Association for the Advancement of Colored People 56, 88, 99
National Rifle Association 89–90
National Voter Registration Act *See* Motor Voter
Native Americans: earliest inhabitants 4; judges, demographics of 199; population 3–4, *16*, 17; West Texas 15
Neal, Margie 141
necessary and proper clause 30–1
Neff, Pat M. 45
New Deal 47, 116
New England 8
New York 213
Nineteenth Amendment, U.S. Constitution 57
Nixon, Richard M. 58, 250
Nixon v. Herndon 56
non-partisan elections 238–9

non-partisan public interest groups 90
non-tax revenue 258–9
North Texas 9, 14–15
northern states 8
Northwest Austin Municipal Utility District No. 1 v. Holder 59
nullification 32

Obama, Barack 47, 127, 132
Obamacare *see* Patient Protection and Affordable Care Act
O'Daniel, W. Lee "Pappy" 17, 77, 117
Office of Attorney General 183–4
Office of the State Auditor 249
Ogden, Steve 254
Oil, Chemical, and Atomic Workers of Texas 87
oil and natural gas severance tax 258, 260
oil industry 14
Open Meetings Law 158
open primary 76
organized labor 86–7, 99
Ortiz, Solomon 127
Osorio, John 138
overriding vetoes 179
"owl meetings" 54

package store distributors 95, 97
Panhandle 9, 15
Parker, Annise 219–20, 236
parks and recreation 268
Patient Protection and Affordable Care Act 32
Patman, Wright 221
Patrick, Dan 90, 110, 133, 151, 160, 183, 254
Patterson, Jerry 182, 185
Pauken, Tom 224
Paxton, Ken 110, 149, 183, 184
"pay-as-you-go amendment" 249
peak associations 85
penalties 258–9
Pennsylvania 213
per diem rates 142, 143, 162–3
Perez, Thomas E. 61
Permian Basin 15
Perot, H. Ross 262
Perry, Bob 73, 74–5, 85–6, 98–9, 103, 211
Perry, Doylene 73
Perry, Rick 247; 2006 governor's race 171; 2010 primary 110; abortion bill 161; agriculture commissioner 186; Amazon case 185; appointee demographics **189**, 190; appointment power 176, 189; appraisal reform